D1328069

Blessed

...I'm So Damned Grateful

By

Raymond M. Saunders
with
Craig R. Saunders

First published by AuthorHouse 10/06/04

ISBN: 1-4184-4583-5 (e)
ISBN: 1-4184-4584-3 (sc)
ISBN: 1-4184-4585-1 (dj)

Library of Congress Control Number: 2004095273

Printed in the United States of America
Bloomington, Indiana

This book is printed on acid-free paper.

Acknowledgments

Special thanks go to: Laura Saunders for her initial transcription, first draft and revealing questions; Karen and Dan Hanson for initial editing and for the title suggestion; Stevie Saunders for her editing expertise; Shirley Danz with the Black Earth Historical Society; Joy Reisinger CG; the Wisconsin Historical Society and the Circus World Museum; Janet and Bill Schmitt for inviting us into their home; Charles Schram, President of the Manilla Centennial Committee and their publication Manilla Community Folks and Facts 1886 – 1986; Randall Saunders and Dick Saunders for the material they supplied; The Manilla Times; The Des Moines Register; Michael Garrett and my wife, JoDee and children for allowing me to write in the depths of the basement while their lives went on without me. — CRS

Dedicated To All My Family and Friends;
Past, Present and Future

Contents

PART II: THE DIARY

Foreword

I am so damn grateful to have had this experience!

Oh my God, it's happening . . .

Slowly, but surely, I have begun to sound like my Father. My wife told me years ago it was happening but, of course, I couldn't see it at the time. I probably didn't want to see it. Furthermore, if the truth be known, my wife's comparison was probably not intended, much less received, as a compliment.

All that began to change several years ago when my father sat down at the breakfast table in the darkness of those early Iowa winter mornings with a hot cup of coffee primed with "too much sugar and too much cream" and began to write his recollections of 'his land' and the people who have lived on it.

Each reflection began as every farmer's day begins, with an all-important quick peek out the window for an up to the minute weather report. This vital piece of information was then combined with a short recap of current events to help plan his day. However, because Dad was approaching 80 years of age, because his age and vision were changing his priorities, he stayed at that table just a bit longer and began recording his memories.

As I read through Dad's writings, a couple of themes kept emerging. First there was the usual recollection of old names and places that pop up in anyone's memoirs. I had heard most all of them as I was growing up and now I was learning where, sometimes for the first time, how and why they fit into our lives.

Second, was an understanding of what my ancestors had gone through to give me the life I have today. Experiencing through my father's eyes and learning about the successes and failures of the people from whom I have inherited my very being gave me a new sense of my role and responsibilities in life. Just as my forefathers have influenced my life, so will my life influence my children and generations yet to come.

Most importantly, however, was a slow realization that perhaps my own Father had discovered the secret of life.

As we read through and reworked the pages he kept saying over and over how grateful he was for the opportunities God had given him. How God had blessed him, how wonderful life was, and how great a wife he had. He kept thanking God for things that, well, quite frankly, to me just didn't seem that great.

As I read his passages about the farm and family, I kept saying to myself, "Dad, look around. Do you see what I see? The farm is really pretty run-down and it has been damn hard to scratch out a living here. You're over ninety-years-old and blind, you have had to pay for this farm at least three or four times over. You owe more on it now than when you first bought in with your father. And our family, well admittedly I have seen more dysfunctional families and while it's also true none of us have ever been institutionalized, incarcerated or in rehab, you have to admit, we certainly have had our times."

As I reread the pages it was, at times, embarrassing. I had lived through some of these moments. I remember feeling embarrassed about being sent into the grocery store because we owed money and our credit was not good. Life didn't seem that great, yet through it all, the recurring theme, "I am so damn grateful . . ." and "Thank God . . ." was surprisingly frequent.

Now, it is I who is thankful. Thankful for the opportunity to have sat down with my father and go over his writings, to relive his life with him. One time, when going over a particularly difficult time during the depression I asked him how he felt about what he has been through, about his blindness, about his poverty.

"Mother and I need a home, love and security more than money in the bank." He said, "No one can ask more of life or need more than we are getting. We just want to help contribute to the future of our farm and our country. We want to make our time worth something." He paused, and then continued, "Sure, I wish I could see, but I am so damn thankful I can walk and talk and think."

It was then that I realized that maybe, just maybe; somehow, someway my own father had found the secret of life. The secret of being happy with what one has, not unhappy for what one doesn't have. The secret of avoiding unhappiness because our wants so far exceed our needs. Not jealous, bitter or resigned, but thankful, a deep to the bone all-enveloping sense of being blessed.

We all know that is the goal; we just don't know the secret of how we ourselves can achieve this elusive goal. Perhaps he is just rationalizing to keep from going crazy or trying to justify a life spent struggling. I don't know, but he is genuinely . . . "so damn grateful."

I asked him if he had any regrets. "I wish I had learned to dance." He said, "I wish I could have taken Trudy dancing . . . she would have liked that."

I am sure, Dad, someday you will dance with her in heaven. As for me, I am taking dancing lessons now.

I am so damn grateful . . .

Craig R. Saunders
Basking Ridge,
New Jersey
Thanksgiving Day,
November 22, 2002

INTRODUCTION

January 15, 2003

My world is black.

Back in January 1989, I sat down to write a bit of early family history. Those were days of rolling green hills, silvery cottonwood trees swaying in the golden autumn sun, red clover and yellow ears of corn as long as my foot. What I didn't realize at that time was that glaucoma was turning my golden years black.

I apologize for my handwriting, spelling, composition and command of the English language. I am a farmer, not a writer, my education derived not from four years on a college campus as I had once hoped, but from working with Mother Nature 92 years on the same Iowa farm on which I was born.

Ninety-two years tempered by 368 changes of season, World Wars, a Great Depression and advances in technology that have rocked the very foundations of our world. But most of all, 92 years tempered by family, friends and God. That makes this not so much a history of a family as a history of a way of life.

Mark Twain once observed, "The difference between the right word and the almost right word is the difference between lightning and the lightning bug."

I once watched my own children chase lightning bugs across freshly mowed fields on hot summer nights. If I can capture only a fraction of the delight and amusement reflected in my own children's eyes by those lightning bugs, I shall be pleased. If, with these words, I can impart to my grandchildren and great grandchildren only a small portion of the wonder of life, if I can impart only a small portion of the wonder of discovery provided by those lightning bugs then I shall be content to leave the lightning to those of less limited talents.

These things and events of my life are as I observed them. They may not be recorded in the perfect order of occurrence, they are recorded in the order I remembered them. I have every reason to believe what I write is very close to being exactly true. The early family history is as I remember being told to me by older members of my family. Several years ago while in Wisconsin with Trudy, we did check out some of the stories and history of the family. We found them to be true almost to the letter.

Please bear with me. I started this endeavor fourteen years ago at the age of 78. Why I waited so long to start is a mystery to me, I do not know.

What I do know is that I was no longer as much help on the farm as I once had been. However, I remember my mother telling me that God may keep someone here on Earth for a hundred years just to do a few minutes' work and I knew in my heart my work was not done.

Today is Mother and Father's wedding anniversary, one hundred years ago today, January 15, 1903.

My father, born John Raymond Saunders in 1880, was six feet tall with a thick dark head of hair atop a slim young farmer's frame. Marie Helen Schoenig, his bride and eight years later my Mother, was two years older and two inches taller with long blondish hair and a stature that bespoke her German heritage.

They were married, most likely by a Methodist minister, in the big house my grandfather built on the original Saunders' farm. I don't think my grandfather or my father ever belonged to a church, but they went when the occasion called for it. My grandmother on the other hand was a stanch Methodist.

If you ate dinner at Grandma's house, you didn't pick up a spoon or a fork until the blessings were given. Of course the wedding dinner was no exception. Her table was always set with hearty helpings of home grown beef and pork. Potatoes dug from the ground the previous fall and stored in the cool vegetable cellar were combined with fresh garden vegetables and fresh home-baked breads and pies, all served on an ever-present white linen tablecloth.

The men around the wedding table were lean and sinewy. Every ounce of strength, both physical and spiritual, they derived from these legendary farm meals was needed to work the land and raise their family.

The women worked no less hard to prepare and present the food the men had provided. Early in their lives as young farming couples the women worked right alongside their men and his horses. As the family grew, sons replaced their mothers in the fields alongside their fathers; only then was the abundance of the family table reflected in the farmer's wife.

Years later women's liberation would become a major social issue. The movement, however, would not begin in the farmlands of Iowa. Here men and women, though recognized as different, were treated as equals, working together, each with their special talents, working with and sometimes battling Mother Nature for survival.

The hired help were also good friends and treated as family. They would have attended the wedding dressed in their Sunday finest. However, on less formal occasions, when dressed for the everyday life as an Iowa farm hand, they would bring to the table a piece of newspaper to put down as a place mat so as not to soil the white linen table cloth, but that was the only concession made for the wedding feast. As usual, no one would leave the table until all were finished, and then only after thanks was again offered for their many blessings.

Although this was my beginning, it all started long before. I have tried to write a bit of early history as I remember it being told to me. I am now totally blind but blessed with a sharp mind. I see these things with the clarity as if they happened yesterday.

This is Mother and Father's wedding picture, although I remember her taller than Dad, this picture clearly does not show it, perhaps because in his later years, his legs bowed or perhaps simply because I was closer to my mother and my memory recalls her as being taller.

PART I: THE HISTORY

Chapter 1

Black Earth

January 24, 1989

To my family –
Many times you have asked me to write a short history of the Saunders family. Due to the fact that I haven't been very active on the farm this fall and winter, I'll attempt to write a bit.

So, at 5:10 this cold January morning, I'll start and hopefully make it worth your time. Perhaps some of my family will take it upon themselves to rewrite my memoirs and perhaps add memories of their own. I'm afraid once over will be enough for me.

I did a bit of simple research, just browsing really, one foggy, gray mist filled afternoon a few years ago in a British Columbia heraldry shop. It was the kind of shop that caters to tourists but the weather was bad and the shop was empty. The owner was happy to have me in his store but more importantly he seemed genuinely interested in my stories – not everyone is.

I learned a new word that day - patronymic. I learned, unlike the more obvious names based on occupations such as Miller, Tanner, Cooper or Smith, the surname Saunders is a name that is based on the first name of the father. They called this type of name "of patronymic origin". In this instance, the Saunders surname is derived from the personal name Alexander.

I learned Alexander was originally a name given as a compliment, meaning a "helper or defender of men." It was first used eight-hundred-years before Christ when Homer, in the Iliad, gave it to a character named Paris for his courage. Five-hundred years later it was a regular family name of the Kings of Macedonia, the most famous of which was Alexander III better known as Alexander the Great.

In medieval Scotland there were three Alexander kings. The grandfather of Alexander I was Duncan, who in 1040 A.D. was killed by Macbeth and made famous by William Shakespeare.

Saunders literally means "son of Alexander" or "Alexander's son." The personal name was often abbreviated and underwent a transformation from "Alexander's son" to "Xanderson" to "Sanderson" to "Sander(s)" or "Saunder(s)" and it is from these abbreviations that our surname was ultimately born.

A hundred or so years after Alexander I the surname Saunders had become quite common throughout all the British Isles as well as the rest of Europe. It is a stretch of the imagination to believe all, or for that matter any, of these Saunders could trace their bloodlines back to Alexander the Great or any of the Scottish Kings. However, they still may have had something in common. It has been proposed "Alexander's sons" may be less literally translated and may refer to "those that served in Alexander's army" or "served under Alexander."

I know little about our early family history. I was told our part of the Saunders family came to England originally from Normandy and that in the early years they lived under the protector of the MacDonald Clan of early Scottish heritage. This particular clan was known as MacDonald of Glenview. They had their own Tartan, which was slightly different from the MacDonald Tartan, as it is known today.

That afternoon in the heraldry shop I also learned of the numerous early instances of the surname Saunders in England. For example, the first was when the Norman Richard de Clare, Earl of Pembroke, nicknamed Strongbow, granted them lands for their assistance in the invasion of Ireland in 1172. The "Selected Documents of the English Lands of the Abby of Bec" refers to a person by the name of Sandre as early as 1248, while one Richard Saunder is mentioned in the Subsidy Rolls for Staffordshire in 1332.

The "original" Coat of Arms[1] for the Saunders family was issued in the year 1520 during the reign of Henry VIII. When son

---

[1] The original Coat of Arms was an emblem woven into cloth (coat) worn over armor (arms) for the purpose of identification. The design was also used on shields for the same purpose.

Craig was studying at the Royal Infirmary of Edinburgh in 1969 he brought back a replica of that Coat of Arms. This particular emblem is quite different from more popular copies I have seen furnished by organizations advertising to trace your family history.

Indeed, in Ireland the Saunders name was (re)introduced when Colonel Robert Saunders invaded Ireland with Oliver Cromwell in 1650. In payment for services Saunders of Saunders Court, County Wexford was awarded 3,725 acres of land, the title Governor of Kinsale and a Coat of Arms in 1666.

This Coat of Arms sported three elephant heads and the Latin motto "Spes mea in Deo" translated "My hope is in God." On the crest of 'our' Coat of Arms is a shield with three bulls' heads and the motto "Invidere Sperno." The motto was a battle cry meaning "I look on my enemies with scorn" however, some where in the back of my mind I remember being told that a less in your face interpretation of the motto is "I scorn to envy". I like that better. I later learned this particular Coat of Arms belonged to a specific branch of the Saunders family originating in West Wales.

I have not researched our English roots; I have no idea if this is the branch of the family tree my ancestors sprang from. However, given the fact that our family business has been raising cattle, this is either confirmatory evidence from on high of our heritage or a shrewd selection in a Scottish gift shop by my son Craig.

I do know my great grandfather, Charles Adolphus (C. A.) Saunders was born in England March 5, 1831 to John and Elizabeth Saunders. When Charles was twenty years of age, on May 4th in the year 1851, he married Louisa Keeley at Brighton in the County of Sussex and the Kingdom of England during the reign of Queen Victoria. His bride Louisa was only eighteen-years-old[2], born on August 2, 1833 to James and Sarah Keeley in Warwickshire.

If this young couple could trace their roots back to any of the Alexander Kings, something had gone terribly wrong in the preceding generations, Louisa would later state that when they married, neither "had any property of any particular value beside their wearing apparel."

The young couple was married in Saint Nicholas Church in the parish of Brighton, a church whose present building dates from the 14th centaury and whose surrounding graveyard contains a mass burial pit from the early 1300's for victims of the Black Plague.

The 1851 marriage registry of Saint Nicholas lists the fathers of both bride and groom; John Saunders' occupation was listed as "carpenter." From the English census taken that same year, Charles Saunders, aged 20, was listed as a "carpenter apprentice" born in Brighton and living at 5 Stone Street with his mother Elizabeth, aged 61, also born in Brighton. However, at this time she was married to Joseph Prior, presumably after being widowed from Charles' biological father John Saunders.

Likewise the marriage registry lists Louisa's father, James Keeley as a tailor. In the same 1851 census, however, Louisa Keeley is listed as living with her mother Sarah. Sarah, born in Middlesex, London in 1813, whose name is now recorded as Fisher, was

---

[2] The marriage registry lists her "Age: 19 yrs" and "Condition: Spinster"

listed as being a widow and living in the home of William George Dowden, his wife Jane and their son William at 20 Dean Street, Brighton, England. Again, presumably James Keeley had died and she married a Fisher from whom she was also widowed.[3]

We have no knowledge of who the Dowden's were, perhaps they were relatives of Sarah's or perhaps 20 Dean Street was simply a boarding house. Both Dean and Stone Streets were the residences and shops of common folks, mostly craftsmen and laborers. The occupations of inhabitants along these streets were listed in the 1851 census as painter, baker, carpenter and carpenter apprentice, shirt maker, 'fancy work', upholsterer, gardener, shoemaker, dressmaker and milkman. We do know Charles apparently moved in with Louisa and Sarah as their marriage certificate listed their residence as 20 Dean Street. Dean and Stone Streets still exist within a few blocks of each other on the map of modern day Brighton.

In November of that same year Charles and Louisa booked passage to America.[6] I remember my Grandfather handing down stories of his parents' crossing. It was a story of rough north Atlantic seas and a quite difficult crossing made that much worse by the crowded unsanitary conditions of their third-class accommodations.

While on board Louisa became quite ill, every morning she awoke with fits of nausea and vomiting that confined her to her cot and permitted her neither food nor drink. On the bad days Louisa was convinced she would never see America. On the good days, when the sea allowed hope, her only wish was to get to America. Like all immigrants, the hopes and dreams of America they had imbedded in their hearts were growing more real with each passing day.

No doubt the rough seas were a factor and it would be very dramatic to say she was with child struggling to get this unborn child

---

[3] English family history provided by Randall Saunders of Westerville, Ohio, great great grandson of Charles and Louisa.

[6] Grandfather told of three brothers coming to America but we have no further details but apparently one brother went to Australia first. This will have to be the subject for later research but it could be interesting, from the end of the American Revolution in 1776 to 1868 not all Englishmen went to Australia as a matter of choice.

Saint Nicholas' Church, was the site of Charles Saunders and Louisa Keeley's wedding May 4, 1851.[4] It is the oldest building in Brighton. A Brighton church was mentioned in the Doomsday Book compiled by William the Conqueror in the latter part of the 11th centaury but it is not known if it is St. Nicholas. In the early 1500's under the reign of Henry VIII, England was attacked by the French and Brighton was destroyed. All that was left was the outline of the streets and the church on the hill – Saint Nicholas. Saint Nicholas of Myra was the patron saint of fishermen and Brighton was a sleepy fishing village until 1750 when a physician published a book praising the healing properties of bathing in seawater. Soon after the Prince of Wales visited for 'the cure' and Brighton's reputation as a seaside resort was secure.[5]

---

[4] This image is an early type of photography called a daguerreotype made by local artist George Ruff between 1850 and 1852. http://www.spartacus.schoolnet. co.uk/Dsphotoday2B.htm

[5] History of Brighton, England, Tim Lambert, http://wwwppicturesofEngland.com/ history/brighton-history.htm

Charles and Louisa's signatures on the marriage registration from
St. Nicholas' Church, dated May 4, 1851.

to America but if that were the case the pregnancy never reached term. The couple's first child would be born in America but not for another year and a half.

I have no way of knowing, but I am certain that Louisa must have been concentrating only on her daily struggle. It would have taken exceptional foresight and understanding for her to realize that, in her womb, she was bringing to America the seeds for our entire subsequent Saunders clan.

When the young couple arrived in New York harbor they were not greeted by visions of the Statue of Liberty or Ellis Island, these landmarks wouldn't be built for another thirty or forty years.[7] No, they would have landed at the foot of Manhattan in the old battery, a fort built for the protection of the city during the War of 1812 and years later turned into an immigration center.[8]

---

[7] The Statue of Liberty was dedicated October, 1886 and Ellis Island was not used for immigration until 1892.

[8] Battery Park now exists at the site but the area was much enlarged with fill dirt from the construction of the Twin Towers of the World Trade Center in the early 1970's.

The new American immigrants settled in Brooklyn, where their first child was born, June 8, 1853. Charles A. and Louisa Saunders named their first-born son William Alexander. William's granddaughter, Lucille Kilpack of Mason City, Iowa, has verified this much for me. In 1856 the family moved to Black Earth in Dane County, Wisconsin.

Why they chose Black Earth is a mystery lost to the years but it could have been chosen for its pure beauty. It was a handsome little village in an area of rolling hills and steep ridges with a meandering trout stream flowing through a green valley of deep, black loamy soil. Ten thousand years ago, during the last Ice Age, a glacier pushed down from the north and it is the clear water springs and the remnants of that last glacier bubbling up through the limestone bedrock that created Black Earth Creek.

The Winnebago Indians were the first to make their home there and were joined by the first Europeans as early as 1833. Between 1843 and 1850 about twenty immigrants from The British Temperance Emigration Society of Liverpool, England joined them. The community was known as Farmersville until the name was changed in 1851 and it adopted the name of the river running through it.

The young Saunders family would have arrived in Black Earth either by foot or wagon train in the year 1856 for it was a full year before the Milwaukee and Mississippi Railroad made it that far west. For the next fifteen years the Saunders' family called this home.

Will, the oldest child, born in Brooklyn, was joined by five more siblings all born in Black Earth – Charles, my grandfather on August 6, 1857, Uncle Ed (Edgar), who for reasons I don't know was called 'Deacon', on June 4,1859, Sarah Elizabeth, who I knew as Aunt Lizzie on November 24, 1860, Aunt Alice (Alice Helena), on September 4, 1862, and Uncle Fred, (Fredrick James) the youngest, on March 4, 1864.

The world they entered was far different from ours; the only means of mass transportation was by rail or water and though ships could span the oceans, the rails did not yet span the young nation. Electricity had been discovered but not put to any practical use save perhaps the telegraph[9], which awaited the rail lines. There were, of course, no cars or airplanes, no radios, stereos, television, movies or computers and forget about a man on the moon. The six Saunders children would be as lost and bewildered in our world as we would be in theirs.

In the world of my grandfather's childhood the '49ers' were in California but they weren't playing football, these were the original '49ers' of the California Gold Rush which was still in full swing. In three short years oil would be discovered in Titusville, Pennsylvania triggering a similar craziness and the beginning of the "Age of Illumination." In my grandfather's youth Samuel Clemens was still a riverboat captain on the Mississippi and Wyatt Earp a teenager in California. During the children's childhood Presidents Millard Fillmore, Franklin Pierce, James Buchanan, Abraham Lincoln, the Pony Express and the Civil War would all come and go. If lucky, one of the kids could spring for a dime novel to keep up on the exploits of Wild Bill Hickok.[10] Other news and entertainment came from what few newspapers were printed in the area plus traveling troupes and medicine shows all of whose prospects improved considerably with the arrival of the railroad.

My grandfather was also quite proud of his Jewish ancestry, which came from the maternal side, Grandma Sarah Fisher. It had always been my belief that Grandma Fisher was the maternal grandmother of Louisa Keeley Saunders making her my great, great, great Grandmother but I guess I must be mistaken. The census records and the article that follows from the Black Earth Advertiser refer to Grandma Fisher as Louisa's mother. She would, therefore, only be my great, great Grandmother.

Likewise, it has always been unknown to me if Grandma Fisher came to America with Louisa, was sent for later as is suggested in the newspaper article or if she was the reason this newlywed couple left the rest of their family in England. I do know at some

---

[9] The first telegraph line was completed between Washington, D.C. and Baltimore, Md. in 1844. The first message – "What hath God wrought?"
[10] James Butler Hickok, born 1837 died 1876.

point Grandma Fisher made her home with Charles, Louisa and their six children in Black Earth.

A review of the U. S. Federal Census helps answer this question. The 1860 census listed 288 people living in Black Earth and included Charles, aged twenty-nine and Louisa, aged twenty-six, with three children, William, aged seven, Charles, aged three and Edgar, one-year-of-age. Charles occupation was again listed as carpenter and a personal estate valued at $500 was recorded. Ten years later, the 1870 census recorded 320 inhabitants living in the village of Black Earth. Elizabeth, Alice and Frederick were, of course, added to the census but so was Sarah Selina Fisher, aged fifty-six, occupation, music teacher. This confirms she was of the age to be Louisa's mother, not grandmother. The 1870 census also tells us Charles' net worth had increased over the past ten years and he now owned real estate valued at $1,500 and his personal estate had grown to $1,000.

Louisa referred to herself as "bred a dressmaker and milliner," apparently influenced by the fact that her father was a tailor. I am told she was a fine seamstress and dressmaker in her own right and ran her own shop with the help of Grandma Fisher. Charles continued to work as a craftsman, carpenter and woodworker by trade.

When the Civil War erupted enough men from Black Earth and its surrounding area volunteered for the Union Army to form two complete regiments. Charles was among them and served as a private in Company "A" of the 49th Wisconsin Infantry Regiment. The Wisconsin Civil War Compiled Service Records indicate that Company "A" mustered in Madison, Wisconsin in February of 1865. He enlisted for one year and was mustered out when the company disbanded at Benton Barracks, Missouri on November 8, 1865.

The records listed Charles Saunders as five-feet-eleven-inches-tall, which was quite tall for 1865. With rare exception his fellow soldiers were listed between five-feet-four and five-feet-eight-inches-tall. His occupation was listed a carpenter and he was further described with hazel eyes, black hair and a fair complexion.

The enlistment papers clearly listed Charles as thirty-nine-years-of-age but he was only thirty-four. That must have been an error, or was it?

The Civil War was the first time in our nation's history that its citizens were drafted into the military yet it was a far different draft than we have experienced in our lifetimes. A Professor Ellison of the University of Wisconsin wrote an article about the attitudes towards the draft in Wisconsin that pretty well summarizes the situation.[11] Volunteerism was considered the honorable thing to do and the draft was used only as a backup, mainly a threat, to get men to volunteer. When President Lincoln placed his first call for 300,000 troops in 1862, the Secretary of War informed Wisconsin's Governor his quota was 11,904 men. If that quota was not met by August 15, the deficiency would be made up through a state draft but only in those counties which did not meet their quotas. It was noted that those counties not meeting the quota were usually those with large immigrant populations.

A year later, when Congress passed The Enrollment Act of 1863 they created the first federal draft but it was still the custom of the time for the President to put out a call for volunteers. There were four such calls, which carried with them the threat of the draft, one in 1863, two in 1864 and the last in the spring of 1865. The federal government was well aware of sentiments against the draft and left several loop holes for evasion. The drafted man could hire a substitute or pay a $300 commutation fee to be excused. Generally the draftee was given 10 days to report during which time many took the opportunity to cross the boarder into Canada. Occasionally more drastic methods were used to avoid the draft. In Ellison's research he came across a 1862 newspaper report of "a woman, not many miles from this village, fearing that her husband was to be drafted, took occasion to deliver him of two of his five digits." Ellison pointed out that "physical mutilation was probably not practiced that often . . . There were too many other ways of avoiding the draft than cutting ones self to pieces."

---

[11] The Civil War Draft in Plover and Stevens Point (Wisconsin): A Study In Efforts, Attitudes, Frustrations, and Results. David Ellison. http://www.pchswi.org/archives/misc/cwdraft.html

VOLUNTEER ENLISTMENT.

STATE OF

TOWN OF

Wisconsin

Black Earth

I, *Charles Saunders* born in _____ in the State of *England* aged *Thirty Nine* years, and by occupation a *Carpenter* DO HEREBY ACKNOWLEDGE to have volunteered this *Fourteenth* day of *February* 1865, to serve as a Soldier in the Army of the United States of America, for the period of *three* YEARS, unless sooner discharged by proper authority: Do also agree to accept such bounty, pay, rations, and clothing, as are, or may be, established by law for volunteers. And I, *Chas Saunders* do solemnly swear, that I will bear true faith and allegiance to the United States of America, and that I will serve them honestly and faithfully against all their enemies or opposers whomsoever; and that I will observe and obey the orders of the President of the United States, and the orders of the officers appointed over me, according to the Rules and Articles of War.

Sworn and subscribed to, at *Madison* this *14* day of *February* 1865. *Chas Saunders* BEFORE *C E Nell* *Recruiting Officer*

I CERTIFY, ON HONOR, That I have carefully examined the above-named Volunteer, agreeably to the General Regulations of the Army, and that, in my opinion, he is free from all bodily defects and mental infirmity, which would in any way disqualify him from performing the duties of a soldier.

O M Blanchard
49th Regt. Wis. V.O
EXAMINING SURGEON.

I CERTIFY, ON HONOR, That I have minutely inspected the Volunteer, *Saunders* previously to his enlistment, and that he was entirely sober when enlisted; that, to the best of my judgment and belief, he is of lawful age; and that, in accepting him as duly qualified to perform the duties of an able-bodied soldier, I have strictly observed the Regulations which govern the recruiting service. This soldier has *Hazel* eyes, *Black* hair, *Fair* complexion, is *Five* feet *Eleven* inches high.

C E Nell
49 Regiment of *Wis. Vol* Volunteers,
RECRUITING OFFICER.

(A. G. O. Nos. 74 & 75.)

The enlistment papers of Charles A. Saunders in the Union Army, dated February 14, 1865. Handwritten in the margin of the upper right hand corner is " . . . and he is entitled to bounty."

As a result the 1863 draft was not very successful, of the 14,955 men drafted state wide in Wisconsin 252 hired substitutes, 6,285 were discharged for medical reasons, 5,081 paid the $300 commutation fee and 2,689 simply did not report for duty. Of the nearly 15,000 men drafted only 628 men actually served in the military.

As stated before, volunteers made up most of the Army enticed by a $302 federal bounty paid to each volunteer in addition to an annual salary of $586 with guaranteed payment every two months plus '. . . all expenses paid'. The federal bounty for volunteers was usually supplemented by additional state and local funds which could total anywhere from $50 to $1,000. The actual amount increased as the war wore on. However, "It had the expected results," as one writer put it, "men volunteered, and it became the standard method of obtaining troops. Even discharged veterans who had enlisted for 'love of country' in 1861 caught the fever and re-enlisted for 'love of money' in 1864."

So what if anything does this all have to do with the obvious error on Charles 1865 enlistment papers? One more bit of information is very important and may well explain the "mistake".

When the 1863 draft was executed in Wisconsin all draft eligible men were divided into two classes. The first was all men between the ages of 18 and 35 years, the second was all unmarried men over 35 but less than 45 years-old. It doesn't take much imagination to realize that Charles may well have intentionally misstated his age by 5 years when registering for the '63 draft. He was only 32 but by adding five years he fell into the second category and being married was therefore ineligible for the draft.

Two years later with the outcome of the war now obvious but still with a Presidential call for more troops and the prospect of a $300-$400-or-more bounty to be paid to each volunteer, all of a sudden military service did not seem quite as burdensome nor as large a threat to life and limb. Charles was an immigrant and as stated before volunteerism was less popular with the immigrants. Perhaps they felt they had less at stake or perhaps because of their European experiences they were both leery and weary of wartime experiences. However, by definition the immigrants were also opportunists and the prospect of an easy and relatively safe $300.00 provide interesting insight into the men and the times.

Historians remember our Civil War as a war that pitted brother against brother but, like all wars, it had many other ways to destroy

The Black Earth Village Hall was constructed by Charles Saunders in 1869-70. It stood in Veterans Park for nearly one hundred years. The bottom floor was used for official city business. The upper floor, entered via the outside stairway, was the cultural center for the village until dismantled in 1961. It contained an auditorium of sorts with a stage complete with a hand painted curtain and was the scene for visiting politicians, school plays, touring actors and traveling medicine shows. Dances, balls and benefits were regularly scheduled in the hall.

a family. Charles returned to Black Earth and his family unable to cope with life without first drawing his courage from a bottle. He had, in fact, become a drunkard.

When sober, Charles was considered an excellent carpenter and when the town's people voted to construct a City Hall in 1869, the contract was awarded to Charles Saunders. By the time of the annual city meeting in 1870 the town had a new City Hall. It was a large two-story wood frame building, "the lower story was used for

The divorce papers as filed in Circuit Court for Dane County.
Louisa's signature as it appeared below on the divorce papers, it
was signed on "this 3rd day of May A.D. 1871." An accompanying
affidavit below attests the Summons for Relief was served by
Wm. Buckley, Deputy Sheriff on May 4, 1871, the twentieth
anniversary of Charles and Louisa's marriage. The fee charged
for this service was $8.60.

town meetings while the upper was rented for concerts, theaters and other purposes . . . the total construction cost was $2,073.68 plus another $600.00 for the lots on which it was built."[12]

Odd carpentry jobs, handyman work and Louisa's dress shop supported the family but civilian life healed neither the scars of battle nor scars of the bottle. Eighteen-seventy-one was the year Mrs. O'Leary's cow was blamed for kicking over a lantern and causing the great Chicago fire,[13] but it was also the year that changed the course of the Saunders family forever. On a hot summer day on the 29th day of June, 1871, in the sleepy little Wisconsin village of Black Earth, the six Saunders children were suddenly and violently orphaned.

The course of events had been set in motion much earlier. Revealing perhaps a small glimpse into Louisa's personality and certainly a large measure of her frustration, on the day of their wedding anniversary, May 4, 1871, she served her husband of twenty years with divorce papers.

The papers chronicle a history of abuse which became unbearable during the proceeding two or three years and deteriorated into an altercation on the afternoon of Saturday the 29th day of April, 1871 that culminated with Louisa leaving the house and providing " . . . for herself as best she might with the assistance of friends . . ." as well as the filing of the divorce papers.

The following are the actual newspaper articles chronicling the event. The original microfilm copy was a poor image, nearly illegible and totally unsuitable for reproduction. What follows is a reconstruction that has faithfully reproduced the articles in the original fonts, size, spacing, punctuation and most importantly the colorful journalism of the day. The first two articles are from the Wisconsin State Journal (Madison).

---

[12] History of Dane County (Western Historical Company: Chicago, 1880), pp888-896

[13] The O'Learys were 'dairy farmers', they kept 4 or 5 cows in a barn behind their house and sold milk in the neighborhood. No one knows exactly how the Chicago fire started, a newspaper article at the time blamed a cow for kicking over a lantern but most agree that was unlikely. A neighbor, Daniel "Peg Leg" Sullivan was for many reasons a likely suspect and it has been suggested that the cow was blamed to keep the angry mob from lynching Peg Leg.

THURSDAY AFTERNOON, JUNE 29,1871.

MURDER AND SUICIDE.

Terrible Tragedy at Black Earth

A Drunken Husband Shoots His Wife and Himself.

From several persons, to whom we are greatly obliged for their promptness in furnishing us the information, we have the particulars of a terrible tragedy, which occurred at Black Earth, this morning, Charles A. Saunders, of that place, having fatally shot his wife, Louisa, and then killed himself.

It appears that Saunders, a carpenter by trade, and formerly a respected citizen of Black Earth, but lately imbruted and de-moralized by whiskey, so as to be almost worthless, had frequently quarreled with his wife, who sought to aid in supporting the family by pursuing the trade of a milliner, and had ill-treated her so that she had made application for a divorce. He was ordered to pay suit money, and refused, whereupon he was cited for contempt of court, and, failing to appear, was arrested and put in jail, where he was held for a week, until the money, $75, was paid. Yesterday he was in this city, and consulting with Hon. George B. Smith in regard to the case. Before going home he drank heavily, and was infuriated with liquor and what he regarded the indignity put upon him.

This morning, about 9 ½ o'clock, Saunders entered his wife's millinery store, and, with a pistol, shot Mrs. Saunders twice, one ball entering her face and the other her neck. He then fired two shots at his mother-in-law, Mrs. Fisher, a music teacher, but she protected herself with a chair, and escaped.

The neighbors, alarmed by the firing and shrieks of the women, rushed with fire-arms, pitchforks and whatever came handy, and in the excitement of the moment would probably have made short work of the murderer, but he ran into his dwelling house adjoining, and into the cellar, where he shot himself, dying almost instantly.

Mrs. Saunders was still alive at noon, but sinking fast. There was naturally great excitement over the fearful affair, and the sympathy of the community was of course all with Mrs. Saunders. Six children were made orphans in one sad moment.

The Black Earth Tragedy.

Black Earth, June 30.
EDITORS STATE JOURNAL: - Mrs.
Saunders, who was shot by her husband
yesterday morning, died at 4:30 o'clock last
evening, and will be buried to-day at 2 P.M.

The body of Charles Saunders was
buried last evening, without any ceremony.

C. Burnett, Editor *Advertiser*

Black Earth Advertiser.

"FORWARD."

BLACK EARTH, WIS., THURSDAY, JULY 6, 1871.

[From the Advertiser Extra, July 1st.]

MURDER AND SUICIDE.

Charles Saunders Shoots His Wife and Himself.

Our usually quiet village was last Thursday forenoon thrown into the greatest excitement by several reports of a revolver and the cry of "Saunders is killing his wife!" Everyone within hearing rushed for Mrs. Saunders' Millinery Store, but only to find their worst fears too full realized. The murderer had thoroughly done his work. Mrs. Saunders was found lying in the middle of the floor, the blood spurting from a bullet wound in her neck and another in the face, at the right corner of her mouth. She was still conscious, and when spoken to, said "Oh, my poor children," and a moment later, when Dr. Stair had arrived, again spoke, "Oh, doctor," and immediately became un-conscious.

In the meantime the excited crowd began to look for Saunders.

The word was given, that he had entered the dwelling house, next door, and into that the men rushed. As he was known to have a revolver with him some care was taken in the search, so that it was some five minutes before he was found. He had gone to the darkest corner of the cellar, and there placed the muzzle of the revolver in his mouth and fired, killing himself almost instantly. One distorted roll of the eyes being the only move detected after he was found.

The cries of the excited citizens were immediately hushed. That he had received his just deserts was plainly depicted on every counten-ance. Not one word of sympathy for him was uttered.

After quiet had in a measure been restored, we set about picking up the particulars of this last scene of a long existing trouble.

From Mrs. Fisher, mother of Mrs. Saunders, and Miss Mariette Warner, one of the shop girls, who was with three other girls in the shop at the time, we were able to get at the facts of the case as near as it was possible for them to remember in the excitement.

At about 9 o'clock Charles Saunders, quite intoxicated, came into the store and seating himself on the counter, asked Mrs. S. if she would go with him to Madison that day, adding that he would make over some property to her if she would go. She partially promised to go, but wished to take her son William, which he objected to. She left the room and he followed to the door and then returned to his seat on the counter. Mrs. S. soon returned, when he commenced abasing her and his mother-in-law in a most shameful manner. After hearing this for a few minutes, Mrs. S. ordered him to leave the store. He refused to do so, got off the counter and faced her, when she took a chair and gave him a push.

He immediately drew the revolver and fired, the ball hitting Mrs. S. in the neck. She fell, when he fired again, hitting her in the face. By this time the girls had all rushed out of the store, screaming. Mrs. Fisher started forward at the first fire, helping herself with a chair, as she is a cripple, when he leveled the revolver at her and she had only time to raise the chair to ward off the shot. Saunders then ran out of the back door, and turning fired at her once more, the ball missing her and lodging in the floor. He then ran to the cellar and shot himself as above stated.

M. C. Burnett, Esq. was informed of the death of Mr. Saunders and at once em-panelled six jurors and proceeded to the place where Mr. S. lay. After holding the necessary examination they declared by their verdict that the deceased came to his death by the means of a loaded pistol deliberately discharged by his own hands.

A Colt's small five chamber revolver was found by his side, and on his clothes was found powder and balls, pipes and tobacco, memorandum book, and a number of letters, one of which proved to be in his own handwriting, wherein he stated his premeditated intention to shoot his wife and himself. It bore a request for the manner and disposal of the bodies, a description of his property and estate.

As no one could be found to volunteer to take charge of the body and give it burial, the authorities made the provisions, and had it buried that evening.

Mrs. Saunders lingered in an unconscious state for seven hours when she died. The ladies of the village rendered every assistance possible before and after her death. Her funeral took place Friday afternoon. The services being held at the Congregational Church, which was filled to overflowing with deeply sympathizing friends.

Charles Saunders was about forty years of age, and Mrs. Louisa Saunders thirty-seven. They were born in England, and married there, coming to this country soon after. They had lived together twenty years, four years of that time being spent in New York, where the oldest son, William, was born, and fifteen years in this village, where the five younger children were born.

Mr. Saunders was a carpenter and joiner by trade, and when sober was a master mechanic. He had built several of the finest residences and public buildings in the village. When intoxicated, which was quite frequent of late, he was quarrelsome and abusive to his family. His wife being unable longer to submit to him, had applied for a divorce, since which time he had been forbidden to enter the store.

Mrs. Saunders had worked at dress making since coming here, and this spring wishing to enlarge her business, he had built a small store and assisted her to purchase a stock of millinery and dress goods. She was highly respected by all, and for several years had been a member of the Methodist Church.

Through Saunders's per-suasion, his wife's mother, Mrs. Fisher, was a few years since induced to leave her home and friends in England and come here to live. She has more than supported herself by teaching music, so that his reports of dependence are entirely unfounded.

The children will probably be left in the care of their grandmother and their oldest brother. The property left is sufficient to keep them in good circumstances. This is the first shooting affair that ever happened in our village, and it is hoped it may be the last.

[Communicated.]

Mr. Editor: In looking back over the fearful occurrence of the past week, we find the following facts remaining as consequences of it. First a community stunned by a terrible crime perpetrated in our mids, in open day, before our very eyes. Second, a helpless widowed mother, far away from the home of her youth and friends, compelled to support life as best she may. Third six orphaned children, forced out into the world, with heart wounded and bleeding, with the shadow of this horrible tragedy resting down upon their pathway for ever. Fourth, a nameless grave, the memory of whose occupant is covered with everlasting infamy, and his name cast out as evil as the instrument through whom and by whom all this has been accomplished. But there is still one other fact to mention, not as a sequel but a stubborn undeniable fact nevertheless, that the author of this crime is still amongst us. Alcohol walks our streets as before, with head erect, bold, defiant, apparently gloating over his bloody work with hands red, not only with the blood of our neighbors but with that of the best of our nation, as his name is legion so he is able to carry on his devilish work throughout the length and breadth of our land. The history of the human race from . . . *(the remainder of this letter to the editor was not available)*

Black Earth, July 3rd, 1871

_____

CARD.
The children of the late Charles and Louisa Saunders and Mrs. Sarah Fisher would take this opportunity to thank their numerous friends for their kindness and assistance in their late sad bereavement.

WILLIAM SAUNDERS
MRS. SARAH FISHER

_____

The only known photograph of Grandma Fisher, the great great great great great grandmother of our youngest Saunders generation. With her is her grandson Frederick, youngest son of Charles and Louisa, perhaps it is his last photo before leaving Black Earth for Iowa.

Charles was forty-years-old when he took his own life and that of his wife. My grandfather was nearly fourteen-years-old when he found his father's body in the basement of their home. For the rest of his life, Granddad remembered that last wild look in his own father's dying eyes. No better reason was needed to turn one's back on alcohol and practice a life of temperance. Indeed, for the next four generations, alcohol would not be served in a Saunders household.

For the next year, Grandma Fisher tried to keep the dress shop open and the family together, but she was now elderly and as a result of having been dropped by her governess when young, had acquired a crippling disfigurement. Running a business and rearing a young family was simply beyond her abilities.

Uncle Will was the first to leave. With his family destroyed and humiliated and no education, he did what all young men dream of doing at some point in their lives. No, he didn't run off and join the circus, he did one better; he ran off and joined what would eventually become known as Buffalo Bill's Wild West Show.[14]

Years later, on our honeymoon, Trudy, my new bride, and I visited Uncle Will. He lived with his son Bill and his daughter-in-law, just outside of La Grange, Illinois. He was quite elderly, a widower, and a minor local politician of some repute. He enjoyed people and loved to talk. Although this enhanced his reputation as a politician, the family was pretty well convinced that age had embellished the tales of his youth. Will insisted this was not the case and at some point in the past had taken his son's family to what remained of a then struggling Wild West Show when it visited near by Naperville.

Bill told us, while walking around the grounds with his father, they heard a thunderous voice. "Well Billy, Billy Saunders you old S.O.B., it's been a long time since I saw you." Startled, they turned to see a goateed, white-haired old man, considerably past

---

[14] Buffalo Bill Cody did not create his Wild West Show, which he called "an educational exposition on a grand and entertaining scale," until 1883. Prior to the official Wild West Show, Buffalo Bill spent a decade or more producing small scale "boarder dramas". The official Wild West Show premiered in Omaha and from there toured around the world. It ran for 30 years, until 1913, and featured American Indians such as Sitting Bull, real life cowboys and trick shooters such as Annie Oakley. Uncle Will would have known them all.

Buffalo Bill's Wild West.

Circus World Museum keeps records of all individuals that have been employed buy this type of traveling entertainment. Their records include Route Rosters on which is listed **"W. Saunders, Stagecoach driver and cowboy in the employ of Buffalo Bill's Wild West Show."**

his prime, but still imposing. It was then that their father introduced them to his old friend, Buffalo Bill Cody.

After that, Bill said, "We pretty much accepted anything Dad said."

My Grandfather, C.A., stayed on in Black Earth for a year after the tragedy but prospects were slim. In March of 1872 he boarded a train for Denison, Iowa.

Earlier, a family of four boys named Theobald had come to Astor, Iowa by wagon train from a small village near Black Earth. The families had been friends in Wisconsin and now they were offering C.A. a home and work on their farm. Help on the farm was always welcome; the four Theobald boys had lost a wife or two along the way and were now supporting seven families! One of the families had five daughters – Bertha, Ruth, Martha, Phyllis and a fifth whose name I can't remember. Eventually, two of the Saunders brothers, my grandfather C.A. and Uncle Fred would marry two of the sisters (Bertha and Ruth) but first they would have to get to Iowa.

Grandpa's train was delayed in Boone, Iowa for two days by a typical Iowa March snowstorm. I suppose it was the kind of storm we have come to expect every March, as a 'traditional' part of the Iowa Girl's Basketball tournament. When Grandpa arrived in Denison he was fifteen-years-old, two days late, with little money and twenty miles of fresh fallen snow between him and the Theobald farm. It would have cost him $1.50 at the local livery stable to rent a horse and buggy to take him to Astor but Grandpa had better plans for that $1.50. Fortunately, all his worldly possessions made a small package, so he walked the old Indian trail they called the Ridge Road from Denison to Astor.

I always thought Uncle Ed followed the next year and then Fred but I have read a couple of accounts that say Ed came first. Eventually the girls came, too.

Elizabeth, better known as Lizzie, went on to prep school at Simpson College. In 1887 she was one of 45 members of the college's freshman class but in December of that year the school newspaper, **THE SIMPSONIAN**, reported "Mis Lizzie Saunders has dropped college work and taken a school." A college education was not necessary to teach and a new opportunity had arisen. With this decision Aunt Lizzie became the first school teacher in the newly formed Manilla school district. She married John McCracken and the Saunders' family tree began to sprout new branches.

Years later, after C.A. had achieved considerable success as a farmer and cattle breeder, he loved to tell the story of how he 'walked into this country.' He told the story so often that people, especially his own family, began to make fun of him.

Brothers working together were one of the key elements that made the Saunders boys successful, but sibling rivalry added its own special brand of stimulus. So, on his 50th birthday, to prove

The adult children of Charles and Louisa Saunders; L – R, Fredrick James, Elizabeth Sarah (McCracken), Edgar, Alice Helena (James), C. A., William Alexander. Circa 1901.

his point, C.A. walked, for a second time, the old Indian trail that brought him from Denison to Astor.

His brother, I'm quite certain it was Ed, steadfastly refused to recognize this feat as anything more than the ramblings of an old man trying to revive and aggrandize his youth. He roughly stated "That's nothing." Grandfather wouldn't let it end there; he re-walked

Uncle 'Deacon' Ed with his wife Mary Ivey Saunders in the back and Grandfather C.A. and Grandmother Bertha Theobald Saunders in the foreground.

that same twenty mile trail[15] for a third time on the 50th anniversary of his snowy arrival in Iowa. He was 65 years old.

Trudy and I visited Black Earth a couple years ago. I had known that Grandpa, Uncle Ed and Uncle Will met back up in Black Earth each year to tend the graves. Their father, a murderer who committed suicide, was not allowed burial in the cemetery. He was hastily and unceremoniously buried on the afternoon of his death in a "Potter's Field" outside the fence of the official cemetery. Their mother was buried the next afternoon in a proper grave within the

---

[15] The first portion of the old Indian trail known as the Ridge Road has now been renamed Donna Reed Road. Donna Belle Mullinger, whose childhood home was along the road, became famous as Donna Reed in such movies as "It's a Wonderful Life" with James Stewart and "Here to Eternity" for which she won an Oscar. She also had a hit TV series in the 60's, "The Donna Reed Show."

city cemetery after a large funeral in the Congregational Church for which the entire town turned out.

Our search for the graves led us to an old hill top country cemetery in the back yard of an aging farm house. Continuing our search for a stone with the Saunders name was not very successful; many of the limestone markers were so aged as to be illegible. This caused us to linger and ponder. Soon a man came out of the house. We exchanged pleasantries and introductions but he knew nothing of a Saunders' grave in his backyard. He did, however, tell us of an old section in the big 'new' town cemetery.

It was dusk as we arrived at the 'big' cemetery. A lone man was walking his dog. He had buried his wife there three days earlier and had returned for a visit. He seemed genuinely helpful, perhaps even grateful for the distraction. "I can't tell you where the Saunders' stone is," he said, "but I'll take you to a person who can."

We were taken to the home of two old-maid school teachers. The door was opened by an elderly somewhat eccentric but distinguished looking lady by the name of Miss Leila Barber. She was tall, as tall as me and straight as a string, before I could say a word she sized me up from head to toe and said "You're a man I can look straight in the eye." I introduced myself and told her why I was there. "Charlie Saunders," she said, "I knew him well."

As fate would have it, she was the sole surviving daughter of a family of Black Earth icons who had been some of the very early businessmen and progressive leaders of the young community. They had known the Saunders family and evidently especially knew Uncle Will before he left Black Earth. The story, as she told it, was that her mother cried for three weeks when Uncle Will left. "Those men," she said, referring to my grandfather and his brothers, "used to come up to my father's house. He cared for the cemetery. They erected a big stone for their Mother."

She directed us to the cemetery, perhaps the most beautiful I have ever seen, meticulously cared for and stretching over two rolling hills with old trees and a sense of peace and dignity rarely found in today's world. The stone was a large gray stone engraved simply with "SAUNDERS," below were the words "Mother" and "Father," no other names and no dates. Alongside was a small, limestone

Modern day picture of the Saunders' Black Earth burial plots. The inserts are enlargements of the small stones marked "Grandmother Sarah Fisher" and "Chas. Saunders, 49th Wisconsin Infantry, Company A." In both instances the actual markers lie just above the upper right corner of the inserts.

marker with the Wisconsin Infantry insignia and the name, "Chas. Saunders." On one of their trips, the boys had obtained permission to move their father into the cemetery beside their Mother. A third barely visible flat stone with the inscription Grandmother Sarah Fisher lay along side.

The next day we returned with paper and markers to do a rubbing of the stones. Before we left Black Earth we went to the newspaper and made a copy of the article reporting the murder/suicide and to the American Legion to get a copy of Charles A.'s discharge from the Union Army.

What Miss Leila Barber and I didn't realize when we first met and what subsequent research has revealed is the fact that our chance meeting was the first interaction in well over one-hundred

The final two paragraphs of the original guardianship papers are reproduced above and bear the date March 2nd, 1872 along with the signature of Sarah S. Fisher.

years maybe in one-and-a-quarter century, between two families whose lives had once been closely intertwined. Leila Barber, we learned later, was a descendent of a man named Thomas Barber.

She was, I have reason to believe, though I don't know this as an absolute fact, the grand daughter of Thomas Barber.[16]

Why is Thomas Barber of any interest to the Saunders family? Well, I'll tell you. On the second day of March, 1872 Sarah Selina (Grandma) Fisher signed a motion for appointment of guardian recommending Thomas Barber be appointed guardian of the Saunders' children. The documents states:

> "The undersigned petitioner respectfully represents that William A. (Alexander) Saunders, aged about eighteen years, Charles A.(Adolphus) Saunders aged about fourteen years, Edgar Saunders, aged about twelve years, Elizabeth Sarah Saunders, aged about eleven years, Alice Helena Saunders, aged about nine years, and Frederick James Saunders, aged about eight years, are minor children of Charles A. Saunders and Louisa Saunders, late of the Village of Black Earth, County of Dane, State of Wisconsin.
>
> That said minors are possessed of some real estate in coparcenary inherited from their said deceased father and also of some personal property, the amount of which cannot at present be ascertained.
>
> That it is for the benefit and interest of said minors that a guardian should be appointed for said minors, to the charge, care and custody of their persons and property.
>
> That your petitioner, being the grandmother of said minors on their mother's side, is the nearest relative said minors have in said county of Dane. Your petitioner not wishing to take upon herself the trust of being said guardian, would respectfully recommend as a suitable person for said trust Thomas Barber Esq. of the Village of Black Earth, County of Dane, State of Wisconsin, and respectfully petition that he may be appointed guardian of said minors accordingly."
>
> Dated March 2nd, 1872
> (signed) Sarah S. Fisher

---

[16] I am not aware that Thomas Barber had brothers in Black Earth but he did have five children; three boys and two girls. His two oldest sons moved to Kansas. The youngest son, David, stayed in Black Earth and went into business with his father. It would be age appropriate for Leila to be David's daughter but I have not confirmed the relationship.

Thomas Barber was born in England in 1817 making him fourteen-years older than Charles (b. 1831) and he immigrated to America in 1847, four years before the Saunders. He moved to Black Earth in 1855, one year before the Saunders, and ran a hardware store. It is interesting to speculate; did Charles Saunders know Thomas Barber in England, were they friends, were they related either by blood or marriage? Was Barber the reason Charles immigrated to America or moved to Black Earth? Or was Thomas Barber simply a respected citizen with a sense of civic duty to whom the guardianship could be entrusted?

These are questions to which the answers may never be known but we do know that he served as co-administrator of the estate along with Grandma Fisher and was the children's legal guardian until 1885. It was not an easy job. As we know, the family began to split apart, excerpts from the estate papers give us an idea just when:

> "...Aug. 3rd,1872 – at which time William A. Saunders the oldest boy of deceased supported himself and has since that time earned his living."
>
> ". . . so as to show the share of Charles A. Saunders and Edgar Saunders, they from that time (December 1873) having supported themselves."

William would have been eighteen, Charles fifteen and Edgar thirteen years-of-age when they began supporting themselves. The younger children stayed in Black Earth with Grandma Fisher and according to the papers filed by William on July 1, 1871:

> "The deceased left goods worth the probable amount of $2,000, and real estate to the probable amount of $1,500. He left debts due and unpaid to the probably amount of about $225."

A small glimpse into their lives can be seen just four days before Christmas in the winter of 1875. It did not foretell of a very Merry Christmas. In a handwritten letter to Judge G. E. Bryant on December 21, 1875, Thomas Barber wrote, on his business letterhead, the following:

> Dear Judge
> I received yours of the 19th and not being posted properly as to my duty in reporting to you, if it be requested, I will make out a full statement of Monies received and disburst. I have no bal. on hand, and taxes are due $25.00. They are without wood – store bill due and the store keepers teasing me. The Old Lady is sick – don't expect her to live[17] – Bill bothering about his share which I think he has had – unless the old lady and children must starve I cannot divide with him at present. Would like full instruction as to my duty – if I am considered as guardian of the Estate, which I have given ample security therefore – I would like to know how far my care or control of the family goes. Bill would not care to see his younger brothers & sisters thrown on to the County if he could only handle the money. Answer this and if it be necessary I will make out a full report.
> I am yours truly,
> (signed) Thomas Barber

Mr. Barber continued as legal guardian of the orphans for another 10 years, a fact that lends credibility to Leila Barber's statements. In 1885 Fredrick, the youngest of the children, turned twenty-one-years-old. On March 9th of that year, Charles Adolphus Saunders, my grandfather and son of the deceased, acting as 'attorney in fact' on behalf of all of his brothers and sisters filed for a *General Release of Ward to Guardian* in the County Court for Dane County, State of Wisconsin. In the final settlement, monies were divided as follows:

---

[17] Sarah Fisher died 10 days after Thomas Barber wrote this letter, on New Years Eve, December 31, 1875. The 'Old Lady' was 61 years old.

Thomas Barber,

THOMAS BARBER,
Dealer in
Shelf Hardware, Iron, Steel,
AGRICULTURAL IMPLEMENTS, PLOWS,
Stoves and Tinware, Bent Wood Work, Mechanics' Tools,
&c., &c.

Black Earth, Wis., Dec 21 1875

Mr Byant

Dr Judge

I recieve yours of
the 19th and not being posted
properly as to my duty in
Reporting to you. if it be required, I will make out a
full statement of Monies
recieved and disburst. I have
no bal on hand. and Taxes
are due $25⁰⁰ they are with-
out wood — Store bills due
and the Store Keepers teasing
me — the Old Lady sick don't
expect her to live — Bill
bothering about his share

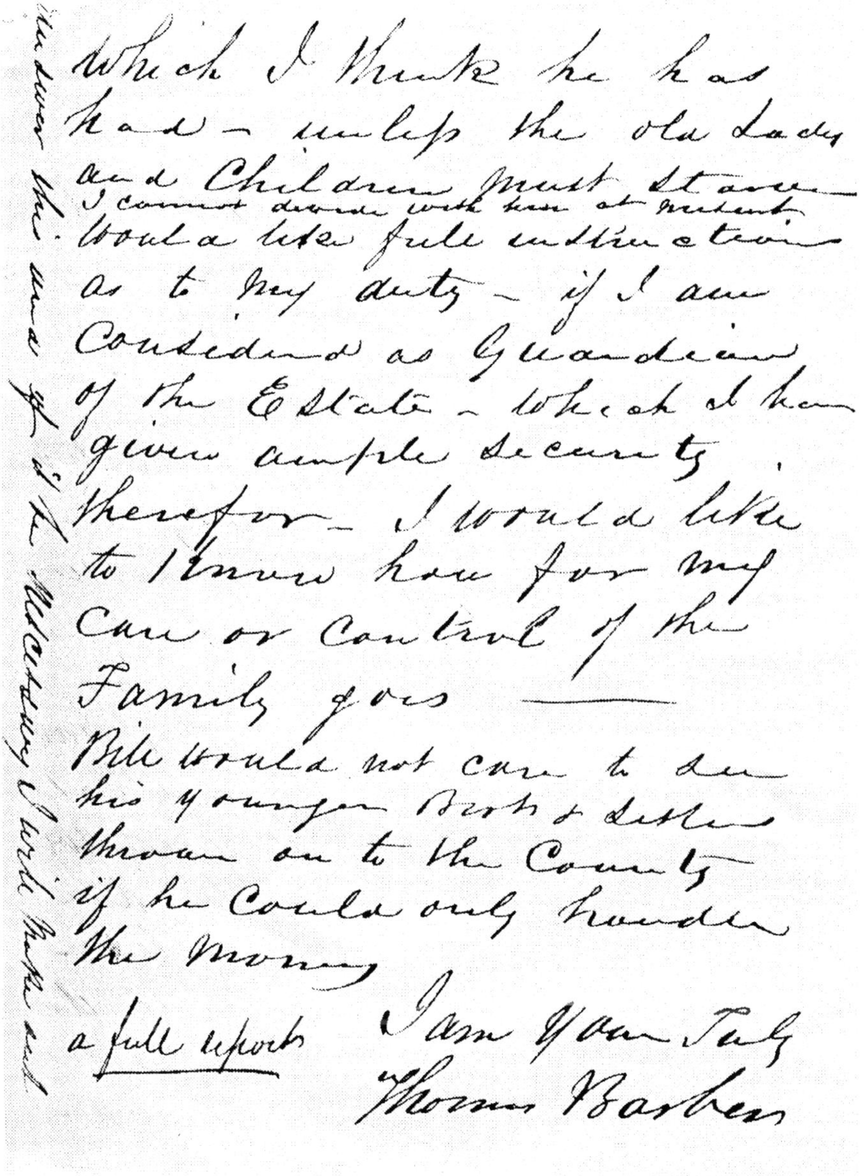

Which I think he has
had — unless the old Lady
and Children must starve
I cannot devise with him at present
would like full instruction
as to my duty — if I am
Considered as Guardian
of the Estate — which I have
given ample security
therefor — I would like
to Know how far my
Care or Control of the
Family goes —
Bill would not care to see
his younger Barts & sisters
thrown on to the County
if he could only handle
the money

a full reports   I am Your Truly
                              Thomas Barber

Edgar Saunders now residing Astor, Crawford County, Iowa $520.00

Sarah E. Saunders now residing Chicago, Cook County, Illinois $338.00[18]

Alice H. Saunders now residing Astor, Crawford County, Iowa $338.00

William A. Saunders now residing Chicago, Cook County, Illinois $522.70

Fredrick J. Saunders now residing Astor, Crawford County, Iowa $338.00

Charles A. Saunders now residing Astor, Crawford County, Iowa $520.00[19]

Save for three graves, all official ties to the State of Wisconsin were now severed but Black Earth still held one more surprise for the Saunders family.

On a more recent visit by some of our family members we were able to view newly discovered documents. A close review of Charles and Louisa's divorce papers revealed;

" . . . That as the product of their joint labors the defendant (Charles) now owns a lot of land in Black Earth Village known and described as Lot No. Seven (7) Block fifteen (15) in Hall &McEwen's Addition to the Village of Black Earth which was bought with the proceeds of a homestead belonging to this plaintiff (Louisa) who had been told the proceeds applied to the purchase of the above described on which the defendant has built a house valued at Two Thousand Dollars and a Shop for the business of

---

[18] Sarah E. is actually Elizabeth Sarah and she never actually lived in Chicago. She apparently was using her inheritance for an education and the Simpson College newspaper, THE SIMPSONIAN, clarifies the question. "Miss Lizzie Saunders, from Astor, who was in last term, being afflicted with weak eyes, was compelled during vacation to go to Chicago for medical treatment. In consequence she is not in attendance this term."

[19] The purchasing power of a dollar in 1885 was roughly ten times what it is today. The children's inheritance would be worth approximately $3,400 to $5,200 in today's dollar.

this plaintiff as a milliner and dressmaker, valued at Five
Hundred Dollars . . ."

Apparently Charles and Louisa homesteaded a plot of land upon their arrival in Black Earth but subsequently sold the land and moved to town.

Review of an 1873 atlas[20] shows Lot Seven, Block Fifteen to be a short two blocks south of the old train depot, which now serves as the museum and headquarters of The Black Earth Historical Society. A quick walk down Mills Street, the main thoroughfare along which most businesses were located, took us to the lot. On it was a house that was a near perfect match of the architectural footprint of the old Saunders's residence as recorded in both the atlas and in an 1876 lithograph entitled, Bird's Eye View of Black Earth Looking From the Northwest.

Could it be that this was the actual house, the home of Charles, Louisa and their six children – the scene of the crime? Surely it couldn't be. The house would have to be close to a hundred-thirty maybe even a hundred-forty years old.

It didn't seem possible yet given the map and lithograph it seemed probable enough to snap a couple of photographs. Accompanied by Shirley Danz of The Black Earth Historical Society, we began photographing the house and noting the similarities between the map details and the building. It was a rectangular two story wood frame house set back maybe thirty feet or so from the street. The narrow front of the house faced east, overlooking Mills Street. On the long southern side of the house was a one story wing, perhaps an addition to the original house.

Soon the back door of the house opened and out walked a kindly lady, she was thin with neatly combed gray hair and wearing a blue dress. She appeared to be in her mid-eighties. Black Earth today is a town of 1,300 people so there are no strangers. Shirley introduced us to Janet Schmitt and explained why we were there.

"He thinks his relatives may have lived in your house." Shirley said.

---

[20] Atlas of Dane County, Wisconsin, Madison: Harrison and Warner, 1873, p.65.

"Oh, I wouldn't know about that," Mrs. Schmitt replied, "but you're welcome to come in if you like."

We declined politely but asked, "How old is the house?"

"It must be over a hundred-years-old." She said, "We have lived here over fifty years."

I explained the history of the Saunders family in Black Earth. She was vaguely aware of the story but knew no details. I thanked her and told her we would be on our way after a couple more pictures.

She retreated into the house only to return a few minutes later with a large file containing the title search for her home. We leafed backward through the pages, the1900's, the 1890's, the 1880's, the 1870's and there it was – "Charles Saunders, Grantee, Warranty Deed, March 21, 1870."

There was no doubt about it, this house, for at least a short period of time was the Saunders home. Clearly it now warranted a closer examination. The present owners added a front porch that is easily defined by the change in siding and slope of the roof. There was also an addition in the rear of the building. You can see a change in the foundation in the photograph on page 47; the original building was only that portion which contains the basement windows and the two long windows. The map of 1873 clearly defines this architectural footprint. Was this small one story extension the Millinery Shop? One newspaper article said the shop was adjoining the residence. The second article stated after the shooting ". . . he (Charles) had entered the dwelling house, next door. . ."

However, a later entry in the Schmitt's title records notes that Charles Saunders was the grantor of a $500 mortgage to Paul Coply and Geo. Carden on May 1, 1871. The description of the property:

> "18 by 26 feet in NE corner Lot 7 Block 15 Hall and McEwen's Addition Black Earth where Millinery Store of Chas. Saunders is standing."

An eighteen by twenty-six foot northeast corner of the lot where the millinery store stood, perhaps the store was separate after all. Did Charles sell off Louisa's Millinery Store? The map of 1873, printed two years after the incident, clearly shows a structure in Lot 6 extending over into the NE corner of Lot 7.

Furthermore, we know from the divorce papers a violent altercation occurred on the afternoon of Saturday, April 29, 1871. The cause was not defined, but could it have been over the sale of the property? Two days later, May 1st, Charles signed the transfer of property that may well have included the site of Louisa's shop. After another two days, May 3rd, Louisa filed for divorce and a day later, May 4th, the papers were served. It is apparent that property had some role because on the fateful day, June 29th, The Black Earth Advertiser reported Charles entered the shop and proposed Louisa accompany him to Madison "adding that he would make over some property to her if she would go."

The rest is history.

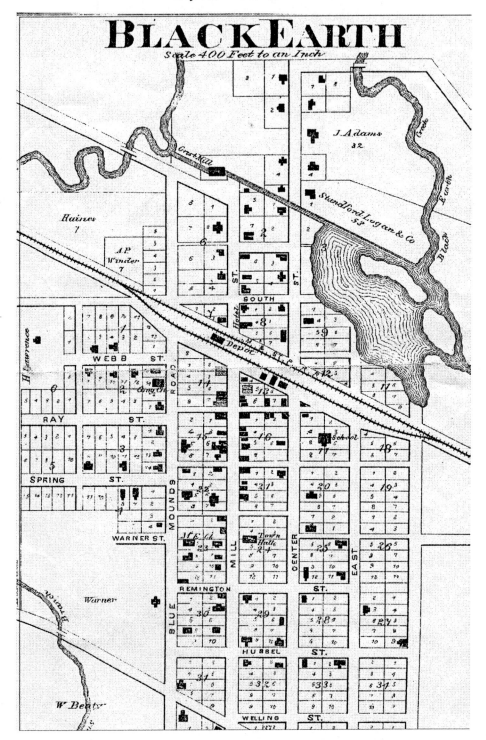

BLACKEARTH
Scale 400 Feet to an Inch

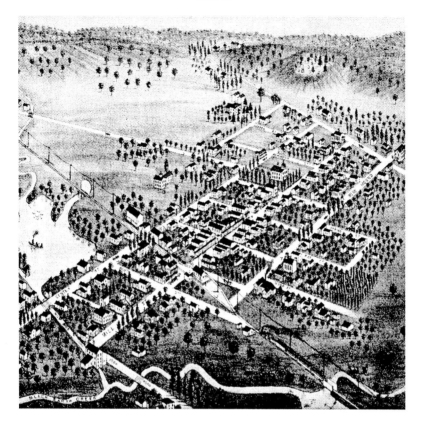

From Bird's Eye View of Black Earth Looking from the Northwest, 1876.[21]
The village was anchored on the north by a grist mill (lower left corner) at
the northern most end of Mills Street and on the south by a cheese factory,
barely visible where Blue Mound Road exits the picture in the upper right
corner. Two blocks south of the grist mill, where the railroad crosses Mill
Street, on the right side, is the railroad depot, the current home of The
Black Earth Historical Society and Museum. Two blocks further south,
on the southeast corner of the block is the home of Charles and Louisa
Saunders and their six children, also on the site was Louisa's Millinery
Shop. Continuing down Mills Street a block-and-a-half on the left is the
Town Hall constructed by Charles in 1869-70. Two blocks straight east
of the Saunders' home, in the middle of the field, is the two story public
school all the Saunders' children attended. One block west and a block or
so north of the house, on the right side of Blue Mound Road is The First
Congregational Church, the site of Louisa's funeral. The Barbers lived a
block east of the depot in the two story house on Center Street.

---

[21] Wisconsin Historical Society. D. Bremmer and Co. Lith. Milwaukee

This ad for a "NEW STORE" appeared in the Black Earth Advertiser April 6, 1871

This photograph was provided by Shirley Danz of the Black Earth Historical Society and appears to be of similar vintage of the image on the next page. They are essentially views of the opposite sides of Mill(s) street. The main building in this photo is Buerki Drug Store but to the right is the Charles Saunders' home. Below is the house today.

BLACK EARTH, WIS.   MAIN STREET.

Charles and Louisa would have recognized this view. The Saunders' home and the site of Louisa's dress shop were just off left edge of this photo, directly across from the two story building on the right. Below is the same scene on a lazy summer Saturday afternoon one-hundred years later.

The "Saunders' house" facing Mills Street in Black Earth as it appears today. Whether the millinery shop was the small southern extension or it stood alone on the northeast corner of the lot, neither had access to the basement. The only basement entrance was from an outside door on the northern side of the residence. After the shooting, Charles would have had to exit the shop regardless of its location and run around the house to the northern entrance to gain access to the basement. The photo on the following page shows the exact stairs down which Charles and his pursuers would have entered the basement. The door at the top is now sealed off and there is a new basement entrance yet these 'nowhere leading stairs' are the original. At the base of the stairs Charles would have turned slightly to the left seeing the second view of the basement and " . . . before he was found. He had gone to the darkest corner of the cellar . . ."

Chapter 2

Cumberland Stock Farm

January 25, 1989

It's now about 5:30 in the morning.
Our forecast is for another beautiful day. Still very mild. A bit of snow yesterday, but will be gone by sundown.
Today I'll try to write a bit about the farm . . .

The 'pot of gold' at the end of Grandfather's train trip from Wisconsin was the John Theobald farm and the rolling hills of western Iowa. The Theobalds had settled in this area only a year or two earlier.

This land was part of the original Louisiana Purchase, bought by President Thomas Jefferson from Napoleon in 1803 for about three cents an acre and explored by Lewis and Clark less than seventy years earlier. Originally, the land was populated by the Otoe Indians; they called the area "Ni-sna-ba-te-na." Ni-sha is the Otoe word for creek, ba-te means boat and na translates as usually or frequently, together they mean "Creek where they (usually) make boats," thus Nishnabotny became the name given to the nearby river as well as the newly formed township.

About the time that Grandfather arrived, a resident of the area advertised in the Denison newspaper:

> "offering pasturage for stock and, as evidence that the cattle would not be disturbed by settlers, said that the day before he had shot an elk and could do so almost at any time."[22]

---

[22] **Manilla Community Folks and Facts 1886-1986**. A publication of the Manilla Centennial, June, 1986

This raw countryside was camouflaged as wasteland with hazelbrush and scrub oak stretching over the horizon farther than the eye could see. Thomas Jefferson thought it would take a thousand years for his Louisiana Purchase to be settled yet the fertile black Iowa soil that lay underneath was some of the best on the planet and was soon destined to feed a nation.

Both our nation and my Grandfather were young and growing up together. The Civil War was over, Lincoln had been dead for seven years[23], and Andrew Johnson had been replaced by Ulysses S. Grant who was now serving as the 18th President of the United States. Three years previously[24] the golden spike had been driven to complete the transcontinental railroad. The Indian Wars were all but over, yet it would still be four years before Custer would be defeated at Little Big Horn[25] and it would be another eighteen years[26] until the massacre of Wounded Knee in nearby South Dakota brought them to a final end. The writing, however, was on the wall and the young country was ready to concentrate on growth and expansion.

C.A. was fifteen years old and orphaned. The burden of a terrible family tragedy weighed heavily on his shoulders, as did the added responsibility of carrying on and rehabilitating his given name, Charles Adolphus.

Fifteen years of age in those days was still young but it was enough to make a boy a man and fate had decided that this young man's childhood had come to an end. No doubt circumstances limited his options but he made the decision that he was done moving and at the tender age of 15 began his life's work.

He worked for room and board on the Theobalds' farm the first year. The second year he earned 25 cents a week and in his spare time rented land from the railroad and put in a crop. With the proceeds from that first crop, he bought two brood mares because the next year he planned to work for other people, too, and a man

---

[23] Lincoln's death was on April 14,1865, five days after Lee surrendered to General Grant thus ending the Civil War.
[24] May 10, 1869 in Promontory, Utah.
[25] 1876
[26] 1890

with a team of horses could earn much more than an orphan just off the train from Wisconsin.

The land my Grandfather rented was forty acres in the Northeast corner of Section Three, in Greeley Township, Shelby County, Iowa. When the railroad came through this country they were given land for development as payment for their efforts. I believe it was every other section of land for five maybe even ten miles on each side of the railroad and by selling off this land the money could be used to build more railroads.

Thanks to the railroad the country was being settled, and thanks to the fertility of the Iowa farmland the farmers were able to prosper and rise above subsistence level, thereby producing extra products for city markets. American agriculture expanded greatly in the 1870's to the 1890's. The industrial revolution had given the farmer new tools with which to work the land. With the railroad, farmers now had a way to get their produce to larger city markets.

The sleeping giant that was American agriculture began to awaken along with the rest of the country. Increased production made food plentiful and cheap, which was, of course, good for the consumers but it also drove down the prices of the farmer's goods. The '80s were also a period of pretty severe drought in some parts of

> *"Fifteen years of age . . . was still young but it was enough to make a boy a man and fate had decided that this young man's childhood had come to an end."*

the country. When times got rough, the railroads, once thought the ally of the farmer, began to be accused of price gouging and unfair business practices. A split began to grow between the farmers and the eastern industrialists. This was the time of the Carnegies, the Rockefellers and the robber barons.

The book **Eyes of a Nation**, published by The Library of Congress, described the times and reminded me of a famous story whose origin has been all but forgotten, a story that I will include for my grandchildren, great grandchildren and all others who have either forgotten or never knew.

The South was rebuilding their economy after the Civil War and new lands were being opened in the west. But farming, despite the addition of new technologies, has always been a hard job, it is now and it was then. Drought, crop diseases and insects, unstable prices and other problems drove many farmers off their land and others deeply into debt. The 1890's were particularly difficult times for the farmers.

For all their problems that couldn't be blamed on Mother Nature, the farmers began blaming the railroad and the eastern industrialists, amongst others. First the farmers formed their own union. It was the first organization of labor in the country and it started in the farm organization that would become known as The Grange. Next they formed their own political party called The People's Party or more commonly, The Populists.

During this time the country's money supply was based on the gold standard. For reasons I can't fully explain, farmers were convinced this limited the availability of money and contributed to their problems. At this time in history the law required each printed-paper dollar be backed up by a dollar's worth of gold in the government's vault. Since gold was so rare, the farmers wanted the more plentiful silver to be the standard.

There was a famous politician from our neighboring state Nebraska by the name of William Jennings Bryan; he was a great orator and debater. Though he was a Democrat, Bryan took up the cause of the farmers and some of the Populists Party causes. One cause he championed was the change from the gold to the silver standard. In 1896 he gave a speech at the Democratic Convention in Chicago, entitled "Cross of Gold" that so excited the convention that he was selected as their candidate to run for President. His platform identified with the farmers, fundamentalist religion[27] and the gold standard, which became a great issue in this presidential election. William Jennings Bryan and the Democrats lost the election to William McKinley. The Republicans stayed in power for the next forty years and The Populist Party eventually failed.

Why am I telling you this story? Because, in 1901 there was a book written about the farmers, politicians, and the gold standard. You know it as the story of **The Wizard of Oz**. It was written as a parable, probably a satire. The Tin man, without a heart, whom Dorothy found in the Eastern Land of the Munchkins, represented the heartless eastern industrialists. The Scarecrow, in search of a brain, represented the farmers. The courage-seeking lion was William Jennings Bryan. The yellow brick road represented the gold standard and Dorothy's shoes? Dorothy's shoes were not ruby red in the book; that was a Hollywood invention. In the original book, the shoes were silver and they were, of course, magical. The silver shoes could get you anywhere you wanted to go in just three short steps. They represented the Populist-championed silver standard as a replacement for the gold standard. And the Wizard, the fraudulent wizard to whom they were all traveling down the Yellow Brick Road in high hopes that he could solve all their problems was none other than President William McKinley.

Grandfather lived these times and this was also the story of his life. All farmers were tied to the railroad. Letters, magazines and newspapers were all brought by rail on the same cars that carried away their produce to market. Four years after Grandfather's move to Iowa, Alexander Graham Bell invented the telephone[28] and the next year Thomas Edison invented the light bulb[29] but it would be a long, long time until these modern inventions would reach the

---

[27] Bryan's last days were spent in the famous "Scopes Monkey Trial." John T. Scopes was a teacher in Tennessee who was brought to trial for teaching evolution. Bryan was the prosecutor and won the case against evolution but died a few days after the trial in 1925. In 1927 the Supreme Court of Tennessee reversed the decision.

[28] 1876

[29] 1877

Iowa farms. Urgent news came by telegraph wires strung along the railroad tracks. Everything depended upon the railroad.

Even Manilla, the town my grandfather and the rest of the Saunders family would eventually call home, was still a corn field and ten years in the future when he began his life a new with the Theobalds. Grandfather would have attended Grange meetings in the brand new little town of Astor, Iowa and later read of William Jennings Bryan's speech and presidential nomination in a newspaper lit by a kerosene lamp.

Actually, if the truth were known, Astor wasn't even a real town yet. Mr. O.A. Olson had established a general store on his farm alongside the Chicago, Milwaukee and Saint Paul railroad tracks. You could buy most anything in his store, it was just like the movies; food, clothing, hardware, and fencing. What ever was needed to succeed on the land was packed into the small general store that surrounded the big wood burning potbelly stove sitting right smack dab in the middle of its single room.

Electricity and telephones were not yet considered practical let alone necessities. Even if you never set foot outside the General Store, this big old potbelly could tell you just about everything you needed to know. Simply by hanging out close by you could hear every bit of town gossip and a continual "town meeting" originated from the surrounding half-dozen or so mismatched wooden chairs. The chairs themselves seemed to have the uncanny ability to predict the weather. When they were pulled up close it was always cold and blustery and when they sat far back the sun shone warmly. When they were empty it seemed the weather was just about right for some kind of work and when they were full, well, more often than not it was raining. If entertainment and excitement were the order of the day, there was always the danger of a checker game breaking out or a stranger wandering up from the depot. If you just wanted to relax and daydream all you had to do was stare at the big shiny nickel plate "Cincinnati Iron Works" logo around the fattest part of the old potbelly and dream of exotic far away places.

Later Mr. Olson also built a grain elevator along the tracks. He would buy grain and livestock from the farmers and ship them off to the city on the rails. O.A. stood of Ole Andrew. He was born in Norway and married Ella Christiansen who had been born in Denmark. Together they tried to help a lot of the Danes, Norwegians and Swedes in the area. At 9 o'clock in the morning all the Scandinavian dairy farmers could be seen descending on Astor with their teams and wagons to meet the "Milk Train." There was no electrical refrigeration in those days so it was a daily ritual to bring the fresh raw milk in cans, each labeled with the farmer's name and assigned number. The train would stop at each little town along the route and load the cans for shipment to the creamery in Omaha. The next day your milk can came back to you empty and clean. It was said that they picked up enough milk in Astor alone to pay for the train to Omaha.

According to the Manilla Centennial History Book Staff:[30]

"The Astor Cemetery was in existence before 1886. Census takers were housed in homes bearing the name of Swan, Bidlack, Saunders, Theobald and Barber. There were 44 males and 54 females registered in 1875 . . .

Astor was plotted in 1882 with thirteen blocks of various sizes on land that formerly belonged to Robert Theobald. By 1884 the thriving community had a Methodist Church, a school, more than fifteen homes of good size, besides smaller homes and apartments above businesses. The population of about 300 people was primarily of German, Scandinavian and Irish descent.

Astor's business district included a flourmill, two general stores, two blacksmiths, drug stores, a grain elevator and a flourmill, a post office, a hotel, a butcher shop, a restaurant, a livery stable and a lumber yard . . .

By 1886 Astor began proceedings to incorporate. However, during this same time, the railroad made a decision that would end the prosperity of this growing community . . . (However) Astor continued to exist for many years as a center of trade for local farmers . . . In 1932 the general store burned to the ground and was never

[30] Jorgensen, Kathy. "Astor", **Manilla Community Folks and Facts 1886-1986**.

L to R: O.A. Olson's house, O.A. Olson Store, hardware store and implement shop of P.C. Petersen, a blacksmith shop and a garage and repair shop.

O.A. Olson farm, Astor, Iowa.

Elevator, Astor, Iowa.

Olson's house and store, Astor, Iowa.

Depot, Astor, Iowa.

This collage of Astor photos was printed in the Manilla
Community Folks and Facts 1886-1986 in celebration of the
town's centennial.

WHICH OF THESE TWO DO YOU THINK RAISES SHORT-HORNS?
THE TOP ONE, OF COURSE!

Grandfather has some fun printing these photos in a 1906 sale catalog. The bottom picture depicts a farmer bringing his milk can filled with fresh raw milk to meet the 'Milk Train' in Astor. The difference between the two pictures could be compared to the 1906 equivalent of a sports car and a pickup truck

This is the first home of C.A. and Bertha, they lived here nearly 25 years until building a new house and turning this into a grainery. Attendees of this family gathering are largely unknown, I believe Bertha and C.A. flank the group; Vic is next to Bertha and my father next to CA. My uncle Chuck, I believe, is the second person to the left of the dinner bell. I'm sure the rest of the kids are there but I can't recognize them.

rebuilt . . . The grain elevator built in 1909 by O.A. Olsen still stands today and is used by the present land owner."[31]

America was making true its promise of a better life. Grandfather was able to buy the forty acres he had rented from the railroad in Greeley Township. The township, just over the county line into Shelby County, had been named after the New York newspaper editor Horace Greeley who advised, "Go west young man, go west."

It was good advice. Grandfather bought a stallion for the two brood mares and began raising horses and added forty acres at

---

[31] The elevator burned to the ground in the winter of 2004.

a time until he owned the whole section except for the northwest corner. He named his farm the Greeley Stock Farm.

On the twenty-fifth anniversary of his parent's marriage, May 4, 1876, at age nineteen, C.A. married Bertha Theobald. Grandma Bertha was only fifteen-years-old when they were married. She was the daughter of John Theobald, one of the Theobald boys who came from Black Earth in the wagon train and the older sister of Ruth Mary Theobald who would later marry C.A.'s younger brother Fred.

The young couple built some new buildings and moved on to their new farm. Years later there would be a story that they lived in a converted grainery during the first few years of their marriage but to my knowledge that was not true. The story grew, I believe, from the fact that after they built their big new house, the old house or at least a part of it was then converted into a grainery.

Family legend has it that Frank and Jessie James may have visited the newlyweds.

Eighteen seventy six was the year that the James and Younger Gang held up the bank just over the Iowa border in Northfield, Minnesota. The James brothers handpicked Northfield's bank because they had a personal feud with the owners dating back to the Civil War. Though the bank was chosen with care the gang should have paid more attention to the town.

Northfield was a small town, populated by tight knit, hard-working Swedes who, though tolerant, were quite suspicious of strangers. They certainly were not the type to stand idly by and allow anyone to take from them the meager rewards they had managed to scrape together from the cold Minnesota prairie. When the townspeople saw the gang ride into town they were suspicious of the strangers and soon correctly surmised that their bank was being robbed. The towns people rose en mass and descended on the bank robbers with whatever weapons they could readily lay their hands on. Using pitchforks, brooms, pistols and shotguns, every member of the gang was either killed or imprisoned; only Frank and Jesse James escaped.

A posse was formed that chased the James brothers through parts of what was then called the Dakota Territory (soon to be called Nebraska and South Dakota), and into Iowa. The posse thought they had the James's surrounded one night in the area of Dow City and Buck Grove, Iowa, several miles northwest of Astor. I think it was in an area once called Gallan's Grove. However, when daylight came the grove was empty.

It took a few days for this news to reach C.A. and Bertha but when it did, it gave them pause to wonder.

The same day the posse had surrounded Gallan's Grove, two strangers had ridden onto the Saunders' homestead late in the afternoon. They were polite, calm and unhurried but also trail-weary and dirty. More importantly, as far as it concerned my grandfather, they treated their horses well, and this was perhaps the most important test of any man's character. The strangers knew Grandfather was in the horse business and they wanted to talk horse-trading. As was the custom, down home hospitality dictated that potential buyers were invited to dinner and as it was late in the day and they were far out in the country, they were also offered overnight lodging. The two strangers, I don't know what name they gave, bathed their horses and brushed them down and fed them before they themselves dined with the young farm couple and retired to their upstairs loft.

The next morning after breakfast the two strangers rode off, clean and rested. They did not do any horse-trading but left with a promise to keep in touch. When Grandma went to clean their upstairs room she found a note that read simply, "For the housekeeper" along with two brand new shiny silver dollars. The strangers were never heard from again and with the exception of the two silver dollars, there was really nothing unusual about this visit. Nothing, that is, until they heard the rest of the story.

Things rapidly returned to normal on the farm although not necessarily in Astor.

Over the years C.A. and Bertha, would have eight children but before they were born a new town was to be born. Again the Manilla Centennial History Book staff tells it best:

"All was quiet and peaceful in Astor until one day some strangers appeared – railroad officials – people soon found out a short cut to Sioux City was their aim. The question was, were they going to build from Astor or Defiance? It was soon found out they were going to build a new town just two miles east of Astor. The railroad bought W.L. Paup's farm, had it surveyed and lots were staked out.

You can imagine the excitement this brought to Astor. The townsmen were bewildered, then decided they had better move to the new town. The sale of lots was held in Nov. and $13,000 worth of lots were sold. Residents of Astor put their business places and homes on wheels and moved to the new town, the moving being done with horses, mules and oxen. It was a lot of hard work. They soon were lined up along the new main street with corn stalks and fodder under their feet. Instead of a gold rush, it was a rush for a new town. With stores still on stilts, they were ready for business. The two blacksmiths, Palmer and Brown, were the first to leave Astor and move their places of business. Their business was necessary for the building of the new railroad as it took many horses, mules and equipment. A boxcar served as depot and freight house all in one. It was a bit crowded but it was all they had.

Lots in the new town sold like wild fire and houses sprang up like mushrooms overnight. E.H. Hanne was the first grocery store to move to the new town. It was located where the Memorial Hall now stands.

The new town did not as yet have an official name. In 1885, Astor celebrated the Fourth of July and one of the program features was a tug-of-war. Since the new town did not have a name, they decided to name it with the tug-of-war contest. There were some who thought the town should be named after Les Paup (who owned the land before the railroad bought it). They wanted it called Paupville.

Until this time, grain had been bound by hand, but the self-binder had just been invented. With it a twist (of hemp twine) had to be used. Mr. Blackburn's Hardware store in Astor was sending out circulars advertising the new twine, called Manila Binder Twine. Mr. Blackburn furnished a

Main street Manilla, Iowa circa 1900. The sign over the board sidewalk between the two buildings says Brokaw & Barstow Hardware. Billy Barstow married my grandmother's sister Martha Theobald. I believe Mr. Brokaw was a relative of NBC News anchorman Tom Brokaw.

Manila rope for the tug-of-war and suggested that the town be named Manila. Some of those pulling for Manila were Cash Crakes (father of Grace Schram), Ad Morgan (Cicero Morgan's father), Luke Tillet, Charley Schroeder and two others. Those pulling for Paupville were Ed Saunders (father of Harry Saunders), Charles Saunders (father of Chuck Saunders), Will Theobald (father of Ed Theobald) and three others.

There are those who wonder how Manilla got its two L's, this seems to have happened at the recording of the town name.

The post office at Manilla was established at the opening of the town. The first postmaster was G.W. Brokaw. In 1886, the postmaster at Astor resigned for nearly all had moved to Manilla."

Back on the Saunders farm the family began to grow. A healthy, strong little baby girl was first to arrive and her father, in a bittersweet moment, named her Louise after his murdered mother. With this act a pattern starts to become apparent even to those of us long

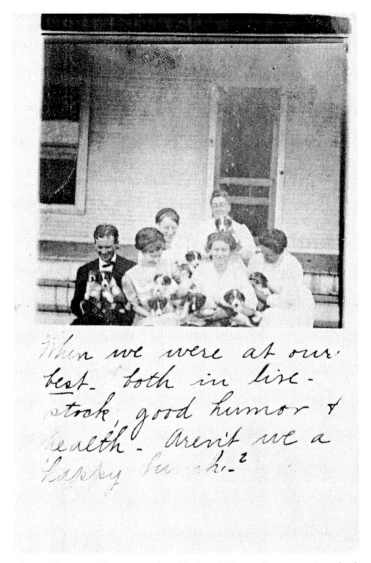

When we were at our best — both in live-stock, good humor & health — Aren't we a happy bunch.?

Aunt Vic sent this postcard to Dad and Mom; it was postmarked May 26, 1913 in Sioux City, Iowa. I believe the people from left to right are Will, Louise, Maude, Vic with Grandma Bertha in the back, the lady on the far right is unknown, possibly a housekeeper. The message on the back read; **"Dear folks: glad to get your card. Sorry you are having so much sickness and hope when the mumps are gone you are 'done for' on the sick list. I have been having some bad days again – lots of pain and fever but guess this weather would make any of us feel bad. Best Wishes to you all. Vic and Jack."**

removed from the early family, a pattern that indicates strong family bonds and perhaps even gives a small glimpse of how painful those first few days, months and even years were after that fateful June day in 1871. With the exception of Will, all the siblings relocated to the same Iowa town and all returned to Wisconsin regularly to tend the graves. In what must have been a pure gesture of love and forgiveness they moved their father's body to lay along side their mother and grandmother. A short time later Charles and Bertha chose the anniversary of Charles and Louisa wedding for their own and then named two of their children after them. Now is not a time to judge but the records we do have, though admittedly one sided, indicate that Charles senior was not a very nice man to say the least yet somehow the six children orphaned by his despicable act grew up with unshakable virtuous family bonds.

Aunt Lou (Louise) grew up on the farm and ultimately married Glen Adams and lived for a while a mile south of the Greeley Stock farm on what we today call the Mark Kenkel farm. They were living there in 1913 when a big tornado hit Omaha; one of my earliest memories is the story of their barn being blown down in the storm. Perhaps I remember it because for years we kept a man's wallet we had found out in the field that spring. It had been carried by the tornado 50-60 miles from Omaha.

My father, John, was the second child brought into this pioneering life. He was named after his English great-grandfather. Father was able to attend country school up to the fifth grade. Some have said third grade but I think it was fifth grade. He attended the same Greeley township school that both I and later my two older sons attended. In a final bit of educational irony, his abbreviated country school education was enough for him, during his adult years, to be appointed Director of the school and responsible for its daily operations.

It was out of necessity, not desire, that he began full-time work on the family farm at about twelve years of age. There was nothing easy about this farm life, and he shared with his parents the heartbreak of watching helplessly as his younger brother and sister died of diphtheria within five years of each other, Blanche aged one year eight months in May of 1887 and Eddie aged one year two months in February of '92. Childhood deaths were not

Bertha and C.A. Saunders with their children, left to right, Victoria, Will, John, Louise, Chuck and Maude, circa 1900. Most, if not all, the people reading this book will, most likely, be decedents of this family. The lesson to be learned from looking at a picture like this is that all these people are gone, the clothes, the possessions, the house and the farm are all gone, yet family remains.

uncommon in those days but that did not lessen the sorrow on the Saunders' farm as the young family, not once but twice, dug small graves for their children.

Charles and Bertha bought the plots next to their two children for $4.00 and today two small little limestone tombstones lay weathered nearly beyond recognition along side their parents' graves in the Astor Cemetery.

Two boys, Will and Chuck, were next. Both finished high school. Will would marry a woman from Lineville, Iowa and manage property in Alabama and South Dakota for my grandfather. Chuck married Pamelia Milligan (Aunt Mille) and worked on the family farm until retiring to city life in Manilla.

Maude and Victoria were the two youngest daughters. Maude married a jeweler by the name of Pease and moved to Smith Center, Kansas. I recall their visits back to the farm and my two Kansas cousins Lynna and Helen. Aunt Vic was the baby of the family and married Jack Anderson, the son of one of the blacksmiths in Astor. They moved to Sioux City where he worked for the railroad, then ultimately returned to Manilla and ran a grocery store.

During this era of development of American agriculture, the land had been settled and there was a great need for livestock to populate the farms. In response to this need Grandfather and his sons became what was referred to as a foundation farm, supplying breeding stock for other farms. They raised horses and cattle but also had a large herd of Poland China hogs, although the hogs were raised mostly as a cash crop for sale on commercial food markets and not for breeding purposes.

Horses were the first business of the Greeley Stock Farm. Everyone needed horses to work the land. They were of course the tractors, trucks and cars of their day. On one of his trips back to Wisconsin, Grandfather shipped back a train car full of horses. At that time if you were shipping livestock, you could ride along in the caboose for free. He wrote back, "There is no money here . . . fence posts are selling for a penny an inch across the top." The horses stayed in Wisconsin and the Greeley Stock Farm was fenced in with fence posts of white Wisconsin cedar.

The two mares and stallion had developed into a fine herd of riding and driving horses. Grandfather also developed large herd of the majestic Percheron draft horses and, of course, race horses.

Horse races were not only part of the entertainment of the day they were important to business. There was no better way to distinguish your breeding stock than a successful day at the track. Racetracks were scattered around the countryside just for that reason; one of them was right there on the Greeley Stock Farm. A half-mile track was located just over the creek on the flat area a little northwest of where the house and farm buildings once stood.

Evidently, as a young boy, my father John was a pretty good jockey for Grandfather's horses. I remember so well Dad's bowed

LERIDA 2D AT THE STATE FAIR

legs but I don't know if they were a result of Dad growing up on horses, growing up without vitamins or just plain old age, but I'd like to blame the horses. Either way, horses were his life-long passion. He cheered along with all the other common folk in the country following Seabiscuit's heroics and television was a great invention to my father's way of thinking, but only because for the last few years of his life he was able to see the Kentucky Derby live from Churchill Downs every May 1st.

One particular story highlights my father's youth. I heard it first-hand years later. We were showing some cattle at the 1948 Iowa State Fair and I had just put up a "John R. Saunders and Sons, Manilla, Iowa" sign over the stalls of two particularly good show heifers. An elderly man saw the sign and stopped to ask me if I knew Jack Saunders of Manilla. Jack was not a name I knew my father by. I had only heard my Uncle Chuck call my father Jack a handful of times but we soon both agreed that the man he was asking about was indeed my father. With that fact established the stranger went on to tell me the following story.

It seems that as a young boy, Dad was riding a horse in a big race at the Iowa State Fair. He would have been only 12-14 years old at the time. The race was a mile-and-a-half and not many horses could compete at that distance. To make matters worse, new regulations had just been passed that all horses had to carry the same weight. For the sake of fairness, saddle and jockey had to be the same weight for all the horses. Today weights are built into

SAUNDERS FARM.

One and one half miles Southwest of Manilla and ¾ of a mile Southeast of Astor.

STALLIONS IN THE STUD.

LERIDA,

The Celebrated Percheron Horse and Prize Winner.

PEDIGREE :

The Gray Percheron Stallion, Lerida, 6780, foaled April 10th, 1884, imported 1887 by M. W. Durham, of Wayne, Illinois; bred by M. Guiot Commune, of St. Aubin Department of Orne; got by Gerome, 3655 (436), he by Vidocg, 728, he by Bayard, 1385, he by Vidocg 483 (732), he by Coco, 714, he by Vieux Chaslin, 713, he by Coco, 712, he by Mignon, 715, he by Franle Blanc, 739, dam L. Amie, 6779, by Bayard, 1385, etc., has been duly entered for registry in Vol. 4, Percheron Stud Book of America, as the property of C. A. Saunders, of Astor, Iowa, and his record number is 6969. — Dated at Wayne, Illinois, November 18, 1887.

LERIDA took 2d premium at Illinois State Fair in a ring of 13, and 3d premium in a Percheron show in France in a ring of 72 of his age; also Sweepstakes at Manning and 1st premium at Harlan this year.

LERIDA was bought of M. Fardonet, President of the Society Hippique Percheronne, of France, who bred his sire, grand sire and great grand sire. LERIDA is a beautiful dapple gray, weighing 2000 pounds.

N. B. I will also have in stud ready for season of 1889 another Imported Percheren Horse, equal in every particular to LERIDA.

PRIZE.

I will also give a prize of $40 to the man who raises the best colt, $20 to 2nd and $10 to 3rd best from my Imported Percheron Horses, to be decided in Manilla about September 1, 1890, by three disinterested judges.

PEDETAR.

PEDETAR is a beautiful Chestnut Sorrel, weighing 1135 lbs.; is high headed, a fine open gaited horse, and the finest road horse in the county; Sired by Antar by Alexander's Abdallah, sire of Goldsmith Maid, Antar's first dam by Brown Chief by Membrino Chief, Sire of Lady Thorne, Brown Chief's first dam, sired by Drowning's Bay Messenger, he by Harpiness, son of Bishop's Hambletonian, he by imported Messenger. Brown Chief's second dam by Hunt's Brown Highlander, Antar's second dam by Bertrand, he by Sir Archey, by imported Diomed, Bertrand's first dam Eliza, by imported Bedford; second dam imported Membrino, Harpiness first dam by imported Messenger. Pedetar's first dam Mollie Dunn by Iceberg, he by Zero, by Boston, sire of Lexington, second dam Irish Mollie by Buckshot, third dam, Maid of Athens, by imported Priam, fourth dam Lady Chesterfield by Arab, fifth dam by imported Knowsley, sixth dam by Imported Dina, seventh dam by Mead's Cellar, eighth dam by Trustram Shandy. Antar sired by Almont 33 (sire of Fannie Witherspoon, 2:16; Piedmont 2:17¼; Westmont 1:13), by Abdallah 15, sire of Goldsmith Maid 2:14, Maj. Edsall 2:29, sire of Robert McGregor 2:17½, sire of Bonnie McGregor 2:16, Roxie McGregor 2:20, Earl McGregor 2:24½, by Hambletonian 10.

PEDETAR is undoubtedly the best son of the illustrious Antar's own brother-in-blood to Flossir G. 2:18½, that has repeatedly shown her ability to trot in 2:15 and was sold for $10,000 last June. Pedetar was bred and raised by Rayse Bros., of Columbus, Wis. For further particulars address

C. A. SAUNDERS,

ASTOR, - - - - - - - IOWA.

the saddle, but in those early racing days, the jockey was required to wear a belt with lead weights to equalize the differences.

Dad's horse won the race in record time. However, as the story goes, the time was so fast that he was accused of dropping the

MY FIRST SHORT-HORN PURCHAS :

LADY IDA 2 D

"MIGHTY OAKS FROM LITTLE ACORNS GROW"

weight belt on the backstretch. His accusers claimed that after he crossed the finish line, he kept his horse going and pretended to have trouble controlling him on the cool-down, either falling off or dismounting as he reached the backstretch. Then, according to his accusers, he picked up the belt, put it back around his waist and walked the horse back to the finish line. Evidently, walking the horse back to the finish line was not an unusual practice in those days, and it was a routine for Dad. When I got home from the fair I asked Dad about the story. He chuckled and immediately knew the man I was talking about. I didn't press him for details but he said, "It was only an accusation, and the record was in the books until 1935 or 36."

It wasn't a horse race that changed the history of Greeley Stock Farm; it was a horse sale. The story my grandfather told was of a sale he attended on a cold rainy December day a couple miles north of Defiance. His purpose for attending the sale was to buy some horses, but they were also selling some cattle. The auctioneer was a distinguished man by the name of Colonel F. M. Woods.

"Buy that cow, young man." The Colonel told my grandfather "sell the bull calves and keep the heifers. In ten years you'll have 71 head of cattle."

My father sent this postcard to my mother on Jan. 30 (1915) he wrote: "This is Tuesday morn. and I have just had breakfast and it is 8:30 and we show for the Grand Champion at 9 so you see I haven't much time . . ."

The words struck a chord in my Grandfather's heart and from that humble beginning, C.A. Saunders and Sons of Greeley Stock Farm, Shelby County, Iowa, went on to establish what became generally recognized as the top herd of Registered Scotch Shorthorn cattle in the United States.

This was at a time of rapid expansion of agriculture and farmers were looking for good breeding stock to make their farms successful. Just as horse races were used to test for the best horse breeders, livestock shows were used to determine the best cattle breeders and the best stock in the country. The show circuit started locally at the county level with the county fairs. After working hard all year, farmers took the best of their produce and livestock to be judged against those of their neighbors. If your cattle were good enough, they went on to the State Fair to compete against the winners from the other 98 Iowa counties. From there it was on to the pros,

The Chicago International, The Kansas City Royal, The Denver Western National, and the International Livestock Exposition at the Cow Palace in San Francisco to name a few.

This was the level of competition that Grandfather thrived on. His cattle were imported or calved from the best imported stock of Scotland, Canada and England and taken to shows throughout the United States. They traveled on trains; the railroad would give them a car and pull it up to a show and leave it there on the sidetracks until the show was over. A typical show herd would consist of 8-10 cattle and always include an older bull, a cow, a summer yearling, a junior yearling and a two-year-old.

Grandfather's first public sale was held Tuesday, February 6, 1900 and was a combination sale of sixty head of Shorthorn cattle and "thirty head of coach, draft and standard bred horses." In the sale bill he wrote:

> "In making this, my first public sale of Short-Horns, I feel assured that the animals enumerated will not only meet the expectations of breeders and farmers in point of breeding, but in individual merit as well. We wish it distinctly understood that this includes every bull raised on the farm during the year 1899, and we believe no sale this year will contain so good a lot of animals. There is not an undesirable bull in the whole lot . . . The Short-Horns have been tried in almost every country and have been crossed on nearly every breed of cattle known and have improved every race of cattle that they have been used upon. History shows that in the times gone by in the prosperity of the cattle business that, in the estimation of the public, the Short-horns have gone to the top. They will do it this time."

The first sale did not go without a hitch and the entire Saunders Shorthorn herd nearly ended abruptly as the following newspaper article reports:

Enraged bull

February 8, 1900—At **Saunders** big sale, near Manilla a mad bull came near being the death of several people. The big tent was crowded with men and when the bull was being sold several men with fur coats stalked about him. Soon one fur coat came near which enraged him and he flew at the man who wore it.

Mr. Saunders grabbed the bull and the animal instantly threw him into the deep straw in the ring. He tried to crush his body with his hornless head. Thick straw saved Saunders' life since the bull could only shove him along through it. The animal then pushed out through the ropes dashing into the crowd and back to his stable.

It seems like the start of the twentieth century was a dangerous time for the Saunders' household. In addition to C. A.'s brush with the bull in February of 1900, in October of 1900 an article was published in The Manilla Times relating another serious brush with death:

TAKES POISON BY MISTAKE

Mrs. C. A. Saunders The Victim –
Has A Miraculous Escape from Death

"Last Saturday about 8 o'clock Mrs. C. A. Saunders living on the Greeley Stock Farm south of this place met with an experience which would undoubtedly have resulted in her death, had it not been for her remarkable presence of mind. She had been feeling badly during the day and went to the pantry to take some medicine from a bottle sitting on one of the shelves. A bottle of carbolic acid was on the same shelf and by mistake she took the dose from this bottle.[32] She discovered her mistake immediately and with great presence of mind, she ate a large quantity of lard and other preventatives to keep the deadly poison from doing its work. Her son was the only one at home at the time, Mr. Saunders being in town, She called to him and said, "well I guess I have killed myself; tell them it was a mistake," and with these words she sank to the floor. Her son almost frantic with grief worked hard over his mother until she regained consciousness and then ran to their nearest neighbor Ed Theobald, who sent a messenger to town for Mr. Saunders, who at once procured a doctor and hastened home. Mrs. Saunders was in critical condition when they arrived but through hard work and the fact that she had taken the lard, etc. her life was saved. At this writing she is still very weak from the effects of the poison, but it is thought that she is out of danger. Her miraculous escape from death is received with joy by the family and by her many friends."

---

[32]The pill form of medicine was not invented until 1909 when the Bayer Company introduced the Aspirin. Prior to that time all medicine was either in a powder or liquid form.

Cumberland 118578 from a sale catalogue from on the Greeley Stock Farm dated Tuesday, December 23,1902. This great bull lived only 10 years, he died March 4, 1904. During that time however, he became the foundation for the greatest Short Horn herd in America.

The first bull Grandfather purchased, a red and white roan, calved October 1, 1894, became the foundation for his herd. His name was Cumberland 118578. He weighed 2,350 pounds and he was a direct descendent of royalty. A 1902 sale catalogue describes the Champion bull:

> "There are few bulls of the Shorthorn breed that carry such a liberal per cent of the blood of the Champion of England. . . .(he is) the greatest that has been known in the Shorthorn history in recent years."

If you walk a short distance northeast of the site where Grandfather built his farm home, you will come upon two large rocks. They are grave markers. When Grandfather's large Percheron stallion, Lerida, died, he was buried right there on the farm. When the great Cumberland died he was buried alongside and the Greeley Stock Farm, which he helped build and the land in which he was laid, was soon after known as The Cumberland Stock Farm.

The early sales on the farm were held in tents. After one of his early sales, C.A. and Col. Woods were walking back to the house in the bitter winter cold and C.A. said, "It's too damn cold to have these sales in a tent." The solution was to build a sale barn as is depicted in the 1906 sale bill. It was, I believe, copied almost identically from the sale barn of the Shelby County Fine Stock Exchange in Harlan, Iowa.

Bertha Theobald Saunders and C.A. Saunders, not only my Grandmother and Grandfather but also cofounders of the internationally recognized Cumberland Stock Farm. (Circa 1919)

On Wednesday, December 19, 1906, Grandfather held a Tenth Anniversary Sale on the Greeley Stock Farm. The sale announcement said, in part:

"It is with pleasure that I offer at public auction, this consignment of pure-bred cattle, showing what can be done in a limited time. This sale almost reaches the ten-year mark, since I first invested in registered Shorthorns.

. . . I must confess it is with reluctance that I offer many of these animals to the public . . . I feel that I am obliged to part with many favorites, in order to be able to offer this desirable consignment of Seventy-One head of choice breeding cattle to my friends and fellow breeders.

The reason of my offering Seventy-One head will be explained on sale day.

. . . I have found the breeding of Short-Horn Cattle to be the most interesting and profitable part of my farm operations. I AM IN THE BUSINESS TO STAY, and it is my ambition to each year be able to offer a better lot of cattle than at former sales, and at the same time establish

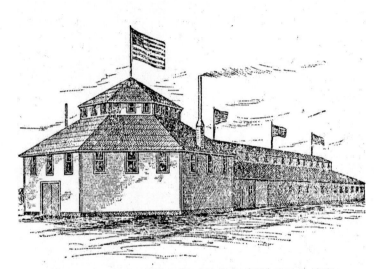

SHELBY COUNTY FINE STOCK EXCHANGE

HARLAN, IOWA

This organization was incorporated May 31, 1902. The object of the association is to promote the interest in the breeding of registered stock.

Our sale pavilion is located on the grounds of the Shelby County Fair Association. The pavilion is heated by two large furnaces, has electric lights and city water. It will accommodate 120 head of horses or cattle and other barns adjacent will accommodate a like number.

We not only solicit all breeders of registered stock to hold their sales at Harlan, but attend the sales held at this pavilion where you will always find the best.

You will also find the latch-string hanging out on every breeder's door.

40 SHORT-HORNS

New Sale Pavilion, Greeley Stock Farm, at 1 p. m.

TUES., JAN. 9, 1906

KING CHAMPION 191878

13 Bulls 27 Cows

...This Splendid Offering...

F. M. WOODS, Auctioneer
SEARS McHENRY, Clerk

C. A. SAUNDERS

MANILLA
Crawford Co., Ia.

Please Post

and maintain a reputation for square and honorable dealing with all my costumers.

. . . Free conveyance to and from sale. All trains will be met, and the comfort of those attending, looked after. Free entertainment to parties from a distance, at Depot Hotel, Park Hotel and Gardner Hotel.

Lunch for 1000 at 11am. Sale to commence immediately thereafter."

True to his word, Grandfather dug a huge barbeque pit west of the sale barn and roasted a steer and fed a thousand buyers, farmers and onlookers. After the lunch on sale day, as promised, Grandfather stood before the assembled crowd and explained his "reason for offering Seventy-One head . . ." the following text of his speech was published in The Live Stock World.

This photo of C.A. and daughter Victoria was in the 1906 sales catalog and captioned "OUR BUSY HOURS. PREPARING SALE CATALOGUES." Note the pictures of Lerida and Cumberland above his desk.

SAUNDERS' TALK TO CATTLEMEN

C.A. Saunders, at his recent sale of seventy-one head of Shorthorn cattle, made quite a talk to the assembled cattlemen and The Live Stock World is glad to give below the many points of his talk:

Neighbors and Friends, Fellow Breeder, Bankers, Auctioneers, Parsons and Paper Men: I wish it was in my power to thank each and every one of you in a way I think you deserve to be thanked for the courtesy, good will and patronage you have shown me in the past fifteen or eighteen years. I say eighteen years, as it is that long since I brought that grand old horse "Lerida" to this country to try and improve the stock of this country. As to how I have succeeded in the horse business I will leave my neighbors for judges. For the cattle business, I consider I have just begun. I say neighbor, as it is the neighbor first. I have always said if I could satisfy my neighbor I'd have the world for a market. I say neighbor, as I see two sons of a neighbor who was the first to use that grand old horse "Lerida" and also the last. For eighteen years he came to "The Greeley" for seed for his horses. When I started in the cattle business he was one of the first men to use a Cumberland bull and has used four from "The Greeley" since. I say again I haven't the language to thank such neighbors. I see another neighbor from over the county line. He, too, was among the first and last to use the old horse and has used four bulls in the past seven years. I can say I am proud to be a neighbor to such people. I say friends, as it reaches further out. I can count you by the score who have bought from one to four bulls from "The Greeley" in the past seven years. I say again, I haven't the language to thank you. Bankers, I wish to thank you, as it would be impossible for me to have done what I have if it had not been for you, as I consider I had lots of help from this source. Fellow breeders, I wish to thank you, as I consider you have done me lots of good. I have never had an animal but what, if you could buy, you were willing to pay a first class price for. Auctioneers and Paper Men, I have been acquainted with you seven or eight years and I have never heard a word but praise and honor for myself and what we were doing at "The Greeley Stock Farm", and I wish to thank you all for your support. Parsons, I do not know if there are any present. (This will seem rather strange to some of you, but I am going to say what I don't think any other

Shorthorn breeder in the U.S. can say.) The quarterly meeting in the M.E. Church of Manilla was once postponed on account of a sale at "The Greeley". Isn't that something for a man to be proud of? This isn't all, I have just heard of a wedding being postponed on account of this sale, Dec. 19, 1906, at "The Greeley". Isn't this an honor of which few can boast? Last but not least, the family. The ladies, you all know what they have done and the boys, where are you? John, Will and Chuck, I do not think the sun ever shown upon three better ones. It might have on one. I wish to say a few words in regard to the cattle. I am selling seventy-one head of cattle. Seventy-one head of as good cattle as I was able to pick from the herd. I could have picked seventy-one which would have brought more money, but I didn't think it just the proper thing, as we have all

kinds of customers, and I like to suit their wants. I am selling seventy-one head for just this reason: Ten years ago the 28th of this month, I was at a sale down near Defiance, at Henry Davis'. It was the first time I met Col. Woods. He was standing in a wagon box with his hat off and the water running down his face. It was raining as hard as it ever rained in the month of December, as he was gaffing for the old cow as I have heard him do a thousand times since. Then I heard him say:

"Buy her, young man, and in ten years you can sell seventy-one head for enough money to buy 160 acres of land."

I bought the cow. The cow has lived, and I have the goods here at your disposal, and I now turn them over to the auctioneers."

This obviously is not a December sale but these scenes depict the free lunch provided to all sale goers prior to a sale and views of Cumberland Stock Farm on sale day. For some of the sales cots were placed in the upstairs hallways for sale attendees who could not get hotel accommodations.

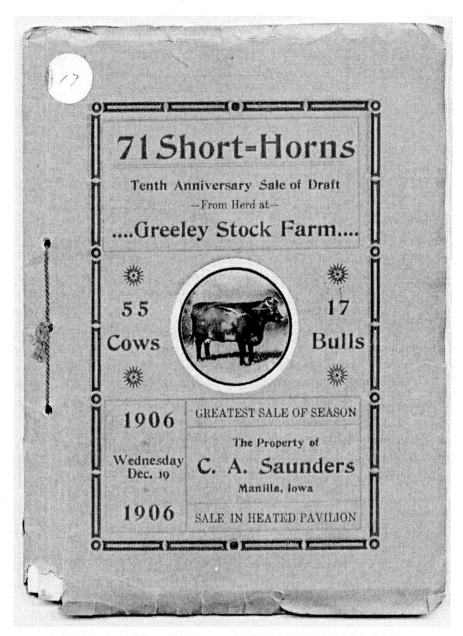

Front cover of the only known surviving copy of the 1906 Tenth Anniversary Sale catalogue.

C.A. Saunders at his desk during his reign as the country's premier Shorthorn breeder. Note the mounted horns above his head; they belonged to his champion bull Cumberland.

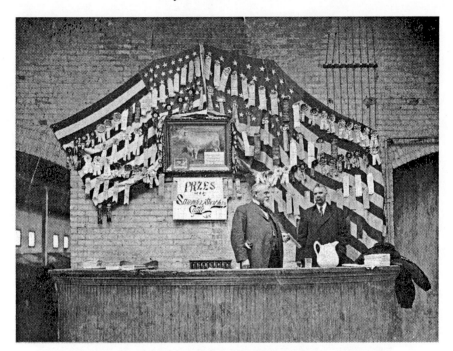

Colonel F. M. Woods and C.A. Saunders on the auctioneers' platform in an Omaha sale barn. The hand lettered sign under the white bull says **"Przes won by Saunders' Shorthorn Cattle in 1908"**. Mark Twain was once quoted as saying, "Never trust a man who can only spell a word one way!"

With the aid of his three sons, an unwavering work ethic and commitment, Grandfather's Cumberland Stock Farm grew a national and even international reputation of excellence. One offspring of Cumberland, called Cumberland's Type, was without question the greatest Shorthorn bull in the world, and a leading factor in ranking Shelby County, Iowa as the number one producer of purebred livestock in the United States. At one time a syndicate of South American breeders sent a representative to buy this bull "but did not bring money enough to take him." However, there were seven buyers from South America who attended a Saunders' Shorthorn sale in 1916 and bought nine head of cattle to be exported back to South America.

Further insight can be gained from a short article written by C.A. in a book printed in 1916, I no longer have the book and cannot reference it but I do have a copy of the article, which reads as follows:

A REVIEW OF THE FIRST 19 YEARS
OF MY EXPERIENCE BREEDING SHORT HORNS

Through the influence of our Grand Veteran Auctioneer Col. F. M. Woods I bought my first cow in December, 1896, of Mr. Henry Davis at Defiance, Iowa, but, at that time, was not thinking much about going into the breeding of cattle, as I raised horses. However, it gave me something to think about in regard to the stock side of farming, and the profits of it. As most of you remember, along in the nineties we farmers and stock raisers had a hard time to hold our jobs. I have bought good, eighteen hundred pound horses for $45.00, and at one time bought eight grade cows and seven good calves for $80.00, and there was not much profit in them at that. I remember of taking horses up to the woods in Wisconsin and Michigan and trading them for lumber at $3.50 per M, shingles 50 cents per M (but they would not handle and load them into cars at that price) and cedar posts at one cent an inch, top measurement, but nothing over 6 cents, even if they measured ten inches. Now, think of having a trainload of such material one thousand miles away from home and no money to pay freight, but we got it some way, and got rid of the products of the woods in the same way.

But, the cattle business is altogether different from what the horse business was in the nineties, and, by way of the following, will tell you the difference: I was signing checks in South Omaha one day to the amount of $12,000.00, the proceeds of one of my Breeders' Sales, and a course commission man said, "Charlie, what are you doing?" I replied, "making these checks so that I can get money on them." He asked me if I knew anything about the men who gave them. I said I did not. He told me that, if any man had given him a check for a horse, he would telegraph ahead and find out if it was good, before he would let the horse go, but not so with the man who is buying cattle, I will accept his check at any time. In all of the 19 years that I have received checks for cattle, I have never had one turned down for lack of funds.

The remarks of that horseman fit well with a story I some times tell: "Soon after I got started in the cattle business, people used to ask me why I quit the horse business and I would tell them that I was the only **honest** one left, so I **had** to quit."

Now, I will go back to the days when I started in with what, I hope, will be the finish of my life-work:

My first cow was a Miss Motte, and a very good one, and my first registered Short Horn bull was Cumberland 118578. The first calf I got I called Cumberland's Chunk, thus showing that he was along the TYPE I was trying to breed, and he was shown at the International at Chicago, winning Champion of the breed and Reserved Grand Champion.

The next calf I showed won fourth and I sold him for $475.00. So you must know that I began to realize that I was breeding cattle that were about right, when I could win in a place like the International at Chicago.

The next time I entered the show ring at Chicago, I showed Cumberland's Banner Bearer, and he stood next to Ceremonious Archer, F.W. Harding's Grand Champion. So I thought that was "going some" for a breeder that no one knew to stand next to this great calf.

By this time, I had begun to get hardened to the show-ring and to know something about what was needed in order to win such big shows as the International. I kept going, and, in the year of 1911, had out young herds that won thirteen first prizes, also get of sire, at the world's greatest shows, a feat that, heretofore, no breeder had ever accomplished.

Now comes CUMBERLAND'S TYPE, who, by his performance has branded himself as the greatest two-year-old Short Horn bull in America, winning 36 Champion ribbons, without a defeat; is sire of the calf-herd and of Modern Type, who won Junior Champion and Reserved Grand Champion of 1915, at the Western Live Stock Show at Denver, and sold for $2,500.00 to David Warnock & Sons, of Loveland, Colorado. When the judge said that (Modern Type) was better than his sire, I felt a pride that I will never forget, for it convinced me that I was improving the breed. Just to think of a two-year-old bull siring calves, the first five of which brought $5,450.00. What more do we want?

Now, just a few things that a new breeder will have to contend with that will embarrass him when meeting buyers and making sales: I recall having had a letter one time from a man from Linn Grove, Iowa, who was coming to see me and wanted to buy a bull. In my mind, I pictured him as a man to whom it would be impossible for me to sell, but, when he came, I found that I was mistaken for I never met a better gentleman to deal with, and sold him a bull for $350.00, and let me tell you this man proved to be one of the best friends I ever had.

I once received a telegram from parties at Lodi, Wisconsin, saying they wanted to buy a CUMBERLAND'S LAST bull. At that time, I felt I was not in a position to meet them, as I knew they would have to have something out of the ordinary. We had a bull that we did not want to sell, but felt that we must put a price on him, and the fact are that they bought him at $1,000.00, and he only five months old; and last year, at Wisconsin State Fair, he won the get of sire. The other bull, Barmpton Cumberland, which they bought at the price of $400.00, was, I think, one of the best breeders I ever sold. I saw fifty calves in their pasture at one time, which was a sight such as I had never before seen and never expect to again. They knew what they wanted, and bought it when they saw it. So, Breeders, when you are in the market and see what you want, buy it and you will always feel you did the best you could.

The breeding of improved stock of any kind is a grand business if it is carried on in a business like way. Think of opening a gate and driving out between $70,000 and $75,000 worth of stock at one time. That has been done on two different occasions in our county.

Not very long ago we heard of the sale of the grandest of all Percheron Stallions, Carnot 66666, when a half interest in him sold for $20,000. Do you suppose the owners and breeders of such stock carry on their business in any other than a straightforward, business-like manner? Certainly not.

Above all see other people's stock with the same fairness you do your own. I never thought much of a breeder who could not see good in any other man's stock than his own. Be fair and honorable in all things.

Yours very truly,
C.A. Saunders, Manilla, Iowa
Cumberland Stock Farm

The Cumberland's Last bull referred to in the article above was sold to Governor F. O. Louden of the State of Illinois and was later bought back by C.A. to continue the blood line on the Cumberland Stock farm.

Cumberland sired a revolution in the cattle industry. M.T. White of the Wallace Farmer and Homestead wrote:

" . . . the original herd of C.A. Saunders & Sons for a quarter of a century was the greatest winning herd of cattle of that day and age . . . (it) was a quarter of a century ahead of the times. This herd, more than any other, was the first to breed a lower, thicker type of Shorthorns, the type we are all wanting today."

That my grandfather was a hard worker is indisputable but he was also a showman and a dreamer. No one reaches the pinnacle of any profession without first dreaming it possible. Showman,

YOUNG BULL BRINGS BIG PRICE

"Cumberland's Last," Sold by C. A. Saunders for $10,000.

Special to The Daily Nonpareil.

Manilla, Ia., March 3.—C. A. Saunders of Greeley township has sold "Cumberland's Last," his junior championship bull. Mr. Saunders does not say what he got for the animal, but he asserts that the price is greater than has been paid for a bull in this country in the past twenty years. The purchaser was F. O. Louden of Chicago. Mr. Saunders has held the animal at $10,000, and we presume he came near getting that amount.

The bull in question is certainly a wonder. He will be two years old in the spring. As a calf he took the championship for calves at the big Chicago international show, and as a yearling he took junior championship, and was by many asserted to be entitled to the grand championship. If nothing happens to him, he is expected to take the championship the coming fall. The animal is snow white in color, and is out of Mr. Saunders' great bull, Cumberland, now dead.

Mr. Saunders will have been in the Shorthorn business ten years next fall. He has certainly made a success of it. He is considered one of the very best breeders in this country.

"That my grandfather was a hard worker is indisputable but he was also a showman and a dreamer"

dreamer, he was also a businessman and perhaps in that order. His word was his bond and could not be broken. Along the way he made many friends and I suppose a few enemies. Auctioneers held a special place in C. A.'s relationships and were perhaps the special link that connected the showman and businessman.

Col. F. M. Woods was the auctioneer that sold C. A. his first Shorthorn cow. He was a portly fellow with graying hair and a white moustache and goatee, the exact image that would later become famous for selling chicken, but this Colonel sold cattle and horses. Col. Woods worked many sales with C. A. as an auctioneer and

Cumberland's offspring feeding in front of the round sales pavilion on the Cumberland Stock Farm founded by C.A. Saunders

"no one reaches the pinnacle . . . without first dreaming . . ."

Over 50 years of breeding of Purebred Shorthorn Cattle by four generations of Saunders are represented in these sales catalogs. The first is C.A.'s first sale catalog dated February 6, 1900, the second is dated Friday, March 30, 1906, note on the top is a hand written note: "Keep This, C.A. Saunders". The final catalog dated March 20, 1950 was the last.

was considered a good friend as well as business associate. The Colonel was also a close friend of fellow Nebraskan William Jennings Bryan but to my knowledge there was little if any connection between Grandfather and the one-time presidential candidate. Another auctioneering friend of C. A.'s was Nels Kraschel from Harlan, Iowa. C. A. had worked closely with him over the years and in 1937 Nelson G. Kraschel was elected Governor of the State of Iowa on the Democratic ticket. The following newspaper accounts are, I believe, from the Manilla Times and self-explanatory.

CHAS. SAUNDERS WILL ATTEND INAUGURAL OF N. G. KRASCHEL

The inauguration of N. G. Kraschel as governor of the state of Iowa won't be, and isn't going to be, complete without the presence of Charlie Saunders, well known stockman who farms south of Manilla. Charlie received a letter from Gov.-elect Kraschel last week in which was tendered a personal invitation to the inauguration in Des Moines in which Kraschel stated "I would not consider the inauguration complete without your presence."

Mr. Saunders told us a story relating to this invitation which we will relate here.

Some years ago when Kraschel was auctioneering and Mr. Saunders was prominent in stock raising, Charlie was present when a bunch of men were "roasting" Kraschel. Standing his friends panning as long as he could, Charlie finally arose and told the group that "before you fellows quit talking about Nels Kraschel he'll be governor of the state of Iowa."

You all know how true this prophecy turned out, and Mr. Saunders and Mr. Kraschel will probably get many a chuckle when they recall the incident.

Meanwhile, Charlie is going to prophetizes a future president for us and left Wednesday evening for Des Moines to be present at the inaugural ceremonies.

HARLES SAUNDERS WRITES ACCOUNT OF STATE INAUGURATION

My trip to Des Moines to attend the inauguration of my friend, N. G. Kraschel, as governor of Iowa, was very pleasing in every way. Upon my arrival at the capital building I was immediately ushered to the governor's private reception rooms where I was warmly welcomed by the host and his family.

Later on I met many of my old friends, some I had not seen for 20 years, all were in a very jovial mood. The Lieut. Gov. Valentine I had known many years and it was indeed a pleasure to renew old acquaintances.

At the proper hour I was escorted to the first seat of those reserved for personal friends. Later three chief justice members were seated by me.

The music was of the best Iowa has—several military bands and a few solos by talented singers.

The entire building was completely filled with flowers. I had no idea of so many, and such beautiful specimens being assembled in one place. They were brought into Des Moines in huge truck loads from all over the state. Many bouquets I'm sure one man would be unable to carry.

I would estimate the crowd at 10,000 of Iowa's good people. It was very educational and would make a perfect vacation for any one who would care to attend. There was no charge for Iowa's inauguration.

I went, I saw, returned, and I know some time in the near future I shall go again; this time not to the "State House of Iowa," but to the "White House of Our Nation." It will again be the inauguration of my friend, N. G. Kraschel, not as governor of Iowa but as "President of the U. S. A."

Your old friend and neighbor,
C. A. SAUNDERS, Sr.

Shorthorn Breeders' Sale

CUMBERLAND'S TYPE 389132

South Omaha
December 14th, 1921

20 head of bulls   35 females

Offering Strong in the blood lines
from Cumberland's Type breeding

C. A. Saunders & Sons
Manilla, Iowa

A. L. Klopping & Son
Underwood, Iowa

Wm. Torneten
Council Bluffs, Iowa

CUMBERLAND'S TYPE, depicted in this 1921 sale bill, was sired by Cumberland on The Cumberland Stock Farm and was without doubt the best Shorthorn bull in the world. He was led into the show ring 36 times and won 36 championships, in fact, he was never beaten and his record has never been equaled.

Junior Champion and Reserve Grand Champion

of the

Western Live Stock Show at Denver, Col.

1919

Owned by C. A. SAUNDERS & SONS, MANILA, IOWA

Third in the line of outstanding bulls was TYPE'S DIAMOND, sired by Cumberland's Type; he was billed as the "greatest Scotch bull living today". In an advertisement he was noted to "be on exhibition at the Shelby County Fair August 16 to 21st, 1919".

Iowa's New "First Citizen"

THE HONORABLE NELSON G. KRASCHEL

C. A. Saunders died in 1941 and in 1944 the Cumberland Stock Farm Shorthorn herd was dispersed at auction. The letter below, written by Will Johnson a writer for The Shorthorn World, was included in the sale bill. We did indeed 'enlist the cause' and in 1948 were back in the show ring with champions.

The Saunders herds at Manilla, Iowa, have been among the best in that great Shorthorn State for almost a half century. The late Charles Saunders bred Shorthorns that, in type and early maturity, were "ahead of their time." He was one of the earliest to recognize the trend toward short legs, compact bodies and consequent early maturity. His cattle exhibited such desirable quality and character that, even though they were somewhat different from the current type of thirty or forty years ago, judges could not turn them down and they won many championships, thereby making popular the present type of Shorthorns.

Charles Saunders' sons, John R. and Charles, have carried on with this type and improved their herds throughout the years, and John's son Ray enlisted in the cause of improvement at an early age and has been one of the strongest factors in making this one of Iowa's foremost herds of Shorthorns.

The "Cumberland" type has come to be the established type among the best breeders in America, and as this herd was the first and foremost example of that type, the dispersion of the herd presents an unusual opportunity to buy Shorthorns that will perpetuate the breed's greatest assets.

The herd is to be dispersed, but I cannot believe that the Saunders name will be missing from the list of breeders of the future. I feel sure that later, when some economic adjustments have been made, that Ray Saunders again will enlist in the cause, and I predict that the herd that he will build up will add new lustre to the Saunders name.

WILL JOHNSON of The Shorthorn World.

From his original rented forty acres, Grandfather, his sons and his cattle built a small empire of sorts. He held properties in several states and his reputation as a cattleman and honest businessman extended through all the states and beyond. Grandfather C. A. lived to be nearly 84 years old before God extended him the privilege of dying in the home he built and on the land that he so truly loved.

The following is the report of C. A.'s death as published on the front page of the Manilla Times, Thursday, June 26, 1941. His wife Bertha died two years later after a long disfiguring illness. Because of it, she could not be laid flat in her coffin and was, therefore, buried laying sideways next to C.A., Blanch and Eddie, their two infant children, in the small Nishnabotna Cemetery southwest of Astor.

Charles Saunders Died At Farm Home South of Manilla

●

Noted Stock Farmer Came to Community in 1873 from Wisconsin

●

Mr. Charles Saunders, one of the oldest and most widely known residents of the Manilla community, died last Friday at his home south of Manilla. Many friends and relatives paid their final tribute at the funeral services Sunday, held from the home at 3 p. m. Rev. F. C. Aldrich officiated and interment was in the Astor cemetery. Serving as pallbearers were Raymond Saunders, Merle Saunders, Glen Adams, Jack Anderson, Arnold Soll and Roy Zimmerman.

Charles Adolphus Saunders was born to Mr. and Mrs. Charles Adolphus Saunders on the 6th day of August, 1857, at Black Earth, Wisconsin, and died at his country home south of Manilla, Iowa, on the afternoon of June 20th, 1941, at the age of 83 years, 10 months and 14 days, after an extended physical disability of some years, due to old age.

Up to the age of 16 years he continued in residence at Black Earth, at which time he came to Denison, Iowa; that is, in the year 1873—by train, and from Denison to this neighborhood he came on foot the same day, and found work as a farm hand with Mr. John Theobald. At 19 years of age he took up farming for himself, spending the first few years on the Ed. Dyson farm west of Astor.

Homesteaded 160 Acres—

When Mr. Saunders moved to the farm which was his home for nearly 60 years, he purchased 160 acres from the government under the provisions of the homestead law. Later more land was added until the farm contained 620 acres.

From early life Mr. Saunders was interested in fine cattle and eventually became one of the midwest's foremost stock farmers, buying and selling animals worth several thousands of dollars.

He originated the Cumberland strain of shorthorns in America and for a long time maintained one of the best shorthorn herds, selling cattle to stockmen all over the world. Many guests and buyers from foreign countries visited the Saunders farm, both to see and purchase his excellent cattle. His herd won him hundreds of awards and honors at state fairs and other stock shows.

Served As Cattle Judge—

Mr. Saunders was in demand also as a judge of fine cattle and many times he was called to expositions to give his opinion on the various animals shown.

Throughout his entire life, he was a staunch prohibitionist and was proud of the fact that he had never used alcoholic beverages.

The deceased was married to Bertha Alma Theobald at Denison on the 4th day of May, 1876, and to this union were born three sons: John R., William H., and Charles Arthur; and three daughters: Lue, Maud and Victoria. Two children died in infancy.

Surviving are: His widow ; the three sons, John R. and Charles Arthur of Manilla; and William H. of Redfield, S. D.; three daughters, Lue (Mrs. C. Hogate) of Owatonna, Minn,; Maud (Mrs. S. W. Artz) of Larned, Kans., and Victoria (Mrs. J. H. Anderson) of St. Paul, Minn. Also a brother, Edward, of Manilla, and 21 grandchildren, and numerous great grandchildren and other relatives.

The heartfelt sympathy of all will be extended, in particular, on behalf of the widow, who has been confined by illness to her room, and for most of the time to her bed, for several years.

Among the out of town relatives and friends attending the funeral were: Mr. Will Saunders, two sons, daughter and husband from Redfield, South Dakota; Mr. and Mrs. Will Saunders and daughter, Lucille, fro mChicago; Mrs. S. W. Artz from Larned, Kansas; Mr. and Mrs. J. H. Anderson and son from St. Paul, Minn.; Mr. and Mrs. Merle Terwilliger from Omaha; Mr. and Mrs. Ed Feick from Sioux City; Mr. and Mrs. Cicero Morgan from Carroll; Mr. and Mrs. Glen Adams and family from Denison; Nelson G. Kraschel from Harlan; Mr. E. L. Klopping from Underwood.

"The pioneer experience and achievements by the late C.A. Saunders have thrilled and inspired thousands of farmers. His word was as binding as his contract. Once given as a promise or threat for assistance or punishment, time nor circumstances did not alter or modify his vow. In the declining years of his life, he often told me that the damage created by the depression of the '30's was not measured by loss in dollars to the farmers, but the irreparable loss was to the integrity of contract. He was a sturdy, unyielding and determined man."

NELSON G. KRASCHEL
GOVERNOR OF IOWA

Chapter 3

MOTHER

January 26, 1989

It's quite early in the morning. I have written a couple pages and I'll start another. I'll try to write a bit about my mother, from both the family's oral history and my own personal memories.

Henry F. Schoenig and his wife Amelia lived in eastern Iowa, near Muscatine when, on March 18, 1877, they became parents for the second time. The baby they brought into the world was a girl. They named their first and only daughter Marie Helen Schoenig. This newborn infant, who was destined to become my mother, would ultimately have three brothers, John, August and Arthur. John was the oldest, Mother was next and Art was the youngest.

I never knew my Grandma Schoenig, she died when my mother was ten-years-old.

It is not surprising, when Grandma Schoenig died, my mother's childhood died too, as did the luxury of her formal education. Grandpa Schoenig was left with four young children. My mother was the second oldest and the only female. At ten years of age she became the woman of the house.

We hear about these things happening, we feel sad for the people and we say something like, "Oh, isn't that a terrible tragedy. Those poor children," and then we go about our business. But think about it. Think about **your** ten-year-old becoming head of a household. Not only that, but a household without the luxury of electricity, where all laundry had to be done by hand, where there was no fast-food, where all food was grown and prepared by hand and with no refrigeration. Think about your ten-year-old being the head of a household with no means of mass communication or transportation other than a horse and buggy.

This certificate of baptism, printed in German and dated August 30, 1878 lists Mother's name as Bertha Maria Helen Schonig, with an umlaut over the o. To my knowledge she was never known as Bertha, only as Marie Helen. The last name was changed to Schoenig by dropping the umlaut over the 'o' and adding an 'e', a common Americanization of German names.

Grandma and Grandpa Schoenig, my mother's parents lived in Muscatine, Iowa.

Grandpa Schoenig did remarry after a time and the children acquired a stepmother. However, his new wife apparently had a hard time accepting the young family. If my mother had the same stubbornness and resolve as a ten-year-old that I saw in her years later, she probably had a hard time accepting another woman in the house too and from that day forward, my mother and her brothers, as she said, "just kind of bounced around."

As I understand, Mother's cousins, Fred, Earnest, Frank and Lena lived in the same area; I believe they were children of

Frederick Schoenig. As my mother told me, "We lived with friends and relatives, and I worked as a housekeeper for my room and board."

At about the time mother was seventeen or eighteen-years-old, she began looking after and living with her maternal Grandmother Schultz. Apparently, Grandma Schultz was widowed at the time. Mother only spent a couple years with her because Grandma Schultz died when Mother was twenty. However, from what I have been told, Grandmother Schultz was a wonderful influence and for a brief period of time she assumed the maternal role in my mother's life.

Grandma Schultz (my great grandmother) is shown above as she appeared shortly before her death. The obituary is unmarked as to date, nor is the paper in which it was published identified. If she died, as I believe, when Mother was twenty, that would place her birth date in 1815 and make her 36-years old when she emigrated from Germany to America.

Death of an Octogenarian.

Mrs. Dorethea Elizabeth Schulz, widow of the late John F. Schulz, died at the family home, near New Era, the 17th of September, at the ripe old age of 82 years and 18 days, of old age.

Mrs. Schulz, or "Grandma" Schulz, as she was known by all her friends, has been an invalid for a number of years. The intense heat of the past summer caused her so feeble health to decline more rapidly. About five weeks ago she began sinking, until one week prior to her death, she became seriously ill. The attending physician pronounced her case beyond medical help, and could only contribute to ease her pain. She sank rapidly until 9:30 Sunday evening, when death, that grim reaper, came to "gather in the sheaf."

"Grandma" Schulz was born in Magdeburg, Germany, and came to this country in the fall of 1851. The family resided in St. Louis for six months, when they came to Muscatine, where they resided for a short time from which they moved to the farm (then a wilderness), where the family have resided ever since. With her demise the "home" is broken, as the children have long ago established their own firesides. "Grandma" was well taken care of the last years of her life by her granddaughter, Miss Marie H. Schoenig, oldest daughter of the late Amelia Schonig. The remaining children are Fred G., of Burlington; Bertha L., wife of A. C. Paul, of Gilmerton, Pa.; Miss Tena, of Kansas City; Frederica C. Parker, of Muscatine; Marie E., wife of Rev. W. Schonig, of Burlington, and Louis R., of Millersburg, Iowa. The remains were laid to rest by the side of her husband in the "Krell cemetery."

This recent photo of grandson Boomer and I shows a vinegar bottle and small chest brought to America by Grandma Schultz. The box still contains a handmade red floral handkerchief of Grandma Schultz. It once contained a thin silver wedding band, which unfortunately disappeared over the years.

Not only were things changing in Mother's life, the life of America was also changing rather dramatically. Although the 1890's were reportedly a difficult time for farmers it was also the era that was to become commonly known as the Gay Nineties and it did so largely because of the growing popularity of what we think of today as a toy. As strange as it may seem to us today, it has been said that the bicycle is what made the Gay Nineties gay.

Two advances made the bicycle, as we know it today, possible. In 1888 an Irish veterinarian by the name of Dunlop, with a sickly young son, was trying make a softer more comfortable toy of his son's tricycle. The result was the invention of the pneumatic tire and ultimately the formation of a tire company that to this day still carries the young doctor's name – Dunlop.

The second was an advance in metal working that allowed the manufacture of small lightweight chains and sprockets so that speed was now achieved with gears small enough to be powered by the human body. No longer did speed depend upon the length of one's legs or the size of the large front wheel. Together, these two innovations relegated the famous bone shaking "high-wheelers" of the 1890's, ridden by men with handlebar moustaches, to the history book.

With mass production the costs came down and the bicycle, which had previously been for the elite and cost a man six months of his salary, now became practical transportation for the common man as well as a popular form of recreation.

Women also began taking up cycling and a whole change in the social order began to evolve. It was not long before Betty Bloomer invented her long legged 'bloomers' and women, who previously had been confined to the more gentile tricycles, could ride this new bicycle and still keep their legs covered. Bicycles and bloomers had a tremendous effect on our western culture. Together they killed the corset and bustle in women's fashion and allowed a more 'common sense' fashion and increased mobility.[33]

In 1896, Susan B. Anthony was quoted as saying:

> "Let me tell you what I think of bicycling. I think it has done more to emancipate women than anything else in the world. I stand and rejoice every time I see a woman ride by on a wheel. It gives a woman a feeling of freedom and self-reliance."

If that was not enough change initiated by a couple of small inventions, keep in mind what, in a few short years, would come out of a small bicycle shop run by two brothers in Dayton, Ohio.

---

[33] http://www.ibike.org/historyusa.htm#chronology

In a scene reminiscent of the movie Butch Cassidy and the Sundance Kid, my mother poses with her brother, August, and their new bicycles. The Gay Nineties was the time of both the famous outlaws and this popular new mode of transportation and recreation.

After Grandma Schultz passed away, Mother took her newfound "freedom and self reliance" and made a trip across Iowa that changed her life. Not only would this trip change her life, it made possible my very existence and ultimately would be responsible for a whole new branch to be added to the Saunders' family tree. Mother traveled by train and horse-drawn buggy to visit a dear friend

My mother Marie Helen Schoenig as she appeared around the time of her trip to western Iowa.

of Grandma Schultz. This lady was Helen Ray, she had married a man by the name of William Ray and had sometime previously moved to western Iowa and was living on a farm two miles north and mile west of Defiance, Iowa.

William Ray had a full white beard that pronounced to all he was quite a bit older than Helen. He was also quite set in his ways so there was little she could do about his chewing tobacco and the dark brown stain it left down the middle of his chin whiskers.

Mother called them Aunt Helen and Uncle Bill. They weren't blood relatives but they were family. There were two boys, Joe and John, and perhaps some girls, I honestly can't remember. I do know that there was one orphan girl, I think from Kansas, by the name of Florence Longnecker who was taken into the Ray household. John Ray would later grow up and marry his "adopted sister" Florence; this story will prove to have a profound effect on our family but must be saved for later.

While visiting 'Aunt Helen' and 'Uncle Bill,' Mother was introduced to some people in Defiance by the name of Schriver. The Schrivers had a lumberyard and a grocery store. Defiance[34] was a thriving town at that time, much more so than Manilla. There was a printing office, which also put out its own newspaper, a bank, a telephone office, a drug store and I think three churches.

I don't know how many saloons there were. My great grandfather had seen to it that this generation of Saunders didn't use alcohol nor socialize much with those who did. In fact, there had been Prohibition laws passed in Iowa as early as 1882 but not all counties enforced them with equal vigor. I am told in Carroll, Iowa they built saloons on skids so they could be moved ahead of the lawmen. However, it was pretty much standard that, in these small Iowa towns, the number of saloons generally equaled, if not surpassed the number of churches.

---

[34] The town of Defiance was originally a stagecoach stop between Harlan and Denison. When the railroad came through a mile or so to the east, it dropped the mail off at Mallory Morgan's farm, making him the postmaster of sorts, the town's people defied the railroad and wouldn't move their buildings to the railroad hence the name Defiance.

"Mother . . . made a trip across Iowa that changed her life. . . and ultimately would be responsible for a whole new branch to be added to the Saunders' family tree."

In fact, the neighboring town of Manning once boasted the longest bar west of the Mississippi. Legend has it that the "Horseshoe Bar" was actually in two adjoining buildings and ran up one side, across the back of the two buildings and down the side of the other. I think that may be an exaggeration; however, I know for a fact that it was 120 feet long, made of solid mahogany with a marble kick plate and had eight bartenders.

Now don't get me wrong, I don't mean to say that the people were drunks. Far from it, they were hard-working Christian men and women but the fact was, there weren't many tee-totaling Baptists in our neck of the woods. Maybe the Presbyterians and Methodists came as close as anyone but as one old barber put it, "This was grain country – it's just that they drank it".

There wasn't, of course, any law, written or unwritten, calling for the number of saloons to equal the number of churches and it wasn't so much that the Catholics wouldn't drink with the Lutherans etc., though they were certainly expected to support their own congregation's establishments. No, I think it was simply due more to the fact that the Germans drank and socialized differently from the Danes who drank and socialized differently from the Swedes and so on.

The fact of the matter was, however, that Defiance was a thriving little town at that time and the Schrivers, with two businesses to run and a new baby in the family, needed a housekeeper and Mother needed a home. She took the job and immediately began fitting into and growing with the community as well as with both the Schriver and the Ray families.

After a couple of years keeping house for the Schrivers, Marie (Mother) made plans to return to eastern Iowa to join her brothers John and August. It was the closing years of the 19th century. Iowa had been a state for more than fifty years, the Indian Wars were over[35] and the government was giving away land.

In 1862 the Homestead Act had been signed into law by Abraham Lincoln. All one had to do to be a homesteader on 160 acres of land of your choice was to be at least 21-years-old, file your intensions with the local land office and pay a $10 filing fee plus $2 to the land agent to temporally claim the land. After five years the settlers "proved up" by finding two friends or neighbors willing to vouch for them and sign a 'proof of occupancy' document. This along with a final $6 fee brought title to your land signed by the President of the United States.

The Schoenig boys had heard of unsettled land in the Dakotas and dreamed of their own 160 acres of prime North Dakota farmland just for the taking. After all, all you had to do was file a homestead claim. Well, almost. You also had to plow the virgin prairie, build a house and farm the land for five years. I think you only had to sleep on it continuously nine months of the year. This allowed three months respite from the relentless bitter cold Canadian winds that blew the freezing snow down across the treeless Dakota prairie.

---

[35] Iowa, named after an American Indian tribe of the same name was a part of the original Louisiana Purchase. Initially part of the Michigan Territory and then the Wisconsin territory, after the defeat of Chief Black Hawk in 1832, the Sac and Fox Indians were forced to give up their rights to the land west of the Mississippi for a small amount of cash, 40 barrels of salt, 40 barrels of tobacco and some blacksmithing services. Iowa became the 29th State on December 28, 1846.

Three months respite was good, but in North Dakota, winter lasts five months!

About this time my Grandfather, C.A. Saunders, who by now had added to his original forty acres and had a large farm with a herd of Shorthorn cattle and a thriving horse business, was building a new home for his family which now included six children. He wanted a housekeeper and cook to help his wife. C.A. had heard about this young lady, Marie Helen Schoenig, in Defiance who, by this time, had earned a reputation of being a great cook and housekeeper.

C.A. had never met this woman, who was destined to become my mother, but he drove five or six miles in a horse and buggy down to Defiance to look her up. In fact, she already had her trunk packed and was about ready to leave and join her brothers for the trip to North Dakota. Although they were two complete strangers he tried to persuade her to come to his farm for a month's trial. Apparently she liked what she saw and heard because they loaded her trunk on the back of Grandfather's buggy and she rode home with him that day to the Greeley Stock Farm.

The home he took her to was a mansion by the standards of the day. It was known as "The Home the Cumberlands Built" and was a tribute to an internationally known Shorthorn cattle business. It was surrounded on two sides by a large open porch and the front door led into a large foyer with an open oak staircase. To the right was a library that led into a master bedroom and bath and to the left was the living room. A total of seven different doors led into the huge kitchen plus a butler's pantry complete with a small sliding service door through which food could be passed directly onto the built-in buffet, which ran the entire length of the adjoining dining room. Sliding double oak doors separated the dining area from the living room. There were six sets of sliding doors altogether and large bay windows in the living and dining rooms.

Upstairs were four large bedrooms plus a suite of two maid's bedrooms with their own stair leading down to the kitchen. A third stairway led to a full attic and a laundry chute ran from the upstairs to the full basement.

Mother stayed at the Saunders farm for some time, over a year, before joining her brothers in North Dakota. They had gone

WHERE THE SHORT-HORN BREEDERS FIRST FOUND US

WHERE THE SHORT-HORN BREEDERS FIND US NOW

In a 1906 sales catalog the original home of C.A. and Bertha Saunders was pictured as *"where the short-horn breeders first found us."* Around the turn of the century a new home was built and pictured as *"where the short-horn breeders find us now."* This was the home my mother was hired to keep, it was known as "The Home the Cumberlands Built."

on ahead and homesteaded north of Minot and had filed a blind claim for her. They, of course, had to live on their properties and made the best of the situation by building a "house" which was actually not much more than a tarpaper shack. The house was built straddling the property line, half the house on one claim and half on the other. To make it legal, a doorless partition ran down the middle of the house which made it a duplex of sorts. This helped relieve some of the loneliness of the North Dakota prairie and helped keep the siblings together.

Now, after time enough to prove residency for the Homestead Act and to get title of the land, Mother was again persuaded to come back to the Saunders' farm in Iowa. I believe there was a clause in the Homestead Act that after 18 months or so you could buy out the land for a nominal fee.

The Schoenig brothers stayed in their tarpaper shack and claimed their land. Uncle John became a station agent for the Sioux Line Railroad and Uncle August stayed on the farms, married and raised a family. Uncle August's first child was a daughter, Helen. She was named after my mother, Marie Helen. She and her husband now own and farm the original homesteads. Soon after Trudy and I were married, we visited Helen in North Dakota and were able to see the original homestead shack still standing.

Mother I believe opted for the homestead buy out to return to Iowa early. This time I think C. A. had a bit of help because, after working another year for the Saunders family, she married my dad, John Raymond.

The year was 1903, the month was January, the day was the 15th, and the new century held a lot of promise for this new family. Not only were things changing on the farm, Teddy Roosevelt was now President and with him came a vision of a much bigger role for America in the world. Teddy was digging the Panama Canal to assure his navy had better access to the Pacific Ocean and the world. This was also the same year a 31-year-old Vermont doctor by the name of Horatio Nelson Jackson drove his used Winton automobile through Denison, Iowa on a dusty rutted road. A road that would, ten years later, become known as the Lincoln Highway.[36] Jackson was making good on a $50 bar bet that he could drive an automobile across the United States. Thirty-seven previous attempts had failed but 64 days after leaving San Francisco Jackson arrived in Times Square, New York City. Years later Horatio Nelson Jackson would be hailed as the Charles Lindberg of the American road but for the time being that comparison was meaningless, no one could have comprehended the comparison for this was the same year[37] where, at Kitty Hawk, the Wright Brothers flew their airplane for twelve short seconds and changed the world forever.

The world was getting smaller but my parents would never fly in their lifetime, nor travel to any great extent for that matter. In fact

---

[36] Predating the Interstate Highway system by fifty years, the Lincoln Highway was the brain child of Carl Fischer, a visionary who developed Miami Beach and later the Indianapolis Motor Speedway. Fischer promoted the concept of the shortest practical hard surfaced route spanning 3,400 miles coast to coast between New York and San Francisco. The Lincoln Highway was dedicated in 1913 and in 1927, the same year Lindberg flew the Atlantic, the Boy Scouts of America placed commemorative markers along the highway coast to coast.

[37] December 17, 1903

Wedding day pictures of John and Marie Saunders with sisters Maude and Vic (Victoria).

my father said one of the things Mother told him when they agreed to put their lives together was, "I'll marry you, but when we get settled, I won't move."

Her mindset was, I believe, in large part due to the fact that after her mother died she and her brothers, as we talked about before, "just kind of bounced around." I think she also saw that her own father, my Grandpa Schoenig, after losing his first wife, could never settle down. He was never satisfied, nothing suited him and he was always looking over the horizon at something he thought would be more attractive.

John and Marie were married and for two years made their home in 'The Home the Cumberlands Built' and made their living on the family farm known at that time as the Greeley Stock Farm, but destined to become The Cumberland Stock Farm.

Between 1903 and 1905 Mother and Dad made plans to start their own home. They thought about going to North Dakota but instead, sold Mom's homestead claim to her brothers. They also thought about some farmland west of where Uncle Bill and Aunt Helen Ray lived, down by Defiance. But true to her word, Mother did not move. Instead they rented 195 acres in Section Two, Greeley Township, Shelby County, Iowa, the section of land on the east side of Grandfather's Greeley Stock Farm.

The land was bare and raw. There were no fences and no buildings. It was owned by a family in Indiana by the name of Goddard. Mom and Dad's first lease was for five years. I don't know the exact details of how much money changed hands but the landlords furnished the material for the fences around the property. All other fences and buildings had to be furnished by Mom and Dad. They also had to pay half the taxes and for half the planting seeds for the crops. Of course the landlord shared equally in the bounty of the harvest.

The young couple needed a home on their new farm so they moved an abandoned two-room shack from the south part of Grandfather's farm on Section Three. I don't know where the shack originally came from or what it was used for but it was located in the area where we later, in the 1950's, built our farm pond. There was a well where the shack once stood and it most likely was the result of someone's failed attempt to start their own farm.

The site they selected for their "new" home was down in the valley, close to a small creek, a little southeast of our present home. They put the old shack on skids and pulled it about three quarters of a mile or more down to the valley site with four horses. Mother drove one team and Dad the other. There was, of course, no basement so they set the shack up on large limestone foundation blocks they had purchased at the local lumberyard. They then added a closet and bedroom with a flat tar-paper roof.

They also dug a well; I remember the wooden pump. It was home-made and consisted of a square wooden 'pipe' with a wooden plunger that had a leather seal. The well was dug by hand and the water was cold and clear.

At the home of C. A. Saunders last Thursday at noon occurred the marriage of their son John to Miss Marie Schoening, Rev. Stire of the M. E. church at Manilla, officiating. The bride is quite well known in Defiance, having lived here at one time. She possesses a refined and gentle nature and industrious habits,—those qualities so essential in a wife and life companion. The groom was raised on the Botna and is a young man of sterling worth, good habits and industrious. The young couple departed on the afternoon train for Kansas City where they will spend their honeymoon sightseeing. They will make their home with the groom's parents for the present. The Enterprise extends congratulations.

SAUNDERS–SHOENING.

Last Thursday, at noon, at the home of C. A. Saunders and wife, south of town, occurred the marriage of their eldest son, John, to Miss Marie Shoening. Rev. Stire, of the M. E church, officiating. The wedding was a pretty home affair, attended by relatives and immediate friends.

The bride and groom, who are highly esteemed, received many beautiful and useful presents, and have the congratulations of a wide circle of friends. They departed for Kansas City to spend their honeymoon. They will reside with the groom's parents on the Greely stock farm.

The newspaper articles of Mom and Dad's wedding were rather limited. Nine years later, when I was one-year-old, Dad's younger sister, my Aunt Vic received a much longer write up in The Manilla Times, it is copied below to give the flavor of a wedding in "The Home the Cumberlands Built".

UNTIL DEATH DO US PART

Miss Victoria E. Saunders and John H. Anderson Wed

DOUBLE RING CEREMONY USED

Was an Elaborate Event and Largely Attended

On Wednesday evening, October 16, 1912 at 5:00 o'clock at the spacious mansion on the Greeley Stock farm, home of Mr. and Mrs. C.A. Saunders, well known and respected citizens of this section, occurred the marriage of their daughter Victoria E. to Mr. John H. Anderson of Sioux City, son of Mrs. J Hendrickson of Reeder, North Dakota.

As he beautiful strains of the wedding march, rendered by Miss Lyda Saunders, floated through the rooms, the bridal party marched to the north parlor. The decorations of the room were most beautiful, the colors yellow and white with delicate and fragrant flowers, intermingled with Cupid's darts and hearts. The double ring ceremony was carried out, Rev. R. R. Moser of the M.E. church of this city speaking the words which united the two hearts for the remainder of life's journey. The ceremony was concluded with a short prayer by Rev. A. M. McIntosh, pastor of the Presbyterian church of this city.

The bride was attired in a beautiful gown of white satin with embroidery chiffon over-draped, wore a band of pearls in her hair and carried a boquet of bride's roses. The groom and groomsman, Mr. Cyril Saunders, the bride's cousin, wore the usual conventional black. Miss Alma Adams, bridesmaid, looked most charming in a dress of white voile over yellow satin. The little Miss Mildred Saunders acted as flower girl and ring bearer and was attired in a beautiful dress.

The bride is one of our choicest young ladies. From a little girl she has grown up in our midst, honored by old and young alike. She is a graduate of the Manilla schools, being a member of the class of '07. She has ever been a bright star in the home circle and has been a valuable assistant to her father in the Clerical work of the Greeley Stock farm, and now she has gone to reign as queen in her own home.

The groom is one of the most popular young railroad men in the employ of the Milwaukee company, and has a run between Manilla and Sioux City, and has recently received notice that he is soon to be promoted to the position of conductor. He is a young man of exemplary habits, industrious, and will make a happy home for his bride.

Before the ceremony Miss Robina Theobald served the guests with a goblet of punch. Immediately after the ceremony and congratulations, the guests were escorted to the beautiful dining room where the color decorations were beautifully constructed, and where the tables were spread. A delicious three-course supper under the supervision of Mrs. Chas. Schroeder of Hornick, as chief chef, who was assisted in the serving by the Misses Hazel Barrow, Adah Van Slyke, Geraldine Perion, Helen Jackson, Gladys Smith and Lillian McDermott.

Mr. and Mrs. Saunders as host and hostess, fully sustained the reputation as to the hospitality of the home on the Greeley, the bride and groom, escorted by relatives and friends, came to town to take the evening train for a bridal tour of the west. The bride's traveling suit was of beautiful brown velvet with shoes, hat, gloves, etc., to match. At the station, as they were taking their departure, they were given a royal send off, rice, old shoes and well wishes were in order.

The esteem in which these young people are held was shown by the many beautiful presents they received on this occasion.

The congratulations on the happy event are numerous and this paper is greatly pleased on this occasion to add its hearty good wishes to those being so freely expressed.

After their return from their honeymoon trip they will be at home at 117 Rustin Ave., Sioux City, Iowa, where they have a little home nest nicely furnished and all ready for their occupancy.

They intend to start housekeeping right, for they have requested this paper, The Times, sent to their address for a year.

———————

They now had a house, but no farm would be complete without some farm buildings. I so well remember the flat tar-paper sheds they used for cattle and hogs, and a corn crib made of willow poles, scrap lumber and wire. The barn was built to house four head of horses, a couple of grain bins, two tie-up stalls for milking the cows and a shed for the buggy and wagon, all in one small building.

There was no paint on any of the buildings except for the cob shed and the outdoor toilet. These two buildings were the only ones built out of new lumber and so needed protection. They were painted barnyard red, of course. I vividly remember, as a little boy, seeing the old wooden bucket of red paint still hanging in the cob shed. I think the reason I remember it was because it was unlike any other bucket I had ever seen. It was bigger on the bottom than at the top, probably an attempt to keep the paint from dripping or maybe from drying out.

The cob shed had a little room for coal and a much larger one for corncobs. There was not much wood to cut around the place. This was true prairie land and still relatively treeless. The cobs were used to heat the house and fuel the cook stove. The corncobs were not only plentiful, they were free, so to speak, and were therefore our main fuel source. However, when they could get it, Mom liked to have West Virginia or Pennsylvania coal in small pieces not any bigger than half a tea cup. Mother had a shiny coal burner in the house. It had glass around it and lots of nickel plate. You poured the coal in the top and it kept feeding the fire at the bottom.

This was a far cry from "The Home that Cumberland Built" but Mom and Dad were happy young newlyweds and they envisioned a future on this land and were willing to work for it. They went to work, they dug, they planted, and they built and they continued to live on this land having one five-year lease and two ten-year leases. They also added willow trees for a wind brake and two lilac bushes, one of which still grows in the same place to this day. Many a spring day, since Mother's passing, I have returned to that site to smell the same sweet lilac fragrance my Mother and I once shared.

Ultimately, when their landlord died, the land went into an estate, not once but twice, with seventeen heirs. An old friend of the family, a man by the name of Ad Morgan[38], walked the three miles out from town one day with the news that there were some people by the name of Paup, descendents of the man whose farm the railroad turned into the town of Manilla, who owned a 1/17th share that they were willing to sell.

In any event, Ad told Dad to buy that share because if he owned it, then the other sixteen shares could not be sold without the Saunders' signature. Mom and Dad bought 1/17th share in their rented farm for $177 per acre. Finally, all the shares were offered for $125 per acre. Ultimately they were bought for $87.50 per acre.

Mother did not go to school after she was ten-years-old and my father didn't make it past 5th grade, if he even made it that far. However, they had what it takes to make a home and raise a family. Hard work, patience, determination, farsightedness and a lot of plain old-fashion stubbornness had paid off.

Together, they had made good on Dad's promise that Mother would never have to move again. I am sure the determination of my mother is one of the reasons the Saunders family still have a home on Section Two and Three of Greeley Township in Shelby County, Iowa.

It is now about 5:30 in the morning January 28, 1989. Our forecast is for another beautiful day. Still very mild. A bit of snow yesterday, but it will be gone by sundown.

As I write these memories, I can't help but marvel at what God has provided for the Saunders family to use and enjoy.

I remember seeing my Dad plow the ground down in the valley with three horses and a walking plow. He would walk day after day, morning and afternoon turning one 18-inch furrow

---

[38] Addison 'Ad' Morgan was of C.A.'s vintage. He actually came to Shelby County a few years earlier with his father Mallory Morgan who was the postmaster involved with the naming of the town of Defiance. Like Grandfather, Ad married a Wisconsin Theobald, Phyllis was her name and I honestly do not remember if she was a sister or cousin of my grandma Bertha. Ad's son Cicero married Lola Milligan a sister of Millie Milligan who married my Uncle Chuck.

at a time. I have also seen my Grandson turn the same piece of ground with five 18-inch furrows behind his air-conditioned diesel tractor in a few short hours.

How many fathers can make that statement?

I, we all, have so much to be thankful for.

We all have nice homes and our families are intact. We have been spared the grief and heartaches of booze and drugs that plague so many lives. Sure, we have our problems and we must work and stick to business, but the rewards are great if you just take a bit of time to think.

More later.

"... I can't help but marvel at what God has provided ..."

Chapter 4

CUMBERLAND STOCK FARM NO. 2

January 27, 1989

Another early morning.

Yesterday was a beautiful day. Trudy and I drove over to Manning where we picked up a rebuilt generator for Doug's D17 Allis Chalmers tractor. It is a 1961 model that we bought in 1962. It was our first four-row cultivating tractor and like Grandpa and Grandma, still on the farm.

We stopped a bit and visited with Milo and Helen Clark. They have just moved off their farm into a newly repaired home in Manning. Their family, Dick, Sue and Lynn, is about the same age as ours. They used to raise a few cattle too and our boys were in 4-H together.

Section Two and Three of Greeley Township, Shelby County, Iowa has been my only home since I was born on the 15th day of February 1911. It has been a home I have learned to appreciate, care for, love and enjoy. It is also the exact spot my wife Gertrude and I now live and where I am writing this morning.

Lucky??

God has been good to me in giving me opportunities.

To use the words of my Cousin C. A. Saunders IV, (we called him Buzz or Buster growing up) "I am the luckiest person in the world." After being asked to explain why, his answer was, "First, I was born in America on an Iowa farm and second, to the greatest Mother and Dad in the world." Buzz was the oldest son of my Uncle Chuck (C. A. Saunders III). He now lives in Columbus, Nebraska.[39]

---

[39] Buzz invented a machine to make archery targets and for a short period of time had his factory in the large brick building, now an abandoned gas station, at the bottom of Manilla's main street. In 1949 he moved the company to Columbus, Nebraska where the grass used to make the targets was more plentiful. Buzz passed away in 1995 and today Saunders Archery USA is run by his three sons, Gene, Tom and Charles (the 5th).

I admit that it is a bit hard to keep all the C. A.'s or all the Saunders, for that matter, straight. Remember, of the six children orphaned in Wisconsin, five of them, three boys and two girls, moved to Astor. My Grandfather C. A. had six children of his own and his brother Edgar had nine and Fred, the baby of the family, had six of his own, five boys and one girl.

The Saunders cousins gathered for some unknown family function, circa 1900. Front row L-R (parent name in parenthesis); Austin, b.1892 (Fred); Clyde James, b. 1889 (Alice); Harold and Harry (twins) b. 1900 (Edgar). Middle row L-R; Charles b. 1886 (CA); Victoria b. 1888 (CA); John b.1880 (CA); Sadie, b. 1887 (Edgar); William b. 1884 (CA); Bessie b. 1889 (Edgar); Arley b. 1886 (Edgar). Back row L-R; Allen b. 1897 (Fred); Elizabeth James b. 1890 (Alice); Wallace b. 1894 (Fred); Lillian b. 1894 (Edgar); Willie Powell McCracken b. 1894 (adopted son of Elizabeth); Cyril b. 1896 (Fred); Lida b. 1896 (Edgar).

When the mailman headed out the south road on his route from Manilla, before he got to our house, there was Uncle Deacon's boy J.A. (Arley), A.C. (Austin), C.A. (Grandfather), C.A.II (Uncle Chuck) and then my father J.R. (John), and that was only 2 1/2 miles of one road. They all went by their initials, I don't know why. There was also over the course of time Fred, Wallace, Austin, Velie, Harry, Dick, Ed, Gene and a host of other Saunders descendants not to mention the Theobald families whose two sisters married into the Saunders family. On top of that were the two girls who came out from Wisconsin, Elizabeth and Alice, who added McCracken and James to the family tree while C. A., Fred and Edgar's girls, added the family names of Anderson, Pease, Grimes, Hughes, Klap, Vrana, Terwilleger and Olsen.

Sometimes it seemed that everyone was related to everyone else. In the 1875 census there were only 44 males and 54 females living in the area so I guess it was a pretty shallow gene pool.

I remember one day, probably in the late 30's or early '40's, I was in the drug store when a pretty young lady by the name of Zona Howorth came up to me and asked me if I was a Saunders. I knew who she was, everyone in town did. Not long before she had moved to town with her parents when they bought Manilla's only movie theater and Zona ran the popcorn machine. I wasn't

One Hundred years later a few of the Saunders cousins descended from John gather at Grandma Trudy's house.

sure what prompted the question, she was just trying to be nice but I gave her kind of a smart-alecky answer. I said something like, "Well, one thing about living here, if your not a Saunders or related to one, you soon will be."

Well, I don't think she appreciated the answer very much and that was the end of the conversation. Sometime later I was in

Abe Meyer's Cash Trading Center. Abe had come to town during the depression and set up this grocery store and would trade for goods. He would buy all the eggs I could bring him and was willing to pay me cash but what ever the going price was, 20,25 or 30 cents a dozen, he would pay me a penny extra if I took it out in trade. I could walk out with 25 cents in my pocket or with 26 cents worth of sugar.

Anyway, I had just carried a full case of eggs into Abe's store when Zona walked in. "Zona," I said, "I just heard you got engaged to Gene Saunders. Remember what I told you in the drug store?" She spouted off something to put me back in my place and left a big grin on Abe's face. Gene and Zona married in 1945 and added four more Saunders to our town.

Not all relationships ended that happily. I was recently reminded of a story about a couple of my cousins. It's not a funny story, in fact at the time it was a considerable embarrassment to all involved but with time the story has developed a character of its own and what ever humor the situation allowed has come to the forefront.

Cousin Mildred, Uncle Chuck's girl and my classmate, and another cousin, I think it was Helen, from Edgar's side of the family dated brothers in high school. The Olson brothers were two of five children of the very prim and proper Joseph and Maggie Olson who farmed down near Irwin. For reasons I don't know these two brothers were nicknamed Red and Blue. Blue dated Mildred our senior year and Red was deeply in love with Helen. After high school Helen enrolled in a Catholic College in Sioux City and as soon as Red saved enough money for gas he drove up to see her.

The women's dorms were strictly monitored in those days and I don't know if he snuck her out of the dorm or just didn't bring her back in time, Which ever it was, the Catholic Nuns found out and Helen was kicked out of college. As the story is told in the Olson family, soon after the incident two of Helen's brothers showed up on the porch of the Olson home asking to see Red. It wasn't so much their words as it was the shotguns on their shoulders that convinced Red of the folly of ever attempting to see their sister again. Red went on to live his entire life on that farm and never did marry.

Years later, my son Craig got into some minor trouble at school with the school superintendent, C.E. Thomas. Neither of us remembers (or are going to tell) what it was all about but Mr. Thomas told Craig that if he didn't straighten up, all the Saunders in the country wouldn't be able to get him back into school. I don't think Craig understood what a powerful statement that was.

Anyway, back to February 15th, 1911. My Mother and Father had waited eight long years since their marriage for me to arrive. Mother told me it was a bright, sunny day when I came to live with them, unusually warm for February with lots of snow and running water. She also told me the day before she helped Dad with some fence repair, perhaps hastening my arrival. I was born at home, of course, in the 'shack' they had rebuilt, but we were not without medical care. Dr. Goin was our old country doctor in Manilla at the time and he made the house call in his horse and buggy to help bring me into the world.

Aunt Grace Schram came out the three miles from town to nurse mother.

They named me Raymond M. Saunders, Raymond after my father John Raymond. I have no middle name, just an initial. The M. is for my mother Marie. I guess they thought R. M. would make me fit in with the rest of the Saunders' initials.

During these years the Saunders' cattle herd had continued to grow and had become very successful, both in the show ring and at auction sales. C.A. Saunders and all his sons were in business together and they held both farm and consignment sales all over the United States. Together they had established what ultimately became recognized as the top herd of Registered Scotch Shorthorns in the United States. Along with a fine herd of riding and driving horses and a large herd of Percheron Draft horses, Grandfather and his sons had become a foundation farm of seed stock for the entire country.

Around 1914-15 my father John and Grandfather C.A. added another quarter section to the Cumberland Stock Farm. There remained 160 acres in Section Three that belonged to a man named Charlie Cornelius. They bought Cornelius' southern 160 acres of Section Three and Grandfather took possession of the remaining

First Photograph

Taken When 6 months old

With his Grand Mother

The following reproductions are from my baby book and filled in by my mother's hand.

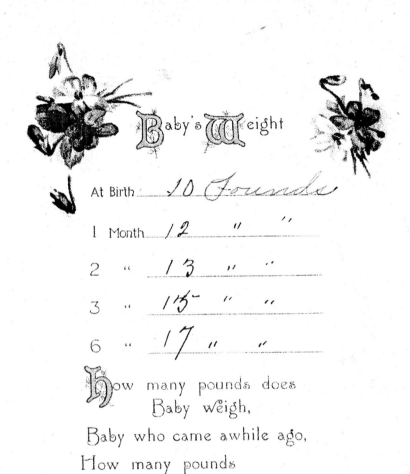

Baby's Weight

At Birth _10 Pounds_

1 Month _12_ " "

2 " _13_ " "

3 " _15_ " "

6 " _17_ " "

How many pounds does
  Baby weigh,
Baby who came awhile ago,
How many pounds
      from crowning curl
  To rosy point of
    restless toe?

Presents

His First Present
was Fair over halls
from his Grand
Father Saunders

He was Presented
with his first Play
thing by his Mother
with a ring and
rattle

Baby Creeps

Date *August 1911*

Baby Stands Alone

Date *Dec. 16 – 1911*

Baby's First Step

Date *Dec 27 – 1911*

Baby's Short Clothes

Date *June 1911*

Baby's First Tooth

Date *Sept 6 1911*

Baby's First Word

Date 7 month Da da

Baby's First Prayer

Date 27 months old

• Now I lay me down to Sleep

Baby's First · Christmas

Presents *Bear cloth coat*

dresses doll. Teddy

Bear number

of presents. Plaything

of Xmas 19

Baby's First Birthday Party

Presents ....

Lrock of Hair

Baby's First Ride

Was to his Grandparents
when 2 months old with
his father and Mother, drove
over buckskin in single bugy

Events in Baby's Life

He fell out of rocking chair
when 9 wks old and fell out
of bed when 3 month old
didnt get hurt either
Time

Baby's Health

Very good up to
22 months of age
Had an operation on his Jaw
when 5 years old. the last of June 1916

Baby's Playmates

Mostly his Mother
and Uncle Julius
and Cousin Mildred who is 8 my
older

Baby's Pets

Foxy his
dog given
him by his
Grand Pa when
he was 2 months old

139

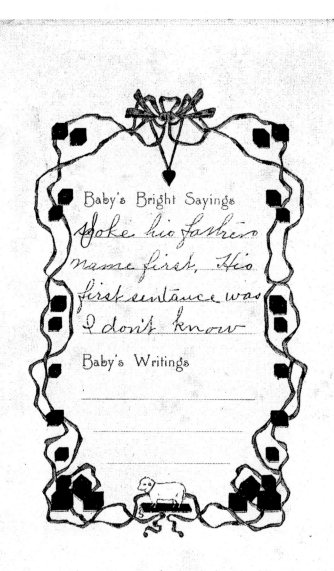

Baby's Bright Sayings

spoke his fathers
name first, His
first sentence was
I don't know

Baby's Writings

(Editor's Note) The Baby's Bright Sayings are the last entry
in the baby book. It is noted on a previous page that he spoke
his fathers name first (at seven months). His first sentence was
recorded as "I don't know." It is pretty much the consensus of the
entire Saunders family and the majority of his neighbors over the
last ninety years that this was the last time these three particular
words were ever uttered in that exact same sequence by Raymond
M. Saunders.

Raymond M. Saunders

acres with a short-term loan. Grandfather already owned 440 acres of this section. Now, with 600 acres of Iowa farmland, my mother's foresight for the future began to surface.

In June of 1916 Cumberland Stock Farm hosted a huge sale of purebred Shorthorn cattle. I am told that people came from all over; in fact, Grandfather was acquainted with the president of the Great

The first picture of sister Margaret and myself most likely taken about mid 1916.

Western Railroad and they ran a train out from Omaha just for the sale. They sold thousands of dollars worth of cattle and the next day, $11,000 worth of remaining cattle were sold to a consortium of buyers from South America. Only 5-6 thousand dollars of the entire sales proceeds was not in hard cash.

With his portion of the proceeds from the "Big Sale" my father bought 120 of the 160 acres Grandfather had taken possession of from Mr. Cornelius. Cornelius was a conductor on the Milwaukee

Railroad and like many people in those days he did not trust the banks but Mr. Cornelius did not want cash either so my father assumed the mortgage for the full amount due on the 160 acres. Dad took 120 acres and Grandfather C.A. took the remaining 40 acres in the southwest corner of the section.

After all of this, Dad still had enough money to build on this property but a site was needed for the buildings. A twelve-acre site was selected on the top of the hill on the west side of the road where the present buildings now stand. This building site was actually in C.A.'s Cumberland Stock Farm but was carved out and surveyed simply by stepping off the measurements. Dad started at one corner and Grandfather at another. Together they stepped off the distances and they say, when they met, there was not four feet difference. Today, that twelve- acre plot of land is the only portion of the original Cumberland Stock Farm still under the Saunders name but that too is another story to be dealt with in a later chapter.

After all these sales, purchases and trades, the buildings on the new farm were begun on July 4, 1917 by a pair of carpenters from Perry, Iowa, Mr. Joe Goodman and a Mr. Becker, whom everyone simply called "Beck." Mr. Goodman was no stranger. He had been the builder of my Grandfather's house and some of the barns on the original Greeley Stock Farm and later he remodeled Aunt Ruth Saunders' home, where Gene Saunders now lives.

There had been another important addition to the Saunders farm during this time. My sister Margaret was born October 16, 1915. The first thing I remember of Margaret is that she made a great friend of Mr. Becker, who was working on the new farm buildings at the top of the hill. Beck would play with her when he came down to our house in the valley for lunch. One day we 'lost' Margaret and couldn't find her anywhere. The yard was fenced in, or should I say we kids were fenced in, but Margaret had found a way out. Mother and I searched the cob shed, the barn, the well and the creek. She was no-where to be found. It was mother's panic I am sure that sears this first memory of Margaret into my consciousness. Finally we found her happily pulling our little red wagon up the hill, going up to the new house to see her good friend Beck.

I also remember the folks telling us how hard it was to get delivery of the building supplies as the 'Great War,' as it was then called, was rampaging in Europe. Nineteen Seventeen was the year the United States joined Britain and France in the conflict. But Grandfather, as always, had laid out plans a long way ahead of schedule. The lumber had been contracted and paid for a year ahead in 1916 with the Green Bay Lumber Company of Green Bay, Wisconsin. The building supplies were shipped by railroad to Astor and then hauled by horse and wagon cross-country to the new farm site.

Once everything was assembled the building started and a short seven months later, February 2, 1918, was moving day. My sister Margaret and I were staying with Grandma Bertha on that day while the adults were putting the finishing touches on the move. I was seven-years-old. I remember about 11 o'clock in the morning either Mom or Dad called down to Grandma's house and told us to look out the east window. There was a large hot air balloon. A lot of people called them war balloons at that time and they were frequently part of the display or entertainment at county fairs etc. I don't remember anything more about it, I had never seen one before, I didn't know where it came from or where it was going on that cold winter day but I do remember that I could see two people in the basket with the ear flaps of their caps pulled down tightly over their ears.

Darkness comes early in the Iowa winter so in the late afternoon we were rushing around getting ready to go to our new house. I remember my sister Margaret standing all bundled up with Grandma Bertha on her front porch waiting for Father to come take us to our new home. It was twenty degrees below zero and we were bundled up for a very cold bobsled ride to our new home.

The bobsled was not what we think of as a sled today. It was a farm wagon with the wheels taken off and replaced with big wooden runners reinforced with a strip of steel along the bottom to make them slide more easily over the snow and ice as it was pulled along by a team of workhorses.

We would have rather ridden in a more fashionable Cutter which is what people these days think of when they think "Over the river

Our towering barn formed the background for my dog Fox and the red wagon Margaret and I shared.

and through the woods to Grandmother's house we go." A Cutter was like a buggy but with runners and pulled by a single horse and it was purely for transportation. I guess if we had been in a Cutter loaded with goods we would have looked like Santa Claus with his two little elves. But we were in a bobsled and this bobsled was for work and we were working, excitedly sitting atop a sled full of baggage being transported to our new house as the sun began to set on that cold Iowa Ground Hog Day.

As we rounded the bend in the road, there it was. It looked like a mansion to us. A big five bedroom house sitting atop a hill in an alfalfa field, there were no trees, no fences, no yards, but there were new buildings and a new beginning. What a sight and what a difference for the family, coming out of a two-room shack in the valley with my mother's willow tree windbreak into a big unprotected home on the top of a hill. The wind seemed to blow from every direction.

I have been told that due to Grandpa's contracting the total cost of the barn, house, garage, a small chicken house was only $16,000.

The house was magnificent as Margaret and I ran through its big new rooms with all the furniture still all sort of mixed up. We ran first upstairs to our own separate bedrooms and then explored the rest of our new home. It was big, with two big colonnades and a china closet; it had a basement and a second floor all with indoor plumbing and three indoor bathrooms. It was even wired for electricity although it would be many years before rural electrical service would be available in that part of the country.

If the house was big, the barn was gigantic, one-hundred-and-twenty feet long with individual stalls lining both sides of a cemented isle running full-length down the middle. This was an aisle through which one could walk to feed the cattle or to bring prospective buyers. Each stall could hold two cows and their calves. Each had a small individual hand-made feed bunk for grain at each corner facing the aisle with a large hay bin running the width of the stall. Each stall was connected inside with a hand-made door resembling a picket fence but made out of 2X4's. A similar door led from each stall to the outside yard. This was the 'summer' door. A second solid door was open during the summer but could be closed during the cold winters keeping the livestock warm and dry. There was a separate window in each stall to provide light, though the barn was also wired and waiting for electricity. The stalls were separated by partitions made of 2X6 planks that rose about six feet. To provide for the circulation of air, the remaining six feet was open up to the ceiling. Above was a second floor hayloft that ran the entire length of the barn and was topped by a wood shingled roof with two giant metal cupolas.

Suspended just below the cupolas ran an iron railing the entire length of the barn, actually extending several feet beyond under a pointed extension of the roof. This railing connected two large hayloft doors located on each end of the building. These huge doors

Our hay cutter was pulled behind father's team, the lugged metal wheels turned a gear box which in turn ran a sickle back and forth through a cutting bar that extended out to the right side. The lever my sister Margaret has her hand on raises and lowers the cutting bar. The strings hanging from the horses harness swing and sway when they walk, discouraging flies from attacking, much like the swishing of his tail.

were attached with hinges on the bottom and during haymaking season they were lowered like a castle's drawbridge until they lay flush with the first-floor walls. Before the days of hay bailers, large loads of loose fresh hay were brought to sit under these doors. From the iron railing above, large iron fingers descended like a gigantic four-legged spider into the hay wagon. The 'spider' was called a grabfork and it would grab a large bite of the loose hay and via a series of pulleys was pulled by a team of horses and later by a tractor, back up to the railing and into the barn. A large trip rope was attached to the grabfork and when the hay reached the right spot in the barn, the man in the hayloft would shout out to the man on the ground. A mighty tug on the trip rope would then with release the hay to fall to the floor. The loft man's job was to evenly smooth out the hay with a pitch fork while the man outside with the rope pulled the 'spider' back for another bite.

The whole process was labor-intensive. Out in the field one

man would drive the team of horses pulling a hay wagon over the windrows of fresh hay. There was science and experience involved in this process, too. The hay would be cut and left to dry a bit before being raked into the windrows. The windrows not only gathered up the hay for loading, they also allowed the hay to lie up more off the ground allowing the wind and sun to further dry it just the right amount. If the hay were put in the barn too wet, it would begin to heat up and ferment and if the temperature reached the critical point it would burn your barn to the ground.

So, when the hay reached just the right brittleness a hay loader would be attached behind the wagon and pulled over the windrows. This hay loader picked up the hay with a series of chains and forked teeth to elevate it into the wagon where two men, again with pitchforks, would stack it for the trip back into the barn. It was best to use at least three wagons so, while one wagon was being loaded, another could be making the trip to or from the barn as the third was being unloaded. That of course took another man or boy to be the driver.

For the unloading, it took a man on the trip rope, a man on the hay wagon to set the fingers, a man or usually a boy with the team of horses or tractor and at least two men with pitchforks in the hot hayloft. There, in the loft, you had to be careful. It was great fun to catch your coworker not paying attention and standing under the railing. With an early well-timed shout to the 'trip man' you could drop a load of hay over your partner's head and watch him scramble in the knee-deep hay to get out of the way or be buried under it.

It is a good thing that the barn was so big. There was a lot of hay to be made. Dad's 120 acres from Mr. Cornelius added to the 195 acres on the east side of the road from the Goddard Estate plus the twelve-acre building site carved out of Grandpa's Cumberland Stock Farm made up our new farm. The barn, like all the new buildings, was painted white, but above the doors and windows and below the eves of the towering roof with its giant cupolas were painted the large black letters:

CUMBERLAND STOCK FARM No. 2
John R. Saunders and Son

All paid for by Shorthorn cattle.

John R. Saunders' home situated on the Cumberland Stock Farm, No. 2, Greelet Twp., Shelby Co.

In 1919 the Shelby County Fair published a Fiftieth Anniversary Edition Catalog. C.A. Saunders and the Cumberland Stock Farm were featured in a special centerfold layout in the 176 page catalog. Included in the feature was this picture of the new Cumberland Stock Farm No.2, as it appeared when we moved in Feb. 2, 1918.

Chapter 5

LIFE ON THE FARM

January 28, 1989

Not quite so early this morning, 5:15 AM. Trudy was up much before me. She has wash already in the dryer and is cleaning out the lower part of her pantry shelves here in the kitchen.

We had a nice Sunday in Spencer, Iowa with Dean's family. Keith had a part in the church services conducted by the young people of their Congregational Church.

We also learned that Keith had won a position on the Western Iowa Debate Team. They will represent Western Iowa in the National meet in Colorado Springs in June. So, it looks like he is getting a good start on his quest for a degree in law (move over Danny Quail).

The drive to Spencer was rather tiring. We had lots of snow and rain, and foggy roads near Odebolt. Very slippery but the sun came out and the pavement cleared. It was almost dry on the way home.

Mother does the driving, and while she isn't any better than she admits, she is an expert driver and really handles her Chrysler Fifth Avenue wonderfully.

We had a nice trip, and a nice home to come home to.

I guess retirement is great?

Our forecast is for another sunny and warm day. Tomorrow, record highs are predicted. This January has been unbelievably warm and dry. We here on the dairy farm don't miss the cold and snow, although we do wonder about moisture for the coming crop year.

Life on the farm is never dull. Perhaps that is what I should write about today. It has been just over a month since we celebrated Christmas; this might be a good place to start.

Christmas on the Saunders' farm has a long tradition and has always been celebrated at the home of the oldest family member. I remember as a young boy going down to Grandpa's on the original Cumberland Farm for Christmas dinner. Their 'tree' was always a branch off one of the big red cedar evergreen trees they planted as a windbreak around their house. It was decorated with candles, popcorn and cranberries.

The days before Christmas were spent in eager anticipation of the greatest holiday of the year and Grandmother helped her grandchildren pass the time by preparing the decorations. Ears of yellow popcorn, grown that summer out in the fields alongside the field corn, were brought up from the fruit cellar. While we sat in her kitchen Grandma Bertha taught her young grandchildren how to shell the kernels off the cobs into a big bowl. This looked like great fun and we were eager to try but our little thumbs soon got sore enough from pushing the kernels off the cob to develop blisters and the adults would always have to finish the job.

The kernels of corn were placed in a large black iron kettle along with a large dollop of butter or lard. Contrary to popular stories, the cobs were not taken to the outhouse for use as toilet paper or even used to make corncob pipes. Instead they were thrown into our large wood-burning stove in the corner of Grandma's kitchen to help pop more corn.

The iron kettle was placed on the stove, shaken and turned with big home made-potholders until the corn was popped. The popped corn was then poured into a big bowl from which individual kernels were strung by little fingers on a needle and thread alternating with store-bought cranberries. Most of the corn from the first couple of poppings did not make it past our mouths and on to the string. Even though it was not smothered with salt and lots of extra melted butter and therefore not as good as our regular 'eating popcorn, it still took at least a couple batches until the majority of the corn made it on the string as Christmas decorations.

When Christmas finally came we all had our dinner in the big dining room. Chuck, Vic, Uncle Will and a dozen or fifteen kids to be sure. The big sliding doors to the parlor were always closed and locked. The parlor was off-limits to the kids; after all, the Christmas 'tree' and all the presents were in there. Grandma Bertha generally had the same gift for all the grandchildren. One time I remember it was our own copy of the New Testament.

After Christmas the big red cedar branch that had served us so well as a Christmas tree was hung out on the porch with the popcorn and cranberries for the birds to continue the Christmas feast.

We, of course, had our own Christmas celebration at home, usually on Christmas Eve. We always tried to go to church and then come home to celebrate the gift giving, never anything elaborate.

After we moved into our big new house, Mother wanted to make sure our first Christmas there was memorable. In July she mail-ordered Christmas decorations from the Sears and Roebuck Catalog. Placing the envelope in our mailbox on that hot July day started our countdown to Christmas. Finally, when December did come around, we went into town and bought our first real Christmas tree. I was about seven-years-old at the time; it must have been about 1917-18. We sat the tree in the front window of the east room. It almost reached the ceiling. All of us kids thought it was so great as we carefully unwrapped the priceless treasures from Sears and Roebuck and added them to our homemade decorations.

The gifts we kids gave each other were usually homemade, but I remember when I was about ten-years-old getting a windup train with a cowcatcher on the front of the engine. I think it is still stored somewhere across the road in the big house.

Years later, Mother's casket would occupy almost the same spot in the same room where that first Christmas tree stood. There is something comforting in knowing that she was well taken care of, that she never had to leave the home she was so proud of. It is these memories, Christmas and others, that make a house a home, a home that is worth working a lifetime fighting to save and to pass on to our own children.

More recently when Trudy and I had our four boys in our little house we continued the Christmas Eve tradition. These were happy days even though we didn't have much. I remember one Christmas we got one truck for all four boys to share. We didn't have a real

The latch hangs free, the door swings wide,
To all our friends at Christmas Tide.
Fire on hearth, good will and cheer,
To greet our friends through all the year.

John & Marie

This undated Christmas card must be from several years later, given
the size of the trees and the shrubs but it clearly shows the love and
pride my parents had for their home.

tree that year either; we just used a branch like Grandfather had,
but we didn't want. Our days were rich and full.

Chores would be finished early on Christmas Eve and we would
all pile into the family car for the drive to church. It seems that after
the kids were in the car there was always one last little chore that
was forgotten and the boys waited anxiously in the car while Mom
or I went back into the house to finish Santa's job. A couple of times
we even proved Santa was real by leaving a pair of new boots out

in a snow bank, suggesting they had "accidentally' fallen out of Santa's sleigh.

As we drove over 'the big hill' just north of our house on these crisp clear winter nights it was an excellent time to slow down and look for the Christmas star. More times than not, a bright star could be singled out by the little eyes and agreed upon by all before the car started back down the hill. Some years 'the Christmas star' would be in the East and some years it was found in the West. It really didn't seem to matter; Bethlehem was a long, long way from Iowa.

The Christmas Eve church service was a combination of familiar Christmas hymns and Sunday School skits with kids in old bath robes, towels wrapped around their heads and fake beards portraying Joseph, the Three Wise Men and, of course, the Shepherds. The oldest of the kids all had proudly memorized lines for the gratification of parents and grandparents. The younger children sang Christmas hymns as a group; however, the program soared in its entertainment value if there was at least one severe case of stage fright and forgotten lines.

Following the program, the children returned to the pews with their parents for a short service of hymns and prayers. As the lights were dimmed the congregation sang **Silent Night, Holy Night** and the light of a single candle was passed person-to-person. Slowly, but surely, candle by candle, a soft golden light returned to the sanctuary as each flickering candle was reflected off the big stained-glass windows. Those windows of deep reds, royal blues, golden yellows and soft browns depicted the life of Christ, and memorialized some of our community's finest children. Written on the bottom of each window was the memorial of a native son, McCracken, Means, Holdsworth and McClaren. Each young man had given his life for his country so that we could enjoy these freedoms.

These were nights without equal!

What gifts!

Life on the farm was good.

Not easy, but good.

We farm folks didn't have some of the problems that plagued the city folks. Working the farm in those days was teamwork. It took not only a man; it took a man and his wife and their children. It took a family, a farm family.

On the farm, everyone had their role. One of the good things about rearing children on the farm was, unlike some of their city counterparts, farm kids always knew what their daddy did for a living. Not only did they know what their daddy did, they also knew where he did it. Unlike the city kids whose father had already left the house for work when they got up in the morning, farm kids not only live at their daddy's work place, they know what his work is and they can work and play right alongside him all day long.

Furthermore, they see the results of their work. On the farm, as in life, you plant, you tend and you harvest. What you harvest depends entirely upon what you plant and how you care for it. It really makes little difference if you are planting ideas or corn you harvest what you plant – if you care for it properly. It's a simple process really and so easy to see on the farm. If you don't feed the pigs, they get hungry. If you don't feed them for a long time, they die. If they die, **you** get hungry . . . Responsibility and consequences for your actions, you learn this at a very early age on the farm.

This is a great advantage. Children learn best by example. Their little eyes are their windows to the world and they look and they see and they learn lessons that shape the way they will live their own lives. For the lucky ones, the ones who have a loving mother and father beside them, who better to teach them? No one will ever love them more unconditionally than their Father and Mother. You don't necessarily have to live on a farm to learn these lessons but it is, as I believe I have pointed out, a great advantage – a blessing.

Living life and rearing children is not about the trips to Disneyland, expensive clothes or toys; it is not about being their best friends. It is not about giving them all the things we never had or making life easy for our children. It **is** about how **we** live our lives. It **is** about the examples **we** set and it **is** about the boundaries **we** enforce. Every parent complains that their children won't listen to them but don't worry. You are speaking volumes and even if their ears don't work, the children are listening with their eyes and their hearts. The children are watching us and learning from us at the times we are least expecting it. To our children, it's the little things that count. My granddaughter Laura wrote the poem on the following page for her father. It was written after she graduated college but it recalled her early days and I believe, says it best.

Sometimes, no, in fact all the time, the responsibility to our children extends to children other than our own.

One day, I think in April, during my fifth year in country school, my sister Margaret and I came home from school, and to our surprise, and I do mean surprise, we had a new sister! A pudgy little girl with a pageboy haircut and a tiny little smile was sitting in our living room with our Mother.

Mother simply said, "This is your new sister" and from then on she was our sister. Wilma Ray Saunders, a seven-year-old little girl, had come to live with us. She slept in the same bed with Margaret that night and the next day she went to school with us. There was no jealously or no anger; there was just acceptance. That was just simply the way we were raised.

Wilma was the granddaughter of 'Uncle' Bill and 'Aunt' Helen Ray, the same 'Aunt' Helen who had been a close friend of my great grandmother Schultz. She was the same woman my Mother, years earlier, had come out to visit from eastern Iowa after Grandma Schultz died. Florence Longnecker Ray was the orphan child 'Aunt' Helen took in and who ultimately married her son John. Wilma Ray was the youngest daughter of John and Florence Longnecker Ray, of Defiance, Iowa.

There was a huge Spanish Flu epidemic in 1918 just after World War I ended. Before the epidemic ended it killed six million people worldwide and got so bad here at home that schools were closed and the mayor issued a proclamation banning public gatherings. People were advised to avoid crowds and not even to gather in groups on the street. The flu was attacking everyone, young and old alike, with a fast and often fatal pneumonia. I had gotten pneumonia twice and there was an old wives' tale that if you got it twice, there was no chance for you.

Father's Day
By Laura Saunders

I cannot remember the first time I met him,
Yet I have known him all my live.
He has always been my driving force.
A constant when my world is shaky
And a cheerleader and coach who watches from the sidelines
Encouraging me every step of the way
In a game called Life.

I remember the early days,
Riding on his shoulders down a path called
Cherry Tree Lane.
A small adventure to the magnificent yellow mailbox
That awaited us at the end of our journey.

I remember playful days outside
As the leaves and snowflakes fell quietly at our feet.
And warm nights
Cuddled up next to him watching M*A*S*H
And learning the intricacies of eating an
Oreo cookie.

And the adventures we took. . .
They stretched my mind to new dimensions
And far exceeded any realm of my imagination.
Each adventure allowing me to observe the world in a new light.

Blessed

A hero of sorts,
He possesses a special power within his essence
That never ceases to make me feel safe, secure and worthy of life.
Strong enough to endure it, and thankful enough
To celebrate all that it has to offer.
He has patience for strength, wisdom and passion for success
And an unyielding grace for the love that he gives so
unconditionally.

He is intense, inspiring,
Committed to all that he does and
Striving for the highest ideals possible.
On a vivacious quest,
He has been under seas,
Crossed continents wide
And has touched the heavens,
Learning their secrets and passing them on.

And yet, through all of his doing and being,
His spirit is light and shines brightly
For all those close enough to feel his warmth.
And, always with a dose of good cheer he asks,
"Are we having fun yet?"
And yes Dad, we are having some kind of fun!

One of the times I was sick my Dad was sick, too – so sick that we thought we were going to lose him. Dr. Loomis brought a nurse out from Council Bluffs on the train to care for my Dad while he and my Mother nursed me back to health. The nurse simply lived in that back bedroom with my Dad. They thought they were going to have to tap his lung but she was not in favor of that and the first thing she did was open the windows to get fresh air. That night old Ad Morgan and the nurse sat up with Dad and he coughed and coughed. He coughed enough to start clearing his lungs and they avoided tapping them.

Dr. Loomis was our local M.D. at the time. He was also President of the School Board. During one of his house calls he stood over me and told my mother, "If we get this kid through this, we ought to make a kid doctor out of him." I was lying in a bed made for me in the front room of our big new house. I remembered Dr. Loomis' statement and took it to heart. It sounded like a lofty ambition.

This was in late January and early February. When we both began to get well, Grandma made ice cream and we had it for my birthday party. I remember sitting beside my Dad at the dining room table eating homemade ice cream and birthday cake with a big heavy quilt wrapped around both our legs.

Dad was still being nursed in the back bedroom. He would ultimately die in that bedroom but not until he lived in that house for another forty years. Wilma's father was not as lucky. He died in the flu epidemic. We had visited the Ray family earlier that year and Mom knew that he was sick. Mom had watched the newspapers real close and on the day his death was announced she hid the newspaper from Dad because she thought it would have a bad effect on him. She didn't want him to know that John Ray had passed away.

Soon afterwards, Wilma lost her mother, again to influenza, leaving Wilma and her three older siblings Glen, Gladys and Meyer alone. The three oldest stayed together with an aunt and uncle but Wilma, the youngest, came to live with us. I remember so well Mother saying many times, "This is my way of repaying Aunt Helen for the kindness she gave Grandma Schultz and me."

Needless to say, Margaret, Wilma and I, like all children, had the usual amount of childhood arguments, disagreements and down right cat fights and I know later they felt that I always had things my own way. However, and I know I can speak for Margaret, too, never from day one did we not consider Wilma our sister.

There was another big change sweeping the country during this time. For the previous seventy years women had been campaigning for the right to vote. After the Civil War they were discouraged that the 14th and 15th Amendments to the U.S. Constitution forbid the denial of rights and privileges based only on race. Black men were given the right to vote but women, of either race, were still denied. In 1872, the year my grandfather moved to Iowa, Susan B. Anthony was arrested in New York for illegally voting in a Presidential Election. Western states were the first to give women the vote but it was not until I was 9-years- old, in 1920 that the 19th Amendment was ratified. It gave all women the right to vote. I remember my mother not being too impressed. She had a lot of political struggles in North Dakota getting her homestead finalized and as far as she was concerned, "they ought to take the vote away from all the men and give it all to the women." She had become pretty fed up with the political process.

Later, after I reached high school, Mother helped me get started in a small purebred Poland China hog project. Grandpa had an old sow die while giving birth to a litter of eight small piglets. I brought them up to our house and bottle-fed them until they were older and could live by themselves. I then fixed up a place for them in the barn. I helped my Dad in my spare time and earned feed for my hog project. I raised them and the next fall took the best four of the eight to the county fair.

John Schram[40] helped me make four crates to hold the hogs. Our neighbor, Otis Manford, brought his old pickup truck over and

---

[40]Joe Schram came from Germany and was our local butcher. He had four boys, Ed, Harry, Charlie and John. John had some injury to his legs as a child and walked on his toes with a cane but it didn't limit him very much. Charlie was the father of our present day grocer Charlie Schram who is also one of the states great sports historians, the local football field is named Schram Field in honor of Charlie.

we loaded the crated hogs in the back and took them to the county fair.

My pigs didn't win a ribbon that year because these hogs were of the old 'lard type' and a new meatier version was now in vogue at the shows, but I won something more important. This was my first trip to the fair with my own livestock and while there I met a young man from Shelby, Iowa by the name of Ed Whaling. I may not have won a ribbon that year but I won a friend for life.

Mom and Dad told me to put a "For Sale" sign over my pen of hogs and even though they were not prize winners, I sold them right there at the fair. This was in the mid 1920's and there was a little time after World War I that times were pretty good. The three boars were sold for $50 a piece and the guilt for $35.

Otis drove back down to the fair in his old truck and found me asleep in the cattle barn. We loaded the empty crates and came

There were no palm-thatched huts and hula girls in my life, only corn stalk shades and my early hog project.

home. The crates were put in the hayloft of the big barn and I believe are still there!

I now had $185, four hogs still at home and the mistaken idea that this was all pretty easy. I opened a small checking account at Uncle Ed's First National bank, called the "upper bank" being that it was built on the upper end of Main Street.[41] I used the money to pay for my clothes and school expenses and started a small fund for a future college education.

Don (last name forgotten), an Auburn University student holds my sister Margaret as I stand along side with my collie dog Fox, given to me by Grandfather when I was two months old.

---

[41] Uncle Ed's First National Bank was on the corner across the street west of the current bowling alley. The big brick building was just recently torn down. The "lower bank" was the Manilla State Bank, which was on the same block but at the lower southwestern corner.

Two years later, in the fall of 1928, I took part of my hog herd back to the Shelby County Fair. Now remember, the Saunders families were pioneers in good livestock and Grandfather C. A. was one of the original stockholders in the Shelby County Fine Stock Exchange which sponsored the fair.

Showing animals at the County Fair was the highlight of the farmer's year and about the only vacation farm families had.

Many people do not realize the value of our state and county fairs as educational events. Fairs and expositions provided young farmers experiences and opportunities that our schools and colleges couldn't. Through these expos, we met many fine Stockmen and educators of the area.

We have already talked about Nels Kraschel, a good friend of C. A.'s, and also a hell of a good auctioneer, recognized as one of the best in America. Col. N. G. Kraschel went on to become Governor of Iowa. The only game of golf I ever played in my life was with one of Nels Kraschel's sons at the Harlan Country Club. He had three sons. One gave his life in the Philippines during World War II.

Herb Kildee was Dean of Agriculture at Iowa State University in Ames. He worked for C.A. when he was going to college and was a good friend of my Dad's. Dean Kildee and our County Extension Directors kept a steady stream of college kids coming to the farm, most from Iowa State but we even had some from Auburn University in Alabama.

Shelby County, Iowa, was an exceptional place to be a farmer in those days. The cover of the 1919 Shelby County Fair Catalog had a banner across the top proclaiming in bold letters:

"Shelby County Is The Color Bearer Of The World's Great Stock Breeding Industry"

On the inside it went on to say:

> "Shelby County, Iowa, is unique in many ways. Of all the counties in the forty-eight states of Uncle Sam's great domain, it stands first in number of purebred livestock produced. There isn't an acre of wasteland in the county.

164

In 1917, Shelby produced 3,420,000 bushels of corn, 1,175,000 bushels of oats, and other grains and forage crops on the same stupendous scale. And that same year Shelby County owned 15,763 horses, 57,358 cattle, 7,555 sheep, 120,519 hogs, 281,000 poultry, practically all pure-bred, and gathered 1,225,000 eggs . . . The fact that she has today more herds of registered cattle, horses and hogs than any other one county in the United States has never been successfully disputed. To this one thing Shelby County owes much of her prosperity . . . The Shelby County Fine Stock Exchange is the largest in the state . . . The county fair held at Harlan is in a class by itself . . . (it) is out of debt, has money in the treasury, has been a liberal contributor to the Red Cross and has a tidy bunch of Liberty Bonds salted away in the strong box."

Both the city of Los Angles and the city of San Diego placed full-page ads in the 1919 Shelby County Fair Catalog. Grandfather was certainly one of the main reasons the county was held in such esteem but there were others. Escher and Ryan had perhaps the best Aberdeen Angus Herd in the United States. Earl Ryan was a hell of a good showman. The Johnson brothers, Harvey and Clifford, raised Hereford cattle of the same world-class caliber. There were many, many others concentrated in the rolling hills of Shelby County, Iowa.

There is nothing that will get a young farm boy any higher than winning at the County Fair in competition with all these good stock men of the area. That fall I came away with the First Prize Spring Guilt, Third Prize Spring Boar and combined with two of their littermates, the First Prize Litter of Four.

I came home on top of the world, convinced that I knew more about the hog business than anyone in the Saunders family and maybe even the county. I just knew that if I raised enough hogs I would be able to go on to college and live all my dreams. However, I quickly learned that there is a lot more to the hog business. I will try to explain later.

Raymond M. Saunders

C. W. Daws, President   L. H. Pickard, Secretary

———OF———

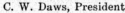

The Shelby County Fine Stock Exchange
Harlan, Iowa

WHAT SHELBY COUNTY IS DOING FOR THE STOCK INTERESTS OF COLORADO

The greatest sale of pure bred cattle ever held in Colorado was the sale of D. Warnork & Sons of Loveland, June 26th, when they sold forty head of Shorthorns at an average of $1,300.00. The top being purchased by a local man at $3,200.00. An interesting feature is that Shelby County figures quite prominently in the event. The larger part of the foundation stock was purchased of C. A. Saunders, of Shelby County, including their present Bull, Model Type sired by Cumberland's Type. He is rated by many competent judges as the most valuable shorthorn bull in America.

The catalog was a work of art. H. E. Lewis of Harlan, Ia., did the photographic work and N. G. Kraschel, also of Harlan, and without a question is one of the leading live stock auctioneers in America, sold the cattle.

R. G. Maxwell of Fort Collins, Colo., a breeder of Shorthorn cattle and Poland China hogs purchased the major part of his stock, both hogs and cattle in Shelby County.

He has for several years been an exhibitor at the Denver Fat Stock Show. The association has given two Grand Champion Premiums each year on hogs, and in five years in succession Mr. Maxwell has won NINE out of the Ten Grand Champion Premiums. He has also taken his full share of premiums on his Shorthorn exhibit.

There are so many good things that comes from Shelby County we are most too modest to claim even that which is coming to us. There is so little for the other fellow.

The county fairs were generally scheduled in the late summer or early fall, hopefully during a week between harvest cycles so that farm work can take second place to the fair. Afterwards, however, it is back to work and the fall of 1928 was my invitation to a long season of work in the cornfields. We picked corn by hand, and soon I found, by concentrating on the job, I could pick corn with anyone here on the farm, and 100 bushels per day was not impossible.

I would start about 6 or 6:30 in the morning. Lots of times the stars would still be shining. My sister Margaret would drive a team of fresh horses, an empty wagon and some lunch out to the field about 9:30 in the morning. By that time I had about 35 bushels in a wagon.

The horses' reins were tied along the wagon and the horses would learn to walk along with you. You wore a husking hook on your wrist, and an old fella from Harlan taught me how to let the corn roll off my hand into the wagon without wrist action. You had to have pretty good strength in your hands. I got so I could pick three rows of corn at a time. Most people would pick only two.

By noon I would come back to the house for lunch and would bring in another 35 bushels. A 26- inch wagon box would hold 25 bushels, about one bushel per inch. We would put on six-inch sideboard extensions and another backboard on the left side of the wagon to catch the high throws.

You had to know what you were doing and care for the horses as well as for yourself. Both were vitally important assets. If either got injured, the crop wouldn't get harvested. If you got the wagon too high you had to throw the corn higher and it took more energy and if you loaded it lop-sided, these high narrow wagons would get top-heavy and prone to tip over on these Iowa hillsides. That could injure the horses in addition to making more work. Besides that, 35 bushels was about all the weight you wanted the horses to pull through the sometimes muddy cornfields.

After lunch, I would take out a third wagon and a rested team to the field while Dad unloaded the first two wagons by hand with a scoop. At the end of the day, I would bring in the third wagon, take care of the team, and then unload this last wagon while Dad did the chores. It would take us about three weeks to get the corn crop harvested this way.

When I look back it is amazing how hard we worked and thought nothing of it.

Dad's team, Doll and Mabel, ready to go back into the field after unloading ear corn in the steel crib behind them. By the time this picture was taken we had the elevator set up and running.

Chapter 6

HIGH SCHOOL

January 29, 1989

I'll try to write a bit about high school this morning.

The first day of school is a big day in everyone's life. As I remember I started in the spring of 1917. We still lived down in the valley in the original house Mother and Dad built when they were first married. Even though this was the year Mom and Dad were building the new place on top of the hill about a quarter to half-mile or so northwest in Section Three, we were not living there yet.

Since we were still living in the old place in Section Two, I started school in Greeley No. 1. It was referred to as the "Sleister School" due to the fact that the school was directly across from the Robert Sleister farm. I don't remember too much about our teacher but I do remember walking down the field and along the creek to the school that was just slightly less than a mile away. I also remember Dad sometimes taking me on horseback when it was raining or muddy. I only went to school that year for what we called the spring term (twelve weeks).

In Iowa at that time, elementary school went up through the 8th grade and in the rural areas all eight grades were in a one-room schoolhouse with one teacher. Each county was plotted out in townships and each township was divided into one-mile square sections. These country schoolhouses were located on one acre-plots in the corner of every other section, making them two miles apart. This assured no students would not have to walk more than one mile to school. The classes were made up of brothers, sisters, cousins and close neighbors, usually not more than a dozen or so kids, sometimes less.

The school day began with everyone participating in fifteen minutes of singing, prayer and, of course, the Pledge of Allegiance. The single room was built around a wood or coal-burning stove for

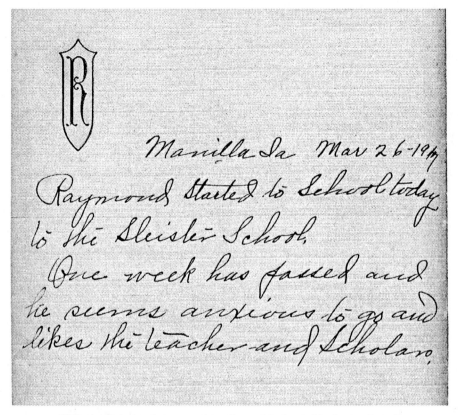

Manilla Ia   Mar 26-19—
Raymond Started to School today
to the Sleister School.
One week has passed and
he seems anxious to go and
likes the teacher and Scholars

This single journal entry, written in my Mother's hand, was found inserted into my baby book.

which the teacher was responsible for the coal. There were desks of various sizes and, of course, blackboards. Each student had a job, cleaning the blackboards, sweeping the floor, keeping the fire burning, or filling the large earthen jar in the back of the room with water. Two identical outhouses were out back, one for the boys and one for the girls. Most students walked to school but there was also a hitching post if you were lucky enough to have a pony.

You know, lots of people think our schools today are a big advancement and certainly there are a lot of good things about today's schools but if you think about it, there were a lot of good things about the one-room country school house. First, the classes were small and even though the teacher was responsible for eight grades she was always available to help and there was always a lot of help from the older students. If you wanted to go faster, there was nothing to keep you from learning from the older students' lessons. Perhaps most importantly we were all responsible to each other.

My fondest memories are of the boys, or scholars as my Mother called them. Henry Hanson, an older boy, was a schoolmate whom I thought was the nicest fellow around. Later he lived north of Irwin and did corn shelling to help make a living. 'Corn Sheller' Hanson was what we called him as there were other Henry Hansons in the community.

Oscar Wetzel, his younger brother, and his sister Annie lived in the same section a little less than a mile down the creek from Mom and Dad's house. I remember them because they were the youngest of a large family. They had a pretty place to live with a big white house and two red barns painted with white trim. I thought they were real sharp.[42]

Oscar used to walk past his house and part way up their pasture with me on my way home. One day, just ahead of us as we walked through the pasture, a startled ground squirrel scurried into his hole. Oscar and I thought it would be just a plain old-fashioned good idea to carry water from the creek in our lunch pails to drown out this stupid ground squirrel. Our plan worked. Oscar was older, maybe five or six classes ahead of me and I think he had done this before. He knelt down on his knees behind the hole and when the soaked little squirrel came sputtering and chocking out of his hole, Oscar deftly grabbed him by the nape of his neck between his thumb and forefinger. I proudly hurried home with the half- drowned squirrel safely in my lunch pail. Mother had a few things to say about that! Somewhat to this six-year-olds' surprise, Mother did not view the trophy of this grand adventure with the same sense of enthusiasm Oscar and I shared when we first conceived the grand scheme. Who would have thought?

Through the summer of 1917 my folks were busy as they began building their new home across the road in Section Three. Living in a new section of the township placed me in a new school and when

---

[42] Years later, when my youngest son Doug returned from the Navy we bought this Wetzel farm from Oscar and added it to Cumberland Stock Farm No. 2.

I returned to school the next fall it was to Greeley No. 2, the same school my father had attended for a short time.

I don't remember a lot about my first year except I didn't like the kids in this new school very much. I think the only good thing about it was that I was joined by my Cousin Mildred, Uncle Chuck's girl, and we continued as classmates through high school.

A local girl, Hanna Christensen, was our teacher in 3rd and 4th grade. Her younger brother, Chris has been a good friend all through my life. Edna Stewart taught three years, 5th, 6th and 7th grades. My father was the School Director and responsible for hiring the teachers. Miss Stewart had a teaching job somewhere down south but Dad was able to hire her after he got a message from someone that Miss Stewart wanted to work closer to home to help take care of her elderly parents.

She lived with her parents in Manilla and walked three miles to our school each day. Miss Stewart was not what you would call a good-looking woman but everyone loved her. Her brother worked for the railroad and oftentimes she was able to hitch a ride on the train down to Astor and thereby cut a mile off her walk. There were a lot of big steam engines passing through in those days and if, on the return trip, the engineer would see Miss Stewart coming down the road, he would wait for her in Astor and give her a ride home in the engine's cab. We learned respect and behavioral manners along with reading, writing and arithmetic from Miss Stewart.

It wasn't all work. We did have some fun and the highlight of Miss Stewart's three-year career in our country school had to be during her last year. Although the school was well cared for it was under the constant attack of young children. One of the favorite things for the boys to do was take shingles off the outhouse roof and with their pocketknives carve darts to throw. It got so bad that while Dad was the director he had to have new outhouses built. These were architectural masterpieces of construction with slanting roofs raised up off the walls to catch the wind and provide better ventilation. They worked fine – unless you were down-wind. Dad let it be known to all if there was any writing on the outhouse walls or any kind of damage, the guilty party would have to answer to the county superintendent. That pretty much solved that problem but what he didn't fix and what provided us with our greatest thrill of the year was the hole in the foundation of the school itself.

The schoolhouse was built on top of a foundation of cinder blocks about two- and-a-half to three-feet high, leaving a small crawl space under the floor. At some point in time, no one knows just when or how, perhaps one of the cinder blocks just simply began to crumble and a small hole developed. Holes can be curious things to small boys and cry out to be explored, so it is not surprising that mysteriously the hole gradually grew and grew.

There was a family by the name of Mickelson living up on top of the hill south of us with two small boys, Irving and Floyd. They were nice kids; I liked them both. Floyd was the youngest, probably seven or eight years old at the time, and I'll be damned if he didn't have the biggest wart you've ever seen growing right on the tip of his nose. Why his parents didn't do something about it I don't know, but they didn't.

By the spring of my 7th grade year both the wart and the hole had grown, the hole to the point that it was large enough to admit a large skunk or a small boy! The boy and the skunk met in the dark crawl space during a cool spring morning's recess, much to the surprise of both. Skunks, more than little boys, don't like surprises but that is not to say that Floyd did not make a hasty retreat. Hasty enough that all caution was thrown to the wind, which I might add was already carrying the unmistakable odor of a surprised skunk. In his rush to exit the foundation's hole, Floyd scraped his nose hard enough to knock the wart completely off.

It bled pretty damned good. The blood ran down over his lips and what wasn't spattered out in front of him or sucked down his windpipe by his coughing sobs, steadily dripped off his chin onto his shirt forming an expanding red blotch on his chest. We were convinced he was mortally wounded. Everyone came running to see what was happening but nobody wanted to get close enough to help because he stunk so bad. The wart, however, was gone for good but the best part was school was dismissed to air out the building and we were gone for the day. I don't care what anyone says, this was high drama, a person can't get that kind of genuine entertainment on television.

Miss Stewart went on and finished fifty years of teaching 5th grade in the Manilla school system. She was there when my two older sons, Dean and Dale, attended the Manilla school. She was a real no-nonsense teacher, one we all remembered and respected but I am willing to bet that day of the skunk was her highlight.

Mary Fuller was the teacher in the 1923-4 school year at Greeley School No. 2 and in February she gave Cousin Mildred, Lilly Olsen and me our 8th grade county exams. All three of us passed.

In those days, after graduating from 8th Grade you could go to any high school in the state and the state would pay your tuition. So, in the fall of 1924, on the first day of school, I took my 8th grade diploma and Certificate of Admission to High School to Superintendent Fearing at the new school in Manilla. Mr. Fearing registered me and this green little country boy started high school and the world opened up to a whole new way of life.

The first friend I made was Gilbert Bohlander. Gilbert lived 1/2 mile north of the Manilla School and even though we were both brand-new freshmen, he had gone to elementary school there and had at least been in the building before. That put him one-up on me. We met in the cloakroom; I didn't know which way to go or anything. He led me into the Assembly Room; I sat down across from him and for four years he was only one seat away. It was great to make a friend so quickly that first day.

I made other friends, Andy Carothers and Louis Vinnick to name just a couple. Thirty-four of us started in the freshman class that day but only fourteen graduated, nine boys and five girls. A few of my classmates dropped out because they just couldn't get the studies, some because they couldn't get along with the teachers. Others went home to help on the farm for economic reasons and some dropped out to get married. Some of these kids we lost touch with. Most of them we lived and farmed alongside after we graduated, but all through high school, Gilbert was one of my closest and most trusted friends. Our class motto was especially true for Gilbert and me, "Together we stick, divided we're stuck".

Gilbert and his family moved to Minnesota soon after graduation. I didn't see him again until our 50th Class Reunion but we took up

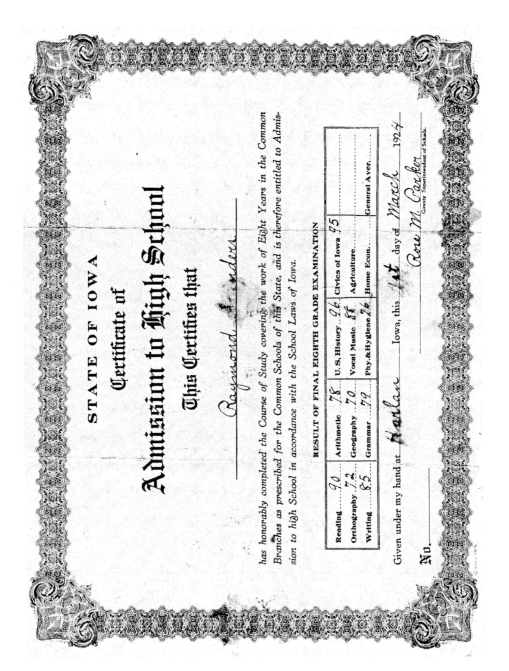

STATE OF IOWA

Certificate of

Admission to High School

This Certifies that

Raymond Saunders

has honorably completed the Course of Study covering the work of Eight Years in the Common Branches as prescribed for the Common Schools of this State, and is therefore entitled to Admission to high School in accordance with the School Laws of Iowa.

RESULT OF FINAL EIGHTH GRADE EXAMINATION

Reading	90	Arithmetic	78	U.S. History	96	Civics of Iowa	95
Orthography	72	Geography	70	Vocal Music	88	Agriculture	
Writing	85	Grammar	79	Phy.&Hygiene	76	Home Econ.	
						General Aver.	

Given under my hand at Harlan Iowa, this 1st day of March 1924

Rora M. Parker

County Superintendent of Schools.

No.

right where we left off. I don't know why Gilbert and I were best friends; we just were, and that is the best kind.

It was quite an experience for a country boy who, up to this point, had only known one teacher in a one-room school house with only ten students. Everything was so new. I had never even been to the new school building. The new school was built in Manilla after joining together two country school districts. They were proud of the new school but it had gotten pretty rough there. Three of the school board members were pretty perturbed and had wanted to do something about it. Dr. Loomis was still President of the School Board and he had heard of a Superintendent of Schools in Onawa, Iowa by the name of Fearing who had done a good job cleaning up that school.

As hard as he tried, Dr. Loomis could not convince the Onawa Superintendent to come to Manilla. However, he did learn that Mr. Fearing had a brother who was just graduating from Grinnell College.

H. W. Fearing was hired right out of college as basketball coach and Superintendent of the Manilla School. He was given a one year contract for $2,800 with the promise that if he cleaned up the school he would get a three year contract and a raise. Professor Howard W. Fearing was a tall, square-jawed man, probably close to 6 feet 4 inches tall and not an ounce of fat on him. He had been a boxer in college.

That first day we got acquainted with Prof. Fearing and his wife, Amy, who was the high school Principal. They let us know that they were the teachers and things would be done their way. He was not a mean man but he made it perfectly clear he was the boss.

Finally established in my new school, my first classes included History, English and Manual Training. These, I thought, would be a snap, but I also had Algebra, which I knew nothing about. I remember well how worried I was that first afternoon going home after school with ten algebra problems I was to solve for the next day of class.

Mother again came to my rescue. "You call Alice Christensen and ask her if she will help you a bit." Alice was a pretty blonde neighbor girl, three-to-four years older than I, who had finished high school that spring. She had been a schoolmate of mine at our Greeley No.2 one-room country school house.

Alice said, "Sure" and I rode over to her house on horseback. With Alice's help, I soon learned how to transpose the numbers and find the value of "x." There were ten problems in that homework assignment, and before I went to bed that night I had them solved and checked. My first day of school was finally over. This kind of hard work and determination was taught to me by my mother and father's examples.

Another kind of example awaited me on my second day of high school. I rode my horse the 3 1/2 miles to school that morning, stabled her and walked across the street to school. I entered through the big double-door southern entrance. In the hallway, just inside the front door, I saw a big football player, Ralph Dyson. Dyson was in the process of saying something to Prof. Fearing. I don't know what he was saying; I wasn't paying much attention but the next thing I knew there was one loud crack and Ralph was laying out cold on the floor.

The 1925 yearbook called The Nishni was dedicated to "Prof. H.W. Fearing who has in every way proved himself a friend and helper to students and teacher alike and who has made possible the 1925 "Nishni" we respectfully dedicate this book."

I honestly thought he was dead.

I had never seen anybody hit like that before. We never fought, at least not like that, in our country school. Finally, Ralph got up on his hands and knees with his head hanging down and his mouth open, a small expanding pool of red tinged spittle forming slowly on the floor below. Fearing paid no further attention to him. Instead, he just continued quietly about his business. Not too many days later, he nailed Burton Holmes in physical education class.

When that class graduated, it was an entirely different kind of school. Professor Fearing got his raise and a new contract. He stayed on for eleven years before he headed for a big-city school in West Des Moines, Iowa. When he came to Manilla High School in the fall of 1925, he struck fear in the hearts of some. When he left in 1936, he left tears in the eyes of all.

Some may call it frontier justice, some barbaric. Others may call it a terribly antiquated and unenlightened educational system. In today's schools people would react in horror and call their lawyers if something like this happened. It would be all over the ten o'clock news. However, before we go passing judgment, we must remember it was a different time and a different world. It is as wrong to judge yesterday with today's standards as it would be to treat today's ills with yesterday's medicine. Furthermore, let me make one thing perfectly clear and remind you that it was this generation, Ralph Dyson and Burton Homes' generation, that also nailed Hitler.

Sometimes, hell, all the time, I worry about the values, morals and fortitude our society and educational system are handing down to our new generations. True, the world is changing. Unfortunately, it has been impossible for Father Time to change the face of the world equally. Some of the world is also staying the same or worse. In some areas of the world civilization is sliding backward and when people reach the point they feel they have nothing to lose, everyone's way of life is challenged. This inevitably will cause conflict in the world of my grandchildren and beyond. I am concerned we are creating a generation of complacency with no fortitude, determination or foresight to stand up for our core beliefs when challenged. I fear for the future of our way of life. I have no solutions; only concerns, but I do believe that education and discipline are a big part of the answer.

Now, back to my second day of high school. I was a greener than hell country kid and I had just learned a big lesson in my first two minutes inside the school house. But Algebra class was waiting for me up in Mr. Schaffer's third floor classroom. I climbed the stairs slowly, bewildered by what I had just seen. With each step my nervous confidence shrunk and the churning swarm of butterflies in my stomach grew larger and larger.

I need not have worried. Alice had shown me how to be sure of my answers and I was the only one of the whole class who had them all right. Gilbert had made one error on his paper and didn't have it quite finished.

Mr. Edwin Schaffer was the football coach and Algebra teacher. To this day I don't know if he believed me or not but he certainly wondered why this country kid got the assignment done perfectly when all the others didn't. He asked me to go to the blackboard and explain to the class how I had arrived at the only perfect paper.

I was given two new equations to solve and explain to the whole class. I knew my lesson. Alice Christensen had done a good job tutoring, and it was a snap. I gained the respect of Mr. Schaffer that day, but I'm afraid I didn't win any new friends in the classroom.

Much to my surprise, Manual Training (woodworking) taught by Mr. Fearing, was my hardest class. By God, it was a son of a buck and I just plain flunked the first six weeks. By the end of the semester I was passing, but it was only on the condition, again my Mother's advice, that I stay after school and ask for some help. It paid off. Mr. Fearing realized I wanted to learn and by the end of the year, my draftsmanship and woodwork was better than the class average.

I learned that schoolwork and education were necessary in life. These early lessons helped me so much through high school that I want to pass them on to my children, grandchildren, great grandchildren and all those who will follow after I am gone. My Mother's blood runs through your veins; learn her lessons well. Ask for advice and get help, then get to work and don't give up until you have done your very best.

Mother saw to it that we were there to learn, not to play. There was no football team, no basketball team, no sports in general for me. They didn't seem as important as getting home after school to help keep the family farm up and running. In my last years there was a little track, however, the lessons came first – and last.

There was a second reason that limited my athletic experiences. During my first-year in high school I was involved in a motorcycle accident. My cousin Buzz had both a Harley-Davidson and what was then the more popular Indian motorcycle. He took me for a ride on the back of one of them down to Defiance. On the way home, while turning the Kenkel corner, three miles west of our farm, a bolt came out of the seat. It threw us violently onto the road and I came up with a broken right arm. I remember riding my horse into town to see the doctor for treatments. The arm healed slowly and from that date forward I was unable to fully extend my right elbow.

Years later we took our infant son Craig to an orthopedist that put him in braces for being bow legged and pigeon toed. The doctor examined my arm also and advised me to have an operation to move the nerve. He told me, "Ray, if you don't, by the time you are 60 you will have lost the function of your hand." We didn't have money to do anything at the time so I just lived with it. Slowly over the years the muscles did weaken, the doctor was right, but it never really slowed me down.

I did go out for Declamatory. I brought home a note about Declamatory but didn't even know what it was. Miss Gregorson, from Defiance, was the school teacher at the country school that Margaret and Wilma were still attending and we had to have her explain to us that it was "public speaking." She persuaded Mother and me that it would be good for me.

Mrs. Fearing was the coach and it was quite a popular extracurricular activity. You were given a choice between humorous, dramatic or oratorical readings. I chose humorous readings because I thought that would be the easiest. After completing the class Mrs. Fearing held tryouts for competition. The home competition was limited to only four presentations per category, and this would be used to determine who would qualify for the county and then possibly the state competition.

Mother was not very pleased with cousin Buzz and his motorcycles when I broke my arm.

Mrs. Fearing invited a Judge from Morningside College in Sioux City, Iowa to spend the day listening and rating the presentations. I gave my class presentation to qualify for the home competition. When I got home after school that day, Mother told me to call Mrs. Fearing. God, I didn't know what was going on but when I finally got up the nerve to call her, she told me I had the highest score and to begin preparation for the home competition.

When the evening for the home competition arrived, Alice Christensen came over and went into town with Mom, Dad and myself. The contest started and when my turn came I strode confidently out on the stage, took one look at the audience and went completely blank. Not just blank; stone cold completely blank. I couldn't say a word. I looked down at Mrs. Fearing and briefly noticed a disgusted look on her face before she diverted her eyes to the floor and away from my 'deer in the headlights' stare.

After what seemed like forever, it came to me. It was something about a kid at the circus and a Miss Morgan. I can't remember anything more except that I only got third place out of four contestants. The fourth one must have been pretty bad.

The next year we had a new teacher. He and I didn't hit it off. Mrs. Fearing returned as coach for my 3rd and 4th years. As a junior I switched to optional speeches and extemporaneous talks and won the home competition. I won the county my senior year. The competition was held in the Ritz Theater now called the Donna Reed Theater in Denison. I competed against Clement Burns of Vail who later became a Doctor of Medicine in Dunlap, Iowa and a boy by the name of Wilhoit of Westside. Both boys were from prominent families in their communities.

The highlight of my trip to the state district competition was a flat tire on Mrs. Fearing's Graham-Paige automobile. The Graham-Paige was a classy automobile, so much so that Prof. and Mrs. Fearing were criticized by the town's people for having spent too much money on a car. I remember Mrs. Fearing telling my mother that other people had the luxury of owning their own homes but as new teachers, their future was not secure enough in the community to allow themselves that luxury so they chose the automobile.

Fancy car or not, it was not immune to the hazards of those early Iowa roads and on our way to the district competition in Missouri Valley, Iowa we got a flat tire. I tried to help change the tire but for the life of me, we were not able to get the tire lugs off. What I didn't know at the time was those early autos had wheel lug nuts that turned one way on one side of the car and the opposite way on the other side. We were dealing with left-handed lugs but how was I to know? We didn't have a car at home. Somehow, however, we did get it changed with ample time after our arrival in Mo Valley to prepare for the competition. This time there was no stage fright.

My speech was entitled "War and Public Opinion." I still remember the last paragraph on the bottom of the first page:

"One glad[43] morning in May, news flashed around the world that Admiral Togo had sunk 17 Russian ships. And now, if you will look into that deep blue sea, you will not alone find those 8,000 corpses, but interworked into every rope, bolt and bar, life, aimless squashed life.

O patriotism, what crimes have been committed in thy name."

The next page was a comparison of peace, I can't remember it fully but it was something like:

"Peace shows a picture of green fields and golden harvests, of populated cities, schools and beautiful churches. . .

It was good enough for second place at the state district competition.

We also had a fine Boy's Glee Club, winning third place at State in Iowa City, with only two second tenors, Albert Carstens and myself.

During my last two years of high school, Vocational Agriculture became available. This was a brand new course that came about by the passage of a bill in the United States Senate called the Smith-Hughes Act of 1917. Smith was a United States Senator from Georgia and Hughes was a Georgian Congressman, both Democrats, together with a professional educator by the name of Charles Prosser and a Republican Senator from Vermont by the name of Carroll Page. They fashioned what is generally agreed upon as the single most significant piece of agricultural education legislation ever written. The Bill provided federal funds for the education of individuals "who have entered upon or are preparing to enter upon the work of the farm." It was officially known as the Smith-Hughes Vocational Agriculture Course but we knew it as

---

[43] The paragraph is referring to the Japanese Russian war and 'one glad morning' refers to a nice day from a weather standpoint, not an opinion of the description of events.

HOME DECLAMATORY CONTEST AT SCHOOL AUDITORIUM FRIDAY

Programs to be Held During Both the Afternoon and Evening

1938

Students of Manilla high will compete in the home declamatory contest on Friday, February 10. There are 11 contestants in the dramatic class 2 in the oratorical and 9 in the humorous. Owing to the large number of contestants part of the contest will be held during the afternoon The program will be as follows:

DRAMATIC—3:15 P. M.
"His Mother"..............Della Armstrong
"An Even Break"...Florence Behrend
"Mother"..........................Lucia Jordan
"The Stepmother".........Selma Lapel
"Death of Jim"..............Leta McMahon
"The Falling of a Leaf"...Selma Miller
"Full Measure of Devotion"..............
..............................Mildred Saunders
"Gun Shy".....................LeRoy Sheffield
"Circumstantial Evidence"..............
..............................Viola Steckelberg
"Cigarette's Ride".....Cornelia Warrell
"Death of Benedict Arnold"..............
..............................Wm. Carney

ORATORICAL—8:00 P. M.
"Why Lindbergh is World's Greatest Hero"...............Buster Saunders
"War and Public Opinion"..............
..............................Raymond Saunders
Music—"Pale in the Amber West"
..............................Boy's Quartette

HUMOROUS
"Sis Hopkins and Her Funny Family"....................Alice Barrow
"Mama Takes Papa on a Picnic"
..............................Beulah Berkemeir
"The Back Seat Driver"....Onalee Grief
"Detour"..................LaVerne Hamann
"His Housekeeping".........Ray Hayes
"Adora's Young Man"..............
..............................Glennie Lohrman
"A Football Fan"...........Alice Loomis
"Jimsella"...................Lucille Miller
"Lena Chooses a Hat"..............
..............................Miriam Vennink

Manilla will be represented in the Extemporaneous class this year by Gilbert Bohlander. The subjects for discussion this year are: Iowa Road Bond Issue; Present Status of Aviation; Farm Relief; Price War in Auto World; Our Big Navy Program; and The Smith-Vare Affair.

COUNTY CONTEST WILL BE HELD IN NEW GYMNASIUM

Declamatory Contest Winners Will Try Again Thursday in This City

The winners of the series of declamatory contests that have been held in the various cities of the county will meet in Denison, Thursday February 23d, and contest for county honors. The program will start at 7:45 and three judges from outside of the county will decide the winners. There will be first and second places in all classes. The declaimers are divided in four classes, namely, oratorical, dramatic, humorous and extemporaneous.

Music will be furnished by the Denison schools.

The program follows:
ORATORICAL
The Constitution ....Paul Cedergren
Kiron
War and Public Opinion—Raymond Saunders
Manilla
The Strike Must Go — Edna Steffen
Charter Oak
DRAMATIC
When the Moon Rose—Elizabeth Malone
Charter Oak
Love Story of Old Madred—Lavinia North
Vail
The Death Disk Eleanor Sandstrom
Kiron
HUMOROUS
Tommy Stearns Scrubbs Up—Hazel Riggleman
Deloit
Jim Cranks the Ford ...Sevilla Slechta
Vail
Billy Brad's Lie ....Roberta Weed
Charter Oak
EXTEMPORANEOUS
Speakers—Louie Evers Gilbert Bohlander, Raymond Malloy, Cyrus Martin, William Slechta.

Subjects:—The Iowa Road Bond Issue. The Present Status of Aviation. Our big Navy Program. Farm Relief. Price War in Automobile World. Smith-Vare Case.

-----THE CIRCUS-----

From "The Court of Boyville"

Hidden by the foliage in the thick of a tree in a three pronged seat, Bud Perkins reclined. His features were drawn into a painful grimace, as his right hand passed to and fro before his mouth rhythmically twanging the tongue of a Jew's harp, upon which he was playing, "To My Sweet Sunny South, Take Me Home." His eyes were fixed on the big white clouds in the blue sky. His heart was filled with the poetty of lonesomeness, that sometimes comes to boys--in pensive moods.

Into the calm rushed Mealy Jones, hat in hand, breathless, bringing war's alarms.

"Fellers! Fellers! It's a comin' here. It's a-goin' to be in two weeks. The man's puttin' up the boards now and you can get a job passin' bills.

An instant later the tree was deserted. Bud Perkins, who was burning with a desire to please Miss Morgan, his foster mother, went to church that Sunday night before the Circus. Any one could see that he was provoking Providence in an unusual and cruel manner. He did not sit with Miss Morgan, but took a back seat. Three boys from the North End came in on the same bench, then Jimmie Sears shuffled in past the North Enders and sat beside Bud, after which the inevitable happened. It kept happening. They passed it on and passed it back again. First a pinch, then a chug, then a cuff, then a kick under the bench. Satan put a pin into Bud's hand and slowly, almost imperceptably Satan moved the boy's arm along back of Jimmie Sears. Then an imp pushed Bud's hand as he jagged it into the back of the North Enders. The boy from the North End gave a howl of pain. But was not quick enough. Brother Parker saw the pin. Two hundred devout Methodist saw his slap his fingers on Bud's ear, lead him down the full length of the church and set him down beside Miss Morgan. It was a sickening moment for Bud.

At eight o'clock the next morning, the town of Willow Creek was in the thralls of the circus. Every where was hubbub. Everywhere the dusty, heated air of the circus. Everywhere save at the home of Miss Morgan.

Here Miss Morgan putters around her morn.'s work vainly trying to croon a gospel hymn. And here Bud Perkins prone on the sitting-room sofa makes paralielograms, diamonds and squares with dots and lines in the ceiling paper. To emphasize his desolation, he left the house and sat by a tree in the yard with his back to the kitchen door and window.

The boys gathered round him. "Why don' yer ast her?"

"I've done astin' her."

"Let's all ast her."

"'Spose she'll let you, Bud?"

"I dunno."

So they all came tramping to Miss Morgan's kitchen window.

"Miss Morgan."

"Well, Wilfred."

"Miss Morgan, can Bud go to the circus with us, Miss Morgan?"

"I'm afraid not to-day."

"Why not, Miss Morgan?"

"Henry misbehaved in church last night and we've agreed that he shall stay home from the circus to-day."

"Oh, don't you believe he's agreed. He's just dying to go."

"They've got six elephants and one of them's a trick elephant, and you'd just die a laughin' to see him."

But Miss Morgan was left high and dry on the island of her determination.

When the boys left the yard it seemed to Miss Morgan that she could not look up from her work without seeing the lonesome figure of Bud.

In the afternoon, the patter of feet by her house grew slower, then stopped. Occasionally a belated wayfarer sped past, and the music

A portion of my first Declamatory Home Competition found in an old picture album during the preparation of this manuscript. Bud did get to go to the circus and while there won a dollar for riding a trick mule, he gave the dollar to Miss Morgan to put in her 'missionary box', leaving Miss Morgan to think he was an angel.

Voc Ag and our junior class at Manilla was one of the first in the State of Iowa.

Prof. Fearing took a summer class at Iowa State and was our Vocational Agriculture instructor. Some of us thought it would be an easy subject, but Fearing again saw to it that we had more than enough to keep us busy and out of trouble.

Our first year of study in Voc Ag was field crops. My project that year was to keep records on a ten acre plot of corn. Because of that project, well at least partially because of my corn project, I met and had dinner in our new house with the future Secretary of Agriculture and Vice President of the United States, Henry A. Wallace.

Henry's father ran a farm newspaper called The Wallace's Farmer out of Des Moines, Iowa. They were friends of my Grandfather C.A. and when they came out to the farm to plan some newspaper advertising for the cattle herd, they stayed for dinner.

Grandpa was fond of my mother's cooking. After all she had started out as his cook and housekeeper, so he brought the Wallace's up to show them the new Cumberland Stock Farm No. 2 and Mom's cooking.

I remember following along with the entourage as they toured the barn yards. Henry was a tall, thin young man with straight dark hair, about 30ish at the time. He was involved in producing hybrid seed corn. He had in fact just formed a company called the Hi-Bred Corn Company, in 1935 he added the name Pioneer and the Pioneer Seed Corn Company was born.

The topic of my corn plot came up and before dinner was over, plans were made for Henry Wallace to give me 1/2 bushel of hybrid seed corn for my project. Well, he didn't actually give it to me; he charged me $12 and that was a lot of money at the time. You could buy a shirt for 98 cents and a pair of overalls for $1.25.

We took that half bushel and planted it in a square in the middle of the ten acre plot. Half a bushel would only plant about 2 1/2 acres so we filled in the rest with the regular open pollinated corn that we grew ourselves. No one knew we had the hybrid corn.

The hybrid corn did well, but I only got fifth place with my project. There was no prize for fifth place, and it was several years before we could afford to buy hybrid seed corn for the farm, but I had learned a lot and had laid the foundation of how to seek out advice and evaluate it for our own well being.

At the end of the school year, there was a Vocational Agriculture Field Day held at Iowa State University in Ames. It was sort of like the county, district and state competition in Declamatory or Music. This was a time that students from around the state gathered and participated in judging contests, viewed exhibits etc, and in general had a good time while competing and being exposed to college and life outside our own little farm communities.

Voc Ag was a two-year course. The first year was field crops and the second was animal husbandry. The first year, my junior year, I came down with a bad case of the mumps and couldn't make the trip to Ames. The second year I was healthy and was able to compete in either the crop or livestock competition. Prof. Fearing put me in the crop judging. He thought judging the livestock would be too easy for me and that I might learn something new in the crop competition. One part of the competition was to identify crops. There were ten stations. We would sit down at each station for about thirty seconds and were given samples of the plants and their seeds.

One particular sample was put in the competition just to see how good we really were and prove to us high school seniors that we didn't know everything. It was a few blades of grass that looked just like Kentucky Blue Grass yet the sample that topped out with the seeds had a distinct reddish hue. Somewhere in the back of my mind I remembered hearing my father talk about Red Top Grass. I had never seen it, but on the other hand, I had never seen anything like this sample either. As I hurried to the next station, I scribbled 'red top' on my answer sheet, more as a descriptive reminder of the sample, with the idea that I would change it if somehow I could get the real answer to pop into my head. Well, nothing popped and I turned in my answer sheet "as is."

At the end of the competition, Mr. Darling, the Voc Ag teacher from Denison came up to our Manilla class and asked who Ray Saunders was. He said he wanted to meet me. After identifying myself, he shook my hand with his left hand and placed his right hand on my shoulder. "Son," he said, "you are the only boy in the state to correctly identify all ten crops. I want to shake your hand."

On one of the class trips Prof. Fearing took us on, and I can't honestly remember if it was to Ames, Des Moines or some place else, he introduced us to his best friend from college. Frank Cooper was a tall, handsome, likeable young man in tweed slacks and a white shirt. Frank had grown up on a ranch in Montana but his parents were from England and his mother was concerned about the rough western influences so she sent him back to England for high school. Somehow or another he ended up in Grinnell College and again I don't remember if he and Prof. Fearing were old college roommates or just best friends.

We listened while Prof. and Frank told stories of their college days. Evidently Frank had fancied himself somewhat of an artist and cartoonist while at Grinnell and did a lot of work on the school paper. His parents had now moved to Los Angles and while he had hoped to work on a newspaper there, he was finding it hard to get any work. He and Prof. laughed about the fact that Frank had hooked up with a couple of his Montana friends in L. A. The joke was that in Montana you could make a few bucks by staying on a horse in the rodeo, while in L. A. a cowboy could get paid for falling off horses in the movies.

It seems that Frank was now having a fair amount of success doing this. Enough so that his agent was concerned that there were two other Frank Coopers working in the movies. She was urging him to change his name and suggested he take the name of her home town Gary, Indiana. As Paul Harvey says, "Now you know the rest of the story." Gary Cooper went on to be Hollywood's leading man for the next 35 years.

Wilma and Margaret followed me into high school. My sisters rode bareback together on a gentle old gray horse called Old Ned that Dad had bought in Omaha. My horse was a smaller mare. She was bought from George Macumber, our postman for 41 years. He had ridden her on the mail route when the roads were too bad to drive his buggy but she was just a little too feisty. She fought the bit in her mouth until Ad Morgan suggested a leather bit and that made all the difference in the world.

We kept the horses in Grandma (no relation) Fuller's Barn directly across from the school. We were about the only kids who rode horseback for the full four years of high school. There were some cars, but no school buses. Busses didn't come until all the country schools were closed, in about 1949.

As my high school career came to an end I had the honor of playing the male lead in the Senior Class Play "A Strenuous Life." This was the same play that Mr. Fearing did when he was in high school; in fact, my part was the same part he played.

This wasn't a coincidence that we did the same play as Prof. Fearing; it was a matter of practicality. It might not have been legal but to save some money, we used his old playbook and made fourteen copies. The number of characters in the play was the exact same number we had in our senior class. Beulah Berkemeier played the female lead opposite me. She wasn't very cooperative as I remember but, hell, I was as stupid as can be, too; we all were. Mildred Saunders played opposite Charlie Barrow. Andy Carothers played a stooped over Chinese waiter and had only one word – "Yiss." Whenever anyone talked to him he always responded with "Yiss." Mrs. Fearing was our drama coach, and believe me, Professor and his wife were hard to please.

I'm not sure I did a very good job, but "A Strenuous Life" unwittingly did its part in preparing us for life after graduation. The time that I was in high school was called the Roaring 20's and for a time we were flying high. In the spring of 1927, during my junior year in high school, Charles Lindberg flew his Spirit of St. Louis non-stop flight across the Atlantic Ocean. He left Long Island an unknown mailman and landed in Paris as "Lucky Lindy," winning a $25,000 prize for being the first to fly nonstop across the Atlantic Ocean and in doing so became the most famous man in America.

It is a little known fact that honor was expected to go to a boy from Denison. Clarence Chamberlain was born in Denison and was the man with the most backing and the man people thought would be the first to make the flight. Chamberlain, along with Admiral Richard Byrd, was waiting for the weather to clear as they watched Lindberg take off into the overcast clouds. Chamberlain made his flight two weeks later and flew from Long Island to just outside

Berlin, Germany. He took the owner of his airplane with him, a man by the name of Levine.

Chamberlain became the second man to fly across the Atlantic while Levine became the first passenger to cross the Atlantic in an airplane. For years there was a Chamberlain Airfield in Denison, south of the Lincoln Highway on the flat land just on the other side of the Boyer River between it and the cemetery, west of the present day golf-course. It is gone now as are most memories of Clarence Chamberlin – timing may not be everything but it is a lot.

In the fall of my senior year, still in 1927, Babe Ruth hit his 60th home run, a record that held for 35 years. In 1928, with little fanfare, Mickey Mouse was born. As I said, we were flying high and roaring through the 20's. None of us could have predicted a year later that rich powerful men would be jumping out of New York skyscrapers as the stock market crashed. At least we had already learned we had to work hard for success.

Today, I thank God for my Mother and Dad, Miss Stewart, Superintendent H. F. Fearing and Mrs. Fearing our Principal. Also of special note was A.R. Edgar who taught math and music and later established the music program at Iowa State University in Ames, Iowa; Coach R.V. Ross and Miss Trowbridge who later became county superintendent in Warren County south of Des Moines. We had some of the finest teachers ever to teach. All were great teachers of Manilla High School during the 20's and early 30's. They were "no-nonsense" teachers.

This was something Trudy and I have tried to instill in our family – lots of love, fun and respect and no stupid doings.

> # *"Together we stick, divided we're stuck."*
> ### *Class Motto*
> ### *Class of 1928*

High school graduation 1928

The Class of 1928 as Freshmen in 1924. I am the good looking kid in knickers at the far left side of the Freshman Class Picture. Back row – Beulah Drake, Evelyn Drake, Andrew Carothers, Mildred Saunders, Garth Fuller. Middle row – Raymond Saunders, Beulah Berkemeier, Estel Golden, Charles Barrow, Waldo Frace, Cassus Crakes, Leyden Swenning, Hazel Theobald, Katherine Clinton, Melroy Carstens, Louis Brockelsby, May Fish, Russel Marr, Mr. Popejoy (there seems to be some confusion in the rows but this is as printed in the yearbook) Bottom row – Mary Knott, Frances Knott, Lily Olson, Victor Weigand, Virginia Long, Gilbert Bohlander, Gladys Randall, Louis Vennick, Leonard Collier.

Class of 1928 Senior picture. Louis Vennick and Andrew Carothers are in the upper left and right corner respectively. For what ever reason, they were both 21 years old and were ineligible for football their senior year. Gilbert Bolander is in the bottom left hand corner. My cousin Mildred Saunders and I make up the third row of our senior class picture.

In 1978 all surviving members of the class of 1928 attended church at the First Presbyterian Church in Manilla, the same site our Baccalaureate Service had been held 50 years previously. Classmates were: Back row – Evelyn Drake Holdsworth, Charles Barrow, Raymond Saunders, Melroy Carstens, Gilbert Bohlander. Front row – Waldo Frace, Kathryn Clinton Brosnahan, Mildred Saunders Blount, Louis Vennink. Mildred and I are now the only surviving members of The Class of 1928. Also attending was the daughter of Prof. and Mrs. H. W. Fearing, Mrs. Rae Gene Fearing Robbins. Prof. Fearing had passed on but Mrs. Fearing was living in a nursing home in Riverside, California. The entire class talked to Mrs. Fearing via telephone, thanking her for her efforts and wishing her well.

Chapter 7

THE [not so] GREAT WAR and DEPRESSION

January 30, 1989.

8:30 AM
We have just had a nice breakfast, and the sun is up. I am about to head out to the barn. I haven't done much at the dairy barn this winter.

Pat has taken over the bottle feeding of the young calves and is doing a better job than I have been able to do.

I help Doug by washing up the milkers and hosing out the parlor. It's good for the hands and gives me something to do.

For a farmer, it is sometimes difficult to tell when a depression starts and when it ends. Whether it is Mother Nature or our fellow man, it seems like there is a long list of forces exerting great powers over farmers, a list over which we farmers seemingly have little or no control. War is certainly high up on that list.

During the first few years of the 20th Century, the war in Europe was known as The Great War. It had been going on for years before the United States officially entered[44] and it exposed the double-edged sword of progress by using new weapons of mass destruction provided by the same industrial revolution that made life easier for the Iowa farmers. It was the most horrendous war ever; more than 6 million soldiers died as well as many civilians. We could not even begin to imagine that a larger war would ever be fought nor that our

---

[44] The United States did not enter the war until April 6, 1917 after the Germans restarted unrestricted submarine warfare and began sinking American ships. History books say the First World War started June 28, 1914 when Archduke Ferdinand, heir to the Austrian-Hungary throne was assassinated, but the stage was set way back in 1870-71 when the French were soundly defeated in the Franco-Prussian war allowing for the formation of modern day Germany. From that point on some historians say it was only a matter of time.

Great War would ultimately be put into perspective and become known only as the first of a series, World War One.

As the United States became involved in the Great War in Europe young men were leaving. Help for the farms was hard to find and things began to get tighter. My Father and Uncle Chuck registered for the draft. Grandfather's grandsons Glen and Earl Adams went off to War. They were Aunt Lou's boys; she was the oldest and had married early. They were my oldest cousins, about ten years older than me. I remember Glen Adams in uniform. Thank God, they all came back.

The day our boys left for war was an important day in the history of Manilla. A reporter by the name of James Weaver from the Des Moines Register was invited to document the events. His article was published in the Register April 24, 1917 and reprinted in the Manilla Times on the 26th. The front page of that edition is reproduced on the following page. The text of the article is as follows:

By James B Weaver,
Des Moines Daily Register
Tuesday, April 24, 1917.

I have today seen the great American melting pot in action, and this is how it came about:

They modestly phoned they were to have a patriotic rally at Manilla in Crawford County, and would I come out by the 5 a.m. train and join the people in bidding goodbye to the recruits who were to leave by the 9:30 train for the Denver training camp?

Of course I would, and did, and I count it a morning beautiful to hold in memory. But I balked at that 5 a.m. arrival and went Sunday evening, arriving at Manilla, (population 1200) at 9:30 p.m. None knew of my coming, so I walked up through the park to a brilliantly lighted corner surrounded by automobiles, for Manilla is in the heart of a rich German farming district.

Rally in Germania Hall.

On that corner stood a great two story double front frame building that was at the moment ablaze with light at every window. I glanced at the broad front of the building and saw there in large letters, "Germania Hall, 1900." As I looked there came from the building a great chorus and they were singing, as only those to whom music is a racian instinct can sing – "The Star Spangled Banner!"

It was the finale to an evening's program, and as the strains of the band and chorus died away and the meeting dispersed, I sought the hotel, murmuring to myself, "Well, God Bless Germania Hall!"

But let me tell you about that meeting. It was a union church gathering. The business men met Friday to get ready to bid the boys goodbye. They appointed a chairman, a secretary and a treasurer in good business like fashion. They called the meeting for Sunday night at Germania hall. The Rev. George H. Mitchell, Presbyterian, presided. The speakers were Rev. Father Francis McNeil of the Roman Catholic, the Rev. A.R. Miller of the Methodist, and the Rev. H. Wendt of the German Lutherans.

Never to Be Forgotten.

There was the band of twenty pieces, five of whom were enlisting. There was a congregational singing of "America" and "The Star Spangled Banner," and five old soldiers[45] sat on the platform with the enlisting youths. The evening was one never to be forgotten by Manilla.

I went to my hotel but at 5 a.m. was fairly blown out of bed by giant dynamite blasts, one for each of the forty eight states and not a soul in Manilla slept after the first shot.

I dressed and went out upon the main street at just 5:30 a.m. and even then they were busy getting the hall ready for the morning's exercises. I walked about with Mayor Saunders and was introduced to the business men. We then gathered at the hall, where a splendid breakfast was served to the recruits and the members of their families. It was a breakfast never to be forgotten, the tables were surrounded by the ruddy faced youths, 17, 18, and 19 years old, their fathers and mothers, their sisters, big and little, the members of the committee and myself.

The boys ate ravenously as boys must, but the mothers and the little sisters were thinking of the separation but an hour away. The boy soldiers seemed very young but I remembered that the boys of 1861 were no older.

Personnel of Recruits.

But let me give you the names of these patriotic young Americans who have answered the nation's call. Note the racial suggestion in these names:

Robert and Allen Hird twins, sons of Isaac Hird, contractor.

Gifford and Victor Theobald, sons of Edward Theobald of the Manilla National Bank.

Max and Frank Berkemier, sons of M.H. Berkemier,

---

[45] "old soldiers" refers to Civil War veterans.

implement dealer.

George Gaumer, son of W.N. Gaumer.

Lynn McCracken, son of James McCracken, stock-man.

Joseph Cooper, son of Harry Cooper, mail carrier.

Leo Perion, son of James Perion, Manager Green Bay Lumber Company.

Allen Saunders, son of Mrs. Ruth Saunders, farmer.

Leslie Currier, grandson of V. Sowles, old soldier.

Ed Algee, son of W.E. Algee and two others who left a few days before.

The hall was filled to overflowing by 8 a.m., the band playing patriotic airs, the whole place alive with expectant humanity. We formed in line, the recruits in advance and with the chairman, the mayor and the few old soldiers, we marched to the platform amid deafening applause. There were the prayers for the boys to soon to go, and for those who are to do the waiting in the anxious months just ahead.

Mixture of Races.

The audience arose and sang "America" and I shall not soon forget that mixture of races that faced me as I arose to speak.

The serious faces, the sense of union of races from all over the world gathered to offer their sons upon the altar of the nation's need, the presence of the old soldiers, the waving flags, combined to remind me of the days of '61 of which mother has told me, days remote and half unreal, but here and now this April morning in this Iowa town became very real indeed.

Three of the boys were given their diplomas – graduated before time, by virtue of a short cut to immortal service.

March To The Train.

The speaking ended; we all sang the Star Spangled Banner, formed in line and marched to the train. There were the inevitable sad partings, the great surging crowd as the train moved away, the boys leaning far out of the windows for one last goodbye wave of the hand-- and they were gone. But with them went, as far as Omaha, a score of citizens, and better still, with them went the tears and prayers of all those Germans, Scotchmen, Irishmen, and Scandinavians – all now for once under the fusing force of freedom's call, Americans under one flag.

If we all did as well as Manilla, Iowa would be sending today 250,000 men to the colors. God bless Manilla, the melting pot, with its militant Americanism!

THE MANILLA TIMES

VOLUME XVII.   MANILLA, IOWA, THURSDAY, APRIL 26, 1917.   NO. 37.

REAL AMERICANISM FOUND AT ITS BEST AT MANILLA, IOWA

Melting Pot Has Done Its Perfect Work in German Community in Iowa.

BOYS OFF TO THE GREAT WAR

Whole Town Ablaze With Patriotism As Tearful Goodbys Are Said

TWO HISTORIC MEETINGS

Sunday Evening Service in Germania Hall Followed By Another Early Monday.

By JAMES B. WEAVER,

In The Des Moines Daily Register of Tuesday, April 24, 1917.

I have today seen the great American melting pot in action, and this is how it came about:

They suddenly phoned that they were to have a patriotic rally at Manilla, in Crawford county, and would I come out to the 5 a. m. train and join the people in bidding goodbye to the recruits who were to leave by that 9.20 train for the Denver training camp? Of course I would, and did, and I count it a surpassing privilege to hold in memory that I basked at that 5 a. m. arrival and went Sunday evening, arriving at Manilla. [population given] ... None know ... the Melting Pot has justifiably liquated community ... surrounded by automobiles, for Manilla is in the heart of a rich German farming district.

Our Soldier Boys and part of their escort, taken on steps of Army building at Omaha.

these patriotic young Americans who have answered the nation's call. Note the racial suggestion in these names.

Robert and Albel Hlbel twins, sons of Isaac Hlbel, contractor.

Clifford and Victor Theobald, sons of Edward Theobald of the Manilla National Bank.

Max and Frank Berkemier, sons of M. H. Berkemier, implement dealer.

George Gammer, son of W. N. Gammer.

Lynn McCracken, son of James McCracken, stockman.

Joseph Cooper, son of Harry Cooper, mail carrier.

Leo Perdus, son of James Perdus.

Three of the boys were given their diplomas—graduated before time, by virtue of a short cut to immortal service.

March To The Train.

Two speeches ended; we all sang the Star Spangled Banner, formed in line, and together to the train. There were the inevitable sad partings, the —

to go, and for those who are to do the waiting in the anxious months just ahead.

Mixture of Races.

The audience arose and sang "America," and I shall not soon forget that mixture of races that faced me as I arose to speak.

The serious faces, the sense of union of races from all over the world gathered to offer their sons upon the altar of the nation's need, the presence of the old soldiers, the waving flags, combined to remind me of the days of '61, of which mother has told me, and now this April morning in this Iowa town became very real indeed.

THE MARINES HYMN.

From the Halls of Montezuma
To the shores of Tripoli,
We fight our country's battles
On the land as on the sea.
First to fight for right and freedom
And to keep our honor clean;
We are proud to claim the title
Of United States Marine.

From the Star Halls of Oaxis
To die Ditch at Panama,
You will find them very ready
Of Marines—That's what we are;
Were the watch-dogs of a pile of coal
Or we dig a mosquito,
Though for battle's hard at every job
Who would not be a MARINE?

Our duty's unturned to every breeze
From dawn to setting sun
We have fought in every clime and place
Where we could take a gun,
In the snow of far-off northern land
And in sunny tropic scenes,
You will find us always on the job
The UNITED STATES MARINES.

YOUR LAD AND MY LAD.

Your lad and my lad
And how he lives today!
In your hand and my hand
And half a world away.
Your boy and my joy
His eyes forever gleam;
Your boy and my boy
Some little mother's dream;

Sky blue and true blue
His eyes still steam aright;
Oh God be his guardian,
His protector thru the night!

Your lad and my lad
And may he live to be,
As were his good granddaddies,
A son of liberty.
Your hope and my hope
And his harvest to be,
And hope there next to his God
His flag that waves on him.
Your heart and my heart
Must breaking at the sight
When "Old Glory" calls your lad
On duty for the Right.

Your price and my —

WILLIAM KRANTZ DROPS DEAD.

Wm. Krantz, who purchased the Jno Walker property in Walkertown and moved here with his family from Erling some ten weeks ago, expired suddenly at his home Monday morning. His death occurred about 6:15. He got up from a chair and started for the door when he dropped to the floor dead. He had not been ill previously.

The deceased was a man past 50 years of age. He leaves a wife and eight children. His son Joe and family rooke here and his daughter, Mrs. Joe Hertman, another married, sides at Jefferson, Iowa. The other children are at home.

Funeral services were held Tuesday morning at the Sacred Heart Catholic church here and the remains taken to Earling. Funeral services were held at Earling Wednesday morning. Interment followed in the Catholic cemetery at Earling at —

The family here —

All was not quite as idyllic as Mr. Weaver made it sound. There were some mixed loyalties in the area. After all, this area of the country was settled by people who, if not born there, were no more than one generation removed from the countries at war and there were German sympathizers in the area. I understand it got pretty hectic up north, around Holstein and Schleswig, Iowa. Hell, even though they had chosen to leave, they had named their new communities after their old.

In Manilla, Germania Hall became a target. Built in 1900 by the German Society, it was a big public meeting place at the bottom of Main Street and the center of the town social life. We had our class plays, social events, town meetings, etc. there. It was a big wooden building with a balcony encircling an open spacious first floor and stage. Before the war was over, there was a big fuss about the name Germania Hall. I remember it as a big problem for the town and they ended up voting to change the name to The Manilla Opera House.

This photo of Germania Hall was published in the centennial book Manilla Community Folks and Facts 1886-1986

Because we were a young country settled mostly by immigrants, most of my grandparents' and parents' generation spoke two languages. English, of course, was not necessarily the first language and that became a concern for some. In the Lutheran Church, the sermons had been traditionally given in German but in reaction to the war that practice ended forever. I also remember the time I was shopping with my Mother at Kerr's Dry Goods Store. We were in the shop when Grandma Schram (they had the meat market and grocery store) came in the store. She could only speak German

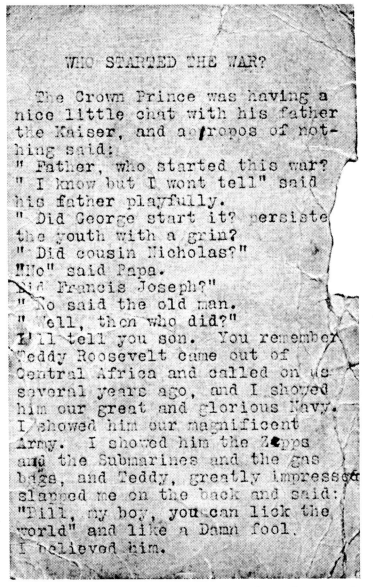

This hand typed 3x5 card was found in a photo album. Hand written on the back was "We don't believe this, do we?" (signed) Ethel.

and Mr. Kerr, who incidentally was also German, wouldn't wait on her unless she spoke English. Mother could speak German and with the aid of another clerk she helped Grandma Schram get her shopping done.

The war, I suppose, in many ways helped our young nation mature, but I laugh at some of the people today who are concerned about people in this county who don't speak English. It has always been that way. All we have to do is wait a generation, even without a war.

The German Army surrendered on the 11th hour. Armistice Day, 11 o'clock in the morning, November 11, 1918. I remember being in my country schoolhouse that morning and at 11 o'clock they let us outside and from town three miles away we could hear the church bells, train whistles and sirens.

The war was over and the people thought nothing could stop the economy. For three years or so the land prices had skyrocketed and prices for goods went wild. But people had overspent and money became a bit harder to get.

In defense of my Grandpa, I'll say he may have tried to help too many relatives and maybe a few too many friends and things just began to tighten up. The market for the Shorthorns and the horses was not as good as it used to be but Grandfather was successful and generous.

Grandfather had helped one nephew, Cyril, with law school. Cyril's dad was C.A.'s youngest brother, Fred. You will remember that Uncle Fred's wife Aunt Ruth and Grandma Bertha were sisters. Unfortunately, Fred passed away at age 46 of a heart attack leaving six children; Austin, Wallace, Cyril, Allen, George and Phyllis.

The June 8, 1911 issue of The Manilla Times carried the following article:

PIONEER CITIZEN GONE

F.J. Saunders, Influential Farmer, is Stricken with Apoplexy

Another of our pioneers is gone. Another name is stricken from the ever-lessening roll of our early settlers, and a solitary woman in the early sunset of life with six children in a lonely home, are left to attest how sadly they will miss him, for F.J. Saunders one of our wealthy and prominent farmers of this section has answered the call.

On Monday he was up town and on his way home he stopped at the home of Mr. and Mrs. John McCracken, the latter being his sister. On entering the house he entered into a conversation relative to his trip to California, which the family had planned with the hope that it would be beneficial to his health for he had been in poor health for about a year, and they expected to leave next Monday, but the unfortunate man, while talking, was suddenly stricken. The loved ones realized that the critical moment had come and he was taken immediately by auto to his home where he lingered until 10:00 o'clock, when he succumbed to the inevitable.

The deceased leaves a widow and six children, three brothers: Ed and Charles of Manilla, and Will of Chicago, and two sisters; Mrs. John McCracken, and Mrs. Robert James of Sioux City, with relatives and a host of friends. He was always industrious and by hard work had accumulated a competency for himself and family. He was one of the influential farmers of this section and was always found working for good, and in his death Manilla loses a most worthy citizen, and all mourn with the loved ones in their irreparable loss.

It must be so. These tender human ties cannot be severed without a pang. In his demise the writer feels a personal loss of a good friend, for he had visited our office almost daily and we visited with him, we knew his ambitions and his heart's desires; we also knew that he was a true friend; he believed in the brotherhood of man and though he might differ with you in opinion, he was charitable and broad enough to grant you that right, and still be your friend.

His life work is now done, and well done, and weary with life's duties and cares, weary of suffering and waiting, he lay down to rest.

"Tired, ah, yes; so tired dear,
I shall soundly sleep tonight,

With never a dream and never a fear,

To wake in the morning light"

He was a man who united sound sense with strong convictions, and a candid, outspoken temper, eminently fitted to mould the rude elements of pioneer society into form and consistency, and aid in raising a high standard of citizenship in our young and growing community, and how much this community owes him and such as he, it is impossible to estimate, though it would be a grateful task to trace his influence through some of the more direct channels, to hold him up in these degenerate days in his various characters of husband and father, of neighbor and friend, to speak of the sons and daughters he has reared, together with the good wife and mother to perpetuate his name and emulate his virtues. But it comes not within the scope of this brief article to do so. Suffice it to say, he lived nobly and died peacefully. The Stern Reaper found him "as a shock of corn, fully ripe for harvest." Not for him be our tears. Rather let us crown his grave with garlands; and let us hope that we will all live as well and that when the summons comes we can say as he did: "All is well."

Funeral services were held Wednesday at the M.E. Church, Rev. A. R. Grant, a former pastor and personal friend, being called from Griswold to officiate. Rev. G.F. Cannom, the present pastor, also spoke and paid a beautiful tribute to the memory of the deceased.

The casket was covered with the most beautiful flowers. At the close of the service an unusual long procession followed the funeral car to our silent city.

To the broken hearted wife and children and to the loved ones, brothers and sisters, who sit in sorrow where his foot steps shall never again find echo, we extend the sympathy of one who loved him, and when they have drained the cup of sorrow, may the peace that passeth all human under-standing, come to them from Him in whom they trust.

———————————

Out of respect for the late F.J. Saunders all of our business houses closed during the hours of the funeral Wednesday.

———————————

Fred Saunders and Mary Ruth Theobald Saunders

On the front page of the same newspaper was an article about the "Prominent Wedding" of Uncle Ed's daughter Sadie A. Saunders to Mr. Ray Grimes. The article ends by saying, "Elaborate preparations had been made for this wedding and invitations were out to some 150 guests, but owing to the demise of the late F.J. Saunders, uncle of the bride, the wedding was a quiet affair."

Grandfather and Uncle Ed helped Austin and Wallace get started farming. He helped his sister-in-law too. Grandfather had sold some cattle and had taken notes in the early 1900's. When the notes could not be settled he took possession of a potato farm in Idaho and established Martha Theobald Barstow (Bertha Saunders' sister) and her husband Billy on the land.

Dad's brother, Uncle Will, and his family had a bit of difficulty getting settled. Will was not necessarily a farmer and I think it is fair to say that his interests lay somewhere other than the cattle business. He had gone to Alabama on a farm that somehow Grandfather obtained interest in, but he got into financial problems and came home with a family. Grandfather built him a house on the Cumberland Farm and he worked there for a while but later moved to South Dakota. A cattle breeder had bought some cattle and took them to South Dakota but times being what they were, they could not pay for the cattle so C.A. ended up taking over the farm and set Will up to care for it. It turned out to be his home for life. Will never came back; he died and is buried in South Dakota.

Due primarily to our age and geographical differences I was never very close to this branch of the family but years later I did have a chance meeting with one of my cousins. It was around the time of the Second World War and I was attending a cattle sale in Sioux City. I was sitting at the lunch counter at the hotel where all the cattlemen stayed. A young lieutenant in an Army uniform sat down and just below his aviator's wings was the name Saunders. To make a long story short, just by chance Uncle Will's oldest boy Howard, a cousin I had hardly known, came and sat down beside me. We didn't recognize each other but soon became reacquainted. Howard had flown into Sioux City on a quick trip back to see his parents and before our conversation was over he had offered me a ride in his plane. It was a two-seater fighter; I don't remember the exact model but we made plans he would get his plane and taxi down to the far end of the runway. A road ran past the area and on our way to the airport he would drop me off there. When he taxied by he would stop to make his turn onto the runway and I would run out and get into the back seat. The plan worked perfectly and in no time we were over the Black Hills. It was my first airplane ride and the last time I saw Howard.

Back on the farm, C.A. Saunders and Sons were still in the cattle business but another problem arose. In order to control TB in humans, it had to be controlled in animals and a law was

Uncle Will Saunders and family.

passed that all cattle had to be tested for TB. Animals that tested positive for TB had to be destroyed and this took a big bite out of everyone's cattle herd, the Cumberland herd was not immune. There was some reimbursement but it was only for a small portion of the market value and did not take into account the extra value of pure-bred cattle.

It took five or six years after the war for things to really go to hell. I suppose now we would call it a post-war recession. There were a couple years of relatively good times that, I suppose, gave people hope and kept them going, but the problems were getting bigger and the money tighter. More businesses began to fail.

Insurance companies had loaned money to the farmers but when the mortgages could not be paid, the insurance companies didn't want to take over the farms because then they would have to pay taxes on them. Yet there was no market and little value in reselling the farms. Frankly, things were in a hell of a mess.

People who didn't live through it think that everything happened in 1929 when the stock market crashed, but it started earlier, with low prices, tight money, even bank closings.

An example of just how quickly things could go to "hell in a hand basket" was a farmer named Weise who lived a mile-and-a-half or so from Uncle Bob. He was a pretty good pig farmer and when his pigs were ready for market, he was offered 23 cents a pound. Earlier that same year, before the spring pigs were born, a price of 25 cents a pound was a fair market price. Weise decided to hold out a little longer for 25 cents a pound so he kept them on the farm and of course had to feed them. Feeding them, needless to say, cost money and within a very short period of time they ate up all his feed. He had to sell and he ended up taking less than 10 cents a pound. A full year's hard work, both livestock and crops, down the drain by market forces few if any farmers understood let alone had any control over.

Prices plummeted. One year C.A. bargained hard to buy corn for $1.50 a bushel; a year later he bought it for 33 cents a bushel.

Sometime later, in the mid-30's the same thing happened to Dad and me. Our plans were to pay off the farm early. We had expanded our hog business and made an early attempt at mass production. We had 600 head of hogs on self feeders, which was something new at the time. At market time, selling them was not as easy as it is today. We had no big trucks to come to the farm; the pigs had to be driven down to the railroad just like the old wild west cattle drives. The first bunch to be sold, about sixty or so, just enough to fill a railroad car, were herded down to Astor and placed on the train. They sold for $4.80 per hundred pounds. By the time we got the last of them to market they sold for $2.65. We had fed all our corn to them, so we were also out a crop.

The check for the hogs was just $423.00, or just barely enough to pay the taxes. It didn't even go to the bank.

Of course, not having your money in the bank was not the worst thing in those days. Beginning in the early 1920's banks all over the country began closing their doors.

Now, my Grandfather, my Dad and my Uncle Chuck had been in the Shorthorn cattle business together, but operating two independent farms, and even though Grandfather's brother Edward (Deacon) was Vice-President of The First National Bank, C.A. did not do his banking there. Perhaps he should have.

Grandfather did not want people to say he got everything from his brother's bank so he did his farming and cattle business at the McHenry Bank in Denison. I think one reason Grandpa went to Denison for his business banking was because the McHenry's were friends and fellow cattlemen although they raised purebred Angus, not Shorthorns. I think also that he just didn't want everyone in town to know his business.

There were two banks in Manilla at that time, located on opposite corners of the middle block of the town's three-block long Main Street. The Manilla National Bank was located on the lower southwest corner and up the hill on the southeast corner stood the First National Bank. They were known as the lower bank and the upper bank respectively. C.A. did his personal banking at the lower bank, Manilla National. My Father and Mother did their banking at Uncle Ed's upper bank, The First National.

This was all perhaps by design, a part of my Mother's foresight, as well as being sure that only Dad and Mom's name was on the title for the land when they built the big barn and new house on Cumberland Stock Farm No. 2. It sort of kept the business from completely being tied up in one spot.

The wisdom of this approach became clear pretty early in this post-war period, I remember it because I was still in high school in the fall of 1925, October 8th to be exact when Manilla National closed its doors.

I remember Grandfather C.A. had gone to Nebraska. At that time he owned a farm in Fort Calhoun and had set up his nephew Austin Saunders in business. The day before he left, Grandfather had sold some cattle to a South American syndicate for $14,800. Because he was leaving the next day for Nebraska, he deposited the money, not in the Denison bank as would normally be his routine, but in his personal account at Manilla National just before he boarded the train for Omaha.

On the train trip home, an acquaintance by the name of Baker said to him, "Charley, I hear the lower bank (Manilla National) is rather shaky."

Grandfather said, "It shouldn't ought to be. I just put in $15,000." He reached into his pocket to show Mr. Baker his deposit slip and pulled out the slip only to find, much to his surprise, a zero was missing. His receipt was made out for only $1,480.

The old steam engines coming from Omaha would all stop at the coal tender built south of the Manilla Depot, to refill their coal cars. That night Grandfather got off the train at that point to shorten his walk home. It would cut off maybe a half-mile or more from his hike.

Upon arriving home he called the cashier of the bank, a Mr. Van Slyke, at his home in Manilla. The conversation went something like this: "Van, there has been a mistake on my account. I'll come in first thing in the morning and we'll straighten things up." Remember, these men were neighbors and business friends and had no reason to distrust each other.

The next morning Grandfather headed into Manilla but the bank doors remained closed and no one could find Van Slyke. Later that afternoon they found him in the public toilet under the stands at the town's baseball diamond – dead. I remember that afternoon when the men came to the school to tell his son Wendell. His father had taken his own life under the grandstand at the ballpark a few blocks from his home on Main Street. When they found him, he was still holding the shotgun that took his life.

Grandfather, like many others, was left 'holding the bag' and this time the bag was nearly empty. That same week, the McHenry Bank in Denison closed. When that happened, Grandfather was effectively out of business though it would take several more years for the bag to completely burst.

I am told there was never any settlement at the bank other than the small payments, about 20 cents on the dollar, made later by a Mr. Helgerson who had been appointed receiver. Many more banks would close their doors in the near future. Between 1920 and 1930 over 5,500 banks closed. Many of them, most all of the early closures, were the small rural banks that could not be supported when the farm prices fell, but it didn't take long to spread to the big-city banks.

At this time, my sisters and I sensed that our parents were having tough goings, and although we had been raised conservatively, I don't believe we knew how tight things were beginning to shape up for our parents. We had a nice home but no one had money to spend. For the next few years we were in school and accepted the fact that there was work to do. It took about all the farm could bring in to make things work. Dad, Mother and I still had a herd of cattle and more horses than we needed. I lived with the youthful blessing of not knowing any better and the optimism that things would get better.

To complicate the problem on a wider scale, many people, and I am not talking farmers here, had plunged into investments in railroad and other stocks frequently buying on margin and borrowing upward of 90% of the purchase price, thinking that good times were here to stay. Despite the low farm prices and difficulty the rural economy was facing, there was some optimism. Our own homegrown Iowan, Herbert Hoover, accepted the Republican nomination for President in August 1928 and in one of the most ill conceived campaign promises ever made said,

"We shall soon, with the help of God, be within sight of
the day when poverty will be banished from the nation."

We were all unaware that we were just a few short months away from something my mother had predicted.

"I lived with the youthful blessing of not knowing any better and the optimism that things would get better"

Grandpa tried to help family and relatives. This photo was taken on the Idaho potato farm on which he helped establish his sister-in-law Martha Theobald and husband Billy Barstow. On the back is written "110 sax of potatoes, #13,000 sold @ 7 cents pr. Pound. Total value of load $910.00. Raised by Barstow & Saunders, Idaho Falls, Idaho."

Raymond M. Saunders, 1934

January 31, 1989

Early morning, 5:00. We have a forecast of sunny and record-high temperature for today. Yesterday afternoon Mother and I made a trip to the welding shop in Audubon for some repair work for Doug. A very nice afternoon, we paid a repair bill at Robinson's shop in Irwin on the way. While in a little coffee shop in Audubon, we met a lady and her husband who had taught school in Manilla about the time that Doug and Craig were in grade school. She remembered Trudy.

Tomorrow, February 1, we have an eye appointment with Dr. Thurlsen, an ophthalmologist in Omaha. Our eyes are getting older.

Now we are about to the time of my life when Mother began to see into our future. These were the years 1929 -30-31-32.

In 1929, the year after I got out of high school, Dad bought a used 1928 blue, two-door Buick with wooden spoke wheels. I thought we were on top of the world, but Mother, more than Dad and I, saw the world changing.

Some time in the late fall or early winter of 1929-30, after the 1928 elections replaced Calvin Coolidge with our own native Iowan Herbert Hoover in the White House and after the stock market crash of 1929, there began what was rightly or wrongly called the "Hoover Depression." In other words, hard times, and it became clear to my Mother that the farms and homes of the Iowa people were in great jeopardy.

Money was scarce and prices for farm products were low. Before long I saw my father sign what was called a "Grant of Possession." This meant that Mom and Dad were agreeing to give up their rights of possession of the farm. Things had gotten so tight for them that the only way they could see out of this was to possibly give up the very home where they had started their life together. The farm that they had bought and together signed a mortgage to the Equitable Farm Loan of Des Moines. This Grant of Possession was a nice name for a Quit Claim Deed; it gave all the rights to the farm to the loan company. The company officers drove their car out into the field where my dad was working and it was signed one bright sunny day in the corn field at cultivating time. After Dad signed the papers he took a deep breath, looked around and realized he was standing very nearly on the exact spot where their first home had been built.

The only good thing, as I see it, was that Dad had three years to redeem the Grant of Possession. This was a process used by the insurance companies so they wouldn't have to go to court. The insurance companies did not want to foreclose because then they would have to pay taxes on the land. They would rather have the money than the farm.

Dad always raised 200-250 hogs a year but this income was being siphoned off for other expenses. Mom and Dad had their names on the two farm mortgages and with prices dropping and many men out of work, Mother knew that all could be lost unless Dad and she could some way make a change, but how?

There were two times in my early life that set the course for me here on Cumberland Stock Farm No. 2; this was the first. I remember it like it was yesterday. It was a cold winter day in early 1930 when Mother called me into her confidence. It was dreary, dripping a little water out of the pale gray sky, just about snowing but not quite. Mother and I were very close; I probably helped my mother more than my dad up until the time I was in high school. Her kitchen was really quite small and we had no kitchen table. All our meals and most of our family business was conducted around the dining room table. I don't know where Dad was at the time, but Mother called me into her dining room and poured her heart out.

"Son, the farm operations here are not in very good condition," she told me in words I can never forget. "I can't tell you a lot about the farm business, but it seems Dad and I can't make it. However, I believe between you and Dad you can work out of it. It will take a long time and a lot of patience."

In her words, "You will have to work for a living some place. The farm is a nice home; we stand a good chance of losing it. I feel if you will begin to get the business end back together and try to get financial aid through the newly-created Federal Land Bank[46] the two of you might be able to save our home."

This was quite a shot for a nineteen year old boy who had visions of some day getting into college. From my seat at the dining room table I could look over Mother's shoulder and see directly into our living room to the exact spot she had made a sick bed for me twelve years earlier during the flu epidemic. For a brief few seconds I could clearly see Mother and Dr. Loomis hovering over me and hearing, "If we get this kid out of this we ought to make a kid doctor out of him." My eyes returned from over Mother's shoulder and were caught in the reality of her own deep blue eyes and I knew it was a dream never to be.

My mother and I gathered up as much of the farm business, bills and information as we could and went to work. We enlisted the help of a young county attorney by the name of Jake Moore in Harlan. Jake's uncle, Tobias Smith, also helped. Mr. Smith was a hard headed old attorney, as I remember him, who had helped my grandfather in some of his business deals.

As a nineteen year old farm kid, I wrote a lot of letters and met with a lot of government officials – Iowa's Governor Herring; future governor and family friend, Lt. Governor Nels Kreschel of Harlan; U.S. Secretary of Agriculture Henry Wallace while he was in Des Moines; Fred Hubble, Shorthorn breeder and President of Equitable Life Insurance Company of Des Moines and Dean of Agriculture at Iowa State, Mr. H.H. Kildee. I got letters of recommendation from all of them.

I made many trips to Harlan to seek these men's advice, always hitchhiking. Our beautiful used 1928 Buick automobile, which only a few months earlier had been such a symbol of my pride of accomplishment, sat gathering dust in the garage. We simply had no money for the luxury of gasoline.

---

[46] Originally established in 1916 to provide easy credit and low interest rates to farmers, 12 regional farm land banks were set up with government money with the idea that the farmer-borrowers would ultimately own the banks. This did not go as planned and it 1923 and again in 1932 the government added more money and resources, organizing all farm credit organizations into the Farm Credit Administration.

This photo of "Uncle Ed's Bank" was another one published in the centennial yearbook Manilla Community Folks and Facts 1886-1996. The caption read: **"First National Bank. R.C. Jackson, cashier, and Fred Breckenridge, teller. The other man could be Roscoe C. Saunders who worked in the bank and married a Breckenridge girl. (The shorthorn in picture was one of Charley Saunders' grand champions.)"**

On one of my hitchhiking trips to Harlan, I was picked up by Dave Kensinger of Manilla and his wife Mabel.[47] I had walked about four miles west of our home toward the newly paved Highway 59 near Defiance when the Kensingers offered me a ride and the big news of the day. The news was the first I had heard of the closing of the upper bank, Uncle Deacon's First National Bank of Manilla.

It looks like breakfast time, more later.

---

[47] Mabel Kensinger was the daughter of Mr. O.A. Olsen. The old store keeper in Astor, Iowa were my Dad and Mother did most of their shopping; trading eggs, butter, corn and hogs for supplies for the years of farm work. As long as Mr. Olson was in business, Mother and Dad did most of their business in Astor with the Olson's General Store.

February 1, 1989

Yesterday, Trudy and I spent the afternoon in Denison. Warmest January 31st ever recorded; a very fine day.

Had lunch at Cronk's Cafe.

Did a bit of banking business for Trudy and stopped to visit Trudy's sister and her husband, Anna Marie and Fred Rabe. It was a fine visit, although it's really apparent that we are all getting old. Anna Marie doesn't walk, but otherwise she is in fairly good health.

The forecast for this morning is for an end to the spring-like weather.

Trudy and I have an eye appointment with Dr. Thurlsen in Omaha. I'm not sure we will keep it on account of the weather and the roads.

Well, I'll see what Doug says later.

Fifty-six years ago today, February 1, 1933 was the last day Uncle Ed Saunders' First National Bank of Manilla was open for business.

We called the First National "Uncle Deacon's bank." Uncle Ed (Deacon) Saunders was grandfather's brother and Vice-President of First National Bank. I guess it would be an understatement to say that the bank closure complicated things. My father did some business there: he had a small checking account and also some notes totaling maybe $2,500-3,500 but fortunately he did not do the big farm business there. So, upon arriving at Jake Moore's office that day I gave Attorney Moore and his Uncle Toby Smith the news.

"Ray," Mr. Moore said, "this will really complicate our job."

I remember Mr. Smith's words. "Yes, it will make a lot more work, but it could also hurry things along, and bring things to a close a lot quicker. I think it depends upon two things; first, will the bank reopen and second, can President Roosevelt gain the confidence of the American people."

The banks were closing because money was so scarce and things got so bad that people did not trust the paper money. The country was still on the gold standard and by law the banks had to back up 40% of their deposits with gold. People began to go to the banks and demand their gold. Soon the reserves dipped below 40% and there simply was not enough.

In November of 1932 Hoover was defeated by Franklin D. Roosevelt in the presidential election but in those days the inauguration was not until March. From November to March Hoover conducted a 'lame duck' presidency during which time he could not or would not introduce banking reform and all hell broke lose. Many states acted on their own to close their own state banks but Hoover did not feel it was the government's role to regulate the economy. He waited and expected market forces to correct it on their own.

Roosevelt didn't wait for anything. Though he felt he could not act while only the President elect, he made plans and prepared. Government normally moves quite slowly but less than a week after his inauguration, in one amazing 24 hour period, FDR introduced legislation, passed it through both houses of Congress and enacted the Emergency Banking Act. He declared a "Bank Holiday" and closed every bank in the United States.

The Emergency Banking Act basically said "we are closing all banks until we can figure out how to fix this mess." Apparently there was a lot of the mess that couldn't be cleaned up because The First National Bank of Manilla, along with a lot of other banks, never reopened their doors for business.

Roosevelt became the leader for American business and a new alphabet soup was born – the AAA,[48] the NRA,[49] the RFC[50] the WPA[51] the CCC[52] and later the PCA[53] took the place of the RFC.

Slowly, the nation's people went back to work and began to gain a little bit of confidence. My friend Andy Carothers was a good example. His father had died early and left Andy and his mother to fend for themselves. Andy wasn't fortunate enough to have his own land to fight for so he went into the CCC to have a place to eat and

---

[48] Agriculture Adjustment Act
[49] National Recovery Act
[50] Reconstruction Finance Corporation
[51] Public Works Association
[52] Civilian Conservation Corp
[53] Production Credit Association

sleep and to support his mother. Along with his CCC colleges Andy built dams across great rivers, tree breaks across the flat prairies and terraces over the rolling hills. They planted billions of trees and rebuilt forests. They built parks and public buildings. In return Andy got a uniform, a place to live, three hot meals a day and I believe he got paid $30 a month and sent $25 of it home to his mother.

Thanks to my mother, we had our work started. We realized we had more to contend with and would be set back with our refinancing plans. But remember, though, due to my mother's foresight, we were ahead of the majority with our work of refinancing. Even though there was a long road ahead, we were beginning to see the light at the end of the tunnel, at least now everyone was **trying** to go the same way. It was slow work but we even made a few friends along the way.

Anyway, this was the process of bringing things back together, trying anything short of bankruptcy. Please understand, we were just a bit ahead of most with our planning, thanks to Mother's prodding.

Over these four long years, we worked hard and tried to bring things around. We also put our faith in the hog business. Slowly, we brought all the accounts together and made applications for all the farm programs.

Two of the most important things in my life were happening to me at this time. First, listed in order of occurrence, not importance, was my mother's talk, which we have already discussed. Second, and perhaps without a doubt the most important, was meeting my future wife who took her place alongside my mother as one of the true great moms of the world. But Trudy deserves a chapter of her own so, for now, suffice it to say, my future wife and I made a quiet trip to Des Moines to meet with the Secretary of Agriculture and the President of Equitable Life Insurance Company.

I also made one trip to Omaha with my father. Father knew the man we were visiting in Omaha. They had been to a dance together in Defiance and I remember them talking about a girl name Kate Atz and how many freckles she had. The meeting went well. On the way home we didn't have money for a 10- cent hamburger after buying gas, but that trip was the finalization of the loan process.

I am sure the only person who knew where we were that day was my mother. She knew how we, as a family, would have to make some big changes.

It paid off.

Eventually the loan was approved and we received only the 6th Federal Land Bank Loan in Shelby County, with the stipulation that both Dad and I sign the mortgages and the notes.

It was a twenty-year loan for $20,000 at 4% interest. We also had what was called a Commissioner's Loan. The Federal Land Bank Loan tied up the land and the Commissioner's Loan tied up all the personal property and assets. This was a temporary deal that ultimately had to be transferred into the Production Credit Association that was formed as a part of the Farm Credit Act. Everything was mortgaged but we had managed to remain in possession of the farm and our home as well as get out from under the Equitable Farm Loan's Grant of Possession.

When word got out around the community, people were sure that Grandfather had pulled some strings. He had not: in fact, he, my Uncle Chuck and the rest of the family, knew very little if anything about the whole transaction. However, the fact that I was C. A. Saunders' grandson hadn't hurt a bit. I know that there were times that it helped when talking and dealing with these people.

C. A. was known as an honest businessman, shrewd, sharp and quick, but honest. I have been told this many times. My Mother may have been his best friend; she got along with him better than anyone and this is one of the times that he should have listened to her. Things wouldn't go as well for him later.

However, Mother, Dad and I had managed the 6th Federal Land Bank Loan in Shelby County and we had accomplished this ahead of most others. We had worked quietly for two years putting the pieces together. We were on our way; Cumberland Stock Farm No. 2 was secure.

Thank God.

The fact that father and son were willing to work together and commit their entire lives to saving their home and way of life was our main promise of survival.

Remember, I was not yet twenty-one-years old but I was convinced I knew more than anyone in the state, I was sure of that.

It's kind of funny how these things work. I'm now nearly 90 years old. I understand more but I don't know nearly as much as I did back then.

> *"The fact that father and son were willing to work together and commit their entire lives . . . was our main promise of survival."*

Chapter 8

GERTRUDE ALFREDA ARNOLD-SAUNDERS

February 2, 1989

Morning, 5:40am
Iowa weather, yes. Two days ago, January 31, record warm weather, 60 degrees or higher all over the state. This morning on our farm it reads 1 degree above zero. However, no snow. A northwest wind, not real strong.

It is Groundhog's Day. Seventy one years ago today, February 2, 1918 my parents moved to their new home on the hill in Section Three, Greeley Township.

It is still dark but I am sitting at my kitchen table, looking out across the road at the house my parents built and lived out their lives in. The house my sisters and I grew up in. The same house we ultimately raised our boys in and now son Doug is raising his family there.

God has been good to us.

Yesterday, Trudy and I drove to Omaha for an appointment with our Ophthalmologist, Dr. Thurlsen. Trudy came home with a new pair of eyeglasses for driving and bright outdoor wear. Also, new tri-focal lenses for general wear. These all made and fitted in an hour's time. The new lenses were fitted into her old frames. She seems to be very happy with them.

After a few stops in Council Bluffs, we headed home a few minutes before five. Quite a change – a paved road, 65 miles an hour in a heated car. Seventy-one years ago, a team of horses and a bob-sled.

We stopped at Mickels' Restaurant in Harlan for a fresh catfish dinner and apple pie with ice cream. Before we finished eating, Merle Greer came in. We had a great visit. Merle worked for us as a hired hand for a few years. He was also a pretty good baseball pitcher on Manilla's Baseball team. Soon his daughter came in with her little girl.

Merle's father and mother moved to the farm directly southwest of our home in 1934-36. They were forced out of South Dakota by dry weather and hard times. A family of eight kids – two sets of twins, Verle and Merle, a pair of girls eleven months younger, Eunice and Joyce, and four little ones. The oldest was no more than 12 years old.

We as a community should really admire their mother and dad; they are in their nineties and are still living together.

A bit more, Merle's boy, Dennis is now married to Gene and Zona Saunders' daughter Nancy. They have had quite a time, a family of his kids and her kids and now they have a little girl of their own who Merle said was in kindergarten.

Now they have their lives put together and are doing well, farming close to Merle's farm.

Life goes on!

On a humid lazy Sunday afternoon in July of 1932 the town of Manilla was abuzz with the news that one of our most prominent citizens was dead. A man who had already touched and changed my life was to do it one more time in his death. Dr. Loomis, town physician and President of the School Board, had been killed in an auto accident. He was only 58 years old and had been coming home from Omaha late the night before, driving one of those new V8 Fords through a driving rainstorm. Just north of Manilla the Milwaukee Railroad tracks crossed Highway 141, and to improve the safety of the intersection, an overpass had been built to allow the train to pass over the highway. Ironically, Dr. Loomis apparently fell asleep going under the highway 141 overpass. He hit one of the wooden pillars and was killed instantly.

My friend Andy Carothers and I were trying to kill time together that Sunday afternoon and we decided to check out the accident scene. There wasn't much to be seen but I do remember seeing the Ford logo imprinted on the wooden pillar Dr. Loomis had hit.

It didn't take long to figure out there wasn't much else to see or do there and it was a nice late afternoon so Andy concocted a plan. He had been working for a farmer in the area, Mr. Dave Comstock, and he had met Mr. Comstock's niece.

M. M. LOOMIS, M. D.,

This time worn cartoon of Dr. Loomis was printed in the Manilla Times sometime prior to his death. He is the man that nursed me through the Spanish Flu and suggested that I become a 'kid doctor'. He is the man who brought Prof. Fearing into our lives and in his death he introduced me to my future wife.

Now Andy was a good-looking guy and was a couple years older and a couple years more experienced. Not only did he have a girlfriend, he had two girlfriends – and they were cousins! I think he liked Linda Jensen better but she was not home that afternoon, so we stopped in to see Mr. Comstock's niece, Trudy Arnold.

Late that afternoon, after some serious negotiations, Andy and I took Trudy Arnold and her friend Ethel Burmeister to the Ritz Movie Theater in Denison.

Color movies were new to the area but we hadn't seen one yet. This movie was in black and white but it was a 'talkie' and it just happened to be the most popular movie ever until "Gone With The Wind" was made. The movie we saw was Al Jolson in "The Singing Fool." In it he sang a popular song of the time called "Rainbow Round My Shoulder."

'Talkies' had come to the Manilla Theater in 1929 a full two years after Jolson had made the very first talking picture called "The Jazz Singer." In that movie he had the famous line "you ain't heard nothing yet", and I guess we hadn't because I was destined to hear a lot more from Trudy Arnold.

Later that fall, I called Miss Burmeister for a date. This time she was the one who wasn't home so I figured if Andy could do it, I could, too. I took a page from Andy's book and called and made a date with Miss Arnold. I wanted to take her to the Shelby County Fair at Harlan. I had quite a few friends there as the Saunders had shown Shorthorns and Poland China Hogs there for many years.

The main reason, however, for going to the fair, besides showing off this new girl, was that I could use my Grandfather's tickets. He was one of the original stockholders in the Fair and always got season tickets. By using the tickets, I not only impressed her, but it didn't cost me to get in.

Let me tell you a bit about that first date. It was the fall season and the harvest was in full progress. When I picked Trudy up, they were thrashing grain at the Arnold farm. As was the custom at that time, this was a community project. Not every farmer could afford a thrashing machine nor the labor costs so relatives, friends and neighbors would pool their resources and travel from farm to farm to get the grain harvested. Every one came to help. The women, of course, came along with the men and prepared the meals.

Blessed

There's A Rainbow 'Round My Shoulder[54]

There's a rainbow round my shoulder
And a sky of blue above
How the sun shines bright
The world's all right
'Cause I'm in love.

There's a rainbow round my shoulder
And it fits me like a glove
Let it blow let it storm, I'll be warm
'Cause I'm in love

Hallelujah, how the folks will stare
When they see that solitare
That my little baby is gonna wear

There's a rainbow round my shoulder
And a sky of blue above
And I'm shoutin so the world
Will know that I'm in love

Hallelujah, how the folks gonna stare
When they see that diamond solitare
That my own true baby's gonna wear

There's a rainbow round my shoulder
And a sky of blue above
And I'm shoutin so the world
Will know

I'm in love, I'm in love
There's a rainbow round my shoulder
And I'm in love

---

[54] Written by Dave Dreyer, Al Jolson and Billy Rose, appeared in the movie "The Singing Fool" and recorded by Al Jolson in 1928

The Arnolds lived right in the center of a pretty close knit German community. In fact, Trudy's Grandfather Henry Niewoehner was the area's German Lutheran Minister. He had come to America from Düsseldorf, Germany as a young man. When I called on Trudy I was invited into the house and with the thrashing crew on the Arnold farm the house was, needless to say, full of German ladies. They were preparing a meal and all talking at once. Some of the conversation was in German and some in English but most of it was somewhere in between. I well remember a Mrs. Stegeman telling of a team of runaway horses. While this was not generally an uncommon or noteworthy occurrence in itself, it was her description that etched a place in my memory, causing me to take notice and remember it to this day. As she was telling this story of a runaway team of horses she was amazed that they did not upset the wagon they were pulling, and using English words with German grammar it came out like this:

"The team ran the gate out, the road up, the corner 'round, the hill down and never sat the wagon up!"

These thrashing scenes were in our photo collection with no identification, they predate my first date with Trudy by maybe 20 years but give you an idea of the job at hand. The above photo was published in a 1906 sales catalog.

Can you imagine a young guy who was trying to impress a sharp looking young lady on his first date? I really began to wonder just what I had gotten myself into.

We made it to the County Fair in our 1928 Buick with the wooden spoke wheels and had just gotten into the cattle barns when Harvey Larson, a young man whose family raised Hereford cattle, saw us and yelled across the barn. His words were plain and outspoken, "My God, Ray, where did you find that good-looking blonde?"

Embarrassed?

I think so, but flattered, too. After all, I did go there to show her off. Later we met Edgar Whaling of Shelby and his date Mada. Remember, I met him for the first time when I was in high school and had brought my pigs to the fair. As fate would have it, we both eventually married our dates of that day. The Whalings and Saunders raised our families through the days of the Great Depression and have had a lot of good times together over the years.

I'll fill in more later. Trudy and I are going to have breakfast now and we are going to Harlan again today. This time to the annual co-op dinner.

Grandma Arnold with her three children, Anna Marie to her right,
Bob and Trudy in the forefront.

A young Trudy Arnold above with her father Gus holding younger brother Bob and older sister Anna Marie in the middle.

An older Trudy with her father in front of the Arnold family farmhouse she grew up in.

February 3, 1989

Going back to the time in my life when my father and I had managed the farm loan and were reorganizing the farm business.

While working on the loans and reorganizing, I became quite serious about my new girlfriend. The entire Arnold family seemed to have a musical knack and Trudy was no exception. She had been somewhat of a child prodigy on the violin and at age nine gave her own recital. Now she was out of high school and had a job teaching school in a one room school house one-and-a-half miles north of her home, at the intersection of Highways 141 and 59. She was making $50 a month and her dad owned his own farm, one that had formally been owned by his father.

Nov. 2[, 1923

Erich Hadenfeld, 22, was injured fatally when the car he was driving ran off the road near Manilla Saturday afternoon. John A. Knott, riding with him, was seriously hurt.

Josephine Kinney will present her pupil, Gertrude Arnold, in a violin recital next Tuesday. Alma Frese and Arnold Finnern will assist with piano and vocal solos.

Fritz and Chris Gierstorf of Morgan township were in Denison this week making arrangements for a trip to Germany.

Attending the Iowa State-Nebraska football game at Ames Saturday were Marie Weiss, Margaret and Bernice Kinney, Joe Flinn, Alfred Rohwer, Al Weiss and Leo Miller.

A barefoot virtuoso at nine years old, Trudy's violin experience is
one of her most proud accomplishments.

Boy, we were almost in love, and things were all going great.
I had met Trudy in the summer of '32 and began dating her that
fall. Now during this time we were raising corn, hogs, had a herd
of Shorthorns and Mother, Dad and I were working on the farm
reorganization. We had a foreclosed farm, so to speak, and a poor
economy along with all our other problems. Two other things were
certain, though. We had plenty of work and no money.

Somehow, our farm loan came through, and by the fall of 1933,
we as a family were much better off. For now we had consolidated

into a long-term operation and at least we knew that we did not have to move off and hunt for another home and job.

I had a youthful optimism. We were going to pay off the mortgage in no time. I was convinced I already knew more than anyone else in the community. I had a few hogs of my own, a partial interest in 315 acres of choice Iowa farm land and a mortgage and notes signed for more money than I ever thought existed. We had increased the hog breeding herd and I had taken the most beautiful blonde to the county fair.

These were the circumstances in which a young man could begin to plan his future. I suppose you could say I had my share of girlfriends even though many more young ladies turned me down for dates than accepted. However, I can truthfully say, I never dated a girl whom I wouldn't consider a candidate for a future mate. I was still interested in that blonde school teacher, so much so that in the winter of 1933-34 when money was so tight, I walked the seven miles over to her home to be sure that no one else was moving in on me. I made that trip religiously every Sunday afternoon and anytime during the week that the weather and farm work allowed.

On one of my treks I carried in my pocket two rings that I had purchased at Tingly's Jewelry Store in Harlan for the unheard of price of $32.50. The wedding band had three little diamonds in it, the big one you could actually almost see. It took me a long time to get them paid off.

I gave her the rings while asking her if she "wanted to eat breakfast with me every morning?" I guess I could not be accused of being a romantic but it worked. She still wears those same stones today although in different settings.

I was 23-years-old and my bride had just turned twenty when we were married June 24, 1934 in the Lutheran Church in Denison, Iowa. I've said many times since that I walked into the Lutheran Church and walked out with the prettiest girl there. It was one of those hot steamy June days that make the Iowa corn grow and a small group of friends and relatives attended. We saved money by not sending out invitations; we just personally asked people we wanted to share the day with.

Trudy gave me this picture as a Christmas present the year before we were married. It sat for years on top our bedroom dresser.

After the wedding ceremony we went out to the Arnold's farm and had ice cream and cake. Someone was going to decorate our car. I remember seeing Uncle Chuck drive it off and I thought "What the Hell?" He took it over to Uncle Fred's house. When we were ready to leave, he brought it back and we were able to drive off into our future without the 'Just Married' sign and the trailing tin cans.

After our engagement we did not go to movies or otherwise waste our money and we were able to save up $40 for our honeymoon. The Chicago World's Fair had been such a success that it had been held over for a year and we decided to spend our honeymoon there to see what all the excitement was about.

Besides, Chicago was a lot safer city now that Elliot Ness had put Al Capone in jail. Although almost one month to the day after our visit, John Dillinger was gunned down on the street outside a Chicago movie theater.

It only cost us 50 cents to get in to the World's Fair and most the things on the inside were free. The only thing we paid for was to get into the Midget Village, this cost us another 25 cents each. Everything there was small. I remember they had little cars and small gas pumps. They had their own grocery store and church.

While in Chicago we stayed with relatives – my great Uncle Will's boy Bill to be exact. Remember I told you the story of Uncle Will, the oldest of the orphaned Saunders children and Grandfather C.A.'s oldest brother. He was living now with his son Bill. Uncle Will, you may also remember, was a local politician and he had received an invitation to the opening of Chicago's new Brookfield Zoo. He took Trudy and me along to the new zoo's grand opening with about fifteen other friends and relatives, all on that one invitation.

We enjoyed ourselves and took in whatever else was free along the way. One stop on the way home from Chicago was for a free tour of Iowa's Fort Madison State Penitentiary. They made Trudy put on slacks for the tour, I guess so she didn't excite the inmates with her bare legs.

Another young couple was traveling across country in 1934 but they were on the other side of the law. This was the same year Bonnie and Clyde were gunned down on a Louisiana roadside. We

There were no invitations and no photographer at our wedding.
These two snapshots are the only 'official pictures'. The maid
of honor was my sister Margaret and the best man was Trudy's
brother Bob. My cousin Mildred's son, Wayne Blount was the
ring bearer.

were more fortunate and were able to return home with still a little
change in our pockets ready to build our new life together.

The old house in the valley that my Mother and Dad built just
after they were married was to be the core from which we would
build our home. It has been setting empty for seventeen-to-eighteen
years but the wood was still good. Two of the rooms, the ones my
parents had originally moved in by two teams of horses, were
again moved to a spot directly across the road from my parent's big
house on the hill top. There was an archway between the rooms
that was maintained and these two rooms made up the living room
and dining room of our new house. The smaller of the two rooms
had been our kitchen in the old house, we expanded it by four

RAY SAUNDERS AND GERTRUDE ARNOLD MARRIED JUNE 24

Ceremony Was Performed at Lutheran Church in Denison Sunday

Raymond Saunders of Manilla and Miss Gertrude Arnold of Buck Grove were united in marriage at Zion Lutheran church in Denison at 2 o'clock p. m. Sunday, June 24, Rev. Wm. Frese officiating at the ceremony.

Robert Arnold, a brother of the bride, and Miss Margaret Saunders, a sister of the groom, attended the bridal couple as best man and bridesmaid and Wayne Blount was ring bearer. Merle Saunders and Mervin Arnold served as ushers. During the service Mrs. Arley Saunders sang a solo.

The church was filled with relatives and friends of the contracting parties, many from Manilla being present.

Following the ceremony at the church the bridal party was entertained at a reception at the home of the brides parents near Buck Grove.

The bride is a daughter of Mr. and Mrs. Gus Arnold, prominent farmers of the Buck Grove community, and is highly regarded by all her friends and acquaintances. She graduated from the Denison high school in 1930 and has since been a popular teacher in the schools of Washington township.

Mr. Saunders is a son of Mr. and Mrs. John Saunders, south of Manilla. Since graduating from Manilla high school in 1928 he has been associated with his father in the management of their farm and has established a reputation for himself as a raiser of pure bred livestock. His many friends in this vicinity are pleased to extend congratulation to himself and his bride and wish them success and happiness.

For the present the newlyweds are making their home with the groom's parents until a new home they are building, just east across the road from the John Saunders home, is completed.

PRETTY WEDDING AT THE LUTHERAN CHURCH SUNDAY

Miss Getrude Arnold and Raymond Saunders Were United in Marriage by Rev. Wm. Frese

CEREMONY AT TWO O'CLOCK

After Their Return From Honeymoon Mr. and Mrs. Saunders Will Reside Near Manilla

The Lutheran church of Denison was the scene of a pretty wedding Sunday afternoon at 2 o'clock when Rev. Wm. Frese united Miss Gertrude Arnold and Raymond Saunders in marriage. Tall baskets of flowers were used on each side of the altar which was illuminated the altar candles.

he ceremony, Mrs. Ar- of Manilla, sang "O Rabe, sister Mrs. Frederick Ra organ ac-Ill., who spent the dayed Arnold home. brid

The bride is the youn of Mr. and Mrs. Gus Ar side south of Denison. St lady of much charm an friends admire her for her position and congenial mann graduated from the Denison school with the class of '30 and a year at home, she taught in the rur at schools of the county for two years.

The bridegroom is the only son of Mr. and Mrs. John Saunders, who reside on a farm south of Manilla. He attended high school there, graduating in '28. Since then he has been assisting his father on the farm and now operates half of the Saunders farm. He is building a new home for his bride which will be completed within the coming month. By industry and persistence, he is succeeding in his chosen work and his many friends respect him for his many fine qualities.

Mr. and Mrs. Saunders left Sunday evening for a ten days trip to Chicago where they will visit relatives and attend the world's fair. Enroute home they will visit in Rock Island and at various points in Missouri. Upon their return they will be at home with the bridegroom's parents until their new home on the Saunders farm two miles south of Manilla is completed.

feet. The old house had a lean-to bedroom attached to it. We took that off and built two brooder houses for chickens. Nothing was wasted.

We also bought a part of the old Manilla Depot, a building 40 feet long by 12 feet high for the sum of $40. We tore it down and hauled the lumber to the farm to use to build the rest of the house.

My new wife and I pulled nails, piled and sorted the lumber. A man from Denison, Ben Boettiger and his helper, a man by the name of Wulf, helped us. Ben at $4.00 a day and Wulf at $2.50, regular laborers were happy to have work during this time for 50 cents to $1.00 a day. With the help of a lot of friends and relatives, we built a four room house from the used lumber, covered the outside with cedar shingles hauled by a stock truck from the Sutherland Lumber Company of Omaha for $1.95 per square.

We used bricks from the chimney of the old depot for our new chimney. We reused the lathe for our plaster walls and even some of the old maple flooring. For the new floor in the living room and dining room, I put in second grade oak flooring which I laid myself at night with the aid of an old gas lantern that Dad let me use after the farm chores were finished.

A man by the name of Webster, from Defiance, helped me plaster the walls of our new home. His paycheck was $40 for the whole job. Again, the plaster was brought back from Omaha on a stock truck back haul.

We were in our new little house, one bedroom, outdoor plumbing and a lot of used furniture. The only new thing in the house was a new wood burning cooking stove and a white sink with a five-gallon pail for a drain and a water pail sitting on the drain board.

The only new lumber in the house was the windows, doors and the shingles. The shingles were used for siding and when we placed them, we stretched them out and covered a third more space, making it a little cheaper.

The summer of '34 was quite hot. We did not raise a big crop that summer but that fall we had Thanksgiving dinner in our new little home. I remember the day. It was a nice bright sunny autumn day and my Mother and Father came across the road to share dinner with us. I'm sure we probably had chicken – we always did, but when dinner was over, Dad commented how good it was.

My mother's curt German response broke Trudy's heart and she has not forgotten it to this day. "Humph – just because you're hungry."

I'll write more later. Mother is around for breakfast. We have had breakfast together every morning since 1934.

Me, Ben Boettiger and Wulf at the old house in the valley my mother and father put together with an old shack they moved there with two teams of horses. We moved two of the rooms up the hill and along with used lumber from the Manilla Depot built our home across the road from my parents.

The final result was our "honeymoon cottage". We raised four boys in one bedroom, ultimately adding running water and an indoor toilet. Our present home is built on this exact spot.

Mr. and Mrs. Ray Saunders

Celebrate 50th...

Ray and Trudy Saunders of Manilla will celebrate their 50th wedding anniversary with an open house Sunday, June 24 from 2 to 4 p.m. at the Presbyterian Church. At 4:30 there will be a "Showing of Memories" at the Manilla Memorial Hall.

The occasion will be hosted by their children and grandchildren.

All friends and relatives are invited. The couple requests no gifts.

Fifty years seemed like a lot but our next anniversary will be our 69th year together.

February 3, 1989

Late afternoon.
The ground is white and cold.

We had a lot to be thankful for in 1934 and 1935 was the year Dad and I were going to wrap it all up. We had a real good crop in '35 but unfortunately, prices for livestock and grain were next to nothing. But the future was ahead, and we were raising hogs. We had lots of hogs that year, some down in the valley and some up on the hill. At that time hogs on a self-feeder was an entirely new idea and Dad and I had 650 head of various sizes on the self feeder.

I had persuaded Trudy to invest $175 into some pure-bred Poland China hogs from the Nebraska herd of Dr. W. E. Steward. Steward was an M.D. who owned one of the top herds at that time. We were not only going to raise market hogs, we were going to supply the whole country with the best breeding stock, just like we had done with the cattle.

We were also making plans for another "crop." In the summer of 1935, June 13, our first son arrived. Dean Arnold Saunders was born in Methodist Hospital in Omaha. Trudy had developed some complications and along with them came anxiety.

Some of the anxiety was natural for a first time mother, and some was contributed by her own mother. God never created a mad mother Blue Jay with more natural fury and inbred protectiveness than He had given Trudy's mother.

Grandma Arnold did not like the doctor in Manilla and wanted her daughter to go to Denison and see Dr. Brennen, but he was about 75-80 years old and that just didn't seem to be the best idea to me. The result was, at the suggestion of Dr. Soe in Manilla that we go to a specialist, a Dr. Taylor in Omaha.

Grandpa Arnold drove us to the hospital and, of course, Grandma Arnold had to go along. We arrived safely, registered in the hospital lobby and got on the elevator to go to Trudy's room. A pleasant young man walked on with us and said, "Boy, it's hot. This weather will sure make the corn grow."

Grandma snapped back, "We're not interested in the corn."

The next morning, at about 4 am, the young man from the elevator delivered our baby boy. It was Dr. Taylor.

Dean weighed seven pounds dripping wet. Dr. Taylor examined him and said, "He's a little premature. We should give him some blood." He proceeded to take 20cc's of blood out of a vein in my arm and injected it directly under the skin on Dean's back. Boy, did it make a big ugly black and blue bruise.

When Grandma Arnold saw it she was furious and gave both the doctor and nurse 'just billy hell.' When she got all through, the only reply the doctor could muster was, "Lady, I've probably delivered more babies than you." It hurts me to admit that by today's standards, Grandma in all her fury was no doubt right.

The nurse, Barbara Heir, was from Oakland, Nebraska. It just so happened that she was the niece of a friend of mine, but she was too young for Grandma Arnold. That didn't bother me much. It was Grandma Arnold's fault that we were in Omaha in the first place.

That night Grandma and Grandpa Arnold stayed in Omaha. I had chores to do so I hitched a ride home on the Davis Bus Lines, it ran twice a day from Audubon to Omaha and back. I knew the bus driver; I didn't have any money but promised to pay him later. He took my arm and said, "Just get in there, sit down and shut up."

In a few days my family came home, too. I remember my Mother's words when we brought Dean home. I carried him from our new little house across the road to Mom and Dad's big house and placed him in my Mother's arms. Her words were prophetic – "Such a little fellow, and so much to do."

Grandfather C. A. walked up from his Cumberland Stock Farm to our own Cumberland Stock Farm No. 2. He had to have been 75-80 years old. I was his first Saunders grandson and he came to our little house to see his first great-grandson. He brought with him a pair of little booties. Trudy wrapped Dean in a little blanket and handed him to his great-grandfather C. A.

A big grin spread slowly under the great white mustache on Grandfather's aging face and without removing his eyes from his great grandson, his words to Trudy were, "You did a great job – a hell of a job."

Trudy and Dean on a Sunday visit to grandma's house.

Grandfather was rather gruff, and Trudy was scared to death of him, but they were friends. He said afterwards that he had "now lived to see four generations of Saunders' boys" as he called them.

One of Trudy's aunts, an RN who lived in Chicago, sent Trudy and me a great big book of instruction on the care and feeding of our newborn son. It was written by some new young doctor whom no one had yet heard of. His name was Dr. Benjamin Spock.

We now had more to look after and a greater future ahead of us.

Dean Arnold Saunders

Chapter 9

Back to the '30's

February 4, 1989

A very cold morning. There is talk of record low temperatures. What a change from just a few days ago.

I went to Harlan with Doug yesterday. He had an appointment with the Agriculture Stabilization Office (A.S.C.) to enroll his farm business in the 1989 Price Support Program. While he did that I started his work with the Soil Conservation Service. This is a soil conservation plan so our farms will remain eligible for the price support programs. It will not be very hard to comply as we use lots of hay and grass in our rotations. It looks like we will remain right on target.

I don't think we could survive without these programs.

We were home early as he had lots of chores to do.

Back to the 1930's.

Remember, 1935 was the year we were going to 'wrap it all up'. We were raising over 600 head of hogs at the time. The reason hogs were such a good cash crop was because it took nine months for a cow to have a calf and a good sow could be bred and the pigs to market by the time the cow had her calf. The saying was "raise more hogs to buy more land, to raise more corn to raise more hogs".

When market time arrived for 1935 hog crop the first car load went out at $4.80 per hundred weight (cwt) in Omaha. This came to only around $13 per head. I guess we should have been happy with that because that wasn't the end of it. Prices began to drop rapidly from there. The load that paid the taxes weighed an average of 269 pounds and brought $2.65 cwt or about $7.12 per head. After expenses were paid, the check was approximately $425. After paying farm taxes, there was less than $10 left from 69 head of hogs. Our crop had been fed and our money was gone.

The pure-bred hogs I had convinced Trudy to invest in didn't do any better because no one had any money. We tried to get $15 for the 250 pound boars. This was nearly twice the market price, but we sold many for $10 to $12. We, of course, had to guarantee that they were breeders and more than one buyer would bring them back in three or four weeks saying that they wouldn't breed and we would have to refund the $10.00. He of course had already used them to breed his whole herd. It got pretty bad. One time Trudy's Dad took a pair of boars right out of some man's trailer, took them home and raised an entire herd of pigs from these 'non-breeders.'

This taught me a lot about the hog business. Matt White was an old field man for the Iowa Homestead magazine, which was bought out by The Wallace's Farmer. He said, "Nothing will get a young farmer any higher, or let him down any harder, than the purebred hog business."

Adding insult to injury, Mother Nature did her part to complicate the Great Depression. A drought began in about 1931 that lasted until 1939 and although we in the Midwest were not hit as hard as the farmers in the southern plains of Kansas and the Oklahoma panhandle, the whole nation felt its affect.

Needless to say, the farm operation got tougher. The summer of 1936 was hot and dry with almost no crop. Dad and I had to sell most of our cattle herd just to make ends meet. We sold them at an auction at the farm on June 30, 1936. We didn't get a lot of money, but we were able to satisfy some of our creditors. We were left with six head of cattle and five milk cows. That turned into sort of a blessing a few short days later.

On the 4th of July that year, the Southwest White Winds turned our crops white. Uncle Chuck and his family had driven to Carroll that day for the Fourth of July Celebrations. The temperature reached 120 degrees in Carroll. He said everything was shut up and people just sat in the shade. On the ride home that evening they drove past cornfields that had been green in the morning but by evening were burned white by the hot winds and blistering sun.

That fall, the normally six-foot-tall corn stalks were only three-feet-tall and with no ears of corn to speak of. Most of it was cut with

Uncle Chuck (C.A.) and Aunt Millie (Pamelia) Milligan Saunders with cousins Buzz (C.A.) and Mildred. Mildred was born in 1910 and Buzz in 1913, dating this photo circa 1915.

a grain binder and used as fodder instead of being picked for the grain.

I saw corn that was planted in the spring not even come up out of the ground until some rains fell in September. Water got very short. We hauled water in barrels from the old well for the horses and what few cattle were left.

No crop, no money.

Nothing.

No work for many people.

These were the Dust Bowl years.

The recession that dropped farm prices after World War I caused farmers to increase production and with the aid of the new machinery available, to cultivate more land. This, of course, cost money and many farmers became deeper in debt but the worst was yet to come. The vast prairie grasslands of Kansas, eastern

Colorado and the panhandle of Oklahoma and Texas had been plowed under for vast fields of wheat and as the drought worsened, farmers kept plowing and planting with the eternal hope that every farmer must have, the hope that everything would get better next year – it didn't. Crops didn't grow, the ground cover was lost and huge dust storms whipped across the fields and literally blew the farms away.

My cousin Mildred got married and moved to Kansas. She wrote back telling us how they would hang wet sheets in front of the windows in a futile effort to keep the dirt out of their house. Piles of dust collected along fences and buildings, drifting just like snow, sometimes covering equipment and buildings. In the winter a new type of storm occurred called a "snuster." It was a blizzard of snow and dust.

In 1934 the Yearbook of Agriculture announced:

> "Approximately 35 million acres of formerly cultivated land have essentially been destroyed for crop production . . .100 million acres now in crops have lost all or most of the topsoil; 125 million acres of land now in crops are rapidly losing topsoil."

While we had the "white winds," farther south they had the "black blizzards" as immense dust clouds blackened the sky. In May of 1934 a storm blew Kansas dirt as far as New York City and Washington, D.C.

Sunday April 14, 1935 started as a clear peaceful day in the panhandle until a black cloud appeared on the horizon. It traveled across the country side at 60 miles-per-hour. That day is still remembered by people in the area as "Black Sunday." It was estimated that 850,000,000 tons of topsoil was lost in the southern plains states during 1935 alone and remember, the Dust Bowl lasted nearly a decade.

The entire area became nearly uninhabitable. Unemployment reached 30% and people sought a way out. There were, of course, no interstate highways at that time but the country's major east-west highway, U.S. Highway 66, also known as Route 66, The Main

Street of America, The Mother Road and Will Rodgers' Highway, depending upon the part of the country you lived in, ran right through the middle of the dust bowl and ended up in California. Many people took this route to what they hoped would be a better life.

John Steinbeck, in his famous book The Grapes of Wrath published in 1939, wrote about these people and their plight:

> "And then the dispossessed were drawn west from Kansas, Oklahoma, Texas, New Mexico; from Nevada and Arkansas, families, tribes, dusted out, tractored out. Car loads, caravans, homeless and hungry; twenty thousand and fifty thousand and a hundred thousand and two hundred thousand. They streamed over the mountains, hungry and restless – restless as ants, scurrying to find work to do – to lift, to push, to pick, to cut – anything, any burden to bear, for food. The kids are hungry. We got no place to live. Like ants scurrying for work, for food and most of all for land."

Steinbeck was not exaggerating. There was a mass migration during these years yet if the truth be known, actually most residents of the dust bowl didn't move on; they just carried on. These were the pioneers and their sons and daughters. They were the people who had settled these empty plains and had learned to make do with what God had given them, however meager.

Once again we found ourselves blessed. We weren't alone in our trials but we were luckier than most and one thing was in our favor. Thanks to Mother. We were ahead of the game and already had managed to get the farm refinanced and had gotten the Federal Land Bank Loan.

Trudy and I closed up our little house and moved in with Mom and Dad throughout that winter to save fuel. Unless you face it, you can never understand. I sit here trying to explain it to you, but unless you live it, you can never understand. Some things in life are like that, some good and some bad. We should pray that the bad ones are few and far between.

People who were trying to salvage their farms at this time were behind the power curve. Those who started later had a harder time to get the loans because money became even more scarce. People kind of laughed at us when we got our loan but thanks to Mom's foresight we at least had a chance. My poor Grandfather was an old man by this time. He had helped so many but now time was running out for him and there was little chance that he could put together anything for himself.

The year of 1936, for most of us at the time, seemed to be the very bottom. Corn sold for 10 cents a bushel and then there was the dry weather.

It seemed pure hell. In California, policemen were sent to patrol the borders to keep out "undesirables" who were fleeing the Dust Bowl.

Franklin Roosevelt's second inaugural address in 1937 was a far cry from Hoover's vision of banished poverty just nine years previously. FDR's vision:

> "I see one-third of the nation ill-housed, ill-clad, ill-nourished . . . the test of our progress is not whether we add more to the abundance of those who have much; it is whether we provide enough for those who have too little."

One of the few good things to come from these times was Congress declaring soil erosion "a national menace" and the establishment of the Soil Conservation Service, which began to set the standard for modern farming practices. In addition there was a project called Shelterbelt that initiated a plan to plant trees across the Great Plains from Canada to Texas in an attempt to protect the land.

Closer to home, people continued to hope for a better year ahead and in spite of it all, life went on and things were changing for us here on the farm. The field tractor was beginning to come into Iowa farming. There were a lot of new changes in the farm equipment and a big change occurred when tractors began replacing horses in the Midwest.

A company in Albert City, Iowa made a tractor called the Theiman that had a Model A Ford engine. If you couldn't afford the whole tractor, it was sold without an engine. It was simple enough to take the engine out of your car; they were interchangeable. But one of the biggest changes occurred when Allis Chalmers Implement Company brought out the first row-crop tractor. It wasn't the first tractor; Hart Parr, Oliver, Farmal and John Deere all sold farm tractors but prior to this time the tractors were just big slow moving engines on big steel wheels. They mainly functioned as stationary power sources albeit on wheels and were used primarily to power or move other equipment like the massive thrashing machines etc. They were too big and bulky to be driven through the fields without destroying the crops. Prior to this, only horses and humans could perform this feat.

The Allis Chalmers Model WC was a tricycle type tractor with two small wheels close together in the front so they could pass easily between the corn rows without causing damage to the crops. These new tractors had a steering wheel, clutch and gearshift. There was a hand brake on each rear wheel and a hard metal seat – really just the bare necessities but much more advanced and selling a lot cheaper than the competitor's models.

Allis Chalmers had also formed an alliance with the Goodyear Rubber Company and were really just about the first to promote rubber tires. Seven-hundred dollars would buy you a steel-wheeled Allis Chalmers; rubber wheels would cost you about $200 more.

Most of the tractors sold in this area were sold by Nels Jensen who conducted business out of his farm. However, he needed a shop in town so he partnered with Earl Hickey in Manilla. Earl had a gas station that had evolved from the old livery stable located a block-and-a-half south of the lower bank, on the same block as the state owned liquor store. Nels sat a tractor in the big front office of Earl's station making it an instant show room and created the first tractor dealership.

Nels sold ten or twelve tractors that spring. Harold Neiman and I were the only two who bought rubber-tired tractors. At that time, you bought a tractor, plow and cultivator for about $1,000.[55]

---

[55] Last week, Robinson Implement in Irwin sold a $150,000 tractor to a 70 year-old farmer.

Now, remember, here was a young 'smart' farmer, a new wife and a new son. Our horsepower was getting older and we hadn't raised much of a crop but the idea of replacing horses and the old machinery with new methods of farming was exciting.

Money was tight but Allis Chalmers had a payment deal. They were willing to help you with credit if you could make the down payment. I sold my team of mules. Jack and Art were my high school graduation present from my Dad. He had bought them in Dunlap eight years ago from a family by the name of Hunter. We got $200 for the team and $40 for the harnesses. I needed $250; I don't remember where the other $10 came from but it was a milestone event in my life. I said a sad goodbye to Jack and Art and hello Allis.

We ran the tractor on the two farms almost around the clock in the Spring of 1937. My Cousin Merle Saunders and I changed off operating the new tractor.

We plowed C. A.'s farm first. I had taken a headlight off an old Buick and hung it over the front wheels so I could see where I was going. I also rigged a little light on the back fender so I could see

How many high school seniors these days can boast a team of mules for a graduation present?

258

where I had been and how the plow was operating. The back light was small and had a switch so I could turn it off and on. I kept it off most of the time to save the battery. The tractor itself had no electrical system and no generator or starter; we had to crank it to start it. In order to provide electrical power for the light I placed an

> *". . . it was a milestone event in my life. I said a sad goodbye to Jack and Art and hello Allis."*

old car battery in a little box on the side of the tractor. Every two days we would take the battery into town to charge it.

I took the tractor about midnight and operated it till noon and then Merle would take over. The reason we did it this way was

All the things that changed my life: the big house I moved into with my parents when I was 6 years old, the little house across the road Trudy and I built for our own home, my first son Dean and of course my first tractor.

because I was married and Trudy would be asleep by midnight but more importantly, Merle was single and liked to run around at night.

The tractor made us more independent. At first C. A. and Uncle Chuck had no interest in the tractor and after their ground was plowed, they still had to work it with their horses. We had an old horse disk on our farm. We took off the front end that was used to attach the horses and adapted the rear end to the tractor. We would plow for a night and half-day and then use the other half-day to pull the old horse disk over the plowed field preparing the ground for planting. Dad would then plant corn with his horse drawn planter while we were plowing more ground with the tractor.

The next year Uncle Chuck bought a John Deere.

We were on our way to modernizing the farm but we were also incurring more debt. To make the second payment, I farmed a piece of ground for Nels Jensen. About thirty acres of barley; I thrashed it and hauled the grain into Denison.

I also got one of the Grier boys to drive the tractor and used it to do some field work on other farms. I was trying to get enough

The use of tractors and horses overlapped, this picture of Dean on one of Dad's team horses was taken a year or so after the tractor arrived. Much of the horse drawn equipment was modified to be used with the tractors.

money to make payments and build some equity in our farm by charging $1.00 to plow an acre of land.

It became a never-ending job.

Bear in mind, during these times, there was a mad scramble for any kind of credit or job with a sure paycheck.

Everyone in Iowa was connected to the farmer so all had problems. Here in Manilla, some of the men worked for the WPA at $1.00 a day with wheelbarrows building the terraced playgrounds behind the Manilla School. Some of the people did not have enough to eat and could not work the whole day.

Still, being farmers, we had it better than some. If we could keep our land we would always have something productive to do and something to eat. My Cousin Buzz Saunders graduated from high school and went into Chicago to go to the Coin Electrical School. He wrote back telling us of workers with ten years experience who were jobless and standing in bread lines.

During this time the government was changing as FDR tried to bring us out of the depression. The mortgages to the Reconstruction Finance Corporation (RFC) were transferred to a branch of the Farm Credit Bank called the Production Credit Association (PCA).

A young man from a large family of boys near Irwin by the name of Wilmer Peterson managed to get himself appointed head of the Shelby County Production Credit Association. The PCA took mortgages on all the assets a farmer owned, plus a second mortgage on any real estate. We people with the Reconstruction Finance Corporation (RFC) and Federal Land Bank Loans were forced into PCA and dealing with Wilmer Peterson. I say forced, because no one besides the government was loaning money and the government changed the RFC to the PCA.

Grandfather, being in his 70's and Uncle Chuck just a few years younger than my father, instead of getting a Federal Land Bank Loan, had later gotten a loan with the large insurance company Banker's Life. This is where Wilmer Peterson got involved with Grandfather. When it became impossible to keep this loan current, they formed a coalition with Peterson whereby he would assume ownership of the farm in order to get financing from the Production

Credit Association with the agreement that the Saunders family could regain ownership.

It's my understanding that Peterson took over the Banker's Life loan at $79 per acre. They went into the cattle feeding business together. His brother-in-law, Jay Colburn, got in on the deal by purchasing the livestock.

The first farm, C. A.'s Greeley Stock Farm, later renamed Cumberland Stock Farm, spiraled into bankruptcy. Whether or not it was before C. A. died I honestly don't remember, but by the time Grandfather did die in 1941, the farm had been lost to Peterson by working himself into the partnership. I am sure it was all legal but somehow or another Peterson got his name on the deed and then he sort of forgot his end of the agreement about the Saunders family retaining ownership. Uncle Chuck moved off the farm and into town, and Wilmer's brother, Vern Peterson, moved up from Harlan and into the house that Cumberland built.

Vern proved to be a good neighbor and friend for many years. For many of those years Vern was a bachelor but during a brief hospitalization he met and married his nurse. Lola had, I believe, three daughters and together they raised a wonderful family and were a joy to have for neighbors.

However, as far as the Saunders family was concerned, Wilmer was a person who took personal advantage of his 'government' office. Perhaps he did a lot of good for other people, I don't know, but he was a man whose word was not to be trusted within the Saunders family, a fact that he continued to reinforce up until his death. Years later when my son Doug got out of the Navy and got married he and his wife Patty visited Wilmer, an oral agreement was made that Wilmer would sell one-hundred acres, including the buildings to Doug when he decided the time had come to liquidate. When the time arrived, Wilmer deeded the entire farm to the State Wildlife Commission.

In a newspaper interview about the donated land Wilmer told of remembering how as a young boy he planted the trees on the farm. Unless he was working for my grandfather at the time, that was either proof his memory was gone or an outright lie. Soon all the buildings were bulldozed down, about a week later a man from the State Historical Society visited our farm, he was looking for the "round barn in Greeley Township", it seems grandfather's sale barn was to be designated as a historical site. Why Wilmer was so intent on erasing every mark my grandfather made upon that land has gone to the grave with him.

Grandfather's own words became prophetic. C. A's good friend and former governor of Iowa, Nels Kraschel had written a eulogy in which he said, "He (C. A.) often told me that the damage created by the depression of the '30s was not measured by loss of dollars to the farmers, but the irreparable loss was to the integrity of contract."

The young people, my Cousins Merle, Don and Buzz, lost whatever interest they had in the farm. Don went off to optometry school and then on to medical school, Buzz invented a machine to make archery targets and started a successful archery business ultimately moving it to Columbus, Nebraska. Peterson had taken over another farm east of Manilla and Merle moved there as a renter.

This did not have a lot of effect on Dad and me; again, Mother's foresight to keep the farms separated paid off, except now we were more on our own and not working with the other farm and an

Sister Margaret and husband Grant Halliday.

important part of our extended family was now going their separate ways

Not only were the times changing but our own family had grown and dispersed, too. You will remember that C. A's younger brother Fred died at age 46, leaving a large family. One of his sons, Allen Saunders, was living in Seattle and soon after high school Margaret accompanied Allen's mother, our great-Aunt Ruth out to Seattle. Once there Margaret kept house for Allen in return for her room and board. She also went to school and eventually worked for Allen in his accounting firm. It was during this time that she met and married Grant Halliday, a career Army NCO.

At about the same time the original forty acres of land belonging to Wilma's departed biological parents, John and Florence Ray, was sold. This gave Wilma enough money to go to West Mar College in LeMars, Iowa. She graduated and taught school at Bronson, Iowa where she met her future husband Roy Zimmerman.

Wedding Day portrait of Sister Wilma and husband Roy Zimmerman.

Regardless of how hard the times were, not all farmers lost out during this time. I remember the story of a man by the name of Hanson Pigally, or something like that, who attended all the farm sales. He always wore a greasy black flat top scotch hat and a dirty jacket and if something went real cheap, probably Hanson would buy it. His stipulation was that if he bought grain, they had to leave it in their crib till the first of October. He bought corn for 8-9 cents a bushel. There was no crop raised that year and he sold the corn for a dollar a bushel. He could not read or write but he sure could figure. He did not trust the banks so he always paid cash but he rarely ever needed more than twenty dollars or so.

A few years later he bought a farm. Keith Moore was his attorney, which is the reason I know this story. He managed to buy a farm off of Wilmer Peterson who again had used the PCA to gain the property. Hanson bought the farm on contract with the provision he could pay any amount on it at any time without penalty. When they got all through with the deal, he sat back and said "Well, I think I'll make a payment on my farm." He reached into his pocket and started counting out his money. Suddenly he turned to his wife and said, "There is only $16,000 in this billfold!"

"Well, Honey," she said, "you picked up the wrong billfold."

As foreclosure sales became common, frustrations grew to the point that in the Spring of 1933, Crawford County made the national news when the governor declared martial law after rioting broke out at a sheriff's sale. A group of local farmers went to the sale to protest. Things began to get a bit out of hand and someone got thrown into a horse tank. It might even have been the deputy sheriff, Hugo Willie. I don't remember for sure but I do remember he was from here in Manilla and ran a service station. In any event things went downhill from there and before the protesters thought better of it, the sheriff, I believe his name was Green, had a noose around his neck and was threatened with hanging.

Fortunately, cooler heads prevailed but still having more frustration and anger than common sense and not yet having gained any degree of satisfaction, some of the protestors went into Denison and took over the courthouse. This is when the governor declared martial law and called out the National Guard. Tear gas and smoke bombs were used to clear out the courthouse and machine guns were set up at the four corners of the courthouse lawn. People were getting pretty frustrated and things got pretty rambunctious in this part of the country, especially between here and Sioux City. I think they called it a Farmer's Holiday.

The foreclosure sales finally ended when the protestors got smarter and better organized. They would go to the sales and bid pennies for whatever was being sold and intimidate anyone who wanted to bid more. By law the sale went to the highest bidder, and after paying 50 cents for a horse, for example, they would give it back to the original owner. In one sale $2.29 bought everything.

There were no sheriff's sales on Cumberland Stock Farm No.2 but just by a slim margin. I was having a hard time. The PCA and Wilmer Peterson were riding us hard. I always felt that he had eyes on our farm, too. Many times Wilmer offered to buy it and rent it back to us.

By this time, Dad, Mother, Trudy, our son Dean and I had the promise of a new addition to our family.

Dale Allen Saunders came to live with us on November 5, 1938, another Saunders boy on the farm started by John and Marie in 1903.

Dale was born in Carroll, delivered by Dr. Marks. To pay the medical bills I sold newly-picked corn that fall for 35 cents a bushel and also shelled some corn that we had in the iron crib. We only needed two or three hundred dollars but it was a hell of a job to get it.

I remember the cold blustery November day when Trudy and Dale came home from the hospital to our little one-bedroom house. We had a small room built right off the bedroom intended for use as a bathroom, but we had no running water and no fixtures so we used it as a second bedroom.

Dean was now three-years-old and baby Dale inherited the bassinet. The problem was now Dean always wanted to sleep with his mother. Somewhere we found the money to buy him a new little bed with side rails and little teddy bear decals on the headboard. The side rails were not really necessary because the room was so small it would have taken considerable effort to squeeze a small boy between the bed and the walls. The bed came for Christmas, along with a note from Santa Claus. It told Dean that this was his bed but if Santa came by and saw that he was not sleeping in it, he would take it back to the North Pole!

It worked. We now had two small boys situated in our little house but no indoor plumbing. There was running water across the road from us, both in the barn and in Mom and Dad's house so we carried water from across the road in five-gallon pails and bathed the kids in the kitchen sink after heating it on the wood burning kitchen stove fueled with corn cobs that we picked up out of the pig pens.

While we were in Chicago on our honeymoon, we had gone into Sears Department Store. It was the largest store in the world at that time. We bought the stove for our new little kitchen. I remember instead of the oven being down on the bottom, it was up higher. We bought it because is was like Mother's, made by the same company as hers and Aunt Mille's but a newer more compact model for our small kitchen. It cost us $35 and, of course, had to be ordered and then shipped out to Iowa by train.

Having things to cook on it was another story. We had to scrape to put food on the table but we were still blessed to be farmers and able to grow a lot of our own food.

Prices were working up a little bit and Dad and I were slowly and steadily building up our cattle herd and raising enough hogs to

The summer of 1939 saw two boys, Dale and Dean in our one bedroom honeymoon cottage but it was going to get even more crowded.

pay the bills. Hogs were our cash crop and raising cattle was our profession. We weren't having great success, but we still had our hopes and dreams and things kept looking brighter for the future. In the forties we began to have a few shorthorns to sell but every time anything was for sale, PCA and the farm loans were there first.

There was no money for extras.

Remember I told you that when Trudy and I built our new little house we had taken the old lean-to bedroom off the little house in the valley and made a pair of small brooder houses covered with tar-paper. In order to make ends meet, we then bought a pair of oil-burning brooders and were raising chickens here on the farm. The farm furnished the grain and what we sold was our salary. The small income from the birds and eggs were what we used to feed and clothe our baby boys.

The chickens became the new life-line for the Saunders family. Mother and Dad had their flock of Wyandott Chickens, too. Dad had gone to Grandpa Arnold to borrow money to buy the chickens. Half the pullets went back to Grandpa Arnold that fall in payment along with one of the chicken houses.

We put the chicken house on skids and tried to pull it over to the Arnold's farm with the tractor but after a mile or so the skids pulled out and broke the floor loose but finally we got it over there and settled.

We changed to a high-grade Leghorn flock and furnished hatching eggs to the Carpenter Hatchery in Harlan and the Lake Hatchery in Manning. Later we candled and graded the eggs and sold them to the Safeway grocery store in Denison.

This looked like a pretty good income so in 1941 we built a new double-decked chicken house just to the south of our own house. We started our chicks on the top floor and set our sights on a Leghorn Hybrid flock of 1,000 to 1,200 layers. Soon both decks were full of layers and we built a new brooder house, one for each family. We kept a yearling flock and a pullet flock.

Trudy cleaned and dressed many chickens to sell to a restaurant in Harlan at 25-45 cents a piece. One fall we sold a bit over $100 worth of roosters to Stowe Produce of Harlan, but that market began to fade and before long we bought only sexed pullet chicks. We used our own eggs for replacements, learning that the ideal time to start the chicks was the 21st to the 23rd of April, in order to bring the new flock into egg production before the weather turned cold. The worst thing that could happen was for a flock to go out of production in the winter; then there would be no money coming in. They would still eat up all the feed and it was hard to get them back into production for the hatching season. Besides that, we couldn't possibly eat that many chickens.

Needless to say, though, we did eat a lot of chicken. Fried eggs in the morning, fried chicken at lunch and leftover fried chicken for supper. We ate our chicken any way we wanted as long as it was

My two boys Dean and Dale in front of our "vine covered bungalow" in 1942. The car was a plain black Hudson that I bought used from a priest in Westphalia, Iowa. I don't remember what model year it was but it served us for many years.

fried. To this day Trudy will still order fried chicken when we go out to eat but as for me, enough is enough. I have had my fill.

In 1939 the rains came and the Dust Bowl became a part of American history as the 'amber waves of grain' returned to the Great Plains. Slowly but surely we were still trying to work ourselves out of the midst of a great depression. But unfortunately there was another large dark cloud looming on the horizon.

Chapter 10

FROM HORSES TO BICYCLES TO MODEL A's

February 5, 1989

Not so early this morning, it is cold, eight to ten degrees below zero and a light powder snow. Just another work day on the dairy farm.

Late yesterday afternoon Trudy and I took Doug's pick up to Denison to pick up some plastic water pipe for him. He is having a problem getting enough water through the old underground pipes. The cleaning and repair work is an on going project for 1989.

It's cold and after the warm January, it's hard for people to adjust. Today there are a lot of cancellations of meetings , etc. Thirty-five to fifty years ago we went about our daily work.

Have modern circumstances made us weak or is it that our modern conveniences afford us luxuries, which by definition, are unnecessary and therefore cancelable?

Before we worked more at a subsistence level, doing what was necessary to survive. We will do the same today, doing only what is necessary.

We never really know what we can do until we are tested.

December 7, 1941 was a nice warm Sunday afternoon. Trudy and I had been in Omaha and were driving home. We stopped in Avoca for dinner and as we were walking into the restaurant, a man yelled across the parking lot in a slurred voice, "Hey, Saunders!"

Trudy was embarrassed and asked, "Who's that old drunk?"

George Lipphold wasn't a drunk; he was a fine old fellow who showed Hampshire Hogs at the county fair but his speech was garbled because he had suffered a stroke and only partially recovered. His mouth was deformed and through his paralyzed lips we heard of the Japanese attack on Pearl Harbor.

We hurried home and found my cousin, Merle, sitting on the back porch of Mom and Dad's house; he had his greyhound dog and rifle with him and had just returned from fox hunting out in our pastures. We pulled into our little house and hurried across the road to tell him the news that Pearl Harbor had just been bombed.

Merle never used big words when little ones worked. "By God we're in it now!" There was nothing more to say.

The next day we all huddled around our radios with the rest of America as we listened to another partially paralyzed man declare:

> "Yesterday, December 7, 1941 – a date that will live in infamy – the United States of America was suddenly and deliberately attacked by naval and air forces of the empire of Japan. . . No matter how long it may take us to overcome this premeditated invasion, the American people in their righteous might will win through to absolute victory. . . With confidence in our armed forces – with the unbounding determination of our people – we will gain the inevitable triumph – so help us God. . ."

For years we had placed our hopes in President Roosevelt's hands to guide us out of the depression. Now we prayed he was strong enough to lead us through another world war.

The photo on the opposite page of President Roosevelt delivering his historic address to congress was published around the world. Sitting behind the President, just above his left shoulder is Vice-President Henry A. Wallace, the same man who ate dinner at our house and helped me with my high school Voc Ag corn plot. Beside V-P Wallace sat Speaker of the House Sam Rayburn.

The war had been going on in Europe for some time and although now, with fifty years of hindsight and full knowledge of the outcome, the decision seems clear and simple. It was not so then. The country had its share of distracters. Hell, I had a father-in-law who thought Hitler would kick everybody's butt. That, however, is the beauty of America.

Final.
Edition
Closing Market Prices
★★★★

Vol. 56—No. 59

Reprint with Permission

ST. LOUIS STAR-TIMES

7TH WAR
EXTRA

Monday Evening, December 8, 1941

28 Pages   Price Three Cents

WAR DECLARED

3,000 Casualties In Jap Attack On Hawaii

Congress Acts In 33 Minutes

Jeannette Rankin Only Member Of Either House To Vote 'No' After F. D. R.'s Dramatic Request

WASHINGTON, Dec. 8—(U. P.)—Congressional leaders will take the war resolution to the White House for the President's signature at 1 P. M. today, St. Louis time, the White House announced.

WASHINGTON, Dec. 8.—(U. P.) — Congress today proclaimed existence of a state of war between the United States and the Japanese empire thirty-three minutes after the dramatic moment when President Roosevelt stood before a joint session to pledge that we will triumph—'So help us, God.''

The senate acted first, adopting the resolution by a unanimous roll call vote of 82 to 0, within twenty-one minutes after the President had concluded his address to a joint session of both houses.

'We Will Triumph—So Help Us, God'

Nearly 1,500 Feared Dead

White House Admits Sinking Of One 'Old Battleship' And Destroyer In Pearl Harbor

MANILA, P. I. Dec. 8.—(U. P.)—Press dispatches reported that 100 to 200 troops, many of them American, were killed at inland cockpit when Japanese warplanes raided Iba, on the west coast of the island of Luzon, north of the Olongapo naval base.

WASHINGTON, Dec. 8.—(U. P.)—Casualties on the Hawaiian island of Oahu in yesterday's Japanese air attack will amount to about 3,000, including about 1,500 fatalities, the White House announced today.

The White House confirmed the loss in Pearl Harbor of 'one old battleship'' and a destroyer, which was blown up.

Everyone can voice their views and help shape public opinion but all in all, when challenged, we pull together and everyone does their part.

Soon after Pearl Harbor we got word that the Japanese had sunk two ships, a destroyer and a cruiser in the South China Sea. Leroy Sheffield my school mate, one year behind me, was on the cruiser. He had entered the Navy right out of high school and completed his tour but stayed on in the reserves and was called up. He was our first fatality of the war.

As soon as we entered the war you couldn't buy anything without ration books. You couldn't buy tires but that didn't matter so much because you couldn't buy enough gasoline to wear out your tires and they quit building cars. All factories were turned into production of war goods. Consumer goods became scarce again and prices were frozen, both on what you produced and on what you bought, by the Office of Price Administration. Sometimes there would be a meeting and they would raise the prices slightly.

I registered for the draft, but I had never served before, had an arm that wouldn't straighten out fully, was over the draft age, had two kids and was supporting my Mom and Dad. Besides that, the war effort needed farmers, too. I was classified 4-F.

Everyone, however, contributed to the war effort and women especially stepped up to fill the vacant jobs on the assembly lines, in the factories and on the farms. Rosie the Riveter became the fictitious spokesmodel made to represent women in the war effort and as always Trudy was there to lend a hand too.

Margaret was with her husband Grant on the west coast. They were transferred to Alabama, then Margaret came home when Grant went to Europe. It was a nostalgic reunion and one that was happening all over America, a solder's last visit home before going off to war. Grant landed in France and went to Belgium just in time for the Battle of the Bulge and when the European war ended he went to the Far East. Once again our family was blessed. He came home and he and Margaret ultimately retired in Little Rock, Arkansas.

Here at home there was no money for extras but we were busy and trying to be happy. Many times I was told to quit the battle. Dad and Mom Arnold were convinced I could make more on a rented farm. No doubt they were right, but this was our home and all of my family's lives

Trudy bore an uncanny resemblance to Rosie the Riveter in the
poster above. She was 28 years old when she found the job she fit
best, in agriculture, right here on the farm.

and dreams were invested in the home farm. I kept on working hard to
save the farm my parents began in 1903.

This rare photo is the only one I have with our entire family together. From L-R: Grant Halliday, Margaret Saunders Halliday, John Saunders, Raymond Saunders with son Dale, Marie Saunders and Wilma Ray Saunders Zimmerman with son Wayland.

In late June of 1944 I was 'laying by'[56] a field of corn just north of our little house when my two young sons, Dean and Dale, came running out to the field to get me. "Daddy, Daddy," they shouted breathlessly, "Mother said you and her have to go to Carroll to get our new baby."

---

[56] A farmers term for cultivating a field of corn for the last time.

Grant, Margaret, Dad plus Dean and Dale

"How do you know?" I asked.

"Dr. Annenberg called and told mother to come and get it, and Mother said, 'Please hurry'." Their eyes were big as saucers and conveyed their Mother's urgency.

On June 30, 1944, Craig Raymond Saunders was born. He was a very happy and pleasant nine-pound, ten-ounce fellow. The weather was pleasant that summer and about all he ever wore was his diaper. I remember how brown he became and how white his hair was. The older boys always wanted him to play with them. These were precious moments for us, but we continually struggled to pay the bills.

The Stamps contained in this Book are valid only after the lawful holder of this Book has signed the certificate below, and are void if detached contrary to the Regulations. (A father, mother, or guardian may sign the name of a person under 18.) In case of questions, difficulties, or complaints, consult your local Ration Board.

Certificate of Book Holder

I, the undersigned, do hereby certify that I have observed all the conditions and regulations governing the issuance of this War Ration Book; that the "Description of Book Holder" contained herein is correct; that an application for issuance of this book has been duly made by me or on my behalf; and that the statements contained in said application are true to the best of my knowledge and belief,

Raymond M. Saunders [Book Holder's Own Name]
(Signature of, or on behalf of, Book Holder)

Any person signing on behalf of Book Holder must sign his or her own name below

and indicate relationship to Book Holder

Gertrude E. Saunders wife
(Father, Mother, or Guardian)

☆ U. S. GOVERNMENT PRINTING OFFICE : 1942 16—28651-1   OPA Form No. R-305

UNITED STATES OF AMERICA
War Ration Book One

WARNING

1 Punishments ranging as high as *Ten Years' Imprisonment* or $10,000 Fine, or Both, may be imposed under United States Statutes for violations thereof arising out of infractions of Rationing Orders and Regulations.

2 This book must not be transferred. It must be held and used only by or on behalf of the person to whom it has been issued, and anyone presenting it thereby represents to the Office of Price Administration, an agency of the United States Government, that it is being so held and so used. For any misuse of this book it may be taken from the holder by the Office of Price Administration.

3 In the event either of the departure from the United States of the person to whom this book is issued, or his or her death, the book must be surrendered in accordance with the Regulations.

4 Any person finding a lost book must deliver it promptly to the nearest Ration Board.

OFFICE OF PRICE ADMINISTRATION

No. 308303 -127

FOLD BACK ← FOLD BACK

8# 43 sugar

Certificate of Registrar

This is to Certify that pursuant to the Rationing Orders and Regulations administered by the OFFICE OF PRICE ADMINISTRATION, an agency of the United States Government,

(Name, Address, and Description of person to whom the book is issued:)

Saunders *Raymond* *M.*
(Last name) (First name) (Middle name)

2
(Street No. or P.O. Box No.) (Number or R.F.D.)

Manilla *Shelby* *Iowa*
(City or town) (County) (State)

6 ft. 2 in. 180 lbs. Blue Brown 31 yrs. Sex {Male ☒ /Female}
(Height) (Weight) (Color of eyes) (Color of hair) (Age)

has been issued the attached War Ration Stamps this 7th day of May 1942, upon the basis of an application signed by himself ☐, herself ☐, or on his or her behalf by his or her husband ☐, wife ☒, father ☐, mother ☐, exception ☐. (Check one.)

Alice Jensen (Signature)
(Registrar)

Local Board No. 83 County *Shelby* State *Iowa*

Stamps must not be detached except in the presence of the retailer, his employee, or person authorized by him to make delivery.

22	20

19

O. P. A. Form No. R-305

UNITED STATES OF AMERICA
OFFICE OF PRICE ADMINISTRATION
SUGAR PURCHASE CERTIFICATE

Not Valid Before 7-11-45
Date

DUPLICATE

Serial No. C 34993544

THIS IS TO CERTIFY THAT:

Name: *Raymond M. Saunders* Address:

City: *Manilla* County: *Shelby* State: *Iowa*

is authorized to accept delivery of

Fifty lbs 50 pounds of sugar

pursuant to Rationing Order No. 3 (Sugar Rationing Regulations) of, and at a price not to exceed the maximum price established by, the Office of Price Administration.

Local Rationing Board No. 83

Date 9-11-45

By _____
Signature of issuing officer

County *Shelby* State *Iowa*

Title _____

To Be Retained by Local Rationing Board

Everyone, men, women and children were issued ration books, without one you could not legally buy any commodity. Above is my ration book, front and back, with three stamps remaining plus a permit to buy 50 lbs. of sugar, dated 9/11/43.

The year was 1944, my sister Margaret and her husband Grant were much involved with the war in Europe. My sister Wilma and her husband Roy Zimmerman were on their own farm at Le Mars, Iowa, close to his dad's home farm. We had three young boys on the Saunders' farm. We were making some progress building up our cattle herd. Although still small, we had a good-sized herd of hogs for commercial sale. Dad was doing the majority of the cattle management; I worked with the hogs and did the majority of the farm work. We were farming with an Allis Chalmers W.D. tractor and had a nice flock of leghorn chickens. We had a home, but still were barely able to make expenses.

Dad and Mom gained three grandsons that summer – Craig on the last day in June, Russell Halliday in July, and Wayland Zimmerman in August. Our own 'infantry' had arrived.

During the 1940's we were busy raising our young boys along with putting every affordable dollar into the cattle herd and the farm. We needed machinery plus a whole new concept of farming the Iowa hills was coming into use.

My father planted just the sixth field of contour corn in the country. The first contour lines we laid out were on the very first field my Mother and Father had cleared of hazelbrush and wild oak forty years earlier, the southwest 40 acres of Section Two, Greeley Township.

We had bought an inexpensive attachment for my father's old horse-drawn John Deere 999 planter, called an automatic hill-drop. With the old method of planting, the seeds were dropped by wire, in long rows 40-42 inches apart, straight across the field from fence line to fence line, up and down the hills. When it rained, each crop row channeled the water straight down the hill, taking with it valuable top soil and massive erosion. This new contour method placed the cornrows on the level around the hill parallel to the slope, and with the new attachment, each row formed a small mound making a tiny terraced area to hold the rainwater and the topsoil. A man from the Shelby County Extension Office in charge of the soil conservation service helped us lay out the first contour lines.

The neighbors stood at the fences watching my father. He sat tall in the seat of his little two row planter, leather reins twisted in his big hands, driving his dapple gray team of horses along the marked out contour lines as they curved around our rolling Iowa hills. They watched and listened to the click, click, click of the planter counting out two kernels of corn every eighteen inches.

I remember my Dad coming into the house for dinner. Dinner was the noon meal on the farm, supper was the evening meal after the chores were done and lunch was a ritual all its own.

Lunch was around four in the afternoon and more often than not, brought to the field by Trudy or the boys. It consisted of Mason jars full of cold iced tea or hot coffee thick with cream and sugar. There were sandwiches, leftover fried chicken from dinner and Trudy always had fresh baked cookies or cake. As you sat there with your family around you in the shade of a wagon smelling the newly turned soil or the freshly mown clover, virtually a picnic every day at work, what better affirmation could there be that you were doing God's work? We didn't need expensive vacations; besides, there isn't enough money in the world to buy this.

Anyway, back to dinner that spring day, Dad came into the house at noon and told Mom, "You know, I planted more corn this morning than I ever have in my life." This was all new to him and that afternoon he would have to go out and plant all the short rows and fill in the blank spots that the contour lines created. But this was all okay because the best part, the part that really sold Dad on the project, was that this was the easiest day's work his horses had ever done, not having to pull him and the planter straight up the hills.

When the corn came up, everyone looked at it and wondered how we were going to pick it. It was harder, no question about it, but contour farming was the future even though it took several years for people to accept this new conservation method. I feel good that we were among the very first.

The next year we won the corn production contest. Today, while cleaning, Trudy came upon a Certificate of Corn Production Achievement awarded to us in 1946 for a yield of 143.55 bushels per acre, this crop was planted in the northeast part of Dad's original farm. In 1948 we produced 170.42 bushels per acre.

These contests were conducted on 10-acre plots and did not necessarily reflect what was happening on the entire farm but we

Blessed

Dean, Dale and Craig above. Opposite is Craig and Russell on their first birthdays.

Sister Wilma and Wayland opposite and Margaret and Russel above

283

continued to implement all the conservation measures we could. It was especially important for us because our farm was kind of hilly. 'Straight row' farmers could produce slightly more corn on their 10 acres but as a man from the District Soil Conservation office said, "If you take care of the soil, it will take care of you."

When I started picking corn by hand for my dad, fifty bushels per acre yield was good. Very few fields yielded over sixty bushels. What progress from 1927 when Henry Wallace gave me a half-bushel of hybrid seed corn to use in my Vocational Agriculture plot.

It was during World War II that I bought our first mechanical corn picker. I had to buy it on the black market. It was out in a guy's pasture; he was dealing in used farm equipment. I paid $800 for a used one, which was a lot of money at that time. If you could find a new one and if you could get a permit to buy it, it would cost you about $600.

Austin Saunders had a mechanical picker that was pulled behind a team of horses and picked one row at a time. Ours was an Allis Chalmers picker that attached to our tractor and picked two rows at a time.

To get our first elevator, we traded Nels Jensen one of our boars, about a 150 pounder, for an old wooden elevator with metal chains. It was attached to his corncrib and in pretty bad shape. Dad and I had to take it off his corncrib and disassemble it to bring it home. Once home, we had to totally rebuild it.

Frank Perry helped me get an old transmission out of a wrecked Buick and we put a pulley on it that was attached by a long belt to the flywheel of our tractor. This powered the elevator to unload the corn into the crib. Now, instead of scooping corn up over the side of the crib, we only had to scoop it into the elevator.

Life was getting easier.

"Lunch was around 4 in the afternoon . . .
As you sat there with your family . . .
   Smelling the newly turned soil
      Of the freshly mown clover . . .

what better affirmation could there be
that you were doing God's work?"

Saunders Win Contour Honors

Manilla Farmer, Son Take Shelby Contest

Special to The Nonpareil.

HARLAN—John Saunders and son, Ray of Manilla, won the 1948 Shelby county 10-acre contour corn contest with a yield of 170.42 bushels, it was announced here Wednesday night.

C. W. McManamy, Nonpareil-KSWI farm director, presented the Saunders' a $25 savings bond as first prize in the contest sponsored by the Harlan Kiwanis club and Shelby soils commissioners.

The Manilla entry topped 21 others and came within 12.6 bushels of equalling the all-time high of 183 bushels made in 1946.

Jack Graves and Frank Arnold, both of Harlan, won second and third respectively in this year's contour event. Graves, a Center township farmer, had a yield of 164.22 bushels, while Arnold, also of Center township, had a 161.16 bushels yield.

Old Bluegrass Pasture

The Saunders' corn was raised on land broken out of old bluegrass pasture. The soil was Monona silt loam with a slope of 16-18 per cent. Graves and Arnold both raised their corn on Marshall silt loam.

Average yield for the 21 entries in the contour test was 144.45 bushels. Seven of the fields made over 150 bushels per acre and 20 of the 21 were over 125 bushels.

Harlan Kiwanis club presented the second award in the contour test, $15 cash, with third prize of 25 pounds of certified brome grass seed furnished by the Shelby conservation district.

Unloading corn into the crib by scoop shovel, the corn was thrown up over the side of the crib through an open panel in the roof. This was the usual way until we purchased the elevator. The small narrow wagon was pulled through the field by a team of horses. The side-boards on the right side are higher than the left, this kept me from over throwing the ears of corn, It was a Sunday afternoon but why I am still dressed in Sunday clothes is a mystery but written on the back is the phrase **"just showing off"**.

February 5, 1989

A cold Sunday morning, ten degrees below zero at 5:10 in the morning. Quite a few public meetings and church services have been canceled. Haven't heard about the Presbyterian Church in Manilla as of yet.

During the late summer or early fall of 1945, the war was winding down. Germany had surrendered May 7, 1945. May 8th was declared V-E (victory in Europe) day and there were massive celebrations and dancing in the streets. We were greatly relieved because Grant was still in Europe. The war, however, was still raging against the Japanese and families here at home were still being notified that they had lost their sons on some far off Pacific island.

We were both shocked and somewhat bewildered when on August 6, 1945 we heard of the bombing of Hiroshima. Three days later, on August 9th we heard of the bombing of Nagasaki. These were just names to us; television had not yet brought war into our living rooms. We had heard rumors of the rush to develop the A-bomb but I don't think any of us fully understood the implications of the Nuclear Age that had just arrived.

Don't get me wrong. Overall we thought it was a good thing. In fact, despite the personal connection, we were, I think for the most part, happy that Harry Truman had replaced Henry Wallace as Roosevelt's Vice President. In our eyes Wallace wouldn't have dropped the bomb and thereby would have extended the war, causing even more death and destruction on both sides. Would that have been better in the long run? Who knows? That's a question for the ages.

Truman, in fact, had been Roosevelt's Vice-President only a few weeks, 82 days to be exact, when on April 12, 1945 he was suddenly summoned to the White House and told that the President had died suddenly of a massive cerebral hemorrhage. Historians tell us when he entered the White House and was greeted by Eleanor Roosevelt, he asked, "What can I do to help?"

Eleanor's response to Truman was, "No, Mr. President. It is now what can we do for you?"

Harry Truman, a man who had started his career as a Missouri farmer before going off to WW I, was sixty years old when be became the 33rd President of the United States and thereby asked to make some of the most crucial and perhaps controversial decisions in history. He was quoted as saying, "I felt like the moon, the stars and all the planets had fallen on me."

The war in Europe had reached its final stage and the war against Japan was doing the same. The Japanese had refused repeated pleas for surrender, in part due to the fact that they believed their emperor to be an infallible god. Faced with the military invasion of the Japanese homeland and with the memories of the fierce battles to rid the Pacific Islands of the entrenched Japanese forces, Truman gave the order to drop the bomb. On August 6, 1945 he announced:

> "The Japanese began the war from the air at Pearl Harbor. They have been repaid many fold."

On August 9th, after Nagasaki, Truman stated:

> "Having found the bomb we have used it. We have used it against those who attacked us without warning at Pearl Harbor, against those who have starved and beaten and executed American prisoners of war, against those who have abandoned all pretense of obeying international laws of warfare. We have used it in order to shorten the agony of war, in order to save the lives of thousands and thousands of young Americans."

Much has been made over the decision to drop the bombs and it indeed was another one of those singular events that changed the world but the fact of the matter is that there was more destruction and more loss of life from the blanket fire bombings our Air Force was conducting over Japanese cities than was caused by the two atomic bombs.

On August 15, 1945 the Japanese surrendered. On August 29th the U.S.S. Missouri[57] steamed into Tokyo Harbor. Aboard this great battleship and with the entire world glued to their radios, the Japanese Foreign Minister signed the formal documents and surrendered to General Douglas MacArthur. The entire ceremony ending the greatest war in history took only 23 minutes.

There was not as much celebration on V-J (Victory in Japan) day as there was earlier on V-E day but we did celebrate the end of the war to end all wars. With the war over and rationing gone, people were more free to travel around the country and although it took us a couple of years to get back on track it now seemed like a good time for Dad and Mother to finally take a much-deserved vacation. Before that time if they got into the county seat or to Omaha once a year, it was a major achievement. They booked passage on the train to North Dakota. They were going to visit my two Uncles, John and August Schoenig and their families, on their original homestead site north of Minot near the Canadian border.

This was a well-earned trip and we were so happy they were able to go. On their return trip home, however, Mother fell on the railroad station platform in Mitchell, South Dakota. The railroad officials took her to the hospital and found that she had broken her right hip. I wanted to move her to Sioux Falls and have a doctor friend that I knew through the cattle business take care of her but the railroad doctor persuaded us to leave her in Mitchell. The railroad paid the doctor bills and we paid the hospital bills.

We didn't expect anyone to take care of us, either the railroad or the government. We simply accepted our responsibilities and did our best to meet them. Were we wrong? By today's standards the

---

[57] When Roosevelt was still alive the ceremony had been originally planned to occur aboard the U.S.S. New Jersey, ultimately however it was changed by Truman to honor his native state. Competition between the two battleships had always been fierce. They were two of only six Iowa Class battleships ever built. Plans called for the ships to be 887 feet long but The New Jersey was built in the Philadelphia Naval Ship Yards on the Delaware River, a lot of the shipbuilders that lived on the other side of the river in New Jersey. As a result they built it a few inches longer so that the U.S.S. New Jersey would carry the distinction as the largest battleship ever built, a fete that was accomplished in only 5 short months.

government, through Medicare, would pay the bills and the railroad would be held liable to the point that we could have paid off the farm several times over. Perhaps we should have sued. Poor Mother stayed in the hospital until next March. The doctor used sand bags and wanted it to heal itself. They did not pin it. When he released her, we brought her home by ambulance, just before the big Sioux City cattle sale, March 4, 1947.

In May she was still unable to walk and we took her to the Carroll hospital for an X-Ray. It showed no healing. In a day or two I was in town and was talking to our vet, Dr. Merrick. He told me of a Dr. O'Donahue, an orthopedic surgeon, whose dogs he had treated. I talked to Dr. Hennessey who made the arrangements and we transferred Mother to Sioux City. The next Monday morning Dr. O'Donahue operated and placed a bone graft from her pelvis to her hip bone and from that point on Mother began to improve rapidly

---

> *"I guess it just never occurred to us to blame someone else for our problems. . ."*

Over one full year after the fall, we finally had her back on her feet and walking. She eventually walked without a cane. Needless to say, our time was well occupied caring for Mother but it was a noble cause. I guess it just never occurred to us to blame someone else for our problems and we were just thankful to have her back with us.

During my mother's rehabilitation, on November 28, 1948, another baby boy was born into our family. Douglas Lee Saunders was born at the Carroll Hospital. Doug was named after one of our war heroes, General Douglas MacArthur, commander of the U.S. Allied Forces in the Pacific during WWII.

Four boys!

Trudy was still a little groggy when she first heard the news that her much wanted girl was a boy. "God knew we had a little house and not much room for a girl so he sent me another boy."

I think God in all his wisdom knew even more. Doug is now a hard working-farmer, farming the land his grandfather tamed and raising his family in the big house that Mom and Dad built. This has allowed Trudy and me to live out our years on this same land we all worked so hard for, all the while being surrounded by our family. For this I am profoundly grateful, eternally indebted and blessed beyond words. But before we could get to this point it would take a lot more blood, sweat and tears.

I have included a letter Trudy's mother wrote the day after Doug's birth. It is significant because it reminds us of an important perspective. Nearly all the people that knew Grandma Arnold are now either dead or only knew her during her final declining years. Often we see pictures and think of these distant relatives who have gone before us as more or less historical figures. If we did not really know them, we fall into the trap of thinking of them as little more than figures, names and dates. It is vitally important however to remember, as this letter illustrates, that they were human beings who cared and loved, who cried and laughed just as deeply as you and I do today. Someday someone will be looking at pictures of all of us. We should all therefore strive to live our lives to preserve our humanity so there is no doubt in anyone's minds as to whom and what we were.

Raising a family of four boys in a little one-bedroom house was no easy task but no one could have done it better than those boys' mother. No indoor plumbing and no running water. Trudy says, "When I think about how much all the girls raising a family have now, I can't believe I lived through it."

We bought a davenport for the living room. It was the kind we could pull out and make into a bed. That's where Trudy and I slept. The two big boys were in the bedroom with the double bed and the two little ones in the 'bathroom.'

We dug a basement under the house and put in a furnace. On the north side of the basement we built a coal bin that could be filled from the outside. We then partitioned it off making one big bin for corncobs to burn and a much smaller one for when we could afford coal.

Monday morning:-

Darling Twidle:-

You know what?!

I'm proud of you.

Am coming to see you one of these days but will give you a chance to rest up a little first.

I stayed to pretty close to the telephone all day yesterday except about one hour when I went to church and prayed for you and the baby. I am so thankful that you have such a nice baby and Ray said you were fine too. He said he would bring Craig in either

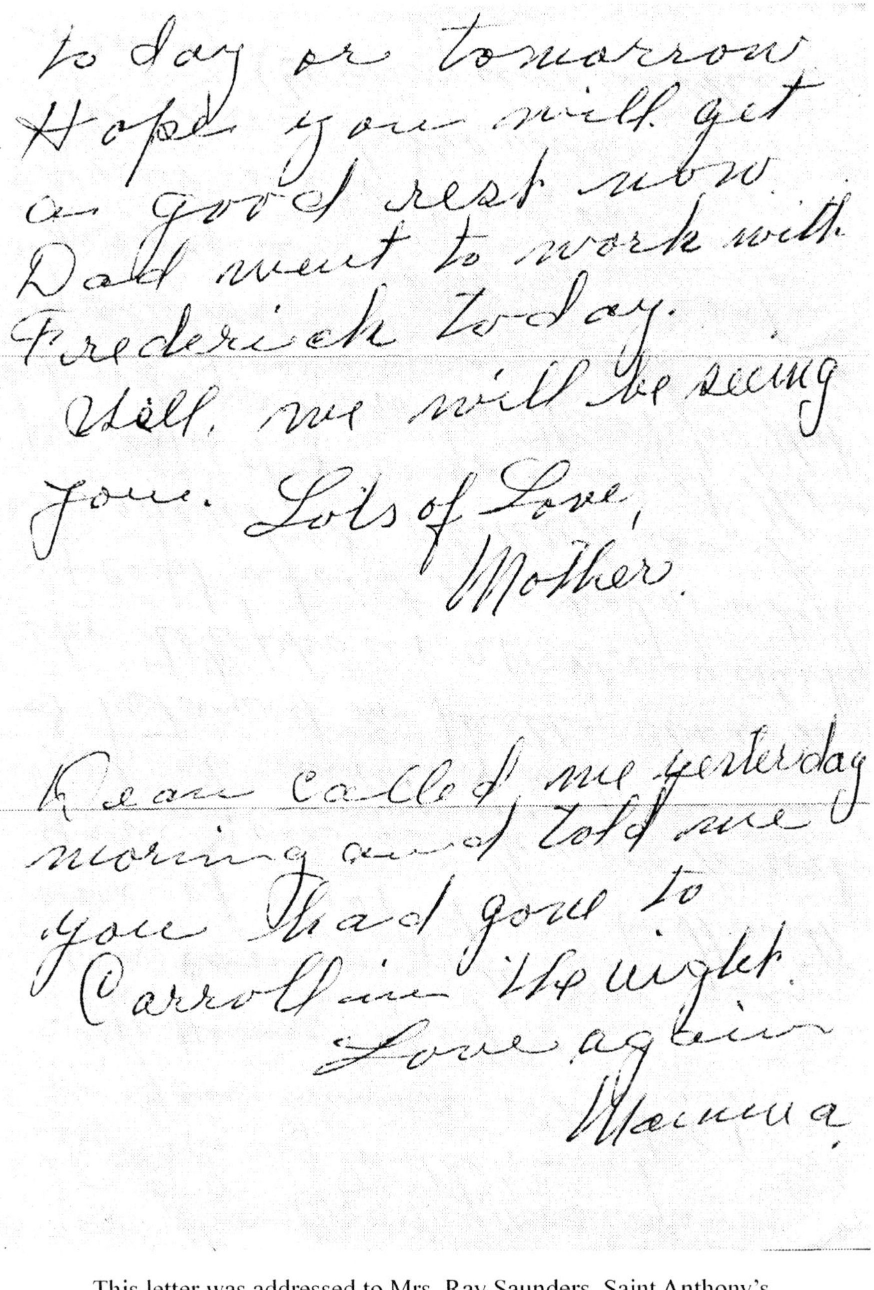

to day or tomorrow.
Hope you will get
a good rest now.
Dad went to work with
Frederick to day.
Well, we will be seeing
you. Lots of Love,
Mother.

Dean called me yesterday
morning and told me
you had gone to
Carroll in the night.
Love again
Mamma

This letter was addressed to Mrs. Ray Saunders, Saint Anthony's Hospital Carroll, Iowa, It's 3 cent stamp was postmarked November 29,1948.

Grandma Gertrude Arnold bringing a birthday cake for one of the boys.

We laid pipe and brought running water up from the chicken house to our house. We then bought a used water pump and water heater and hooked up the sink. We still didn't have an indoor bathroom but we hooked up a garden hose with a shower head and hung it up over a beam in the basement so we could take a shower. We also had some old pipe left over from the depot. We ran that out to an old barrel that we had cut holes in and used that as our septic tank.

Electricity was another problem – we didn't have any. When Mom and Dad's new house was built in 1917-18 it was wired for electricity. Manilla had just three or four years earlier passed a $20,000 bond to build the Manilla Light and Power Company but there was no source from town. Grandfather had built his house about fifteen years earlier and had not wired it but he had electricity because the generator in Manilla also sent current to Defiance and Irwin and the power lines ran only a short distance from his house. In those days you had to pay to run the wires from the power line to your house and for Grandfather it was only a short distance so he wired his house and enjoyed electric lights.

Mom and Dad's original plans were to put a small gas generator in the basement. There were quite a few farm light plants (generators) around the country. They were used to charge large batteries also stored in the basement. A lot of people would run these generators every day by putting in just enough gas to let it run just long enough to charge the batteries. If you had company that night, you put in more gas. Delco Light was one of the companies that supplied these systems.

We used kerosene lamps before that. First they were those little wick-type and then the Aladdin-type lamp. They worked with a mantel instead of a wick. We never had a gasoline lamp nor did we use gasoline lanterns. I am not exactly sure why, Trudy's parents used them. We did use a lantern at the barn. We would carry it out and hang it on a nail wherever we needed the light. The lantern burned a mixture of air and gas, not liquid like a lamp. Most all of them had reflectors behind them to reflect the light out into the room.

I can't tell you exactly what the year was but we sold some cattle or hogs and had some extra money so I invested it in a wind generator or wind charger as we called them then. I got the dealership for Windcharger. This was a wind generator not unlike the ones we see today as a source of alternative energy. The system cost around $500 but I got a pretty good discount by signing a contract to be a distributor, although I never sold one. A lot of people had little wind chargers on their house or garage in those days but most were for a little six-volt battery to power their radio or perhaps one weak light.

This Windcharger was a 32-volt generator that had sixteen lead and zinc batteries in the basement. These batteries were attached to the generator atop a sixty foot windmill tower. We found a used tower near Dallas Center. We took it apart, brought it home in pieces and reconstructed it behind the garage. We put it together lying down and painted it with aluminum paint. We then poured cement anchors in the exact position the tower would stand and fastened the south two legs of the tower on a big hinge with a single bolt to the two southern anchors. We then made a big A frame with a couple telephone poles and set that up north of where we wanted the tower. Next we ran a rope from the top of the reclining tower up over the A frame, (we had to have the A frame to get the rope off the ground) to a tractor. Slowly, Trudy drove the tractor forward. It wasn't very heavy and as soon as we got it started it was no problem to pull it up. All we had to do then was balance it just right and get the northern legs fastened to the ground.

The next step was to put what people call a sky-hook on the platform at the top of the tower. It stuck up about eight feet over the platform. We ran a rope over the sky hook and tied it onto the generator as it sat on the ground. This rope ran through a couple of pulleys before it was fastened to the tractor. We also had to have a second rope to hold the first rope away from the tower. Trudy again drove the tractor and slowly pulled the generator to the top of the sixty-foot tower. I was up on the tower and the generator was already above the platform. We only had a little bit more to go; we were using a four-rope block and tackle. I remember when we got it up there it had to be bolted on to a turntable with three bolts but Trudy's foot slipped on the clutch and the resulting lurch of the tractor broke the rope. I had on big heavy gloves and quickly reached over and held the ropes as the generator hit the platform. There was only a small clearance. I told Dad we had to finish it now because I would be too scared to come back up on top of the tower.

Dad and Trudy spliced the rope and we got it back up and secured. The generator had three blades that had to be attached and balanced. It looked just like a three-blade airplane propeller. The system worked pretty well and we used it quite a while. The thing about 32-volts, you had to have heavy wire as well as special light bulbs for 32-volts. We also had to be careful not to try to light everything up at once. Old Mr. Potter in Harlan sold us the wire and he guided me on how to wire the barn. The house, you recall, was wired when it was built. We had to have three wires, one of which was a ground wire. Mr. Potter didn't want more than three lights on a circuit so as to not pull the batteries too hard. One other thing he wanted was all the connections stripped, twisted and soldered then taped over with electrician's tape. A fellow by the name of Clifford Nobel from down by Defiance helped wire the barn. We got aquatinted with him because Dad was a director of the country school and Clifford had married the schoolteacher.

After we got lined up and knew what we were doing it went pretty well. We got nearly to the end of the job and that afternoon we rigged it up so Mother and Dad had electricity. They had electric light a couple nights before the rest of us. I remember looking across the road and seeing Mother's house being lit up. She was so proud.

We also brought electricity to our little house at the same time and being at the end of the line our electrical supply was a little erratic, to say the least. If the wind didn't blow, the lights didn't work. If you had the lights on and it was real windy the lights would brighten up because you had both the battery and charge. If the wind blew too hard the generator had to be turned off for fear the blades would fly off, which they did on occasion[58], and we were out of lights again. I remember we were always careful to keep lights turned off when we weren't using them so as not to waste the batteries. We finally backed the Windcharger up with a little gas generator that we got for nothing. All that did was charge a battery but couldn't put out enough to light the house.

Several years later, sometime in the early fifties when the Harlan REC (Rural Electrical Co-op) finely extended their lines way up to the county line we made up our mind that we should pay to get the line to the house. A farmer northeast of Des Moines bought the Windcharger from us and we were out of the energy business.

This made it a lot easier raising the boys but by the time Doug was four-years- old, he had all the childhood illnesses and problems and some to spare. One winter about Christmas time, he caught

---

[58] "The wind sure blew today, broke the blades off the Wind Charger, I sure worried for fear the wind would break the cottonwood tree north west of the house and they would strike the house."
Mother's diary dated March 24, 1949.

Douglas Lee and the Black Measles.

a cold and by Easter he had the flu, chicken pox, pneumonia, whooping cough and the measles. One night at about one o'clock, Dr. Hennessey made a house call. By that time the measles had hemorrhaged under his skin. I remember the Doctor's remarks to my little sick three year old, "Son, if anyone ever says black measles to you, you tell them you had them." It reminded me of my bout with the Spanish flu and pneumonia.

Doug was a very sick little boy but his mother nursed and loved him back to health in a small little home, all the time caring for three other small boys.

Now that we had four boys, our little home did not impress my mother and father-in-law as they kindly told me. Grandma Arnold was not very happy with me. She was a wonderful lady, a preacher's granddaughter and all, but sometimes it seemed that she just looked for something to worry about.

Perhaps I am wrong to say that she didn't like me but I know in my heart that it would have made things a whole lot better, at least in her eyes, if I had been a good Lutheran boy.

Our family attended the First Presbyterian Church in Manilla and Sunday morning services would get out a little after noon. This caused us some problems as Sunday was always a day for big family dinners at the Arnolds' house. They all attended the Lutheran Church in Denison, which got out a half-hour earlier. This

The entire Arnold family gathered for Sunday dinner, this time at the Saunders' house. From L-R. Trudy's father Gus Arnold, Bob Arnold holding their oldest daughter Dorothy with wife Garnet looking over his shoulder, Ray Saunders with Trudy's mother Gertrude partially obscured next to Anna Marie Rabe and husband Fred. In front of Fred are the children Dean and Dale Saunders and Arnold Rabe. Trudy apparently was taking the picture.

meant that everyone had usually started eating dinner by the time we got there. One Sunday we came at our usual time after church but this time we had brought the main course. Naturally it was fried chicken. Everyone was waiting for us. Dean walked in, saw that they had not started eating yet and blurted out, "A-hah, we got you this time. We have the meat."

They didn't catch on right away, or at least didn't let on, but after that day they always waited for us before starting Sunday dinner.

Be that as it may, Grandma Arnold's concerns perhaps were not unfounded. Grandpa Arnold had their farm paid for and for one thing, they didn't like our debt. Nor did they like the idea that their daughter had a big family in a little house. We had four children in a one-bedroom house with no bathroom. They wanted us to change homes with my parents. No doubt they were one-hundred percent correct but I never mentioned it to my mother and father. How could I? They had worked all their lives to build their home.

At one point we laid a cement foundation for an additional bedroom to the little house, but it never materialized. Too many things came up and took all the possible income.

The cattle herd was doing fairly well, but not a lot of income. We were keeping all the females and were trying our best to bring back the Saunders' Shorthorns.

In February 1948, we showed the champion bull at the Omaha Spring Consignment sale. The champion was sold for $1,250 to Carahan Brothers of Elkton, Colorado. The Carahan herd had been started years earlier using seed stock from C. A. Saunders and Son's Cumberland Stock Farm.

Trudy had driven down for the show and the sale and the evening of the Cattleman's Banquet, our two oldest boys accepted the Championship Trophy. This made four generations of Saunders in the Shorthorn arena.

March of the same year, we again had the show champion and top sale price at the Tri-State Show and Sale in Sioux City, Iowa.

Again in April we had three young bulls entered into the Sioux Falls, South Dakota show. One of our bulls won his class and was in contention for top honors. I'll always feel that the top sales officials began to think enough was enough for the Saunders Shorthorns and they wanted to give it to someone else. Our calf was young; he was good enough to be champion but he didn't win. He did end up being the second highest selling bull of the show.

That fall at the Southwest Iowa Sale at Red Oak, Iowa, we slipped in and won the top prize, Grand Champion bull. This bull went to the Bellows Brothers in Granger, Missouri. Their father, George Bellows, was also a customer of my grandfather C. A. Saunders.

Three champions in one year, but it had all started about three years earlier. I don't remember exactly the blood line of cattle we had at that time but we needed a good bull rather badly. It was understood that when I went to the Sioux City sale that year, if I could get one, I would.

There was a bull in one of the younger classes from a fellow by the name of Greg. He was a pretty good bull and I bought him for $300. But there was a second bull, his name was Don Hill Ransom.

Win Top Honors At Shorthorn Show

John R. Saunders and son, Ray, showed the grand champion Shorthorn bull at Omaha February 17.

The bull, Cumberland Ransom 4th, was raised by the Saunders'. The champion was purchased by Carahan Bros. of Elkton, Colo., whose carload of Shorthorn fat cattle were judged the best at the 1947 International Livestock show.

This was the 33rd annual Shorthorn show and sale, which has now grown to be the largest sale in the United States. Prize cattle from seven states were shown on February 17 with the sale being held on February 18. The cattle were sold to buyers from 11 states, the largest shipment, 32, going to a California ranch.

On the evening of February 18, Mr. and Mrs. Ray Saunders and sons, Dale, Dean and Craig, attended the Shorthorn breeders banquet at the Rome hotel in Omaha, where the boys accepted the plaque presented by the Knights of Ak-Sar-Ben for achievement in agriculture. The boys represent the fourth generation of Saunders' in the Shorthorn business. .

IOWAN EYES 1948 CORN KING TITLE

Shelby Countian's Yield Hits 180 Bushels; Best on Contour 170 Bushels.

Harlan, Iowa, Nov. 13. (Special)—Shelby county corn yield entrants foresaw the possibility of another national corn king from Shelby county Wednesday night when Forrest Adams of Kirkman was announced as the winner of the county straight row 10-acre corn yield contest with a yield of 180.38 bushels per acre. Adams' yield topped the 27 entries in the 1948 contest sponsored by the Shelby county Farm Bureau.

At the same time John and Ray Saunders of Greeley township were disclosed as winners of the Shelby county contour corn yield contest at the announcement dinner.

The Saunders yield was 170.42 bushels per acre to top the 21 entries in the contest sponsored by the Shelby county soils district and the Harlan Kiwanis club. In winning the contest they topped all previous contour corn yields in Shelby county and came within 12.6 bushels of equalling the all-time high of 183.0 bushels made in 1946.

The Saunders' winning entry in the contest was made with a Pfister hybrid planted on land broken out of old bluegrass pasture. The soil was Monona silt loam with a slope of 16-18 per cent. This was the Saunders family's first time in topping the county contest.

1948 may have been our best year ever on Cumberland Stock Farm No.2. We had four boys, three Grand Champion Shorthorns and the top contour corn yield in the county.

Don Hill Ransom, "Sire Supreme" and father of the fourth generation of Saunders Shorthorns.

He only placed third in his class but he came from a good breeding line. Both his Mother and Dad were sired by the same champion bull in Perth, Scotland. His big problem was that he was a bit long-bodied but I studied his pedigree and I wanted him. The bid was run up to $700 and they could get no more. I bid $720.

There I was. Now I had two bulls and no money except for the three head of cattle I had brought to the sale. I went to the sale manager and asked if there was any way I could resell the first one. He thought a short time and said he didn't see why not. After the sale the Auctioneer called the crowd to order and announced that Ray Saunders was here and that he had bought two bulls and he was going to offer one for sale. He sold that bull for me for $80 more than I paid for it.

I came home and told Dad that I had bought a herd bull. "Did you buy that Ransom bull?" he asked. "That is the one I would have bought." Dad knew the cattle business and was a good teacher. Don Hill Ransom was the sire of our three new champions.

John Saunders and Son Shorthorns were alive and well on Cumberland Stock Farm No. 2 but there was still not enough money coming in. There were more expenses than ever on the farm machinery and automobiles were now a necessary expense. There was just not enough income for any surplus and my young family needed so much more than we could gather up. The war was over, prices were on the decline, we were producing but the expenses continuously loomed over us.

One of the things that keep a parent going, however, is the fact they always wish for and work hard to make a better life for their children. Indeed, this has always been part of America. In America we are not limited by family, title or class. We can always dream of a better life for our children. This is instinct for good parents and we were working hard for this American dream on Cumberland Stock Farm No. 2. We were making progress but sometimes the steps of progress are small and slow.

We have talked about the typical country schoolhouse dotted every two miles across the countryside with its pot-belly stove and all eight elementary grades crammed into its one small classroom. This was the most efficient way to educate the people as I was growing up but as time progressed and when attendance dropped below five students per school, one by one these schools were closed.

Because of this our two older boys were transferred out of the country school into the Manilla School. Instead of riding horses like my sisters and I, they rode bicycles and left them at Uncle Chuck's house. We bought the bikes in Sioux City when we were at a cattle sale, along with some yellow rain slickers. Sometimes progress comes in very small steps.

When our son Craig was ready for school, I believe the year was 1949, Dean was fourteen-years-old and capable of driving. Dean had learned to operate a tractor not too long after he learned to walk, so we bought him a Model A Ford to drive to school. We bought the car from my sister Wilma's brother-in-law, Nobel Zimmerman. I don't remember what we paid him, though it seemed like a lot at the time, but the car was in good shape. Nobel and his friend had overhauled it and driven it to California and back.

Dean was fourteen-years-old and the car was twenty. At that time in Iowa a student could get a special school driver's permit, good

Douglas Lee and Craig Raymond Saunders

to drive to and from school only. He passed his test, got the permit and was given specific instructions not to drive up Main Street. He was to go only up the side street one block south. Furthermore, he was instructed to go directly to Uncle Chuck's house and park. He was not to drive around town. He was to leave it parked and always come home on the same route immediately after school and most importantly, give no rides except to his brothers.

In a few short years we had gone from horses to bicycles to a Model A. In looking back, this was an awesome responsibility to put in the hands of a fourteen-year-old. However, these were not ordinary boys, these were farm boys. Dean had already successfully learned to drive a tractor and operate farm equipment and he had been responsible for the care and well-being of livestock. When a father and son work together daily, side-by-side on the farm, responsibility and mutual trust comes early and comes easily. Dean got along fine. Oh sure, there was the one time that he took a little detour and somehow drove off the road, down a bank and through Ed Theobald's fence, but that was a cheap lesson – as well as a great adventure. It just didn't seem so at the time.

Later, after Doug started Kindergarten for half-days, Dean would drive him home at lunch time. The other boys would come, too, and Trudy would have their lunch waiting for them. Then it was back into the Model A and back to school with a home cooked meal under their belts for the rest of the school day. They were great boys. They paid attention and did what was expected of them. A few years later, the school buses were added and the boys were able to board right here at the farm.

Of course that, like everything else on the farm, depended upon the weather. We lived on one of the poorest roads in the county. On

A prize cow and calf with Dean, Dale and Craig.

the good days it was surfaced with dust; on the bad days, mud. Our road at that time was a simple dirt road with no grading. When it rained or snowed, it became impassable. The school bus wouldn't attempt it and we would have to leave our car at 'the corner'.

'The corner' was just a little over a half-mile north, up over 'the big hill'. Both were important landmarks in our lives. 'The corner' was the intersection that marked the Crawford county line with its surfaced roads. 'The big hill' was the obstacle situated between our home and 'the corner'. Whether we were coming or going we had to go up and over 'the big hill'. And so, ladies and gentlemen, 'the big hill' is the reason when my boys tell you they walked to school in mud and snow, uphill both ways, you better believe them!

In bad weather we would leave our car parked at 'the corner' and walk the half mile of mud up over 'the big hill' to home. For important events when the forecast was bad, we would park our car at 'the corner' in anticipation. If Trudy and the boys had somewhere to go, they would walk that first half-mile or I would drive them to 'the corner' on the tractor.

Going to church or the in-laws for Sunday dinner became a special effort, with my wife and boys sitting on the fenders and hanging off the back end of the tractor. Not only did I have to keep it from slipping and sliding on the narrow path between the ditches, I also had to drive with just enough speed to get through the mud and up over 'the big hill' but slow enough not to throw mud up off the wheels and into the Sunday casserole. This was especially important for the first 100 yards or so of the trip when the tractor wheels were caked with manure from the barnyard! If the road was impassable with the tractor, there were always the horses.

During this time, our County Supervisor, Mr. Tom Barrett of Irwin, came to me with a plan. He explained how he thought we could get our road graded and surfaced. Barrett said to do it quietly so there would be no competition. "If you take a petition to the township trustees, they will have to take it to the Board of Supervisors," he explained. He was helping me because I had done so many things and knew so many people.

When the Township Trustees had their next meeting, we presented them with our petition. The two landowners and three renters living on three miles of dirt road all agreed to move our fences and set them back to the sixty-six foot line. The road right of way was originally laid out to be only forty-four feet wide. There being no other petitions or requests at the meeting, the trustees were forced, reluctantly, to recommend our petition to the county board.

Mr. Barrett, true to his word, persuaded the Board of Supervisors to schedule the new road work. We were pleasantly surprised as we lived on the very edge of the county and for the most part our road work was pretty much neglected. However, the fence project had to be faced, and our outside fences had to be taken up and reset. Again, once more in my life, we were a bit ahead, but the new fences and my mother in the hospital continued to drain our finances.

We just couldn't seem to put even a little bit of money away. It seemed we were in a never ending struggle. Later we were able to oil our road. These days we pay to have oil spills cleaned up but in those days big tanker trucks came and sprayed a thick tarry type of crude oil on the graded road to give it a hard, but not immune to potholes, type of finished surface. It was cheaper to oil the roads because there were no gravel pits in Shelby County. If we paid the initial cost of surfacing the roads, the county agreed to maintain the road.

More cost to us, but all for the better, and we were a bit ahead of most as the oil road stopped a few feet south of our farm driveway.

By this time Mother was home, managing fairly well and improving. It began to appear that we had things going again.

Summer 1947, Mother was home from the hospital, cars still had fenders and Craig was three years old and sitting on our fire engine red 1946 Hudson. I traded off the 'priest's car' and brought this one home from Mitchell, South Dakota while on a visit to Mom while hospitalized for her broken hip. In the background, behind the garage you can just make out the outlines of the Windcharger tower. "It began to appear that we had things going again."

Chapter 11

. . . A GREAT HOLE.

February 6, 1989

Eight degrees below zero this morning. Not much wind, but a cold day on the dairy farm.
Doug still has his hands full. I hope I can do him a little good today.

Sometime, in the later part of 1949, after Mother had recovered from her hip surgery she began to feel poorly again. At first it was just fatigue that seemed explainable by all that had and was still happening to her, but she never really got better. In her own words:

> "Was invited to Austin's girl's wedding, planned so much on going. Haven't been feeling too good lately. Dr. gives one the impression its all in your head.
>
> But I try not to complain to much as we should bear our burdens with God's help and not always complain.
>
> Got down in bed a few days the last of August, also Dad. Had Doc out and he said I should go to hospital or clinic at Carroll so finally went September 26, '49 and there found I had sugar diabetes. Blood sugar was 4+. So sent me to hospital and was there 12 days and got on a diet and came home Oct. 7, '49."

For a few short years things returned to normal and we enjoyed our lives working together with Mom and Dad on our Cumberland Stock Farm No. 2. In February of 1953 we celebrated Mom and Dad's Golden Wedding Anniversary with a huge celebration in their home. Trudy decorated the serving table with a beautiful cake she made with fifty hand-made frosting roses. Friends and relatives from all over the Midwest filled the house to overflowing.

However, by May of that same year a familiar pattern of fatigue and just plain feeling poorly again became my mother's common condition. We took her to Dr. Couley at Mercy Hospital in Council Bluffs. After exploratory surgery he explained to us that she had developed pelvic cancer. He gave us little hope, yet she came home and she and Dad continued to live together in the big house.

A few months before she died she penned in her diary these words of love for her home:

> "Had been feeling rather mean, went to see (Dr.) Ryan, and he sent me to Mercy Hospital was there eleven days was there 5 day(s) when they operated to remove a tumor from lower stomach They all claimed it was just a tumor but I knew better and it was cancer.
>
> Some thing had to come to bring an end.
>
> Came home May 24 and went down May 7, '53 I sure had a siege for 3 or 4 days. But when I came home I walked into house from car and to my bed. It felt good. I was so weak.
>
> It was a very hot sultry day Wilber Jahns brought me home Helen Gravseth from Souris, N.D. came with Ray to bring me home This is July 1, '53 and am feeling as well as usual My worst trouble is giving up my home You will never know the heartache it has cause me Dad and I worked hard to gain it and even thou I can only live a short time I would like to keep house for Dad and I. I have always loved my home and was so grateful for it. But one can't take it with them so I am hoping neither of us will linger to long and be a burden on our children. This was written July 1, '53. "

We looked after them. Trudy and I would take meals across the road to them. Our whole family cooperated. This is the one thing I must not forget, the total cooperation of our whole family in these times. There were many examples, but they weren't necessarily unusual; that is just the way we lived.

One day in May while Mother was in the Council Bluffs hospital, Trudy and I returned to the farm in the late afternoon. Perhaps Dad was with us, I don't remember for sure. What I do remember is driving through the back roads of Shelby county and coming up over the hill and seeing our farm come into view.

Long time neighbor and friend Elsie Manford presents Mother with her 50th Anniversary corsage while Dad looks on. The serving table below is decorated with Trudy's first big wedding cake and homemade mints.

Out in the field, we saw two young school boys on two W.D. tractors. They had taken it upon themselves, without anyone telling them to do so, to get the field ready to plant corn the next day. Dean and Dale were in the field and the two younger boys were doing what they could to start the evening chores.

Our good friend, Ray Hayes, came the next day. The boys were up and going early. It was a Saturday and there was no school. Ray and Father both planted corn that day. I remember Ray asking, "How do you want it planted?"

My answer, "Just like you would on your own farm." Ray was a conservative farmer and knew better than most how to lay out a contour line. He and Dad had no problems planting even though one was on a tractor and the other was still driving his team of horses.

I stood in the fresh-turned Iowa soil that morning, I watched my boys, I watched the tractor and I watched the horses. I could feel the sense of change clawing its way into my heart, the sense of impending loss gnawing in my stomach but in my mind's eye, I saw a vision of a woman. A stubborn woman. A woman who knew what she wanted and who had fought her entire life for her home and this little section of God's green earth to secure a way of life for her family.

It rained that evening and by Tuesday afternoon, when it was dry enough to get into the fields, the corn Ray and Dad had planted on Saturday was spiking through the ground.

Things were as they should be.

The cycle of life was continuing.

On Mother's last Thanksgiving on earth she recorded these words:

> "We went over to Ray's and had dinner. It was real muddy under foot so Dale took me over on the stone boat[59] (sitting) on a bale of hay and Ray brought me home at 5 pm. It was a dreary day but we were all happy.

---

[59] A stone boat is a small skid pulled behind a tractor. Its purpose is to haul in rocks that are turned up when plowing and otherwise preparing the ground for crops.

I sure had a jolt when Ray wont let me raise my own chickens. It hurts but guess I can take it as I have taken a lot. I hope I can do my own work again soon, life isn't worth much when you always have to be waited on. Life can be beautiful when you are well."

Late in the fall of 1954, Mom's brother, Uncle August and his wife Aunt Flora, came to visit. They brought along their daughter, my Cousin Helen, who had been named after my mother, and Helen's infant daughter. I remember the visit well. We all had dinner together in the big house around Mom's dining room table. We talked about old times, about working together and about friends and family. After an intensive visit with her brother and his family, Mother and the rest of us were still sitting in the dining room. Helen was nursing her daughter but was the first to notice that Mother was not real sharp. She suggested that perhaps we should call the doctor.

We wheeled Mother into the bedroom. I lifted her out of her wheelchair and laid her on the bed. Helen closed her eyes. Dr. Hennessey was there already. He looked over at Dad, took his hand and said "John, I am afraid she is gone."

I remember that afternoon so well.

I did the only thing I knew how to do.

I went out into the corn field.

I knew Mother could not stay forever. We had to take fluid off her abdomen several times before just so she could get her breath. We had made some plans and she had made a list of what she wanted the girls and me to have.

When she came home from the Sioux City Hospital after breaking her hip, she rode in Walter Huebner's new ambulance. In those days, before paramedics, the funeral homes also used their hearse as an ambulance and this was Walter's first trip in his brand new 1946 Pontiac ambulance/hearse. The significance of this was not lost on my mother, and always being the one to plan ahead, she talked to him, in German, thinking I wouldn't understand.

"Walter," she said, "when I leave, I want you to lay me away."

Walter conducted the services from our farm home on a beautiful fall day in mid-November. We brought Mother home one last time and placed her coffin in the living room on the exact same spot where she had nursed me back from pneumonia and where we had once, on a much more joyful occasion, so proudly placed our first real Christmas tree. The house was overflowing with family and friends. Many were seated in chairs on the lawn with a speaker system set up so all could hear.

Dad was alone now in the house he and Mother had built and worked so hard to keep. Trudy, the boys and I moved into the big house slowly over the next few months. Trudy felt lost in the big house because she did not have to pile things up on top of one another.

My Mother came from a home broken by her own mother's death when she was but ten years old, yet she established her own life, raised a family and secured a home. As best she could she gave us children the tools to assure our success. She had a successful life, to be sure, and she made a better place of her own little corner of the world but when she left us it left a great hole.

Had been feeling rather mean Went to see Ryan, and he sent me to Mercy Hospital was there eleven days was there 5 day when they operated to remove a tumor from lower stomach They all claimed it was just a tumor but I knew better and it is cancer

Some thing had to come to bring an end came home May 24 and went down May 7 53 I sure had a seige for 3 or 4 days But when I came home I walked into house from car and to my bed, It felt good I was so weak,

It was a very hot sultry day Wilbur Jahns brought me home Helen Gravseth from Souris N.D. came with Ray to bring me home This is July 1 53 and am feeling as well as usual My worst trouble is giving up my home You will never know the heartache it has caused me Dad and I worked hard to gain it and even thow I can only live a short time I would like to keep house for Dad and I have always loved my home and was so greatful for it But one cant take it with them so I am hopeing neither of us will linger to long and be a burden on our children, This was written July 1 53

Two pages of Mother's Diary telling her thoughts of learning she had cancer.

Mom and Dad

Trudy and me

Dean and Dale

Chapter 12

I BELIEVE. . .

February 7, 1989

It's now 5:10 in the morning and it is still cold. A few degrees below zero.

Doug phoned from across the road last evening about 8:30. It was too cold to walk over; said there was another heifer calf born.

He told us the old D17 tractor had handled the cold quite well.

The new diesel tractors, however, will not start mostly because our farm fuel supplier "goofed up" and did not fill our tank with winter fuel. I guess we will have to haul the tractors into Irwin to be warmed up and have the oil filters changed, etc. This could have been avoided. I'm sure Doug will watch it next year. It's been such a warm December and January, I guess everyone thought there was to be no winter this year.

Last evening Doug's three boys, Chris, John and Matt had supper with us – homemade chicken noodle soup and chocolate pudding. They really seemed to enjoy it; everyone had second helpings. Their mother, Patty, had taken their sister Jennifer to Denison for her weekly dancing lesson.

It's great to have them enjoy staying with Grandpa and Grandma.

It makes me feel that the two lifetimes of work and sacrifice, first my Mother's and Father's and later Trudy's and mine, have been worth it.

To keep the home and farm together, to be responsible for providing security, opportunity and a future for a whole new generation is an awesome responsibility. I feel blessed that God has been pleased with our work and given us the opportunity to help do it again with our grandchildren.

319

It enriches our lives to have such deep roots in the land and it keeps us young having the youngsters so close. I believe we should be grateful for the opportunities we have had, regardless of how difficult – God never gives us more than we can handle.

During the early years while our boys were in school, we were barely able to gather enough money for our growing family; we were always short of money. The farm and building repairs continually kept us broke.

We did, however, have a lot of distractions that helped us remember how to smile. During Dean's early elementary school years he went to the one-room country 'Sleister School', the same one where I started my school career what must have been about thirty years earlier. You may recall it was about a mile away and Dean would usually walk but one winter day, after a particularly bad ice storm, Dean took his sled. It seemed like an innocent enough idea until he fell off going down a steep hill and pretty well scratched up his entire face. He didn't think much of it and he continued on to school but by the time he got there a bit more blood had frozen on his face giving it a close resemblance to a pound of fresh-ground hamburger.

His teacher and his mother simply freaked out but there was no serious damage and when it began to heal I thought it might have the makings of a good memory. This was right at the end of the war and fashion was dictated by current events. The boys had matching bomber jackets, I had a leather jacket and Dean, Dale and I all put white muffler scarves around our necks and went off to the photography studio. My mother and I thought the pictures showing the scratches were pretty funny but Trudy would have nothing to do with it. I ended up having to have two pictures made, one for Dean's grandma with the scratches and a touched up one for his mother.

When Craig was born, Trudy took her copy of the picture and placed it on her bedside dresser. A well-meaning nurse stopped to chat with Trudy. She asked if Trudy had any other children, Trudy told the nurse there was a picture of her boys on the dresser. The

nurse picked up the picture, stared at it for a few seconds and asked, "Is your oldest boy in the Air Force?" We all thought that was pretty funny – except Trudy.

A few years later, Trudy decided she wanted a photograph of herself with the two youngest boys to complete the set of family portraits. She dressed up Craig and Doug, combed their hair and took them off to the studio. All went well until the exact moment of the exposure when Craig took it upon himself to goose Doug in the rear. The photo was printed with the two boys looking straight into the camera as instructed but mischievously biting their lower lips and Doug's right hand a blur in the process of hitting his brother in the groin. We should have had a movie camera.

As Craig grew up he seemed to have inherited some of his mother's talent and aptitude for music. To be honest, I don't know how much was aptitude and how much was parental pressure but the poor kid consented to piano lesions, first by the Catholic Nuns in Manilla and later by a Mrs. Potter in Harlan. He spent every Saturday night of his formative years, up until about junior high, going with his mother to Harlan for piano lessons. As a reward he was allowed to go grocery shopping with his mother afterwards, he seemed to enjoy that.[60]

He also had a singing career. When he was young he had a nice soprano voice perhaps aided by his brother's groin shot. Mainly, however, it was a 'career' that he was coerced into when he was too young to know enough to resist, but that didn't last too long. When he was about nine or ten years old we began entering him in local talent shows, these usually were held at the county fairs. I am

---

[60] "Actually this turned out to be not quite as bad as it sounds. It was at the magazine section in the grocery store that I saw my first Playboy magazine. There is nothing quite as memorable as an adolescent boy's first sight of a bare breast, I had to wait a lot of years to see a real one, but for now, this was quite enough. I can still feel the burning flush that rushed to my face the exact instant of my discovery. With my heart pounding to bust out of my chest I immediately, as quickly as possible, put the magazine back on the rack only to return a few short minutes later after determining that Mom was still safely several aisles away in the produce section. The experience turned into a Saturday night ritual, Mom thought I was looking at the sports magazines because I always asked her to buy me one- -to cover my tracks!"– Craig R. Saunders

Craig, Doug and Trudy

sure visions of her own violin recital at that same age churned in Trudy's mind. One year when he was in 3rd or 4th grade he sang at the Shelby County Fair and was invited to appear on TV in Omaha. WOW-TV had a local show called "Talent Sprouts." I think it was fashioned after a national show that was hosted by Arthur Godfrey called "Talent Scouts." In any event Craig was invited to sing his county fair song, "Here Comes Daddy's Little Cowboy" on TV. The whole town was abuzz and when the appointed day arrived we took Craig out of school early to go shopping in Brandis Department Store. New cowboy boots and hat completed a whole new outfit complete with six-shooters and then it was off to the studio.

There was no rehearsal; either we were too late or there wasn't one, I honestly don't remember; however, we were informed that Trudy could not accompany Craig on the piano, as she usually did, because she did not have a union card. Showtime arrived and when it was his turn Craig came out and sat on the couch with the host for a short interview. It was then that I first realized we just might be doing something terrible to this poor kid.

Craig handled the interview in a pretty serious manner but got through it and then rather stiffly walked to his mark on center stage. The music started but it was not his mother's music; it was a much more flowery and professional introduction. Craig didn't have a clue when to begin singing. After what seemed like forever, he turned and with his spurs jangling, walked over to the professional accompanist and said, "I think you made a mistake!"

That was all that was said. He turned and walked again to center stage, This time the music started in a more recognizable form. I had seen this situation before. My freshman year Declamatory home class competition flashed across my mind and I thought I could help. I positioned myself behind the main camera and began directing Craig and mouthing the words. When his eyes contacted mine a slight smile returned to his face and his confidence began to return. The show went on, but all this was just too good for the director to pass up. I may not have had a union card and I didn't know a quarter note from a ransom note but there I was, a big dumb Iowa dirt farmer on TV directing my son's musical number.

Needless to say, we didn't win any prizes that night but if the truth were known, most people watch shows like that for the same reason they go to car races – to see a wreck. We were the hit of the show but stardom is a fickle thing. For weeks afterwards Trudy was too embarrassed to show her face in town. I was luckier – I only had to face the cows.

"Here comes daddy's little cowboy, isn't he a sight.
All dressed up in his western outfit lookin' for a fight
. . ."

It was at about this time that we finally decided to sell the pure-bred cattle herd. Farming practices were changing and the market for breeding seed stock had dried up. Anyone who was in the business now was only in it as a hobby. The pure-bred business had to be supported by something other than itself; it became something for the rich to dabble in and our pure love of the business could not pay the bills. We sold by auction in Harlan, Iowa. It was no great sale, but we were able to clean up a part of the expenses.

I had made up my mind when we had to sell that I would never go to a sale or show again. It was a hard decision to make and it was made out of equal parts anger, disappointment and, of course, jealousy as we had had a fair amount of success and pure-bred Shorthorns were a rich part of our family history but we just could not go on. Thankfully, the two older boys had real good 4-H careers with the cattle and it had been an important part of their education.

The 4-H's are head, heart, hands and health. The motto is *"To Make The Best Better,"* and the pledge is:

I pledge
*My **Head** to clearer thinking,*
*My **Hands** to greater service, and*
*My **Heart** to greater loyalty,*
*My **Health** to better living,*
For my club, my community, my country and my world.

The 4-H creed further elaborates:

I believe in 4-H Club work for the opportunity it will give me to become a useful citizen.

*I believe in the training of my **HEAD** for the power it will give me to think, to plan and to reason.*

*I believe in the training of my **HEART** for the nobleness it will give me to be kind, sympathetic and true.*

*I believe in the training of my **HANDS** for the ability it will give me to be helpful, skillful and useful.*

*I believe in the training of my **HEALTH** for the strength it will give me to enjoy life, to resist disease and to work efficiently.*

I believe in my country, my state, and my community and in my responsibility for their development.

In all these things I believe, and am willing to dedicate my efforts to their fulfillment.

Sure, sometimes we had a hard time finding two nickels to rub together but what more could parents ask for? We were blessed, living in America with values like this. With our church and with our devoted family we had all the things that money couldn't buy. It was hard to understand how we could be so short of money and so rich in family life. For me it has always been about the family and I have tried to make the family farm fun rather than work.

Dean Saunders and his 1949 Iowa State Fair 4-H prize winning heifers. He was the fourth generation of Saunders to show Shorthorns at the fair.

Dean had been an accomplished 4-H showman. While in 4-H, he and his brother Dale took eleven head of Shorthorn cattle by rail to Phoenix, for the Arizona National Livestock Show. It was the last of the Saunders' pure-bred herd on tour and reminiscent of C. A.'s old show tours. They had two white steers in the herd, one light-weight and one heavy-weight. Both won their classes. It takes a good showman to accomplish those things. At the end of the show the boys sold the cattle and returned home by train.

It was a very successful show but one that almost didn't happen.

Earlier this morning I listened to a short sermon given by a Jewish rabbi from somewhere out in radio land. His talk seemed to reinforce my belief that God guides you always. Not only in church, not only in Sunday School and not only while you are in meditation, but always. It seems to me that He continuously gives us guidance and opportunities, not always in a comfortable fashion, but it is always there, if we just listen.

I can't help but think of the time in Trudy's and my life when God quickly demonstrated that fact to us.

It happened at the time when Dean was a senior in high school. We were just beginning to pick corn in early October. It was a crisp clear autumn Saturday morning, the kind with football in the air. My two eldest sons were both capable and anxious to get things rolling and get into the cornfield.

Later that morning Trudy just happened to be looking out the window from our little house and she caught a brief glimpse of our son Dean driving along the south road about a half-mile away. From her vantage point he was visible only for a few short seconds before he passed out of sight behind a hill. He was bringing in a load of freshly-picked ear corn but he didn't come back into view nor make the turn at the corner as soon as Trudy thought he should, so she walked up to the corner to investigate.

She found him lying in the roadside ditch. He had run off the road and the tractor, the load of corn and Dean were down the embankment.

Trudy helped him back up to the road's edge and then in a panic ran the nearly half-mile back to the farm house. She alerted my mother and sent Dale who just so happened to be in from the field at that time, back out to get me. Trudy then drove our automobile to the accident scene. Together we helped our son into the back seat of the car. Mother had alerted our family doctor, Dr. John Hennessey.

We drove into town and stopped in front of Dr. Hennessey's office. He came out to the car, took one look at Dean and his only words were, "Follow me to the hospital." He immediately left his office full of patients and we began the thirty mile trip to the hospital. Dean recalls the doctor poking his head into the back seat of the car, but that is the last thing he remembers.

Somewhere along the way, on Highway 71, State Patrolmen were stopping cars. After a brief conversation with the doctor, they cleared the way for us. As we drove up to the entrance of Carroll's Saint Anthony Hospital, an emergency crew was waiting.

Things happened so quickly!

When we took him out of the car he was as white as hell. He was beginning to slip away. Dr. Hennessey came back out of the hospital and asked permission to operate. "I think he has a ruptured spleen," he said. Immediately, our son was rushed onto surgery.

I will never, never forget the comfort the Catholic Sister offered us. If it is true that angels sometimes walk amongst us, then surely she was our angel of mercy. In her crisply starched white habit she appeared to us seemingly out of nowhere yet she was well-aware of the situation, perhaps much more than we were. She smiled and her presence was comforting. She offered us a place to sit and rest, she held our hands and asked us about our other children. In doing so she gave us a brief respite from the emergency at hand while at the same time, I believe, she was preparing us for the fact that we might not save this boy.

Dr. Walter Annenberg and Dr. Hennessey went to work immediately and removed a ruptured spleen and set a broken left arm. Afterwards they came out and said "I think we were successful. Don't worry (about the spleen). Other parts of the body will take over for it."

Then, for a second time in our lives, doctors inserted a needle into my arm and took my blood to give to my first born son.

When they took us in to see him, he was so much different, all the difference in the world. He looked alive. We stayed at his bedside all that night.

Dr. Hennessey remarked how fast Dean recovered. Ten days after his accident, Dean went to a Friday night high school football game and we haven't had a death in the Saunders family since 1958.

It took some time for us to become fully aware of what God was telling us but for the time being we were rejoicing in the fact that He gave us our son back.

Why do I write these things and why do I believe?

First, answer these questions.

Why did Dean's mother see him for the few brief seconds that he was visible out our dining room window over a half mile away?

Why did she notice he had not turned the corner?

Why was my second son available so quickly to summon me from the field?

Why were my Mother and Father available to care for the younger boys?

How did Mother realize to alert Dr. Hennessey so quickly?

Who gave Trudy the strength to run a half-mile for the automobile?

Why did Dr. Hennessey leave his other patients so quickly?

Why were the Patrolmen there to escort us to the hospital?

Why was the Carroll Hospital and Dr. Annenberg ready so quickly?

And why was the Catholic Sister so comforting?

I believe because God had work for us to do.

I believe He was telling us to tend to business, keep our eyes open and pay attention.

I believe He expects us to look after and take care of the gifts that He has given us.

I believe we have so much left to do for the families God has given us to look after.

I believe these are the things that He expects us to do.

I don't know why, but He does.

Perhaps those who read this will think I am preaching – I am not.

This is simply what I believe.

I love you all.

> ## "We were blessed . . .
> *living in America*
> *with values . . .*
> *our church . . .*
> *our devoted family*
> ## we had all the things
> ## money couldn't buy."

Chapter 13

. . . And Pray I Do

February 8,1989

Another early morning but not quite as cold. Slight wind.

Yesterday Trudy and I mailed some soil samples to the soil lab at Iowa State University in Ames.

Doug was able to get the Allis 7000 started. Diesel tractors are sort of a problem in prolonged cold weather.

He cleaned the free stall barn and ground a load of feed for the cows. I am sure it was quite late when he finished chores last evening.

The next winter after Dean's accident he attended the Farm Operator Winter Course at Iowa State University. It was designed to teach the young farmer the necessary business skills during the winter months when the farm did not demand as much personal attention. But money was so scarce, the following year he left the farm and took a job in Fort Dodge, Iowa. He went to work for a finance company; the irony of that has not escaped me.

I know that part of the decision was made because of the accident and concerns about his physical ability to lead the farmer's life. However, Dean was a keen observer of life and I have always wondered if he didn't decide, consciously or unconsciously, to be on the other side of the money game, loaning money instead of the constant struggle of trying to pay off loans.

That left son Dale and I running the farm.

In the meantime Trudy was doing everything possible to bring in a little extra cash. She had begun sometime previously baking birthday cakes for friends and relatives. Her first big cake was for my parents' Golden Wedding Anniversary[61] and it was such a hit that she soon became the unofficial wedding cake baker for the whole

---

[61] See picture in Chapter 11

countryside. Three or four tiers of home-made cake decorated with pure white frosting, hand-made roses and enough loving attention to get any marriage started off on the right foot.

In the fall months during football season, Fridays were caramel apple days. She would buy apples by the bushel then combine pounds of brown sugar, corn syrup and butter to make huge vats of caramel on her kitchen stove. Wooden sticks were bought by the thousands and inserted into the apples by Trudy and the two younger boys. A family assembly line was formed and the apples were dipped into the caramel when it was just the right temperature. As they cooled on large sheets of waxed paper, some of the caramel pooled around the base. This assured a pretty steady labor supply, at least while the boys were hungry, because their little fingers would scoop up the excess caramel as the apples were placed in paper cupcake cups.

This process would actually begin on Thursday and by Friday at noon the trays were loaded in the backseat of Trudy's car and delivered (in several trips) to Manilla, Denison, Harlan, Manning, Avoca and Irwin. The Junior Classes of these little Iowa towns ran the concession stands at the Friday night football games. Trudy sold the caramel apples for 10 cents and the students resold them for 15 cents. They used their profits to fund their Junior Prom; we used ours to run the farm.

Later she made donuts. The most wonderful donuts ever made, the melt-in-your-mouth, fit-for-a-king kind. There have never been any better, before or since. On our trips to Omaha we would buy fifty pound bags of donut mix and frosting. The dough was deep fried in large cookers filled with Crisco then fresh out of the deep fat cooker the frosting was applied. Hot fresh glazed donuts and cake donuts dripping with chocolate, vanilla, or maple frosting, once again assuring lots of helpful little fingers 'cleaning' the trays. Trudy never wanted for help on donut days.

She stacked the donuts on their sides, two deep on huge trays and sold them to the schools for the Friday night football games along with the caramel apples. They were enough of a success that she began to make them twice a week and sell them at Charlie Schram's grocery store. He would set them on the counter at the checkout stand. At 50 cents a dozen, no one could resist them. The town was small enough that it was no great effort to drop in at Charlie's anytime but soon, people began changing their shopping day to donut day.

Trudy also started selling toys on the party plan representing a company called Toy Parade out of Marshalltown, Iowa. The party plan was like Tupperware parties and this was long before Toys-R-Us. She used the family car and would pack the trunk full and then pack the back seat and front passenger's seat to the roof with boxes of toys, crafts, games, stuffed animals and small gifts. She turned our car into a regular Santa's Sleigh on wheels.

She would drive her toy-packed car to the party hostess's house, unpack it and carry the boxes inside. Over coffee and dessert she would show and explain in detail each toy to the guests, then pass it around for their inspection. At the end of the night she would gather up the order forms, repack the car, drive home and unpack the toys in the garage.

Sometimes she would do this two or three times a week during the Christmas shopping season. If she were really busy, she would leave the car packed and we would find some other way to get where we were going, or more frequently, just unpack the front passenger seat and put the two young boys in the single seat for their trips to school or wherever. No one had even thought of seat belts in the family car in those days.

Trudy would combine two or three parties before sending the order off to Marshalltown. When the boxes arrived it was Christmas all over again. The little kids loved to help open the boxes and unpack the toys and sort the orders. There were boxes and toys all over the house. Sometimes there were toys damaged in shipping or just worn out by the constant packing and repacking, these toys would be the boy's payment for their help. Even today, when grandchildren and great-grandchildren visit Grandma and Grandpa, they play with games and toys left over from the Toy Parade days.

After sorting the orders, Trudy would pack all these boxes back in the car and drive back over the same old country roads to deliver them.

This eventually turned out to be very successful for her. She used our family car so except for wear and tear there were no extra expenses. She paid for her gas and insurance and whatever was left over was hers to save. The first year she had $322 at the end of the season.

This was a turning point!

Trudy saved and invested her toy money in Investors Diversified Securities (I.D.S.). Her business grew for a few years and she was promoted to area manager. This business allowed her at least a temporary escape from the house and the farm problems. It satisfied her urge to be on the move and she thoroughly enjoyed the socializing and the friendship of the entire organization.

She stayed with Toy Parade for 17-18 years until its owners Myrtle and Bill Eberhart, sold out to a New York company. Myrtle and Bill retired and moved to Rodgen, Arkansas. Trudy stayed on and worked for the new owners for one year before 'retiring' herself. We hear from the Eberharts often and are thinking of visiting them later this year (1989).

Trudy's efforts gained her a bit of independence and for the first time a little bit of money of her own to spend. Her years of sacrifice and doing without made her watch every penny, and not a one of them did she spend on herself. She helped me out on the farm on occasion and in later years she was once again ready and willing to help Dale and Johnet when they found themselves in deep financial trouble.

In a recent letter to one of the boys Trudy recalled her 'working' days;

"g'pa and g'ma's 50th wedding anniversary was my first cake. I made 50 roses for it which took me weeks, I think, to get them as perfect as I wanted them – later I could make 50 roses like that in a matter of hours. I have kept count of the cakes – weddings, anniversary, birthdays etc. I have done around 300. Have to tell you about a birthday cake I made for Dorothy. We had just gotten a station wagon (to help me with my toy business) – I wanted Dad to go with me to deliver it but with a station wagon he thought I could do it myself. Well, its sort of hard to steady a cake and drive and while going around a corner it slipped and my hand went into the cake. Had to come home and do it all over – I was so mad at your Dad I could have killed him, all because he just didn't want to help out. So it has been some 40 years ago or more since I did all these cakes. I look back now and wonder how I managed it all. I wish I would have labeled the pictures of each cake, but of course at the time I thought I could remember them all.

So much for the cakes. . . . then, I used to make caramel apples and donuts. I also did farm surveys and took the census, anything to make a little extra cash. I so wish I could have done more for you boys as you were growing up – but money was scarce and it seems Dad always found a place for my earnings.

Then I sold toys for 17 years. I also knit or crocheted 35-40 afghans for the grand kids as they graduated and for other gifts etc.

Played the church organ for 44 years without pay and bought my own music too. A time or two they gave me a check but I gave them back, I felt if God had given me this talent, this was one way I could repay. I was moderator for our Presbyterian Women for several years besides being president of our Women's Club and also our Country Club (this was a club of farm women, not a golfing club). . .

Oh yes, I taught school for $40 a month – yes $40. That's what the substitute teachers now get for a day. Oh I know a dollar went further then. . . Didn't need a college degree, you were required to take a 'Normal Training Course' in high school and then take a State Board exam which was pretty stiff.

So I guess my life has been pretty full . . . wish I were worth more now.

I made that remark to (granddaughter) Laura . . . that I wished I could do more for my sons and grand kids.

She said, "You can Grandma – you can pray for us."
And pray I do."

For over forty years Trudy was the organist for the First Presbyterian Church in Manilla, Iowa. Although she learned to play the violin as a child she never had any piano or organ training, she felt that this was a God given gift and never accepted payment, she even bought all her own music, she felt it was the least she could do in repayment. She wrote in a letter, **"It was a sad day for me in December 1988 when I played the organ for a church service for the last time after 40 plus years. I've enjoyed playing – I was not perfect. I made my share of mistakes – some I could cover up – others were obvious. Whether the congregation realized it or not, but for my postludes I always tried to play a familiar hymn. I was trying to send out a message to the people that when they left the church – God's House – the message in the song – like "Praise the Lord", I've A Story To Tell The Nation" and others would continue to ring in their ears for the coming week."** (This photo was my 1961 Christmas present along with the following card – Craig R. Saunders)

338

Son -
Here is something
I wish to share with you.
Your mother, doing one of the many
things she loves to do.
In time this can be one of
your most cherished possessions.
Lots of love Dad.
"Christmas 1961"

Chapter 14

It Seems Strange . . .

February 9,1989

Nice day, cold, clear, south wind. As soon as I finish this I'm heading for the barn.

I want to go back again to the time we got out of the Shorthorn business. After selling the cattle herd, we bought 200 Columbia Ewes through Producers Commission Company of Omaha. These big ewes cost us $12 per head. After giving us a big crop of lambs the next spring they sheared $9.60 worth of wool per head. Perhaps we had found something that would give us a little breathing room as far as the finances were concerned.

Cumberland Stock Farm No. 2 had changed forever. The pure-bred cattle and the proud horses were gone, replaced by sheep. Although Grandfather C. A. was probably turning over in his grave, I think my father understood. But Dad was becoming increasingly frail. Arthritis from his horse-racing days and years of hard manual farm labor bowed his legs and made his trips to the barn fewer and fewer. First he was confined to the house and ultimately to his bed.

After Mother died we had moved into the big house and lived with Dad. When he became bedridden we cared for him. It was hard on Trudy taking care of him. We had a big double-tub washer in the basement to wash his clothes; I bathed him, cut his hair and shaved him. A day or two before he died, Dr. Hennessey was out helping us get some diapers. Someone suggested a nursing home. Dr. Hennessey said that "no one in any nursing home got better care than John did and he was certainly a lot happier."

A few days later he had a vision of Mother coming to get him and he died in his own bed, at the age of 78. We were expecting it.

Trudy tended to everything. I had been in Harlan on business that afternoon. As I drove home and came over the top of the last hill, the farm buildings came into view. I noticed smoke from a little fire down by the chicken house. I soon learned they were burning Dad's mattress and bedding. Dad died in the north bedroom of the big house in the same room where we thought we might lose him to the Spanish Flu forty years earlier; the same house he had once built and shared with my Mother. He had earned the right and thanks to the efforts of our family, mainly Trudy, God allowed him the privilege of never having to leave his home. He died on the land he loved and had worked so hard for his entire life. Another blessing.

When we moved my father's body from the house, he never returned. The funeral was at the funeral home. This was Trudy's house now and she did not want a funeral in it. We buried him in the Astor Cemetery, next to my mother, his parents C. A. and Bertha and his two young siblings Eddie and Blanch.

Soon after my Father's death I got a letter from an attorney in Harlan. I had worked this land all my life and struggled to keep it in the Saunders family. My labors had earned me half-interest in the farm. Margaret and Wilma had left to lead their separate lives but now they wanted their half of the estate.

Some thought that wasn't quite fair and perhaps I could or should have worked with Dad while he was alive and arranged better estate planning (for me) but Mom and Dad loved my sisters just as much as me and wanted to see to their well-being too. During my parents' lifetime their ability to provide for their three children seemed to decrease over time. As we grew older and our needs increased, there was very little they could give us. They, however, had given me opportunity. Now, who was I to deny my parents the opportunity to provide for my sisters in death what they couldn't during their lifetime?

The only way I could settle the estate was to take out a new loan and buy back my sisters' half of Cumberland Stock Farm No. 2. Over the years, working with our attorney Jake Moore and his brother in Harlan, Dad and I had the Federal Land Bank loan paid down pretty low. We only owed about $16,000. But the Federal Land Bank was not making new loans and the only way I could pay for my sisters' share of the estate was to take out a new loan and refinance the farm through the Metropolitan Life Insurance Company of Des Moines, Iowa.

The interest rate was higher, as was the principle payment. To make things a little harder, the man in Harlan's Metropolitan branch office was a Mr. Carver and he was tougher than H-E double L. Sometime in his early business life he had gotten into a head-to-head confrontation with my grandfather. Needless to say, Carver got set straight in no uncertain terms and in short order. But later, when he found out the Ray Saunders on the loan application was C. A. Saunders' grandson, life with Metropolitan became no picnic. No smiling happy Met Life Snoopy cartoon character here.

Carver was also a close friend of Wilmer Peterson in the Production Credit Association. Wilmer had taken over grandfather's farm and I know that between the two of them they would have loved to add Cumberland Stock Farm No. 2 to their holdings.

It wasn't easy. There were no favors. I was three days late one year with my farm payment and Carver sent the check back because there was no interest payment on those three days. I sent the check back, but this time I went over his head and sent the payment directly to Des Moines. It worked for that year but each year thereafter, prior to each payment, I would get a hot letter from Carver demanding payment on time. Finally, I wrote back. I said I understood but that he should also understand that I would never, never ever pay him one day ahead of time.

We now worked for Metropolitan.

During this time, my second son Dale became interested in raising hogs and sheep. They were his favorite 4-H projects and he did very well, receiving the Showmanship Award one year. He had learned his lessons well from his experience showing pure-bred cattle; it was in his blood. Later in life he would become one of the better commercial hog producers in the community but the road would not be an easy one for any of us.

The year after Dale graduated from high school, he married his high school sweetheart, Johnet Weber. She was a beautiful young lady, one year younger than Dale and had just graduated high school. Her family hadn't lived in Manilla too long. They had moved here to start a dry cleaning shop in the big brick building on upper Main Street, kitty-corner from Uncle Deacon's old bank building and across the street from the new bowling alley. It was the building that Dr. Soe later occupied for his dental practice. Her father was a big man who loved music and playing the piano. Johnet had a beautiful singing voice. She inherited her musical talent from her father and her good looks from her mother.

There was no stopping these two young teenagers. They married December 1, 1957, with both her parents and our blessings. The Webers didn't have the means to help the young couple and the only way in God's green earth that Trudy and I could help them get a start in life was to offer them a share of the farm operations.

This was a share of the work, a share of the debts but also a share in the future. Our plan was for a gradual increase over the years so that their share would increase to a full half-share of the personal property over a period of fifteen years. I told them, "It is up to you. How hard you work and how smart you work will determine how much you have."

The circle of life was completing itself.

Trudy and I were living in the big house my mom and dad had built in 1916 and Dale and Johnet moved into the little house across the road. Life was optimistic as the young couple stripped wallpaper, painted and patched the walls preparing for their first home together. This was, of course, the same house Trudy and I had originally built in 1934 when we were first married.

You may remember we had assembled it from the scraps of the old Manilla depot and first home my parents had built down in the valley when they themselves were first married in 1903. My son and his new wife were the third generation to live within those walls, perhaps even the fourth. I have no knowledge of the origin of those first two rooms my parents moved. I was, however, proud to have something to pass on to Dale and Johnet and excited about a future of working with my son.

Dean had moved on to become assistant manager of the finance company in Fort Dodge but I must say I thought it still possible that Dale and I would be able to put things together as my Father and I once had. I still had visions of the boys running the farm.

It was not to be.

Johnet wanted a contract, a guarantee so to speak, and it was not altogether an unreasonable request, so Jake Moore began writing it out. After typing a few pages he pulled it out of his typewriter and said, "I have worked with your Dad for years . . . it's like when he started."

I was approaching fifty years old and had been farming this land for over thirty years. I was conceived and born on this land and hoped someday to be buried on it. I was there and working when the land was originally purchased from the Goddard estate. With Mother's help, Dad and I had refinanced and kept it in the family during the depression and I had recently refinanced again to settle the estate with my sisters. I had worked hard to assure that the farm would be available to share with my sons, the fourth generation of Saunders boys on the Cumberland Farms – it was hard work, but it was the only thing I knew and I was living my dream.

Considering all this, fifteen years for a half-share did not seem unreasonable to me. However, to young people, just approaching their twenties, fifteen years is over half a lifetime and looks like forever, especially when the first few years were subsistence and there was barely enough income to pay the farm expenses.

Dale and Johnet became increasingly frustrated. I can understand their frustration, especially from a girl who was used to town life, going to work at nine in the morning and closing up shop at five in the afternoon. Hell, my own wife wanted our life to be more nine-to-five but on the farm the work never ends and the rewards are frequently more directed towards the heart than the pocketbook.

Viewed from the little town lots on which they build their houses, townspeople think, often mistakenly, that because farmers control a lot of property, they are rich. Unless they have lived the reality of farm life and fought its battles, unless they have experienced the hard reality and understand the vast difference between assets and liabilities that plague farmers; unless they have carried the huge mortgages and borrowed money to plant the spring crops on the gamble that there would be a harvest in the fall; unless they have lived the farmer's life, it is easy to see why they may think this to be true. It is, therefore, equally easy to see why the young couple became so easily and completely discouraged.

As the first year stretched into the second and the honeymoon period of our agreement wore off and the reality of the situation became more and more evident, Dale came to me with an idea. He could get an FHA Farm and Home Loan if we would agree to lease him the land. Trudy and I still had two boys in school. I couldn't retire or give him everything but in order for Dale to get the loan he had to have a three-year lease. After much debate, Trudy and I agreed. I leased them the east end of the farm on a crop-share basis. Because this was a farm and home loan, it had to include everything necessary to be a successful farmer including a share of all the farm equipment in addition to all the farm buildings, including the barn and the hog houses. Everything except the chicken house.

Someone once said "the difference between happiness and unhappiness was the difference between expectations and reality." Dale and Johnet became more and more dissatisfied as the gap between reality and expectations continued to widen. Finally, after two years, although they lived just across the road, a registered letter arrived in our mail box addressed to Mr. and Mrs. Ray Saunders. The letter stated that they were going to terminate their lease.

Dale left the family farm and moved to a rented farm north of Manilla. Because the farm equipment was on the FHA loan and because he needed it to continue the loan on the rented farm, he took all the equipment with him. He took the best tractor, the disk and the plow.

Trudy was reduced to tears for weeks and blamed me for my stubbornness. She went into a depression, elements of which have lasted to this day. Since that time there has not been a holiday or family gathering at which she has not lamented the schism that developed within our family and I know for a fact that she goes to bed each night praying to God for reconciliation. It seemed my whole family was mad at me. While trying to give them everything I thought they needed, I never even came close to giving them everything they wanted.

These were the days of our lives that were filled with raw emotions. Every father wants to raise a child and impart to them the independence, confidence and knowledge to be successful. That is as it should be; it is the role of a good parent.

In the grand scheme of things God has created a world where each new generation greets the world's problems anew with fresh ideas and untapped energy. To a certain degree the new generation is not responsible for the current conditions and is given the liberty to shed some of the baggage the older generation has picked up along the way. That too is as it should be. It sets the stage for, or at least the potential for, progress.

However, it is also true that it can be painful when a child's youthful exuberance and enthusiasm completely negates the father's hard earned experience. Hell, I wanted Dale to be more successful than me and in doing so not have to repeat the same mistakes I made. Perhaps that is where I erred.

Is it possible that, in my good intensions, I was unknowingly leading him down the same path I had taken simply because it was the only path I knew?

The son is quick to see a father's mistakes, not only because they are not his own but also because they are viewed from the lofty perch of hindsight. It is easy to criticize but sometimes next to impossible for the son to learn the lessons from the father's mistakes. The lessons learned give value to a father's experiences and he so desperately wants to pass them on. Therein lies the difficulty; for a mistake is a mistake only if a lesson is not learned. As difficult as it is to learn from one's mistakes it is oh so difficult to learn from other's mistakes.

The fact is, sometimes there exist relationships in which the cultural background, the genetic make-up, life experiences, age differences, hopes, dreams and expectations, even the very synapses in our brains are so different that, for whatever reason, there can never be a meeting of the minds.

Mind you, different does not necessarily mean wrong nor does it convey any sense of blame; it simply means dissimilar, diverse, unlike and poles apart. For better or for worse, for reasons I don't or can't understand, this best explains my relationship with my daughter-in-law. We just plain see things differently and there seemingly exists between us an underdeveloped sense of compromise. Whatever the cause however, we were both just trying to do what we thought best.

I fully understand that there are two sides to every story and I will be the first to admit that not only did I inherit my Mother's stubbornness but as the years went by and my roots grew deeper and deeper into the soil of Cumberland Stock Farm No. 2, my trademark streak of "Saunders' stubbornness" became so refined and perfected within my very soul that I had little conscious control of it. I understand that I can be hard to work with. Therefore, please remember, I am writing this history from my point of view and perhaps others were not aware of all the problems nor, after all the frustration, did they care to find out the whole story . . . nor perhaps did I.

However, if they have a different story they will just have to write their own book. As for me, I started all over again, for the fourth time!

Trudy and I were now more than financially broke; our hearts and spirits were broken too. I am sure most people expected us to quit and I can't say that we didn't think about it. Hells bells, I wanted to escape so bad I looked into buying a fishing camp in the north woods, up on The Lake of the Woods, but what did I know about fishing? Farming was all we knew. Mom and I needed money to put food on the table. Remember, we still had two young boys to finish raising.

During that last year, however, by a stroke of luck and God's good grace, we became acquainted with the field manager of the Lytton Creamery of Lytton, Iowa and through him we met, what turned out for us, the greatest banking family in Iowa.

We had no collateral; only debt, but T.J. Tokhiem, President of the Lytton Savings Bank, was willing to loan us 100% of the money to buy ten head of Holstein bred heifers, a used milking machine, milk cans and a cooler. We were in the dairy business. All we had to do was milk the cows morning and night.

We were up and running by late winter or early spring. The milk went to the Lytton Creamery and one-half of the milk check went directly to the bank to pay off the note and one-half came home to the farm. Twice a month like clockwork, the checks arrived. For the first time in our history we had a regular and at least semi-reliable cash flow. By May of that year, Mr. Tokheim was pleased with the way we were operating and provided the money to buy fourteen more calves in the fall.

We were back in the cattle business only this time it was milk cows and we were also back to farming the entire farm.

Everyone pitched in.

That summer, Craig and I custom-baled hay and loaded the bales on hay racks for $0.12 per bale. Some people paid us in hay, which we brought home for the milk cows. Craig used his share, 4 cents a bale, for tuition that fall at Simpson College in Indianola, Iowa where he had also won a football scholarship.

With a minimum amount of machinery and Craig off to college, that fall Mr. Tokheim once again came to our rescue. He loaned us $85 to buy an old W. C. Allis Chalmers tractor that allowed us to haul our corn in from the field.

Trudy was also selling toys at this time. She loved to be on the go, meet people and party. She would pack the trunk and back seat

> *". . . a mistake is a mistake only if a lesson is not learned."*

with toys and be off. She didn't make much money but it was more than we had before and it certainly gave her an escape.

Needless to say, this all took a bit of the pressure off me.

The two younger boys, Craig and Doug took an interest in the dairy and were a great help. If they had not learned it by then, they by God now learned the value of hard work.

It seems strange how God's plans work.

Chapter 15

. . .OUR BOYS WERE GONE.

February 10,1989

Looks like a beautiful day. Sun is going to shine.
Doug is shelling corn today. He just called his mother from the milk parlor, "Mother, I have an errand for you. Will you take the alternator to Manning for me?"

This was, I believe, the last photo taken while all the boys were living at home. L-R: Dean, Craig, myself, Doug, Trudy and Dale.

A year after Dean left the farm, he met Rosemary Bellingter and on September 2, 1959 they were married in Fort Dodge, Iowa. A promotion took the young couple to Sioux City, Iowa, where, in mid-August 1960, Karen Marie Saunders came to live with them. Dean had accomplished something I had been unable to do; he added a girl to our family and Trudy finally had the baby girl she had so desperately wanted. Our first grandchild and a girl! Our Saunders family, myself and two sisters, had eight boys and only one girl, so Karen was very welcome. As I remember, she was a

TRUE girl, too. She wanted her own way (and got it), cried a lot and almost wore her parents out.

As a newborn Karen developed a bad case of colic, maybe mixed in with a bit of the flu and when I say a bad case, I mean bad with a capitol B. The doctor told Rosemary the baby would normally be hospitalized but since she didn't have other children in the home and she could devote all of her time to the new baby, he felt Rosemary could give the undivided attention the baby just couldn't get in the hospital, and boy did she need it.

Little Karen had a Bad (remember the capitol B) case of diarrhea and lots and lots of crying. Sometimes they changed diapers three times an hour or more during what seem like unending crying episodes. They took her off the formula and all she got was boiled water until the diarrhea eased a bit, they then added skim milk only to have the diaper changes and crying start all over again. She lost a lot of weight and oh, did I mention the crying – it never stopped.

Now Rosemary had a very close relationship with her Grandmother Bellinger. Rosemary was the oldest child in her family and she had a brother and sister that were born just 13 months apart, this took a lot of her mother's time so Grandma Bellinger helped out and was like a second mother to Rosemary. In fact, after high school Rosemary had a secretarial job at the Quaker Oats factory in Fort Dodge and Grandma's apartment was just a short distance away on the second floor above the Salvation Army building. Rosemary would walk those few blocks and climb the stairs every day to have lunch with Grandma and on Fridays would stay just a bit longer to fix Grandma's hair. Therefore, it seemed only natural Grandma wanted to see her new great granddaughter and help care for her.

Grandma was a German Catholic from Josephstal, Russia. Originally Germany was a loose collection of warring states where all land was owned by and all commoners worked for the nobility. When Catherine the Great wanted to settle the vast open plains of Russia she offered the German farmers the promise of free land, freedom of religion, and exemption of taxes and military service. She allowed, even encouraged, them to keep their own language and customs.

The promise of owning their own land was a powerful force. However, by the early 1900's there grew a real resentment on the part of the Russians towards the Germans, this resentment escalated into an 'unofficial public policy' of looting and confiscation of German property. We hear a lot about the Russian Jews being forced from their homes but it wasn't just the Jews, German Catholic families, who were able, left Russia in droves, forced to leave all behind. Grandpa Bellingter had already left two or three years earlier to make a place for his family in America and Grandma Bellingter plus Rosemary's mother and father were on the last ship to leave Russia before the start of World War I.

Grandma was a short woman, when she sat in a chair her feet couldn't touch the floor; she had to have been less than 5 feet tall and just as wide. She spoke only German but could understand English. Rosemary spoke only English but could understand German. Together they communicated perfectly. Dean could speak and understand only English but when Grandma Bellingter cursed him out in German he also understood perfectly what she meant.

Rosemary was special to her grandmother so when Grandma wanted to come help she couldn't be refused. She took the train from Fort Dodge to Sioux City and in the late afternoon Dean went down to the railway station and brought Grandma to their little home and new baby. Grandma walked into the house and took one look at her first great granddaughter, saw the diarrhea and the crying and said in her thick, heavily accent, using English for extra emphasis, "Gonna die, gonna die, baby's gonna die."

While on the boat to America Grandma came down with a serious case of chicken pox and apparently nearly died. While being treated, she was transferred from her third class accommodations to the boats infirmary where she also witnessed all the sick children. With this as her major source of medical education, Grandma sat, feet dangling in mid air propelling her body back and forth in Rosemary's rocking chair, watching poor little Karen in her crib and saying over and over again, "Lots of kids on the boat had that, they all died. She's gonna die too. She's gonna die."

Rosemary didn't believe it, she had lots of faith in her doctor but can you imagine the effect this had on the new parents? By 2:30

the next afternoon Rosemary called Dean at work, "I can't take it any longer," is all she said.

Dean came home immediately and Grandma went back to the railway station.

Dean had the ability to hold and cuddle baby Karen to give her some relief and soon all was back to 'normal'.

It's a hard job training new parents but Karen, who later had the help of two younger brothers, did a great job. Recently, Dean retired and the kids threw a big party for him. I have never witnessed three more respectful or responsible children. They all, Dean, Rosemary, Karen, Kevin and Keith, did a great job. I count them, as I do all my children, as one of my great successes in life but I am getting ahead of myself.

After four boys of her own, Trudy finally got the girl she had dreamed of. Granddaughter Karen Marie Saunders was born August 13, 1960.

Another promotion moved Dean's young family back to Fort Dodge where they bought a small home still under construction. To complete the landscaping, Dean rented a sod cutter and we cut virgin bluegrass sod from the hillside just north of our farm pond. We loaded the sod on our stock truck and hauled it to Fort Dodge. Somewhere today, in Fort Dodge, Iowa, there exists a small piece of Cumberland Stock Farm No. 2.

It was not long before Dean capitalized on his farm background and moved from the financing business into the farm equipment business and became one of the top salesmen. Through his farm machinery business we were able to get many good used pieces of farm equipment at trade in prices. We needed the help because, after Dad passed on and I settled the estate then Dale left home and we resettled again, we needed so much and had so little cash.

After renting for a few years Dale and Johnet were able to buy their own farm two miles west of Manilla. They raised two fine boys there, Robin and Jay, now both with families of their own. I am as proud of Dale as I am of any of my four sons and I am so pleased that I arrived at a place in my life when I could finally help him out.

There were three times that I recall.

When Dale bought his own farm he built a new hog house and went into the hog production business. However, as I learned for myself at his age, prices fluctuate while expenses continue to rise. Rasmussen Lumber Company put a lien on the building for $6,000. With some of Trudy's money and some of my own, we were able to pay it off.

Later, during a time of high interest rates, I think during the Jimmy Carter administration, Dale had bought a bunch of hog feed in Harlan at 20% interest. Needless to say, hog prices did not go up 20% and when the note came due . . . well, there was just no way. I went to Harlan and sat in the feed store manager's office. I told him "There is no way on God's green earth that you can collect from that guy (Dale) . . . he just doesn't have it." Dale's bill with interest had accumulated up to $7,800, a huge portion of it interest. I told the manager, "I'll make this offer today and give you $4,000 cash, but when I get up and walk out, that is it." He knew I was telling the truth and he took the deal.

Doug was in on the feed deal. The money came out of our farm account. I can't remember the third thing . . . oh yeah, I bought him a tractor. $4,800 at an auction, an Allis Chalmers 190, in pretty decent kind of shape . . .

Why do I write this? Was I feeling guilty? No, I was just trying to help the guy out. It happened at a time when we were pretty short but still able to get it done and I was thankful for the opportunity. These were gifts for both of us, for me to give and them to receive; I don't want to collect and I am not bellyaching about it but since our failed partnership, Dale and Johnet's relationship with the rest of the family has been a bit strained. I guess that happens in a lot of families, especially ones that try to do business together. I just wish God would answer Trudy's prayers.

Perhaps it is my fault. Trudy says that there are probably a lot of things that they don't like about me. I understand that. I am not complaining or hollering. They have a nice home, Johnet is a great decorator and housekeeper, and she is a good cook and a good mother. I just couldn't do business with her. I wish it didn't have to be personal. Her family is gone as are so many of our friends' families today and what do we have if we don't have family?

I write this with no animosity or sorrow. I'm sure the opportunity was there for them to have worked with the rest of the family; it's just that God's opportunities were interpreted differently.

Yet He loves us all.

The times were changing rapidly. In early October 1957, just a couple months before Dale and Johnet were married, the world woke up to a very faint but strange beeping noise every 98 minutes. The Soviet Union had launched Sputnik, earth's first artificial satellite and once again in my lifetime the world was changed forever. These were the years of the cold war[62].

Then came the decade of the sixties with the dawn of the space age, the Cuban missile crisis and the space race with John Kennedy's vow to put a man on the moon. Farm work, businesses

[62] The cold war lasted from 1945 to 1991. From the end of the Second World War to the collapse of the Soviet Union and the tearing down of the Berlin Wall. It included the Korean War, Vietnam War, the Cuban Missile Crisis and the space race just to name a few highlights.

and even school classes would come to a halt when there was a space shot. Televisions were set up in the school gymnasiums and classes suspended so all the students could watch as John Glenn became the first American to orbit the Earth in February of 1962.

It's little wonder that this generation of school children began to think far beyond the fences of the family farm. During this time of my attempted partnership with his older brother, Craig established himself as a student athlete in school yet he also made time to help with any and all of the farm work. In his spare time Craig would build home-made rockets. He and a school friend, Bill Reiff, son of our local hardware store owner, would go to the hog house and catch small mice to send up in their rockets and parachute back to earth.

Upon graduation from high school in 1962 he was one of twenty-five students from through out the United States who earned an invitation to a two-week conference at Cape Canaveral. There he met a couple of the original seven astronauts and other members of the NASA Mercury space team.

In the fall of 1962 Craig became a full-time student at Simpson College. A football scholarship and a job cleaning the gym showers and dressing rooms along with his earnings from hay bailing got him started. Two-a-day football practices began a couple weeks before school started so we took him down to the campus early. The first day of football practice the entire team had to run a mile. This was nothing and Craig distinguished himself by leading the pack and ultimately earning a starting position as a freshman. This was not big-time football but there were still important lessons to be learned.

One such lesson came just a few days later. In a practice scrimmage Craig made a tackle only to get up and find his little finger sticking out at a right angle from his hand. He told me later his first thought was that he would get a couple weeks off from the grueling practices. He approached his coach holding his right hand in his left while the rest of the team backed away in a shocked silence. He said "Coach, I think I broke my finger." The coach, in one sudden deft move, took Craig's hand in his and reset the little finger. He then taped it with two small strips of tape to the ring

The Des Moines Register

The Newspaper Iowa Depends Upon

Des Moines, Iowa, Wednesday Morning, February 21, 1962—28 Pages—Two Sections

Price 10 Cents

Comics	21	T.V., Radio	22
Editorials	20	Weather	22
Markets	21	Women	14

THE WEATHER—Snow today, heavy in northwest, diminishing tonight; high 20 north, 30 south. Snow flurries Thursday. Sunrise today 7:02; sunset 5:55.

***

GLENN ORBITS THREE TIMES, BACK IN EXCELLENT SHAPE

BY THE ROCKET'S RED GLARE

PLAN HUGE WELCOME IN WASHINGTON

'A Wonderful Job,' Says Kennedy

WASHINGTON, D. C. (P)—The U. S. government came to a virtual standstill Tuesday during the takeoff and landing of the first American to orbit the Earth.

Clerks and stenographers, bureau chiefs and cabinet members kept an eye on the television screens while shuffling the papers on their desks.

"Most Proud"

After it was all over, President Kennedy came out into the White House Rose Garden and saluted Astronaut John H. Glenn, Jr., as "the kind of American of whom we are most proud."

Mr. Kennedy returned to ...

LIFTED FROM OCEAN AFTER 5-HR. FLIGHT

Next: 2-Day Check In Bahamas

By Jack Wilson
(Of The Register's Washington Bureau)

CAPE CANAVERAL, FLA.—John Glenn parachuted to a safe landing in his space capsule Tuesday after three trips around the world.

The Mercury capsule, with the pilot still inside, was hoisted aboard the destroyer Noa 20 minutes after it hit the water off the Bahamas, about 700 nautical miles east of here. Glenn was reported in excellent condition.

The 81,000-mile trip, from the instant the capsule was launched on the nose of a ...

FOR GLENN'S FAMILY, THE HAPPIEST DAY

His Wife Admits She Worried

ARLINGTON, VA. (P)—"It's the most wonderful day for my family," exclaimed Mrs. Anna Glenn, smiling and happy, after her astronaut husband's historic triple orbit of the Earth Tuesday.

The children are so proud of their father and the Mercury man and everyone else who made this possible," the petite, 41-year-old brunette told reporters about an hour after her husband completed his flight safely.

Call From Kennedy

For all Glenn three was most joy to come ... from President Kennedy ... from her husband. At ... 3:30 p. m. Glenn called ...

It Was A Long, Long Day ...

Astronaut John H. Glenn, jr., smiles as he rests on a bunk during examination aboard the U. S. de...

finger and sent him back into the scrimmage. I think there is good reason to believe that had Craig sat out two weeks he would have lost his momentum.

Best case scenario, he would have lost his starting position. Worst-case scenario it would have been a good excuse and a lot easier not to return to the tough practices. In either case he would have been in jeopardy of losing his scholarship and quite possibly his college education.

Perhaps that is not giving my son enough credit but as it was, Craig didn't even miss two plays, let alone two weeks. Before school started, however, there was still one even larger hurdle weighing heavily on his mind. The two-a-day football practices were easy for Craig to deal with but as registration day for the new college year approached he did not yet understand where the money would come from for this college education. The night before registration Craig walked the streets of his campus and strange new town well past midnight, feeling lonely and empty but thankful that there was no moon to make visible the tears in his eyes.

The next morning his Coach, Ken Heizer, again came to his rescue. Craig sought him out in the crowded gymnasium where registration was proceeding and naively told him, "Coach, I may have to go home. We can't pay for all of this." Mr. Heizer assured him there was a monthly payment plan and promised to help him apply for a student loan. Two weeks later Craig was elected President of his incoming freshman class.

His sophomore year was yet another year that changed the world. November 21, 1963. It was one of those days in which everyone remembers exactly where they were and what they were doing. I was in the basement of a clothing store in Carroll, Iowa buying a pair of overalls when I heard the news John F. Kennedy was assassinated. In rapid succession his brother Bobby and then Martin Luther King were assassinated. The sixties were a world gone crazy but somehow we survived it, both as a nation and as a family.

Doug looked after the cows and farm so that many times we were able to go to Craig's football games. For the next four years summer jobs spraying herbicides on country roads, student loans

The Des Moines Register

THE WEATHER—Generally fair, colder today, high in mid-30s. Clear, quite cold tonight. Partly cloudy, warmer Sunday. Sunrise 7:15; sunset 4:49.

The Newspaper Iowa Depends Upon

Des Moines, Iowa, Saturday Morning, November 23, 1963—20 Pages—Two Sections

Price 10 Cents

CHARGE PRO-CASTRO SNIPER WITH MURDER OF KENNEDY

President Is Shot In Head and Neck

DALLAS, TEX. (UP)—A furtive sniper armed with a high powered rifle assassinated President John F. Kennedy Friday.

An hour and a half later, Vice-President Lyndon B. Johnson took the oath of office as the thirty-sixth President of the United States.

Mr. Kennedy, 46, was shot through the head and neck as he rode through Dallas in the presidential limousine in what had been a triumphal motorcar.

"Oh, No!"

When the shots were fired about 12:30 p. m. (CST) and the chief executive slumped forward, Mrs. Kennedy turned in the seat beside him and cried, "Oh, no!" in anguish and horror. He blood indicated her left stocking.

She tried to cradle his head in her arms as the limousine took off at top speed for Parkland Hospital, where Mr. Kennedy died about half an hour later.

Within the hour, police arrested a 24-year-old man after the fatal shooting of a Dallas policeman.

The man, Lee Harvey Oswald of Fort Worth, was charged late Friday night with the assassination of Mr. Kennedy.

Oswald, described as chairman of a "Fair Play for Cuba Committee," defected to Russia in 1959. He returned to the United States in 1962 with a Russian wife and a baby girl.

Oswald also was charged in the slaying of the policeman. He was seized in a movie theater about three miles from the assassination scene.

Oswald checked in the building from which the assassin's shots were fired. His supervisor said Oswald was there at the time of the assassination.

Oswald denied any connection with the shootings.

Triumphal Tour

The assassination occurred just as the President's motorcade was leaving downtown Dallas at the end of a triumphal tour through the city's crowded streets. There were few spectators in the shooting area.

His special car — with the protective bullet-proof bubble down—was moving down in an incline onto an underpass that leads to a freeway route to the Dallas Trade Mart, where he was to speak.

Witnesses heard three shots. Two were believed to have hit the President, one in the head and one in the neck.

The third shot wounded Gov. John B. Connally of Texas in the side. His condition was reported not critical.

The motorcade slowed and then sped forward as bracketed speed for 3 minutes to Parkland Hospital near the Trade Mart.

Onlookers, terrified at the sight and sound of the assassination, dived for protection onto a grassy park at the entrance of the underpass, fearing more shots. Police swarmed onto the scene.

Suit Still Neat

At the hospital emergency entrance, a reporter saw the President stretched out face down at full length, motionless on the back seat of the car. His suit still looked neat—but there was blood on the floor.

Secret Service men helped Mrs. Kennedy away from the car. Hospital attendants aided Connally and his wife.

It seemed evident that there was some planning behind the assassination.

In the Texas School Book Depository building, overlooking the underpass, officers found an old foreign-made rifle with telescopic sights, spent cartridges and scraps of fried chicken.

The rifle, described as a bolt-action, 6.5-mm. weapon, apparently of Italian make, was partly hidden behind

KENNEDY— Continued on Page Five

Cancel Iowa-Notre Dame Game

IOWA-NOTRE DAME football KENNEDY is fourth president game today at Iowa City to be slain by an assassin's has been canceled by agreement of officials of the shows that presidential two schools ....Page 13

THE BODY of President Kennedy is returned to a sorrowing capital, where it will lie in repose at the White House today. A funeral mass will be said Monday in Washington, D. C. ....Page 8

TEXAN ONCE DEFECTED TO SOVIET UNION

Seized in Theater; Officer Killed

Leased Wire to The Register

DALLAS, TEX. — Lee Harvey Oswald, a 24-year-old warehouse worker who once lived in Russia, was charged late Friday night with assassinating President Kennedy.

Police Chief Jesse Curry said Oswald was formally arraigned on a charge of murder before a justice of the peace in the homicide bureau at police headquarters here.

Three Miles Away

Oswald was arrested at 2:15 p. m. Friday, nearly two hours after the assassination, as the suspected killer of a police-man on the street in the Oak Cliff district, three miles from where the President was shot. Oswald also was charged with murdering the policeman.

District Attorney Henry Wade said the case against Oswald in the slaying of the President probably would go to a grand jury next week. Wade refused to say whether fingerprints found on the murder weapon matched those of Oswald.

Oswald faces a death sentence if convicted.

A former Marine, Oswald went to Russia in 1959 with the declared intention of living his life there. Leaving the U. S., he said, was "like giving up prison."

In 1962 Oswald returned to Texas with a Russian wife and an infant daughter. He was identified as an adherent of the leftist "Fair Play for Cuba Committee." Both the House Un-American Affairs Committee and the State Department, it developed, knew of Oswald.

Oswald was seized in a movie saloon after a policeman to death on a street nearby.

Murder Charge

In police headquarters, while being escorted through a corridor, he shouted at reporters: "I haven't shot anybody."

Captain Will Fritz, head of the police department homicide bureau, said Oswald was employed in the Texas School

GUNMAN— Continued on Page Two

Ban Commercials Out of Respect

NEW YORK, N. Y. (UP)— The nation's three major television and radio networks scrapped all commercials and entertainment programs and all signs of respect for the death of President Kennedy.

The National Broadcasting Co., and Columbia Broadcasting System all damned their entire network radio and television programs Friday to news of the assassination and all allied incidents.

The Mutual Broadcasting System said it would ban commercials and entertainment features until after the President's funeral.

ABC said its commercial and entertainment ban would remain in effect indefinitely. NBC said it would observe the commercial and entertainment blackout until after the President's funeral.

CBS said it would not return commercials and entertainment programs to the air until after the President's burial.

KENNEDY— Continued on Page Five
GUNMAN— Continued on Page Two

A Wave--Then A Mortal Wound

President John F. Kennedy waves to spectators lining motorcade route in Dallas, Tex., Friday. Also in car were Mrs. Kennedy and Gov. John Connally of Texas. About one minute later...

... Three shots rang out and the President slumped in his seat. Here his face is partially hidden by rear-view mirror, his arm is raised. Connally, wounded seriously, is in left portion of circle.

The President, mortally wounded, slumps in the seat and his wife stands over him. Man on bumper is not identified. Car sped directly to a hospital, where the President died about 30 minutes later.

JOHNSON, 55, IS SWORN IN AS PRESIDENT

'I'll Do My Best,' He Tells U. S.

By Richard Wilson

WASHINGTON, D. C. — President Lyndon B. Johnson took his constitutional duties Friday night as the head of a saddened and troubled nation.

"This is a sad time for all people," the new President said. "We have suffered a loss that cannot be weighed. For me it is a deep personal tragedy. I know the world shares this sorrow that Mrs. Kennedy and her family bear.

"I will do my best. That is all I can do. I ask your help—and God's."

President Johnson, who is 55 years old, made this brief statement after arriving at Andrews Air Force Base from Dallas, Tex., aboard an Air Force jet that also brought back to the capital the body of the assassinated President, John F. Kennedy.

The body of the President was taken to the Bethesda Naval Hospital with Mrs. Kennedy, while President Johnson and Mrs. Johnson boarded a helicopter for the White House, 20 miles away. President and Mrs. Johnson arrived on the White House lawn a few minutes later and entered the executive mansion.

Schedules Conference

At the White House, President Johnson scheduled a conference with Secretary of Defense Robert S. McNamara and national security adviser McGeorge Bundy. Then he met with a bipartisan group of congressional leaders and other executives and congressional officials.

The grim-faced new President acted swiftly to take over the order of the death of President Kennedy.

After he was sworn in by Federal Judge Sarah T. Hughes in the forward compartment of the presidential plane at Dallas, Mr. Johnson said: "Okay, let's

JOHNSON— Continued on Page Eight

Lyndon B. Johnson "I Ask Your Help"

Cancel D. M. School Events for Weekend

Des Moines schools canceled all extra-curricular activities for the weekend, including several football games, school plays and other events. They will be rescheduled, said Dr. John H. Harris, superintendent.

and a job driving a school bus kept him going. He studied the biological sciences in the building named after one of the college's most famous students, George Washington Carver. His study habits and willingness to work earned him a Bachelors degree and entrance to the University of Iowa's College of Medicine in 1966.

Between his first and second year of medical school he came home and worked at the Iowa Beef Packing Plant in Denison, Iowa, lugging freshly slaughtered quarters of beef on his shoulders, loading train cars and truck trailers bound for big city markets. He was usually off work by three P.M. and in the fields helping Doug and me with our farm work. He was saving his money for something special.

Craig and Virginia Ann Harrison of Indianola, Iowa were married that fall, August 26, 1967. They lived in the old tin quonset huts originally built for WW II veterans in the shadow of Kinnick Stadium on the University of Iowa campus.

Between his junior and senior year in medical school he had the opportunity to study at the Royal Infirmary in Edinburgh, Scotland. It was there, the young couple sat in the common room of their bed-and-breakfast on July 20, 1969 and watched with the rest of the world as Neil Armstrong made "one small step for man, one giant leap for mankind."

Killing two birds with one stone, Craig joined the Air Force and received second lieutenant's pay during his senior year in medical school and then went on to intern at Lackland Air Force Base, Texas in exchange for three years as a flight surgeon. His interest in aerospace medicine, however, gradually gave way to his interests in surgery and he ultimately completed fifteen years of training to become a heart surgeon. Early in his training we were able to contribute a total of about $350 to his education. Later with student loans, scholarships and odd jobs, he didn't need anything from us. It certainly may have been one of the best investments I ever made.

While in high school Doug developed a love for the farm and the Holsteins and upon graduating from high school, enrolled in the winter Farm Operation Course at Iowa State. While at Iowa State,

The Des Moines Register

The Newspaper Iowa Depends Upon

Des Moines, Iowa, Monday Morning, July 21, 1969—22 Pages—Two Sections

Price 10 Cents

Where to Find It:

Comics	4-5	TV, Radio	10
Editorials	12	Weather	11
Voters	1-5	Women	9

MAN WALKS ON MOON!

Yanks First to Make Lunar Visit

THE WORLD'S FIRST MOON MEN

Neil A. Armstrong

Edwin E. (Buzz) Aldrin, jr.

Michael Collins

'Fantastic' Trip By Armstrong And Aldrin

Leased Wire to The Register

TRANQUILLITY BASE, THE MOON — Man landed on the moon and walked its dead surface Sunday, July 20, 1969, for the first time in his two-million-year history.

Two men, wearing American flags sewn to their left shoulders, landed on the Sea of Tranquillity at 3:17 p.m. (Iowa time). One of them, Neil A. Armstrong, 38, of Wapakoneta, Ohio, was the first to set foot on its alien soil warming in the lunar sunrise.

His first words at that moment, 9:56 p.m. were: "That's one small step for man, one giant leap for mankind."

"The surface is fine and powdered, like powdered charcoal to the soles of my boot . . . I can see my footprints of my boot in the fine particles."

Twenty minutes later, his companion, Edwin E. (Buzz) Aldrin, jr., 39, of Montclair, N.J., stepped to the surface from the spacecraft, Eagle. His words were: "Beautiful, beautiful, beautiful. A magnificent desolation."

Millions on their home planet 240,000 miles away watched on worldwide television from a camera on the side of the spacecraft as the two sat on a show that will long be remembered as a truly beautiful experience.

Armstrong was out of the spacecraft for two hours and 14 minutes; Aldrin for one hour and 44 minutes.

The two planted their nation's flag on the moon, gathered soil samples, and talked to their President on earth by radio telephone.

President Nixon's voice came to the ears of the astronauts from the Oval Room at the White House.

"This has to be the most historic telephone call ever made," he said. "I just can't tell you how proud I am . . . Because of what you have done the heavens have become part of man's world. As you talk to us from the Sea of Tranquillity, it inspires us to redouble our efforts to bring peace and tranquillity to man."

"All the people on earth are surely one in their pride of what you have done, and one in their prayers that you will return safely . . ."

Aldrin replied, "Thank you, Mr. President. It is a privilege to represent the people of all peaceable nations." Armstrong added his thanks.

Steps Cautious at First

Armstrong's steps were cautious at first. He almost skidded.

"The surface is fine and powdered. His powdered charcoal to the soles of the feet," he said. "I can see my footprints of my boots in the fine sandy particles."

Armstrong read from the plaque on the side of Eagle, the spacecraft that had brought them to the surface. In a steady voice, he said: "Here man first set foot on the moon, July, 1969. We come in peace for all mankind."

In the moments he walked alone, Armstrong's voice was all that was heard from the lunar surface.

He appeared phosphorescent in the blinding sunlight. He walked carefully at first in the gravity of the moon, only one-sixth as strong as on earth. Then he tried wide gazelle-like leaps.

Aldrin tried a kind of kangaroo-hop, but found it unsatisfactory.

"The so-called kangaroo hop doesn't seem to work as well as the more conventional pace," he said. "I would get rather tiring after several bounds."

In the lunar gravity of the moon, each of the men, encumbered on Earth, weighed something over 25 pounds on the moon.

Armstrong began the rock picking on the lunar surface. Aldrin joined him using a small scoop to put lunar soil in a plastic bag.

Keeps Lonely Patrol

Above them, invisible and nearly forgotten, was Air Force Lt. Col. Michael Collins, 38, keeping his lonely patrol around the moon for the moments when his companions blast-off and return to him for the trip back home.

Collins said he saw a small white object on the moon, but didn't think it was the spacecraft. It was to the wrong place.

Back in Houston, where the nearly half-room rode the sky to its zenith, Mrs. Joan Armstrong watched her husband

MOON— *Please turn to Page Four*

First Words as Man Stands on Moon

'That's One Small Step for Man, One Giant Leap for Mankind'

First Man on the Moon

This is how astronaut Neil Armstrong appeared on a television picture sent through some 240,000 miles of space Sunday night as he became the first man to set foot on the moon. This picture was taken by an Associated Press cameraman from a television picture received at the Manned Spacecraft Center in Houston, Tex. Armstrong is shown from waist up as he stands at the foot of the lunar module. Moon horizon is visible in the background. A PAGE OF PICTURES: Page 2.

MORE MOON STORIES

EXCERPTS from astronauts' reports After landing on moon — Page 3

DRYDEN collects $25,000 on the bet that man would land on the moon before 1971 Page 3

ESTIMATED 500 million persons in homes, autos and parks follow landing on moon Page 4

NATION'S leaders pray for astronauts at White House church service — Page 4

'IN THE beginning —' Page 5

ONLY THING between astronauts and death is $300,000 suit — Page 7

TEXT of Nixon's conversation with astronauts Page 6

LUNA, Soviet spaceship, changes orbit Page 6

HORNET, the carrier that will recover Apollo astronauts, makes many discoveries of its own Page 14

...And on the Earth

SOVIETS SHOUT 'HOORAY!'

LONDON, ENGLAND — Crowds streamed joyously in London's Trafalgar Square, Chinese flowed in the streets, and Russians shouted "Hooray" — almost everyone on earth unified by man's arrival on the moon.

Pope Paul VI praised America's three astronauts as "conquerors of the moon" minutes after the landing.

The pope said town new leave the expanse of earthless space and a new destiny."

Soviet media did not stress the landing but it was revealed that reports were buried in Soviet newscasts behind other news of the day. Muscovites cheered and expressed congratulations to Americans in the Soviet capital. "Hooray," one said. "It's a great day," shouted another.

In the war-torn Middle East, Arab radio stations interrupted their bulletins of a major war to REACTION— *Please turn to Page Six*

NEIL'S MOM: 'PRAISE GOD!'

Leased Wire to The Register

WAPAKONETA, OHIO — Stephen and Viola Armstrong watched with varied emotions Sunday as their son Neil and Edwin E. Aldrin, jr., landed on the moon.

"Praise God from whom all blessings flow!" said Mrs. Armstrong as she and her husband appeared arm in arm in front of their home after the landing.

"I'm very thankful for the successful landing," said the proud father of the moonflight quietMaker. "I hope something good comes of this. I hope a whole lot of good comes from the day. Marvelous.

A KIND OF HUSH IN DES MOINES

By James Risser

While two American astronauts made history with man's first steps on the moon, the people of Des Moines spent a typical, if somewhat quieter than usual, July Sunday.

The astronauts' walk on the Sea of Tranquillity was marked by a tranquil day here as almost everyone stayed home, spellbound, to watch the moon show on television.

Police reported less crime than usual and downtown traffic was light. Radio dispatchers at the police and fire stations

DES MOINES— *Please turn to Page Seven*

Moon Holiday: No Mail Today

There will be no mail deliveries and all federal offices will be closed today in honor of the lunar landing of Apollo 11. All non-essential state offices will be closed this morning but

open in the afternoon. The banks will be closed all day. Government offices. But Polk County offices will be open for business as usual. Banks and post offices are expected to be open stores are expected to be open

Doug met the former Dean of the College, Mr. H. E. Kildee. Dean Kildee now resided in a hotel suite in downtown Ames but when he was a college student he had worked for Doug's great- grandfather C. A. Saunders. He knew my father and the Saunders family well. Holsteins were Dean Kildee's real love in the livestock industry and he was able to give Doug valuable advice on Holstein breeding.

Our Holstein heard was growing and we had more work than we ever thought possible, yet we had a steady income and we had gotten rid of Production Credit Association and Wilmer Peterson.

By now Doug had a good herd of Holsteins going and had the makings of a promising dairyman. As we talked about earlier, he attended the winter farm-operating course at Iowa State University. Many weekends while in college, Doug would come home to help on the farm and leave early Monday morning so he could be in classes by eight o'clock. Half a world away, other young men were fighting a war. As long as Doug was in classes he was deferred but a few days after finishing his classes he received a letter from Uncle Sam indicating that he would be drafted for the Vietnam War. In order to have some control over the situation, he enlisted in the Navy. They allowed him to be on a deferred list so he could be present for the spring planting and fall harvest. He would be allowed to stay on the farm until November.

That summer was the time we made the decision to build a milk parlor. The thinking was Trudy and I could more easily handle the cowherd and keep the cash flow coming in during Doug's absence. Once again we bought used equipment and worked all summer getting it set up in the big barn. In mid-September Doug received his Navy orders to report for induction on September 23rd. We were able to get the parlor ready so we could milk in it the Saturday night before he was to report for duty.

Craig had come home from Iowa City that weekend to see him off and to help start the cows through the parlor. Sunday afternoon Doug spent all by himself, painting the holding pen fence . . . and thinking.

Doug had to be in Omaha the next morning so, after the chores were done that night, we packed his small bag in the family car and started one of the longest most heart-rendering journeys of our lives. It was a stormy dark September night in which we said our goodbyes and handed over our youngest son to Uncle Sam. A cold, soaking rain fell all night, making it as wet and dreary as our tear-soaked souls.

None of us remember what was said that night. It was not a night for words; it was a night for silent prayers and countless tears. We prayed for his safe keeping and deep in my heart I was kind of glad that he was in the Navy, hoping he would be safer than in the Army.

Doug's Uncle Bob (Trudy's brother) and Aunt Garnet accompanied us that night, as much to see us home as to see Doug off.

The next morning Trudy and I were in the new milk parlor, doing the milking. I remember saying "Maybe we have spent too much money and made a mistake."

But we hadn't. It was hard to hire help to replace the boys. Trudy helped with milking the cows and the cows learned rapidly to adapt to their new surroundings.

Trudy was a great help to me at this time, and we were perhaps closer than we had been in years. Though neither one of us said it aloud, our boys were gone. The little house we built for ourselves across the road was standing empty and falling into disrepair. The big house seemed bigger and emptier now than it had on that cold February day fifty years earlier when my little sister and I ran through it searching out our new rooms. If you had asked Trudy at the time why she was out in the barn milking cows with me, she would have said something like . . . "Well, the parlor is new and kind of fun but you need the help, too."

I'm sure that was all true, but I know she was there with me because her house was empty and it was a time that we both needed each other. I'll say it again; I never met anybody that I would want to put my life together with other than Trudy.

God never asks more of us than we can give and he never takes without giving back in return. We were home alone with a lot of debt and work ahead of us. Trudy and I both worked the milk parlor, bred and cared for our cows and Trudy was still selling toys. While at a party in Sac City she met a young couple, Wayne and Judy Baldwin, who were looking for a better job. They moved down and helped us for about a year-and -a -half before moving on to Colorado to manage a hog farm. Two outstanding young men followed, Doug Bro from near Exira and then Doug Jensen from near Irwin. They were God sends that helped us keep the farm going, but one of the nicest things happened to us the following March.

Craig was in the Air Force stationed in San Antonio, Texas. Dean and his family came down to look after the farm for the weekend while Trudy and I flew to San Antonio. It was our first real vacation in years and the very first airplane flight, except for the ride in my cousin's fighter, for either of us. I was 59-years-old when I walked through that aircraft door and into a different world.

We were both nervous and excited as we fastened our seatbelts and placed our trays and seatbacks in the upright position. Soon the roar of the jets and the almost imperceptible first movement of the aircraft. For those first few seconds it reminded me of that old Chinese proverb that says all of life's greatest journeys must begin with but a single step. I thought of my great grandfather stepping on to the boat with his new bride, taking them from their home in England to an unknown life in America. I thought of my Grandfather stepping onto the train in Black Earth and stepping off in Iowa and taking those first steps to his new life. I thought of the cold February afternoon my Father picked up my sister Margaret and me in the old horse-drawn bobsled and the first steps of our short journey to our new life and new home on Cumberland Stock Farm No. 2.

I began to think of life as a series of entwined journeys and my mind began to play the who, what, when, where game. I began to wonder who now was taking what unknown first steps that would begin what as yet unimaginable journeys, and when, at journey's end, where would our country, my family or I be?

We had taxied to the southern end of the runway and took off to the north. A slow right turn carried us over the Missouri River and into western Iowa. I looked out the window. There was snow on the ground and I realized I was looking at the same snow covered land that Thomas Jefferson purchased and Lewis and Clark explored two hundred years before. It was the same snow-covered ground my Grandfather had walked into on another cold March day nearly one hundred years ago.

These men had followed the winding contours of the Indian trails that followed the animal paths over the hills, the rivers and the streams. These pathways had now all but given way to the square patchwork quilt of civilization. The land I saw was divided up into perfectly square one mile sections to facilitate the taming of the prairie, mobilization of its produce and the education of its new citizens. I looked for telltale signs of the old country schoolhouses built every two miles but they were gone too.

As we flew farther south the snow disappeared and slowly the land got greener and greener. I marveled at the thought of drinking a cup of coffee sitting five miles above the earth, traveling over 500 miles per hour but I am a farmer, attached to the land and my thoughts flew backwards to "my" land and "my people."

I thought of my parents. They were married 67 years earlier. The year was 1903, but the really big news that year was about a couple of brothers named Orval and Wilber who, on some obscure sand dune called Kitty Hawk, made the first powered flight. Mom and Dad never flew and it took me nearly sixty years to get my feet out of the dirt. Guess we were just too busy trying to scratch out a living. Besides that, up to now, there really hadn't been much of a reason. But now with two boys in the military, our family was being scattered. Craig was a young Captain interning at the big Air Force Hospital in San Antonio and Doug was a Navy airman aboard the aircraft carrier USS Oriskiny.

As the aircraft door opened in San Antonio we were met by hot dry Texas air offering no resemblance to the cold windy March Iowa day we had left just a couple of hours earlier. Little did we know that half a country away, the USS Oriskiny was coming into port at Hunter's Point in San Francisco. Doug knew we were going to be in San Antonio and without telling anyone, except his brother, he got a weekend pass and early Saturday morning phoned his brother Craig to come to the airport to pick him up.

Mother was up early. As usual, she was afraid she might miss out on something. I was still in bed Saturday morning, taking full advantage of my first vacation when someone came bursting into the bedroom asking why I wasn't up milking the cows. It was Doug. Imagine my surprise. We spent a wonderful weekend in the warm Texas sun. I remember the Alamo, the River Walk and the Air Force Base. What a reunion, and over all too soon.

It was hard for us to return home that weekend and leave our boys in these strange places. The thought of two of our own family in the senseless Vietnam War was difficult to understand. When our Manilla boys gathered at Germania Hall and marched off to WW I everyone understood the cause. When they marched off to WW II, Pearl Harbor was fresh in our minds and we understood. But this . . . this seemed much more difficult to understand.

Craig spent three more years as an Air Force Flight Surgeon, making many flights into the war zone. Doug spent four years in the waters off Vietnam. It was hard to understand the necessity, much less right, for the United States to have our boys in SE Asia.

We were, however, Americans and long ago we had put our sweat in the soil and our faith in our country. We hoped and prayed that faith was not misplaced. We were not alone, and we were more fortunate than some.

Our boys came home!

Son Doug in his Navy uniform and on the flight deck (foreground) of the USS Oriskiny

Son Craig as a U.S. Air Force Flight Surgeon on the right and in the rear seat.

Chapter 16

. . . A NEW SIGN WENT UP. . .

February 11,1989

Four long years later Doug was discharged from the Navy at Subic Bay in the Philippine Islands. Mother and I went to the Omaha Airport to pick him up. Our excitement turned into anxiety as we watched passenger after passenger leave the plane. Doug was the last one off. I will always remember the sight of him walking off that plane. He was wearing a handsome Navy uniform he had tailor-made in Hong Kong, but he had spent over 24 hours sleeping and traveling half-way around the world in it, hopping military and commercial planes to come directly home. He didn't look very neat, but he looked oh-so wonderful!

He walked off the plane with his discharge orders in his hands, throwing them in the air and yelling, "The war is over!"

People were startled at first but then, slowly, a few began to clap their hands until soon the whole terminal was welcoming him home. I couldn't believe the number of people who came up to shake his hand.

Doug ducked into the public bathroom and changed into civilian clothes right there in the airport. He always knew what he wanted to do and as we approached home, at the bottom of the hill was one of our tractors sitting out in the field. He asked us to stop the car. He got out of the car and on to the tractor – he never even came into the house. Thereafter, he hardly even went into town, Trudy asked him why he didn't go places. He said, "I've been to the other side of the world and I don't care about going anymore."

The day after Doug came home from the Navy we began to make many plans for the Cumberland Stock Farm. New fences were made, a new silo was erected as was a new free-stall barn along with cement feed bunks. We even began to cement the cattle yards to try to get control of the mud and manure problems. The Holstein herd had grown a little each year. Trudy and I had managed to hold things together.

I now had the pleasure of walking and planning alongside a young man, just as my grandfather had done with my father and my father had done with me. Now it was my son and I planning to continue the Cumberland Stock Farm traditions.

We began to think along the very same lines. We planned a sale and sold off our surplus stock in an auction held right here on the farm. We tried to minimize our work and increase cash flow.

In the meantime, a quarter section of land adjoining our farm in the northeast corner of our Section Two came up for sale. The farm had been owned by a family by the name of Hinkelmen, They had been our neighbors for years but their sons had all moved on and now the farm was in estate.

We tried to interest my second son, Doug's older brother Dale in buying the farm in some sort of a partnership and working with Doug in the farming operation, but it was not to be. I spent a day-and-a-half working directly with the Metropolitan Life Insurance Company in Des Moines and we spent a full day with Dale and Johnet. Mr. Hinkelmen's son-in-law was the administrator of the estate and he visited us two or three times but I could not get Dale and Johnet convinced.

Johnet still had a bad taste in her mouth from our previous dealings and Trudy was surprisingly not much in favor of any kind of partnership. She hoped and prayed every night for reconciliation with Dale, but perhaps she saw this as potential for further problems. I don't know.

It didn't matter. Johnet complained the buildings were not perfect and turned thumbs-down on the deal. With the Saunders out of the picture, the farm was placed up for public auction. They only wanted $400 per acre, it was not over priced.

I did not go to the sale. I stayed home and was loading manure with a pitchfork when Dale came over after the auction. "Dad, where were you today? They were stuck at $375-380 per acre. It didn't sell," he said.

"There was no need," I said. Finally, the farm was sold privately; today that land is worth well over $2,000 per acre.

Doug and I had our hands full with more than we could handle. We were not in a position to take on more. The timing was just not yet quite right to take on this new venture alone. We were committed to our own farm improvements and were reinvesting by replacing some of the machinery. In fact, Doug and I were investing all we made, sometimes faster than it was coming in.

We continued on with our nose to the grindstone. We bought a couple of used Allis Chalmers D19 tractors. They were not the most popular of tractors. They had been only made for three years and they had a six-cylinder gas engine, but they could be bought for fewer dollars per horsepower than any other on the market. We bought a used feed wagon from one of Dean's dealers and pulled it home from up near Spencer, Iowa behind Dean's car.

One year later on a cool October evening in 1974, I walked into our milking parlor, the parlor we had built when Doug left for the Navy. "Dad, do you want to buy a farm?" Doug said as he looked up from his work. "Mr. Scott, the real estate salesman, was here. Oscar Wetzel wants to sell his farm. He will be back later tonight to discuss it with us."

It was quite an abrupt conversation. The Wetzel farm joined our land in the southeast corner of Section Two, just south of the farm we missed buying a year ago. Oscar had been a neighbor for as long as we had lived here. I went to school with him. He was the one that helped me drown out the ground squirrel. Most of his adult life was spent as a bachelor farmer with no family. He had married late in life and along with the marriage came an instant family but no one to carry on with the farm.

Mr. Scott stopped in before we were finished with our chores. Nothing unusual about that; hell, it seemed our chores were never finished. He told us the particulars and how Oscar wanted his money. Twenty-nine percent now and a ten-year contract on the balance at 6% interest. With our experiences of a year ago fresh enough in our minds, Doug and I talked it over and asked Mr. Scott to come back at nine o'clock the next morning.

At 8 A.M. the next morning I went into Manilla to use my Aunt Sadie's telephone. Party lines were still the norm for our country phones. Instead of each user having their own private telephone line, several users used one telephone line and anyone could listen in on your conversation simply by picking up the phone. To be honest, though, that was less a concern to me than who might be listening in my own kitchen!

I called T. J. Tokheim, our banker friend in Lytton, Iowa who had helped us purchase our original milk cows nearly fifteen years earlier. He listened and said, "I'll tell you how to handle it. Obviously, Oscar is getting older, wants to retire and needs some money. All you have to do is make sure that you don't overpay. They want a little more money than the farm that was sold a year ago but, by taking out the half-mile of fence that separates Oscar's and your farm, it will increase the value of both farms by $50 per acre."

Tokheim advised me briefly on how to write the contract to make it stick. "Generally, the buyer wants escrow money of about $1,000 which he holds till March. (March is the beginning of the fiscal year for farmers) They want money quickly, without listing the farm, etc. You give them a check for $5,000. Tell them as long as they want to live there and pay the utilities they are welcome to stay. If they want to mow the lawn, that is their prerogative. But what I want you to do," he continued, "is not to pull one staple on that fence or make one change till March."

Tokheim's last words were, "You write out the check to both the realtor and Oscar. Have the realtor endorse it so he can give it to Oscar then all Oscar has to do is take it to the bank. Don't worry about the check. I'll see to it that it clears."

Mr. Scott came at nine o'clock that morning, just as planned. We gave him a $5,000 check and signed an agreement for the balance of the down payment on March 1, 1975 with possession at that time.

In less than an hour, Scott was back with our contract, and a gift certificate for steak dinners for four at the Holiday Buffet in Harlan. Doug and I had bought a farm. Then we told the rest of the family.

Word got out quickly and it wasn't exactly pleasant for a while. Trudy, of course, was worried and upset that we hadn't included her and the rest of the family but we had already learned our lessons and I knew that fast decisive action would be the only way to get this job done.

When Oscar's heirs found out that he had sold the farm, some of them thought it was for too little money. Our neighbor Mark Kenkel stopped in at the farm a couple days later. "I was down in Irwin today," he said, "heard the farm deal didn't go through."

Dean called, and said, "The land deal didn't go through."

But I had signatures of both Mr. Scott and Mr. Wetzel and they had the money. The old banker Tokheim was 77-years-old at the time and he had set up a deal that stuck.

The next spring, Doug and I took out the fence. The new farm fit in well and before many years passed, it was worth three times the purchase price.

There was one more addition to the Cumberland farm that spring. Doug was taking a course in Manning, learning how to use artificial insemination in our cattle herd. While eating lunch at one of the local restaurants he became acquainted with the waitress, Miss Patricia Fisher.

It wasn't long before Doug came to us and said, "Dad, Mom, I want you to meet Patty."

We, of course, agreed and one April evening Mom, Dad, Doug and Patty ate those four steaks Mr. Scott had given us. In all honesty, I must say I was surprised. Such a little girl, but smart and knew just what she wanted. Doug and Patty were married the following December 14, 1975.

We bought a used trailer (mobile home) for Doug and Patty and set it up just south of where Trudy and I had built our little home in 1934. I would have loved to have them move into our little house but by then it was in too great of disrepair. The kids did as we had years before; they went to work and made do with what was available.

Never could a family ask for a more pleasant and cooperative daughter-in-law. Perhaps somewhere there exists some as good, but none better. She was and still is a precious jewel. Doug, who had been homesick half way around the world while on the USS Oriskiny, now had the world by the tail. I truly believed it.

We farmed a father-and-son business, we discussed our problems and made our plans in the milk parlor and a new sign went up on the barn:

CUMBERLAND STOCK FARM II
Saunders and Saunders

The sign may never have to be changed as he now has three sons and a daughter to follow on in the Saunders and Saunders Family Farm tradition.

My Father and Grandfather experienced this before me and now I am blessed to be experiencing the same feeling.

What a great feeling!

> *"Farm life is*
> *family*
> *intertwined with*
> *work."*

Two generations of change. Above Dale and Dean show their
prize winning Shorthorn heifers. Below, their nephews, Doug's
youngest boys Matt and John, the fifth generation of Saunders
boys, with a Holstein milk cow and calf.

Chapter 17

. . . Grace and Dignity . . .

February 12, 1989

Another early morning. 4:10 am and I have already had a cup of Butternut coffee.

Could be a heat wave today. The thermometer is 20 degrees above zero this morning, a lot different than 15-20 below less than a week ago.

Busy day yesterday. Doug got his 1985 corn shelled and delivered to town. Mother took his alternator to the shop in Manning. I washed up things at the milk barn and rode over to Manning just before dinner and got the alternator repaired, then ate dinner[63] with the corn shelling crew at Doug and Pat's.

Mother went into the beauty shop for a permanent and then to Denison for something for the house.

After dinner I took Doug's AC7000 and picked up a big bale of hay from the old Wetzel place, set up Doug's milkers for evening and then came home to work for Trudy. The new hairdo looks pretty nice.

Today we are going to Harlan for our driver's license, groceries and perhaps dinner.

Farm life is family intertwined with work. All the boys stayed close to the farm except one. Doug is of course here at home, Dale has his own farm in Manilla and Dean has spent a career in the farm equipment industry and has a small farm of his own.

I think Craig secretly wishes he had a farm.

---

[63] On the farm, dinner is what lunch is to the rest of the world. A farmer gets up in the morning to some fresh coffee and maybe some pastry or toast. After chores and the rest of the family is awake it is time for breakfast. Noon is dinner time and the big meal of the day followed by a lunch at about 4 o'clock. Supper is at night after the field work and livestock chores are done. Of course there is always room for a bowl of popcorn or ice cream before bed.

After four years of active duty Craig left the Air Force with the rank of Major, but not before his first little girl, Laura Morgan Saunders, was born December 1, 1971, in the Madigan Army Hospital, Fort Lewis, Washington. Laura was our second granddaughter and we took our second airplane flight the following March to meet her.

Trudy was quoted at the time, "I thought there should be a law that requires grandkids to live near their grandmother . . . "

Upon his discharge, Trudy flew back out to Washington to help Craig and Gin move their new baby and household back to Iowa where he began a surgical residency. Craig became deeply involved in his four years of general surgery. Ginny not only worked as an Occupational Therapist during that time, she managed the family.

Four years later this young family included little Emily Harrison Saunders who put in her appearance at the Saunders' household at 6 Melrose Circle in Iowa City on December 10th 1975. She was a delightful little girl born just four days before her Uncle Doug married Aunt Patricia Fisher.

Craig was the groomsman at the wedding so he and his three-year-old daughter Laura drove out to Doug's wedding on December 14, 1975. They drove back home in one of the worst Iowa snowstorms on record.

After Craig finished four long years at Iowa he then spent two additional years learning heart surgery at The Cleveland Clinic. Ginny and the girls remained at their home in Iowa City. Craig would fly home for holidays and short visits but in just plain words, the marriage began to deteriorate.

The Saunders' men can be faulted for being stubborn and Craig was no exception. He placed his goal of being a heart surgeon above all else. At the time it seemed a lofty goal for this young Iowa farm boy. Although I know for a fact he now regrets and sees the folly of that approach. Ginny, with two young girls to care for and a full-time job of her own was tired of playing second-fiddle to Craig's career and I am sure longed for just a few of her own needs to be met.

After completing his cardiac training in Cleveland, Craig interviewed with Dr. Neil Arbegast in Bakersfield, California. Craig took his wife with him on one of the interviews but when the time came for him to move to his new job, Ginny elected to stay in Iowa City.

We all felt so sorry for Craig that hot July day in 1980 when he stopped at the farm with his two little girls. They were spending the summer with him and traveling to California in their ten-year-old Buick station wagon with rusted-out side panels. Somewhere near Las Vegas, the entire muffler system fell off the car but they finally made it. He established himself in a small apartment, gave his station wagon up for a used brown and tan Buick Regal and went to work.

We visited him in November of that year. He was 36 years old and for the first time since he started his surgical training six years earlier, he could come home every night and sleep in his own bed. No more in hospital night calls as a resident, finally a bit of spending money and most of all he was beginning to win the confidence of all the other doctors in the area.

One of the great friendships of our lives developed from that November trip to California. Craig took us to Porterville, California to the DeJong Dairy where we met Tom and Janet DeJong and their family. Tom Sr. was my age and five weeks earlier my son had done a triple bypass on him. Actually it was Tom's second heart operation but he was recovering well. Needless to say the DeJongs thought the world of the young doctor; in fact, a year or two later Craig would also operate on Grandma DeJong. So, when he asked if he could bring a couple old Iowa dairy farmers to tour their California dairy, they were delighted. We all became very close friends, always visiting the DeJongs whenever we were in California.

The young doctor was on his way. He, like his family before him, began to command the respect of those who worked both for him and with him. It was time for him to get the rest of his life in order. Looking back, I am sure that both Craig and Ginny have since endured times tougher than what they were going through. Certainly the rest of us have, but they were young, living life the best they knew but not knowing how to keep their lives together.

One early April morning, a phone call came to the farm. The young doctor could hardly speak. Although his mother and I had made several planned trips to visit him in the various sections of the country while he was studying, something, I think it was God, said, "Ray, he needs his father now . . ."

I made reservations on the next flight to California. A heartbroken young man met me at the Los Angeles Airport. Craig was learning the hard way that his selfish devotion to his own personal goals and career had torn apart the fabric of his personal relationships beyond the possibility of repair. He had learned to be a fine heart surgeon but he was going to have to learn all over again what it meant to have to deal with is own heart . . .

On the ride to Bakersfield we talked and talked, then rode many miles in silence. We both had a hard time sleeping that night.

Early, and I mean early the next morning, we drove up into the mountains through the Kern River Canyon. Never in my life had I seen so many wildflowers. The wild poppies were in full bloom, glimmering in the bright sunlight – red, yellow and orange. It looked like God had opened his paint can and just poured it all out over those mountains. It was beautiful beyond my ability to describe.

On the way back into town, we noticed a young man with long hair and dirty jeans lying on the edge of the road with his dog. When we drove up he seemed to be sound asleep. We weren't even sure he was alive. With a toot of the car horn he sat up. We asked him if he was okay. He said he was sick and yes, he would accept a ride for the three or four miles back into town. He said he had a sister living there.

The dirty stranger and his dog rode in the back seat and the trip was made in almost complete silence. He seemed reluctant to talk. His only words upon arriving in a very questionable part of town were, "Let me out here."

I shall never, as long as I live, forget the sight. A long-haired, unwashed young man, dirty clothes and a mangy dog walking away from the car leaving a layer of dirt, dust and dried grass in his wake.

Nor can I forget my own son's remark, "Boy, and I thought I had problems."

I could hardly believe what God had shown me. Two young men, about the same age, one a promising young surgeon, the other apparently a drug addict, and he loved them both. It was hard for me to keep my silence and let Him work.

I believe God has a plan for all of us but he leaves it up to us to figure it out.

We went on to the hospital where Craig spent a long time visiting patients and getting things in order for a big day of surgery scheduled for Monday morning. The next morning we drove to the hospital. There I met and visited with Dr. Neil Arbegast, the doctor who had originally asked Craig to join them in California. He was well aware of the personal problems the young doctor faced.

That day I was a guest in the operating room and I had an experience that I would guess only a very few fathers in the history of the entire world have ever experienced. I stood at the head of the operating room table and watched my son hold another human being's heart in his hands, stop it, repair it and start it up again better than new. Three times that day he preformed this miracle. I marveled at the concentration, skill and dedication. I thought of the sacrifices and the broken home. I wondered if anyone or anything could have prepared him to successfully manage his professional and his personal life. I suppose many do but I wondered if it was I who had failed him. Could I have made him stronger, given him better values?

A parent always wonders.

By five or six that afternoon three heart surgeries were over but the physical endurance, the psychological stress and the burden in his own heart had taken its toll. Dr. Saunders was so tired he could barely speak, let alone walk. I sensed it was not so much a physical tiredness as it was a sense of loss. After having accomplished so much and at such great expense he had lost the ability to reap the reward of sharing his accomplishments with the people he cared for the most.

We returned to his empty apartment and both laid down to rest. I dozed off thinking of the wonderful gifts life had given my son and prayed for only one more, the ability to enjoy his accomplishments.

About eight o'clock, Craig woke up with a different look on his face. "Dad, let's go out to eat." He was a different person. His problems were still with him, but it seemed as though he was back in command. We went to a local Basque restaurant where many people knew him and we were joined by a young couple for a modest family-style meal with red table wine in screw-top bottles. I believe all of us were watching our pocket books.

The next morning I left Bakersfield and started my way back to Iowa in a ten-passenger commuter plane bound for Los Angles. Before we took off, the young lady in the seat ahead of me turned and asked, "Are you Dr. Saunders father?" She was a nurse who worked at one of the hospitals and knew of his work. She and her son were on their way to meet her husband. It seemed to me that everyone knew the young doctor.

I have often since wondered.

Why did God show us those beautiful wildflowers?

Why did we find that young man on the side of the road?

Why did three patients need open-heart surgery that day?

Why did the first person I met after leaving ask, "Are you Dr. Saunders' father?"

Why?

My Grandfather once said, "God and politicians work in odd ways. Most people don't listen and the rest of the people can't understand them." Frankly, I think Grandfather put politicians in much too lofty company. However, I believe this was God's way of showing us that we are not alone, that he will show us the way if we will just pay attention, listen and obey.

I believe He was showing us with His flowers what a beautiful world He had created for us. With the young man he demonstrated just how blessed we were. With the surgeries He reminded us what great gifts we have and all the good we can do with His help, and with the stranger on the airplane He let us know that our work was not unrecognized.

This was one of the very few times I had really spent time alone with one of my sons. It was difficult to relate these experiences to the rest of the family when I got back to Iowa.

Trudy has been heartbroken over the divorce of Craig and Gin. We have remained close to his family. His daughters, Laura and Emily, have spent their summers with their Dad and have been to visit us many times both in our home and in their Dad's home in California. It would be hard for anyone except a successful heart surgeon to supply the opportunities he has for them. I believe he has been granted that privilege because he has used the time God gave him to help others.

God will point the way.

Eight years later, the first Sunday in September 1988, Craig married Miss JoDee Ditter, a young student originally from Grand Island, Nebraska, another Midwesterner. He met JoDee after having performed heart surgery on her stepfather. Two weeks after the wedding, he was on his way to China to perform open-heart surgery. His new wife stayed home to attend to her studies and classes. Now the house isn't so lonely when he comes home.

February 13, 1989

Not so early this 13th day of February 1989. Yesterday was Sunday morning, the day of the big Home Community Club Valentine Dinner.

The dinner was at Cronk's Café in Denison, Iowa. It's a good thing we have a nice car, money for gasoline and paved highways. Much different than fifty years ago; then it was a luxury. Now it has become a necessity.

It was fun.

The Home Community Club was started during the depression years of the early 1930's. Originally, it was part of the County Extension program out of Iowa State University. It was an attempt to organize the farm ladies. In addition to the social aspects they conducted cooking lessons, sewing demonstrations etc.

My mother was one of the first members and today there will be three generations of Saunders present. Trudy and myself, Doug and Patty plus their children Chris, Jenny, Matt and J. C. There are only a few of the members still living on their farms.

Things and conditions have changed so much. Fifty years ago there were no thoughts of Holsteins on Cumberland Stock Farm No. 2. I wonder what Dad and Grandfather would say. I feel they know and approve. The family and farm homes they worked so hard for nearly a century ago are still in good hands and growing.

Trudy has been a great help through the years and I have grown increasingly dependent upon her. Perhaps for that reason, perhaps for others, she had grown increasingly stubborn. No doubt there are many things she would like to have different but as I look back I can't see anyone in the area that has a nicer home or family.

We are the only family of all the young people that we grew up with who are still together in our farm homes. The Harold Neimans are the only ones still alive. Andy Carothers, Louis Vennick, Melroy Carstens, all gone. Harold Justice, Jim Theobald, Wilber Jahn gone, too.

I don't give a damn what anyone says, you can't find a farm that has been lived on and looked after like this one.

Blessed

We have so much to be thankful for.

Looking back, perhaps one of the most important things that we should be thankful for is our ability to change, yet we fear it so much. The world changes around us. We can either be a part of that change and continue to grow or we can choose to become obsolete. When we lose the ability to change, we begin to die. Perhaps not suddenly, but surely, slowly we begin down the path of extinction. You know, Charles Darwin was misquoted. It is not "survival of the fittest" as is often quoted. He actually said something like "It is not the strongest or the most fit, it is those with the most ability to change that survive."

When Mother, Dad and I managed to get only the 6th Federal Land Bank loan made in Shelby County, we had in a sense bought back our 315 acres and managed to get things drawn together. We had our home pretty much secured, a $20,500 mortgage, a place to live and most importantly an opportunity.

My visions of college and becoming a 'kid doctor' changed when I signed the notes and mortgages on the farm along with my father. Instead of a carefree college student, there I was, not yet old enough to vote yet owing more money than most any other farmer or for that part, more than anyone, or so it seemed.

I might add, when we were refinanced and all the bills were paid, I had $417 in the farm account at Harlan National Bank, but the problems were not over. There were many years of struggle ahead.

However, we were one of the few who had managed to hold onto our farm and home. I believe this was in large part due to my mother's ability to foresee the problems, and being ahead of the great rush for help during the great depression plus the fact my parents were very conservative and hard-working.

One good thing about all the changes which occur while one is engaged in life's struggle just to survive and grow old, is that one gains perspective. I have always thought it was one of God's little jokes on mankind that daily we put ourselves in a position to struggle and strive to do the one thing that so many people fear the most – growing old.

But with age comes, if not wisdom, at least perspective. If, when faced with our insurmountable problems of today, we step back and look at our insurmountable problems of yesterday, we gain the perspective that they were not impossible. The seemingly overwhelming, the impossible was possible.

That is the lesson to be learned.

God does not give us more than we can handle. We have lived through and conquered the 'impossible' tasks of our past and we will also conquer the present and future, including I might add, our own deaths.

Secure in this knowledge, it becomes our challenge to face these tasks. It becomes our challenge to live life, with as much grace and dignity as humanly possible.

PART II: THE DIARY

Family Values

February 16, 1989

It's bright and sunny again this morning. It's 8:00 am and it is ten degrees above zero. Not too bad.
I wish you could hear Trudy at her organ. She is practicing the music for church. It is great.

Yesterday was quite a day; I now have my 78th birthday behind me. Dale called and alerted us that Uncle Bob and Aunt Garnet were planning on coming over. Trudy was at a United Presbyterian Women's board meeting at the church. So Bob came over, Trudy came home and Patty came from across the road with Jennifer and John and we all had lunch together. Later, Doug, Chris and Matt stopped by.

Just as Trudy and I were leaving for Lenten church services, Ruth Manford brought us our airline tickets. We are planning to fly to California on March 1 for about ten days with Craig and JoDee.

When we got home from church, my sister Margaret called. So that is my 78th birthday, all on paper.

Tomorrow we plan on driving to Des Moines for a visit with Dean. He just had some minor thyroid surgery, nothing serious. He will be fine. We will stay at our granddaughter's house, Karen and her husband Dan Hanson have a fine home and a good outlook on life. Karen's remark was that they ". . . only have to make thirty-five more years of payments." I suppose that's true but it is a beautiful home and having fought my entire life to keep the home and the land that my parents fought for, too, I can tell her that it is worth it.

When we have a family so close and caring, it's great to be around. We may be getting old but we still have a life to live, children to look after and grandchildren to bring into the world. A close, caring family, good honest work and the joy of planning for the future of both the family and the farm is what keep Trudy and me going.

I don't know how others survive without it.

I guess maybe they don't.

We are about the only ones left.

> *"God and politicians*
> *work in odd ways.*
> *Most people don't listen*
> *and the rest of the people can't*
> *understand them."*

February 25, 1989

A typical February day. A slight mist in the air. Sanding trucks were on the highways.

I am so happy to be home and to know the family is in good hands.

So far, the month of February has been the exact opposite of January. We have had some winter. No big storms, but cold and light snow for the past few days.

Many days in January the temperature reached the forty-to-sixty degree range and was very dry. February has been in the teens to minus 35 degrees with a bit of snow on the ground.

We had a fine trip to Des Moines this past weekend but it is wonderful to be home. Dean is feeling well after his thyroid surgery and beginning to think about getting back to work for New Idea. He ordered his seed corn and sort of complained that it was going to cost him $77 per bushel so he is looking forward to spring and the future.

While in Des Moines, Janet Clevenger, Ginny's younger sister from Indianola, brought her two girls up to see us. They are such a beautiful set of twins, two-years-old this coming April. They were born prematurely, weighing less than four pounds. Katie and Kimberly are so pretty and so active. Janet's husband Murry is the plant supervisor at Meadow Gold, in Des Moines.

At noon, Dan Kahl, Dorothy Arnold's son, Trudy's niece's boy, joined us at Karen's house for dinner. He is going to Diesel Automotive School and working nights at Burger King to finish school in June.

After dinner I rode into the hospital with Rosemary to spend more time with Dean. Dean is now 54-years-old, has raised a fine family, Karen, Kevin and Keith. This past week at his company's promotional meeting in Chicago, he received six company awards.

Yesterday, Doug, Pat and I went to Harlan, the annual Uncle Sam payment day. It was a nice day and the weather forecast seems to be favorable. This morning the thermometer reads about twenty-two degrees above so maybe winter is on its way out. I hope so. It will help Doug with his dairy business and make it easier to get things ready for fieldwork.

We leave Wednesday on American Airlines out of Omaha to visit Craig. Always fun to see him, and also great to come home again.

What a change from thirty-five years ago.

March 17, 1989

Trudy and I had a wonderful trip to California and visit with Craig and JoDee.

Mother and I spent a couple of days in Ventura in a condominium on the Pacific Ocean where Craig and his colleagues stay when they are taking call for the hospital there.

It's a different world there. So much traffic and so many people. It makes me happy to be home on the farm in Iowa.

Yesterday Trudy went to Denison and while she was there, she visited her sister Anna Marie. I stayed home on the farm and emptied Doug's manure spreader and did a few things here on the farm. It's easier for Trudy to get around town without me and I have nothing to do there.

Today she and I went to Irwin and picked up some tractor parts at Robertson Farm Equipment Company. They were having their spring party. Our son Dean was there as the White Farm Equipment representative. That evening he stopped at home for supper. Son Dale plus Bob and Garnet stopped later. It was Trudy's seventy-fifth birthday party.

How short life has been.

March 19, 1989

Sunday.
Kind of early, 5:15 am.
I woke up and decided I couldn't do much in bed so I shaved, made a cup of coffee and read a bit in the Hoards Dairyman . . .

It seems there are a lot of people beginning to realize that as you get a bit older, you don't have to have the biggest herd or the most acres, etc. I suppose that goes for a lot of other things besides farming and the dairy business.

It's sometimes hard to convince your creditors and financial people that more isn't always the answer.

A man from the state of Kansas writes about how he enjoys this eighty acres and forty cows. Although some of my family have disagreed with me through the years, I have always felt there is a time to reduce your herd. It is my theory of marketing your product and feel that is why our sales have been fairly successful. It doesn't take long for the herds to increase in size and with genetics and care, the new offspring should get better with the years.

It's always good to see and hear of the problems as well as the successes other dairymen have. Hell, I guess I am saying that it's good to be educated no matter what business you are in. Sometimes we fall into the trap of thinking we are the only ones with problems or the only ones who have to work for a living.

Son Doug and I have talked of how this year we want to repair the big barn and finish, or at least make a big attempt to finish, the fencing around the new machine shed. We also need to get the water system repaired and in top condition. These things will lighten the workload through the next winter.

Also, a new breeding program is being contemplated. We want to bring in frozen semen from some of the top bloodlines from eastern Canada.

If this program is started now and is fairly successful, in about four-to-five years, when Doug's family really begins to take a real working interest, the herd should have an ample supply of good heifers to enter the milking herd and those that are for sale will be of the breed that is in demand. If, that is, there are any dairymen left on these western Iowa farms.

March 28, 1989

6 am. A lot has happened since we left California.
Record high temperature this morning.
WHO Radio reported an all-time high on the Omaha cattle market at $80 per hundredweight. The feeder market is very active.
One wonders just where we are headed. Our plan now is to send 28 steers to Dunlap Auction for Tuesday's sale. They are Holsteins and are not fat but they will bring good money and should come close to bringing Doug's farm and dairy operation into the black side of the ledger.

Doug and Pat are doing well. Their family is growing and they seem to be happy. Yesterday while Patty went to a school conference, Doug took Trudy and me and all four kids to Harlan for a short conference with the A.S.C. and to get a few parts for the machinery.

Trudy and the kids went to the park for a while. I wonder how many other 75 year-old grandparents have the opportunity and advantage to spend free time with four grandchildren in the park.

When we were ready for home, Grandpa treated all to a chocolate shake at Hardee's Drive-in. We enjoyed the fellowship with them. It keeps us young.

Easter Sunday Trudy and I joined the young people of the two churches of Manilla for sunrise services and breakfast. We then drove to Ogden, Iowa to meet Karen and Dan. Together we drove on to Algona, Iowa and ate dinner with Kevin. He prepared pork chops, baked potatoes, creamed green beans, salad, hot rolls, cream puffs, ice cream and strawberries.

His dinner table looked so nice. I wish we had been able to take a picture but like a lot of other times none of us thought to bring a camera, yet I will picture it in my mind forever. Maybe that is the best picture.

A happy occasion for Grandma and Grandpa.

It was wonderful!

March 29, 1989

Today is quite foggy. We need rain. Being selfish, I would like to get our new alfalfa and oats seed in and then rain.

Sunday evening upon returning from Easter dinner with Dean's family, Doug called. He had quite a day. He was about to join his family for a short trip to Carroll to have dinner when he discovered the farm was completely out of water. The well that had given us problems in January had caved in completely.

Luckily for us we had sort of prepared for an overhaul of the water system. Doug had a new well drilled in January but unfortunately had not gotten it hooked into our water system yet. So, he had to hook up the stock trailer to his pickup, load the portable water tank and spend Easter Sunday hauling water.

He arranged for Carroll Kalvig of Irwin, who does our pump work, to install a new pump in the new well and hook it up to the water line. Carroll came soon after dinner on Monday, with his backhoe. He dug the ditch and was successful. He remembered close to where the water line was. By late afternoon there was water being pumped into the cistern from the new well.

Almost immediately we had water at our house. What a relief. We could have been out of water for many days had we not had the foresight in January to get started on our water system overhaul. Now we need to complete the job soon.

Last evening Trudy talked with our Michigan friends, George and Shirley Hazel. They are planning on being here on our farm for a weekend visit. So, we will have a fun time renewing our old acquaintances. We are sure to have a great time.

Looks like it is about 7:30; time for another cup of coffee. More later.

April 10, 1989

Monday.
Early Morning.
A lot has happened since Easter Sunday.

We have our new well working and although there is a lot of work to be done on the water system, we seem to be fortunate.

George and Shirley Hazel of St. Johns, Michigan visited us for the weekend of April 1-3. They are also dairy farmers and they brought with them their daughter Kathy and grandson Dana Mathew, twelve years old.

The whole family enjoyed their visit. We went to church and then took them on a short trip through the hills of western Iowa. We stopped at the National Wildlife Refuge at Desoto Bend and the museum of the sunken steamboat Bertram. Many of the pre Civil War artifacts are interesting.

Wednesday of last week we were back in Des Moines. This time we attended the finals of the Iowa State High School Mock Trials. The Spencer, Iowa team of which grandson Keith was the prosecuting attorney, placed fifth among 24 teams from various regional competitions throughout Iowa.

It is always a pleasure to be a guest of Karen and Dan Hanson. Their home in Des Moines is a far cry from the little apartment they first lived in. They seem to know what life is all about.

On our return trip, we stopped for a cup of coffee and a roll in Stewart, Iowa and called an old friend. Roy Gillman had taught Vocational Agriculture at the Manning High School during the early 1930's. During the last of the 1940's and for part of the early '50's he had been an Iowa Shorthorn Fieldman, then he became the Secretary of the Hampshire Sheep Association.

We had a nice but an all-to-short of a visit.

Time goes by so quickly.

April 15, 1989

Another early Sunday morning, 4:50 am.
It was very cold here in Iowa this last weekend, cold and dry.
Had a bit of rain Monday night or Tuesday morning, about one-fourth of an inch.
Still dry and cold. Nothing real drastic yet but it is quite a cause for concern.

Quite a bit was accomplished here on Cumberland Stock Farm this past week. For one thing, we finished the oats and alfalfa seeding. While Doug tended to the chores and the seeding, I enjoyed doing the disking of the corn stalks. It's a lot different sitting in the heated cab of an Allis Chalmers 7060 and a 21-foot disk than it was years ago when I was Doug's age. When I was his age, I sat on the cold iron seat of a small tractor exposed to the cold spring winds in my long underwear, heavy coveralls and thick work gloves pulling small equipment and working long, and I mean long, hours.

We had some sad news this last Thursday. Trudy's brother, Bob Arnold, had a farm-related accident. He was pinned between a tractor wheel and corncrib wall. We visited him in the hospital Thursday evening. He was lucky but still had three broken ribs, a bruised lung, a separated shoulder and various cuts and bruises.

At 4 am on Monday morning, Trudy took him up to St. Luke's Hospital in Sioux City, Iowa. Some of his tests showed a spot on his kidney and apparently they thought they were going up for some X-rays and observation. However, by noon Trudy called home to tell us he had his right kidney removed. Is it possible that this whole accident was a blessing that saved Bob from a more serious illness?

God works in mysterious ways and not always the way we have planned. There is an old Jewish proverb, "Man plans, God laughs."

Sunday we went to church and then ate lunch in Denison before going to the hospital to visit Bob. He is slowly recovering and lucky to be in as good of shape as he is. He has had a lot to contend with the past two or three years. It makes Trudy and me realize just how fortunate we are. We all know he is seventy-two- years old, but even then, if we were in his shoes, who knows what we would be doing. I really feel sorry for him and especially for his wife, Garnet. She is seventy-four or five-years-old and has never driven a car and is now sort of alone with the farm and family problems.

Again, it is easy to tell others what they should be doing, but oh so hard to be told!

Personally, I am so thankful for my family.

It would have pleased me to see our two farmer sons and their sons working together. I feel Dale's boy Jay would have made a great future for his family had he elected to work with his Dad (not necessarily bigger, just better). Of course, I am sure he will make a great future for his family however he chooses to live his life.

The past week Trudy has won high score at bridge, attended her Woman's Club meeting, got her hair done and is going to church for the Presbyterian Woman's Meeting and tonight we plan on taking Chris and Jennifer to Irwin to see the school play.

So, it seems to me that we are very fortunate.

Doug has started to clean up the lots where the steers were kept over the winter. He says the dry weather is perfect for that yard. I worked the silage ground with the spring tooth plow. This will allow the water to soak in if and when it does rain.

We have to do something. God can't do it all.

April 19, 1989

It's early Wednesday morning. Another of those mornings when grandpa wakes up and that's "it."

Ten years ago last night, just before midnight, our little granddaughter came to live on our farm. Doug and Patty left here around 9 pm. Just after midnight he called to tell us that he had a little girl.

"Oh, Doug, it can't be," I said, but it was.

Jennifer Ann was born April 18th, 1979. She was a pretty little baby. At last, not since my sister Margaret has there been a Saunders girl on the Cumberland Stock Farm No. 2.

Fortunately for her, she already had some help breaking in these new parents. Two years earlier on November 5, 1977, her big brother, little red-haired Christopher Douglas, came to live on the same quarter section of Greeley Township where, nearly 75 years earlier, his great Grandpa and Grandma started their lives together.

Patty had a hard time conceiving Chris. After he was born she told Doug, "I want four youngsters and I don't want to wait for them."

She didn't have to wait long. Jenny was to get even more help soon. Jonathan Charles was born June 1, 1981. He had the honor of having both his Great Grandpa's and his Great-Great-Grandpa's name, John R. Saunders and Charles A. Saunders. Little Matthew Lee was born July 31, 1982. Matthew's name goes back to Trudy's grandfather, Matt Arnold. Grandpa Arnold was actually Matthias; however, he was called Matt by his family and friends when he came to America from Germany over 100 years ago. This naming may be pure coincidence, but it does make a great story.

Today, the four grandchildren all board the Manilla School Bus at the same place where their dad did thirty years earlier.

It is a pleasure to have them so close and to watch as they grow and learn to follow their life's work.

May 6, 1989

What a lot of havoc has transpired in the past two weeks. This morning, record lows. We may have escaped the frost, but it is cold. Mother and Pat have all the garden plants covered.

The past few weeks we have had storms all over the country so who knows what is in store.

It's still quite dry. We were lucky to pick up a real good rain about a week ago followed by some showers and cool weather but it is still dry.

A person really wonders how to plan the future.

We are painting 2x6s for the fence around the machine shed where the old hog house was. I painted some in the morning while Doug worked the calves. I then took the big 7060 tractor out and started the last field we will plow, a field called the Cistern Hill on the old Wetzel farm. It was really fun for a 78 year-old. I didn't need to hurry even though it was cold. A big tractor, cab, heater/air conditioner, etc. What a change from the one-bottom sulky plow and four head of horses, then a few years later an old W. C. Allis Chalmers and two fourteen inch plow bottoms.

I know I have said this all before and I will no doubt say it again several times before I am finished, but I still marvel at what has transpired.

What a change.

It looks like if we can get one more good rain by June we will be able to get a fairly good cutting of alfalfa. A silo full of good haylage will be worth a lot this winter.

It's fifteen-to-six, I have to turn the furnace up.

September 24, 1989

It has been quite a while since by last writing. A lot of fine things have happened this past summer.

On June 24th Mother and I had all our family here for our 55th wedding anniversary.

We all attended church in Manilla where all our four boys had grown up. We still attend and Trudy plays the organ most every Sunday. Only one boy missed out, Dean and Rosemary's youngest. Keith had been on a youth exchange trip to Germany and arrived home the day after our party, but he returned home safe and had learned so much.

After services we had a family dinner at Cronk's in Denison. My sister Wilma, Trudy's brother Bob and his wife Garnet, sister Anna Marie and husband Fred Rabe were with us. I wish my sister Margaret could have been with us. She is widowed now and lives in Little Rock, Arkansas and is not in the best of health. Her son Russell teaches at the University of Nevada, Reno.

In the afternoon many of our old friends came out to the farm. Ed and Mada Whaling of Shelby, Floyd and Phil Fanning of Nemaha, Lloyd and Merle Davis of Oakland, Jim and Dorothy Theobald, Melroy and Lucille Carstens and Selma Vinnick plus Dale and Phyllis McCone, all of Manilla. Murray and Janet Clevenger of Indianola were there with their beautiful twin daughters Katie and Kimberly.

These are only a few of the many friends who joined the family in the afternoon here on the Cumberland Stock Farm No. 2, the farm were we had started our married life together fifty-five years ago.

Mother and daughter-in-law Patty had prepared a beautiful buffet lunch. How wonderful.

Now back to the heartaches and problems of everyday life. What would life be without family and friends to share the good and the sad with?

We are so fortunate and must remember to count our blessings.

We had our family picture taken in our home, again, on the same spot where we began our married life together in 1934.

It was a great day.

Perhaps this will be the last time the entire family will sit down to dinner together.

"Man plans,

God laughs."
Old Jewish proverb

September 26, 1989

Early morning and another wonderful day. Beautiful fall weather.

We are bailing hay. Doug's New Holland bale wagon is working fairly well, but it has needed some minor adjustments.

Doug needs more time and a good young man who wants to try and is willing to learn. I hope in another few years he will have a boy of his own who can run the place.

Last evening after school, Doug's three boys helped unload a load of hay and then went with their dad to look at a 396 Chevy engine for Doug's '69 Camero that he is trying to rebuild. This is the one hobby or diversion that Doug has. After they came home, the boys went to the pasture to get the cows while Doug went after another load of hay. The hay is wonderful but I wish we were cutting corn silage.

Guess we always want more.

We may want more but we are all busy with what we have. Pat has taken Jennifer to Denison for dancing lesions.

This past weekend was busy with something my Mother and Father could never have dreamed about. On Friday afternoon about 4 pm Craig and JoDee pulled into the farm with four Chinese doctors.

Drs. Alfred and Joan Li with their daughter Dr. Catherine Li and Dr. Chongxian Liao, the doctors are all originally from China. Dr. Catherine was raised and educated in China but came to the U. S. and spent two years studying at UCLA. She has been working with Craig's heart team for the past two or three years and is responsible for engineering Craig's first trip to China in 1988 with his whole California heart team. Dr. Liao is the head of the heart team they visited and worked with in China.

Saturday morning we had a late breakfast then the Manilla and Denison newspaper reporters were out to meet and interview our friends from another country.

The afternoon was spent in the cornfield and I am willing to bet that we are the only farm in Iowa that has had a Chinese heart surgeon driving their tractor in the cornfield. He had the biggest smile I have ever seen and it was hard to get him off the tractor for a quick trip to the antique farm equipment Steam and Gas Show south of Irwin.

Sunday morning Dr. Alfred Li gave the sermon in our Presbyterian Church. He talked about China and went back 4,000 years in their history. All of us sitting in the church pews that day remembered celebrating our country's 200th birthday in 1976 and I don't believe the irony escaped many of us. Alfred[64] talked about the many changes that have occurred in China during all that time and made reference to the short period of time, about fifty years that his country has been communist. Dr. Li praised former President Nixon for helping open the door between the East and West. He also talked about change in the future and stated he was certain that our two countries would get together in the future. He only hoped it wouldn't take another 4,000 years.

This was all very interesting because Dr. Liao graciously attended the service, though he declined to speak because, as he put it, "my English is not so good." He no doubt has beliefs that are significantly different from ours and could not have reached his high position without the cooperation and permission of the Chinese Government. That is just a realistic fact of life in modern-day China.

Craig and he have become good friends.

We had a wonderful weekend but all too soon they were back on the plane to California. Craig had open heart surgery scheduled for Monday morning.

To me, one of the main, if not *the*, highlight of the visit was when on the spur of the moment I asked my eleven year-old grandson Chris, to ask God's blessings before our Sunday meal. He did it with no questions and without falter.

It was impressive to all.

[64] Alfred, Joan and Catherine are all Americanized version of their Chinese name that they were given when they first started English classes in China. Dr. Chongxian Liao remains in China and has no American name but told me it was okay to call him Charlie, if it made things easier for me.

Blessed

We have a great family and we are so lucky that Doug found Patricia Fisher.

Manilla, Ia. Times Thursday, Sept. 21, 1989 Page 6

Ray & Trudy Saunders Host Visitors From China

Members of the Saunders family are pictured with their guests. Left to right: Doug, Ray, Jennifer, Dr. Liao, J.C., Chris, Trudy, Matt, Dr. Joan Shen, Dr. Alfred Li, Catherine Li, Dr. Craig Saunders, Patty, and JoDee Saunders.

Thanksgiving Day 1989

It is early. I have a habit of waking early.

Today Trudy and I are driving to Spencer to be with Dean and his family for Thanksgiving Dinner. I would like to stay overnight but Trudy thinks she has to be home. Her sister Anna Marie's husband, Fred Rabe, is in Omaha's Clarkson Hospital and is very ill. Combination of stomach, liver, kidneys, etc. Trudy has been taking her sister to Omaha and feels she needs to be available.

Our weather has been dry. Doug has a little bit of corn to pick yet. I know his position; I have been in his shoes. It is not easy with a family plus a Mother and Dad to sort of look after in addition to hired help that can be a pain in the neck as well as the pocket book. He is doing a great job, though. It's just that he has so many chores with the milk cows plus up keep on all the farm equipment.

It is hard when you have so little to work with but perhaps we need to thank God for what we do have. I know.

I just wish I could help him more. We have to make room for his youngsters so they have an opportunity here on the farm. He is so lucky to have the wife and family that he does. Many people have problems rather than joy.

Dean's family is doing well. Karen is an elementary counselor in the Des Moines schools and her husband Dan is a credit man for Northwest Bank. Kevin is following in his father's footsteps and starting a new job in the credit department for Ford/New Holland farm equipment in Kansas City. Keith, the youngest, is still in high school but well on his way. He has won seventeen debates in a row and is looking toward the state and national debate finals. He wants to attend the University of Northern Iowa followed by the School of Law at the University of Iowa.

Dale's boys, Robin and Jay, have both graduated college, have good jobs and are married to wives who are school teachers. None of our boys have been in any kind of trouble.

Craig called from his car on the way home from the hospital last night; he is so busy. I sometimes wonder why all the Saunders seem to burn the candle at both ends. His girls are doing well. Laura is a senior in high school in Eugene, Oregon. She is a great swimmer and captain of their swim team. She wants to go to University of Southern California next year. Emily is a freshman, doing well in her studies. I understand she is studying the violin. I sincerely hope she succeeds. She has had a stormy past few years. Apparently she loves her Dad more than anyone else and has had a rough time accepting the divorce. I believe, however, she is on the right road.

We all have so much to be thankful for this year of 1989. I pray Trudy and I will be here for many more of them.

Looking back, a lot has happened since the day in 1931 when my Mother and I made up our minds to, shall we say, "Save the family farm and home."

I really thank God for my family and the opportunities. As I look back, few are as fortunate.

Thank you, God.

Be there in the future for all of us.

Please.

We need you.

November 28, 1989

To my son Doug, whose birthday is today.

Happy Birthday, son Doug.

A few short years ago on November 28, 1948, God sent you to join three brothers, your Mother and Dad, and yes, Grandma and Grandpa Saunders here on Cumberland Stock Farm No. 2.

We were a poor family and had little, but oh, we were so rich in family life. It was hard to understand at first why God hadn't granted your mother her wish for a baby girl.

God knew what he was doing. It's been a great joy to be able to live a big part of my life so close to you, your wife Patty and your beautiful children. Few men get the chance to live and enjoy that close fellowship. I now realize what my Mother and Father enjoyed; having a young family here on Cumberland Stock Farm No. 2 when you and your brothers were growing up.

We came so close to losing that family heritage so many times.

A few days ago, I had the fun and pleasure of using your big tractor and chisel, plowing the exact spot I was born on February 15, 1911. Without God and family, this is one of the pleasures we could never enjoy.

Take care of it and don't lose it.

Time is getting shorter for Mother and me. We thank God for all He has made possible for us. Each day we realize how precious our family heritage is to all of us.

Son and family, take care.

Enjoy it now and always.

God Bless you all.

As ever,

Your Dad.

December 27, 1989

Sort of early. Christmas is over and 1989 is almost finished.

Best of all, the cold weather of the past two or three weeks has at least given up for a few days. It's partly cloudy, but warm, almost 40 degrees. December 1989 set cold records all the way to Texas and Florida.

Once again, most of the Saunders family sat down to one table for Christmas Dinner. Mother prepared a big brunch for us on the morning after Christmas. Seventeen people in all sat at one table.

Christmas Eve we enjoyed a midnight supper with Doug's family. This has become sort of a tradition after attending the Christmas Eve Candlelight Service at church. What fun for the youngsters.

Christmas Day, Dean's family came mid-afternoon. They joined us for the evening meal and stayed overnight. Dale's family came mid-morning on the 26th.

How thankful we need to be. I hope this will be repeated many times. It is great to know they care.

Doug, Patty and the two older children made a quick trip to Des Moines with the pickup and livestock trailer to exchange a Holstein bull with Tom and Marge Sullivan. We just needed a bigger bull. Perhaps it was my fault since we got him in early fall.

The two younger boys, John and Matt, stayed with Grandma and Grandpa. What a joy to have them. They helped Grandma take down the Christmas tree.

Craig and JoDee arrived back home in California the day before Christmas. They had been on a trip in the Caribbean. He was back in surgery Sunday morning. His girls were to join them on the 26th then they are off again to Chicago on the 29th for his partner's, Dr. Dominic Tedesco's, wedding.

I think the whole Saunders family will be glad to see 1990 in hope that things will begin to settle down.

February 17, 1990

Another Birthday passed.

Seventy-nine years, a good home, a wonderful family, grand kids and above all, a wife and partner with whom to share God's blessings.

Had a nice letter from sister Wilma, and a late evening phone call from sister Margaret who lives in Little Rock, Arkansas. Trudy's brother Bob and wife Garnet came over in the evening

Sunday and Monday were beautiful, warm days. We have about four inches of snow on the ground now and it is quite cold again. Only a short time till spring though and as of yet, we have had no big storms in western Iowa.

So nice.

Doug has been cleaning the calf stalls, a job we have to do by hand here on this farm.

Trudy and I have had a lot of things to do during our fifty-five years together. A lot of them seem endless, but, oh, God has been good to us. I thank him for the opportunity to have been born in America and to my Mother and Dad. My hope now is that our grandchildren and great-grandchildren can carry on.

The boys and their families have avoided the heartaches of drugs and alcohol that are so rampant today. We are so very fortunate.

Trudy and I are in fairly excellent health. Trudy enjoys her automobile, her bridge games, church and her lady friends. I enjoy going to the barn each day, washing up the dairy equipment and cleaning up the milk parlor, then being able to come in and enjoy a wonderful home, grandchildren and a few close friends.

I hope I can help Doug some on the farm this summer. He really needs almost a full-time man, but no one wants to work, especially on a farm, and few young people know enough to try.

I hope I live long enough to see Doug's boys show the world how a real farm needs to be operated. Dale McCone made the statement once, "They are in the buggy; all they need to do is pay attention to their dad and learn how to drive."

Interesting?

Think about it.

Makes a lot of sense in this world of 1990.

Trudy and I are looking forward to flying out to California for a week at the end of March. Laura and Emily will spend their Spring vacation with their Dad and we plan on being there the last few days of their break and then a few more days with Craig and JoDee.

In June, Laura will graduate form high school in Eugene, Oregon. We are planning a visit at that time with the girls and their mother, Ginny. We then hope to spend a few days with Trudy's Cousin Verona and Clarence Nickles of St. Helens, Washington. They are from North Dakota originally. It has been quite a while since we visited them. The last time was when Craig was in the Air Force and Laura was just a newborn baby.

Tomorrow, Sunday, we go to Denison for the Home Community Club Valentine Dinner. My Mother was one of the early members; now my wife and Doug's wife carry on the tradition.

We will have a nice, enjoyable dinner.

I've spent an hour and I'll now write Margaret and Wilma. Perhaps later I can go back to sleep. So long for now.

"How fortunate we are

in the

United States of America."

March 14, 1990

How time flies, and what wonderful things God gives us to enjoy.

Yesterday, mid-morning, while I was cleaning up the milk parlor, Doug came in and said, "Go over, change your clothes and ride with me to Dunlap. I'm going to take a cull cow to the auction."

How wonderful to know your son would care to take Dad along. After all, I am seventy-nine years old and I don't see very well nor walk perfectly.

Before long he had his trailer hooked up to his four-wheel-drive Dodge pickup and we were on the road. It was raining a bit and Doug was not able to work in the field but we were thankful; it had been dry for so long. It rained a little more along the way and within thirty minutes of when we arrived at Jim Schaben's auction yard, the cull cow was in the bank for $697.60.

What a change!

It used to be that I would be lucky to get somewhere from $75 to $125 after shipping a cow to Omaha on a truck along with a few head of cattle from several other farmers. We would have had to combine our stock to make a truck load. Then they would sell the next day and we would wait for the commission house to mail a check.

How fortunate we are in the United States of America!

While at the sale we chatted with other local dairy farmers and learned of one who had sold his herd on the butcher market. Not everyone has the patience or know-how to look after a dairy herd. So much depends on management and of course hours and hours of hard work.

Doug and I had a nice roast beef sandwich at the sale barn lunch room before driving back home in the much-needed rain. I finished up in the milk parlor and set up for the evening milking and then went back across the road to our little house.

Trudy was home from playing bridge. "No luck."

Before I was completely relaxed, son Dean, who travels for White/New Idea drove in and offered to take us to dinner. He was in the area visiting dealers. We picked up an old friend, Dorothy Theobald, and ate supper in Denison at a new truck stop.

To finish the day, Mother got a call from the Vail Iowa Church Ladies. They asked her to bring the tapes from the TV show of Craig's China trip to show at one of their afternoon meetings.

We also made plans to meet some of our family in Storm Lake on Sunday the 18th for Trudy's birthday dinner.

More rain.

What a perfect day.

April 9, 1990

The Easter Season is upon us. Fair crowd at the Palm Sunday service. Once again, Trudy was at the organ. She seems to get much more out of that old organ than anyone in the community. Something she can do and that she truly loves.

We had a wonderful trip to California last March. We timed this trip to coincide with Laura and Emily's visit with their Dad. They are young ladies now. We are planning to visit Laura, her mother and sister Emily in Eugene, Oregon for Laura's high school graduation. Seems like only last week she rode on my shoulders when we visited Craig and family. He was in the Air Force and lived in a log cabin in the woods of Washington State. It must have been sixteen, maybe seventeen years ago.

Time marches on; we don't live forever.

While at Craig's, Emily played her violin for us. She is shy, but Trudy, who played violin as well in her youth, said she did very well. I sincerely hope she works hard at it. She needs something she can do that others can't.

We all do.

Talking of music, while we were in California, Chris and Jenny attended their first music contest – Chris on the drums and Jenny on the saxophone. They couldn't wait for us to get home to show us their superior ribbons.

They are all growing up so fast.

Chris loves to be with his Dad. Doug took him to the field yesterday while he disked and prepared the 'south of the barn field' for oats. He told me last evening that Chris drove the 1060 (tractor) on the whole field except around the outside. He will soon be taking my place here on the farm.

I hope God gives me a chance to see him and his dad working the farm together.

I believe my Dad and Mother would be pleased with the way their grandson and great-grandsons handle the Cumberland Stock

Farm No. 2. It has been a pleasure for me to work with Doug's family.

Not much more going on here on the farm. Cattle prices are around $80, hogs $55 per CWT, corn $2.30 per bushel. It's all far different from the $2 to 3.50 per CWT and $0.10 corn when Trudy and I were trying to get started in 1934-36. What a change from the one-row walking cultivator and the tractors here on the farm today.

All for the good, I hope.

It is 7:30 in the morning now, and beginning to get light. Cloudy, but I don't believe we have had rain as yet. Rain will be welcome, even if it does delay the oat seeding.

April 18, 1990

1990 Easter has passed; it is a beautiful day.

Mother and I visited Gene Saunders in the Denison Hospital. He had a stroke in November of '89. He seemed to be progressing well but fell after therapy and injured his back. I guess he also has a trace of Parkinson's Disease. He is not quite sixty-five-years old, a young man by my standards. I know he worries a lot about his health, his home and his farm. His son Keith is there, doing a wonderful job. Nevertheless, he has a lot on his troubled mind.

We stopped to visit Fred and Anna Marie Rabe, Trudy's sister. They both use wheelchairs and walkers. Their son and daughter and their families were there as were Bob and Garnet.

Nice Easter.

Certainly makes me realize how fortunate Mother and I are. Seventy-six and seventy-nine-years-old.

Mother hosted a group of ladies for a Bridge game on Monday night then played in Manning on Tuesday and is going to Denison today. She sure is busy.

We need to begin making plans for our trip to Oregon. The time will be here before we are ready. That is for certain.

> *"I believe my Dad and Mother would be pleased. . ."*

April 25, 1990

Cold and windy.
I put fertilizer on the alfalfa fields. They are coming along well. Six weeks and the hay will be ready to cut.
We have some moisture and a promise of rain the past few days. Doug's oats are nice and green. Looks like his grain drill worked okay earlier this spring.

One of the nicest days of my seventy-ninth year on the Cumberland Stock Farm No. 2. was when our little grandson, Matthew, ate dinner with us yesterday. He hasn't felt real well the past couple of days and has missed a bit of school. He had a bout with flu and colds and just has had a hard time shaking it off. Although a husky chap, he reminds us much of son Craig when he was a child. Always a smile.

His mother was busy with the older children's school schedule both in Manilla and Irwin. She also had the Presbyterian UPW Circle in her home last night in addition to her chores of bottle-feeding all the baby calves. Patty was a busy girl, so Matt ate dinner with us. When I came in from the field, he beat Grandpa in a checker game, five to one. After dinner we started another and have it on the board to be finished later.

What a blessing to have grandchildren.

In the afternoon I drove Doug's big 7060 Allis Chalmers tractor and plowed the alfalfa sod on the southeast corner of the farm with a five-bottom plow. Not often have I plowed sod in the spring that worked so nicely. Hope to finish the plowing today. Doug will be ready to apply anhydrous ammonia. Even though I am seventy-nine years old, he puts up with me and it's a pleasure to work with him again.

I wish my Mother and Father could see our farm now, sixty years since the Great Depression.

May 18, 1990

Early morning.
What a beautiful day; showers forecasted by the weekend.
To be a part of the Cumberland Stock Farm No. 2 is certainly one of the most gratifying parts of life.
It's been a busy week.

Tuesday Doug loaded twenty-five Holstein steers on Don Ewoldt's big truck and sent them to the sale barn in Dunlap, Iowa, twenty miles west of the farm. He was kind enough again to ask me to go with him at noon. Those twenty-five steers brought almost as many dollars as my father and I borrowed from the Federal Land Bank for our farm back in 1932-34. We had secured a loan of the unheard of amount of $20,500; those twenty-five steers brought home close to $18,500, with all expenses paid.

The price of corn has risen from 10 cents a bushel to $2.50 a bushel but we have had to pay for all the equipment, too. Wednesday, Doug finished spraying the west pasture for thistles using a low voliant chemical, 2-4-D Ester, mixed with water and sprayed over the top of the field using a $3,000 sprayer and a $15,000 tractor and this was our 'cheap' equipment. These days it costs more to overhaul a tractor than it used to cost to buy a new one.

Now, with the purchase of the Wetzel farm, the building of the milk parlor and operating expenses, we owe over $200,000.

Progress?

Sometimes I wonder.

Has it all been for the better? Yes, certainly.

No, it was never better in the 'old days' and I never yearn for the 'old days.'

Some aren't here to take part in the change. Again, I wish my Dad and Mother could see and know what has taken place in the past sixty years since the time we made the decision not to give up.

As I look out the window and across the road from our new home,[65] built on the exact spot Trudy Arnold and I built our first little home out of the two rooms Mother and Dad used to live in when they first started, I am more than amazed and overwhelmed by God's gifts to us.

I am thankful for the little things which, when you stop and really think about it, are really the big things.

I am thankful for lights and water, for good roads and the comfort of a warm home. I am thankful to have been a part of the change and to be able to plan for the future.

Beautiful sunrises, white fences, and the old home under good care of Doug's wife Patty and four wonderful grand children waiting for the school bus.

All God's gifts.

> *I am thankful for the little things which,*
>
> *when you stop and really think about it,*
>
> *are really the big things.*

---

[65] In 1981, the original one bedroom no bathroom house built in 1934, in which all four boys were raised, was torn down and a new house was built on the exact same site.

May 19,1990

Another wonderful morning on the Cumberland Stock Farm No. 2.

Looks like a trace of rain, cloudy, sort of foggy and almost 60 degrees.

Mother is up, stirring up some kind of breakfast and has walked out and checked the rain gauge. About three quarters of an inch.

How fortunate we are.

Once again God has been good to us.

Yesterday, the man from Irwin who does our custom herbicide spraying had a breakdown, that put us three or four hours behind schedule but we got the Eradicane applied on the field we call Oscar's Windmill Bottom. At about 4:30 pm I was about to cover it with the 7060 and disk. Rain had been forecast for about 6:30-7:00 and the western sky was beginning to darken.

In the meantime, Trudy and the grandchildren had brought Doug his afternoon lunch and a cold drink of lemonade. Doug had just finished planting corn on the hill we call Oscar's Cistern Field. Quite a sight to see your wife and grandchildren leave the field in Mom's Chrysler, Doug with the Dodge pickup and fertilizer wagon, then right behind them, Grandson Chris, twelve-years-old, moving the 185 Allis Chalmers and our four-row White planter to the next field we call the North Bottom; a total of over $50,000 worth of equipment by today's process.

I was able to finish covering the Eradicane. It had gotten quite dark before I finished, but no rain. When I came in from the field, the weather news reported flash-flood warnings and heavy rain in the Denison area. Water was over Highways 141 and 59; around 7:30 pm they had two-and-a-half inches of rain in less than thirty minutes. The radio reported cars in the ditch east of Denison because of water and debris on the road. They also told of a farmer that lost a hundred head of hogs.

Again, we must thank God for help and guidance. I keep thinking of the scene yesterday of everyone leaving the field, Chrysler,

Dodge, wagon, tractor and planter, all moved by Dad and Mother's family.

Perhaps tomorrow Trudy and I will drive up to Spencer to Grandson Keith's baccalaureate services. He is bound for the University of Northern Iowa this fall and wants to study law.

We have our flight reservations for our trip to Oregon to attend Laura's high school graduation. She is Craig's oldest girl and our second granddaughter. She will attend the University of Southern California; no definite major decided yet. She is a good swimmer and captain of her team in Oregon. She hopes to make a mark at USC. How time marches on.

We're so fortunate that Dad, Mother, my wife Trudy and I did not give up. I often wonder where we would be if we had, and more importantly, would we be as happy?

I think not.

Breakfast time, more later.

May 22, 1990

7:30 AM
A beautiful morning, damp from the recent rains, light fog and sun just breaking through.
Four grandchildren outside waiting for the school bus.
Trudy is just getting around. She is in her red pajamas and has a pleasant disposition. She must have had a good night at her Bridge game.
What more can a grandpa ask for?

This past Sunday we spent with Dean's family. Keith's baccalaureate graduation service was one of the most pleasant evenings of our life. We stayed overnight and stopped for pancakes the next morning in Storm Lake, then stopped to see Trudy's sister Anna Marie and Fred Rabe for a few moments.

Doug was mounting his chopper when we arrived home, getting ready to harvest his alfalfa for haylage. It is silo-filling time again and the hay will surely grow in this moisture. He has some corn to plant, as well as all his soy beans. It's a bit late for planting, but everything will really grow and this beats hot, dry weather.

Breakfast is ready. So long for now.

"We're so fortunate that (we)...

did not give up."

June 15, 1990

Getting used to Iowa time and weather again.

We had a wonderful trip to California, Oregon and Washington. We flew to California, met Craig and JoDee and had a few days with them. On Tuesday, Clarence and Verona Nickels, Trudy's cousins from St. Helens, Washington, picked us up and we drove with them up through the dry San Joaquin Valley. We stayed overnight somewhere north of Sacramento before heading up to their home. We spent a couple of days there and on Friday they drove us to Eugene where we met up with Craig and attended Laura's high school graduation. Afterwards we celebrated with a nice salmon dinner with the girls and Ginny.

Sunday the Nickels picked us up again. On Monday we had a wonderful trip to Mount St. Helens. It had been ten years since the volcano eruption. We then stopped at the nuclear power plant and flew home Tuesday, June 12.

Patty and her family met us at the Omaha airport.

It's great to be home.

California was dry, Oregon rainy and Iowa has been wet and stormy. A lot of flooding; however, our farm has fared pretty well.

We brought home some wonderful news from Craig and JoDee in California – "A little one is on the way." due in December.

Doug said, "I hope it is twins, a boy and a girl."

Raymond M. Saunders

June 20, 1990

We have had a lot of rain.
Manning, Manilla and Astor flooded Sunday.

Sunday was a great day. Doug and Chris took Grandma and me to the west pasture. The grass was up over our knees. Plenty of water and thirty-six nice heifers in the pasture. Later Trudy and I drove to Denison, saw Fred and Anna Marie, Bob and Garnet and stopped a bit at Dale's.

Quite a Father's Day.

Monday we visited Jim Theobald at the Manilla Manor. Jim and Dorothy Theobald were no doubt our best friends during the past fifty years. Jim is a descendent of the original Wisconsin Theobalds, the people my Grandfather came to Iowa to work for and whose daughter he ultimately married (Bertha Theobald). I guess that would make us some kind of distant relation by marriage but I have never bothered to figure out the details.

Jim has Parkinson's disease. He is younger than I, but can hardly walk and he takes a ton of pills. It's depressing to see such a big vibrant man and such a good friend reduced to a shuffling, mumbling shell.

God help me, we don't want to look forward to that kind of future.

Today we were able to get into the field. The boys from Irwin sprayed herbicide. I was in the field real early and got it ready for spraying. Dale came down about nine o'clock and drove the tractor and spring tooth harrow.

Doug was planting corn this afternoon and I had the privilege to ride a bit on the planter. I couldn't drive because I couldn't see the planter marks in the fresh earth. This could very well be my last year in the fields. I can't see the best and I am getting old.

Sometimes I feel worthless.

Worthless in the sense that we started with so little yet there is so much left to do. When I started, there were areas of the farm where erosion was so bad that it could not be crossed with horse or equipment. The farm has been improved, terraces built and covered with grass, yet there is so much to be finished.

I still owe money, more than when we started. I have been told many times 'if you are so damn smart why aren't you rich?' Well, Mother and I need a home, love and security more than money in the bank. No one can ask more of life or need more than we are getting. We just want to help contribute to the future of the farm and in doing so, the future of our country.

We want to make our time worth something.

Perhaps the most important lesson in life is to be happy with what you have, but in order to do that, you must also have dreams. You must find the proper balance in life to be satisfied enough with the present to live your life fully, but dissatisfied enough to have dreams of making the future better. Dreams are important. Without them you exist, with them you live. When your dreams are gone, you cease living and begin waiting.

Within the margins, between our dreams and reality, dwell our emotions and the good news is it is within our power to make of them what we want. How we perceive and deal with that discrepancy between our dreams and our realities defines our emotions. Happiness, love, jealousy even hate and hostility all dwell in that margin of discrepancy between our dreams and reality.

It is the old question, is the glass half empty or half full. It makes little difference if it is perception or reality, people can use the same data to arrive at completely different conclusions, what makes the difference is how one thinks.

I have come to understand that one's thoughts and dreams are a person's most valuable possession. Earlier, when writing about my Grandfather I wrote, "No one reaches the pinnacle of any profession without first dreaming it possible."

What makes men successful businessmen? What makes a man a major league ball player? For that matter, what makes a man run for the Presidency? Sure, they all must have the necessary skills but lots of people have enough skill. What separates those that make it from those that don't is the simple fact that first and foremost they think they can – they have a dream.

As important as our positive thoughts are to us our negative thoughts can also shape our destiny. Too often it is simply the fact that we think we can't.

I'm reminded of the story of my granddaughter Hilary when she first learned to ride her bike. The shiny new bike had been a Christmas present but she and her father waited for a warm spring day to take it out. The neighborhood school playground was the perfect place for her to quickly learn all the skills of balance, starting, stopping, turning and braking. The grin on her face grew and grew as she mastered the wide open spaces of the playground.

The path home, however, was a narrow sidewalk and some of her newly found confidence began to fade only to disappear completely when she saw a large bush growing halfway out into the sidewalk in front of her. She had plenty of room and possessed all the skills to safely navigate the obstacle – she just didn't think she could. In a panic she yelled "DAAAAD" took both feet off the pedals and steered directly into the bush.

She survived, of course, but the new bike had some new scratches and it was several weeks before Hilary would successfully travel that path again. But that's life isn't it? We meet some obstacles and we acquire a few scars and we go on.

The key is in the "go on" part of this lesson and this is exactly where your thoughts and dreams achieve their supreme importance in your life. Your thoughts and dreams are the roadmap for how you will live your life and the beautiful thing about living in the United States of America is you are free to think and dream as you please.

This is one of our most basic freedoms and if anyone, be it governments, religions, parents, teachers or coworkers limit our thoughts or suppress our dreams they become the most sinister of thieves robbing us of our most valuable possessions. They become obstacles that must be dealt with in order to live a rich and full life.

This is an important lesson because in America "we the people" are the government, the parents, teachers and coworkers. In America we have the freedom of religion so it behooves us all to be careful and diligent guardians of this privilege.

I am so thankful that I still have my dreams. What a privilege it has been to live here on Cumberland Stock Farm and help my Grandfather, my Mother and Father, my sons and grandchildren live their dreams.

We want to keep the dream alive, always dreaming of a better future.

> *" . . .Mother and I need*
>
> *a home,*
>
> *love and*
>
> *security*
>
> *more than money in the bank."*

June 24, 1990

Today son Dean and his whole family are coming to our farm home. The same place Mother and I started on June 24, 1934. They will share dinner with us.

Dale and Johnet have a commitment at their church in Denison. Perhaps they will stop by.

Dr. Craig and JoDee are in California. Their great news is a baby in December. Emily is expected to be there for the summer, Laura will be a freshman at USC this fall.

Doug and his family have taken a few days off and are in Jackson, Michigan for today's auto race. We expect them home sometime on Tuesday.

To my family –

Fifty-six years ago today, your Mother became my wife. A lot has happened since June 24, 1934. I am so very thankful to all. What a great life we have had together. Years of fun, work and play. Much laughter and many tears, but in all, a happy life and I mean that.

God has blessed us and given us great opportunity, but no more than He has offered to anyone else. He has given us our time together.

As Ever,
Your Dad

"Dreams are important.

   Without them you exist, with them you live.

When your dreams are gone,

   you cease living and

      begin waiting."

August 14,1990

Another early morning. Hard to go back to sleep.
Our summer has been cool and wet.
Mother and I made a trip to Carroll for hay rake parts yesterday. Perhaps that trip could have been avoided had someone taken the time and filled the gear box with grease when they took it out of the shed this spring or even last year. It's hard to remember to look after everything.
The farm seems to always be behind on work, but we seem to have more than enough of everything.
Two bull calves born this last weekend. Both came backwards, with front legs back and needing help. Thank God Doug knew how to handle the problems. Many would have lost them.
Hope his boys learn as well as he has.

Anna Marie has been gone for one week. She died in Lutheran Hospital in Omaha after a long time in a wheel chair. She never walked after back surgery, something about a disk.

It seems almost impossible. I really feel for Trudy. It seems her family depended on her so much. In fact when Anna Marie died, the hospital called Trudy, not Fred. Trudy called Fred and told him we would pick him up and take him down early in the morning. We stopped by and picked up Bob, too. We knew she had passed on but none of us wanted to break the news to Fred. When we got to the hospital they went into the room and her body was still there.

We had a little service for the family. Fred adjusted well.

I fear that we are fast approaching the time when we will be a bigger burden on our families. So far our health has been pretty good. Our eyes are our immediate problem, although Trudy came home from the eye exam in Carroll last Tuesday with 20/20 vision wearing her glasses. Seems to me that is pretty good for a seventy-seven-year-old who had cataract surgery approximately a year ago. I have glaucoma and don't have anywhere near that kind of record but how thankful I am for my family and the health and opportunities I have had.

Sure, I wish I could see better, but I am so damn thankful I can walk and talk and think.

Anna Marie Arnold, Trudy's older sister.

August 21, 1990

It's Tuesday morning and still wet. It rained a bit during the night.

Doug and Chris were able to finish the straw bailing on Sunday afternoon and put the bails in the shed and got the wagons under cover.

How we would have welcomed some of this 1990 weather in 1988 or even last year. Shows how a farmer depends on God and the great weather machine.

I thank Him for life and family.

Sunday was quite a long day. Bob and Garnet went along with us to take Fred Rabe to the AM Pride Truck Stop Restaurant for dinner. He really seemed to enjoy it.

On the way home we stopped to see my friend Jim at the Manilla Manor. How depressing.

Yesterday Trudy and I did something perhaps we will never do again. It was sort of a rainy day. We drove Doug's Dodge pickup truck to Perry, Iowa to pick up a pair of boys' 24 inch bicycles.

Doug found these a couple of weeks earlier. He had taken his family with him when he went to Nevada, Iowa to look at a 585 International tractor and scoop. The family stopped for lunch at Hardee's and for some reason, Doug went into a resale store across the street. By a quirk of fate, they had two identical bikes that had just been brought in. They were perfect for Matt and John, his two youngest. $103 for the pair originally priced at $111 each.

Doug bought them and placed them on layaway. Of course he couldn't bring them home with the two boys with him. So, we picked them up yesterday. They will be used as Christmas presents. He saved some money, we had a nice trip in the rain and the boys will be so happy.

How wonderful for Trudy and I to be able to make such trips.

September 7, 1990

Quite hot.

This summer has been one of Iowa's wettest. Many acres of hay spoiled. I thank God we on put our early alfalfa into the silo. Even though we are usually late in harvesting, we always end up with good feed.

Kind of a foggy morning. We hope to bale hay this afternoon. Big round bales. I'll tell you later how we made out.

Each year we try to do better. Although I'm seventy-nine-years -old, I hope I can see several more harvests.

Yesterday Doug and Pat took Chris to a special dentist in Spencer, the same one that looked after Dean's Karen and Keith. This made for a great day for Grandpa and Grandma. Jenny, John and Matt came to our house after school and we had supper of fettuccini and meat sauce, fruit, Jell-O salad and milk. It's wonderful to have grandchildren so close. It keeps us young.

Yesterday afternoon I set two posts between the two north silos. Perhaps the last post holes I'll ever dig. It was late afternoon and in the shade but still hot.

I thank God I can do some of these things, and have a place to do them.

Also, a family who appreciates having Grandpa around.

> *"... I am so damn thankful*
>
> *I can walk and talk and think."*

September 12, 1990

Beautiful sunrise.
Looks like another September day that makes one glad to be alive and live in Iowa.
Kids just left on the school bus. Always a happy time when all are healthy.

Yesterday started off with a phone call from Craig in California. He had his appendix removed the night before. Craig said he was going home today. We thought him to be sort of kidding, but last evening around 7:30, JoDee called and Craig was home. As I understand it, before he went home, he did an open-heart surgery that afternoon.

His mother's comment, "Typical Saunders. Can't tell them anything. They'll have it their own way."

Doug and Patty asked me to go with them to the pasture mid-morning, we sorted out six head of heifers to bring home. Some will calve soon, others will be bred to calve in June 1991. Doug's cattle look real nice. Plenty of rain this year and lots of grass.

It's a real joy to be asked to go along. It's also great to be able to go and to be in good enough health to enjoy the farm. Again, how wonderful to be nearly eighty-years-old and be wanted and physically able to enjoy our Iowa farm home.

May God help us all to listen and to understand Him.

Mother has another Bridge game today, choir practice tonight, club at Patty's Thursday and Friday we are planning on going to the Spencer Fair with Dale and Phyllis McCone.

It's a good thing we raised our family forty years ago.

There wouldn't be time now!

September 30, 1990

Dear Family – It is the last day of September 1990. Someday you will understand why I love my family so much. You have all spared us some of the many heartaches some parents have to accept. Never a day goes by that we aren't thankful to God for you. Every one of you.

The past season has not only been busy, it has been very trying. Many things have shown us how close God is to us.

If things go well, Doug and Chris plan to change the head on the Uni Harvester from hay to corn. Would have been nice if we could have gotten this done two weeks ago, but we didn't.

Late yesterday afternoon, Doug and Chris managed to get the one heifer, which is due to calve soon, in from the west pasture. They have tried many times. Others yes, but not her. Perhaps things are changing for the better.

We have a grandchild due in about eight weeks. It will greatly change Craig and JoDee's life. We also have a great-grandchild due in late February or early March at Karen and Dan's house. These two events easily overshadow all of the harvest and other problems here at the Saunders' farm home.

The four youngsters here on the farm, Chris, Jenny, John and Matt are growing. All are willing to lend a hand to their Dad and Mother. Chris is with his dad a lot. I'm sure he will be able and well-qualified to replace Grandpa in a very short time, should he elect to join his dad in farming. They won't have to add a lot of acres. Some, yes, but what a dairy farm they could have and operate if they can get along together as they do now.

Those grandkids have a wonderful mother. I'm afraid, though, they will never find a replacement for Trudy. She is, and has been, super. God was with me when we met.

I'll write more later. We have to go into the Manilla Manor today. Mrs. Austin Saunders' (Calahain) 100th birthday.
So long. More sometime.

October 29, 1990

A lot has happened since I wrote a month ago.

The silos are full and yesterday Doug started combining soy beans. Everything went along fairly well. It was a great pleasure and admiration to see grandson Chris working with his dad.

I am sure my Mother and Dad would be proud of the family and farm they started when they married in 1903.

Doug's cattle have continued to sort of give him a rough time. Many calves have been born backwards and it seems that uterine problems are a big dilemma. Patty and the younger children drove the pickup trailer to Audubon, Iowa with a cow called Pinky. We could use a real dairy veterinarian. I guess the way to get one is to send one of the kids to veterinary school. Granddaughter Emily has shown interest in this field of work.

Mother (Trudy) has had a demanding and tiring summer. After our trip to California and Oregon for granddaughter Laura's high school graduation, she spent many days taking Anna Marie to Omaha to see Fred who spent quite a few days in the hospital. Then Anna Marie was in the Omaha hospital and her death in August just about wore Trudy out.

To top it off, in early October I spent a week in Clarkson Hospital in Omaha and had her driving and worrying all over again. Sunday afternoon, Oct. 1, I was working in the field bailing hay. Trudy brought lunch out to the field about four o'clock and along with it, a Mason jar filled with hot coffee. It is a memory I shall never forget, that rich coffee smell, the warmth of the jar in my hand and the dark creamy brown liquid colored with our farm fresh-milk and with too much sugar – just the way I liked it – and the taste of that last cup of coffee I will ever bring to my lips.

I drank it all down and did not bale another fifty bales until I got so ungodly sick. Somehow I managed to stop the machinery and found myself on my hands and knees in the fresh cut alfalfa. It was then that I threw up. It was a big blood clot that looked just like a sponge, full of holes and kind of red.

No one, at least no one in their right mind, wishes for or plans their own demise, yet what better plan could there be for me to meet my maker suddenly, working out in the fields doing the things I love? That thought, however, never crossed my mind at the time and somehow, I don't remember how, I made it back to the house.

Monday morning I was feeling a bit better, at least not vomiting anymore. Dr. Hennessey made a house call and I went into his office on Tuesday. On Wednesday I went into the hospital in Denison because that was the day the x-ray tech came down from Fort Dodge to do studies. Dr. Hennessey asked me to come back to his office on Thursday and he called the hospital but could not find out anything – no reading. Dr. Hennessey cursed and I told him. "I will go anyplace and do anything with you but I have lost faith in the Denison hospital. I'm going to Omaha or California!"

He referred me to Dr. Schafer at Clarkson Hospital in Omaha and that afternoon he went to work and ran me through every test you could think of. I had bleeding stomach ulcers so bad that at first they couldn't distinguish the ulcers from cancer but Dr. Schafer came into my room Sunday morning. I was eating my breakfast and he informed me the biopsies were benign and the worst thing for me was that I was going to have to cut down on the coffee.

It's been almost one month since Mother brought that delicious jar of coffee to the hay field. It was really good, but I have lost all desire coffee. I am home now and feeling better than I have for some time. I still have eye problems, glaucoma, and must see the doctor again this week, but my family will never know the good feeling I had when you all called and wrote when I was in Clarkson Hospital.

I hope mother can take things a bit slower. She seem to have someplace to go every day.
So long.

December 1, 1990

A beautiful, crisp clear early winter day.
Not a cloud to be seen.

Doug is still working hard picking corn. Chris drove the four-row New Idea Uni Harvester on the same fields where his great grandfather, John R. Saunders, and me, his grandfather, hand-picked corn seventy-five to eighty years ago. What a change!

We were able to pick ninety-to-one-hundred bushels by hand in a full day. Now, we are able to equal that in one to one-and-a-half hours, picking four rows at a time with the Uni and wagons that hold from one-hundred-fifty to two-hundred bushels,

I used the AC 7000 and spent the afternoon hauling in the big round bales of shredded corn stalks. Doug will use them for cattle bedding this winter. I have two more to haul in and I am finished.

Now for the greatest news of all. The baby that we have been expecting in California arrived this morning about 9:30 California time. So the "Li'l Boss" is ready to take one on at 1780 Glenwood Drive, Bakersfield, California, home of Craig and JoDee Saunders. Hilary RaeAnne was born on her Mother's birthday as well as her big sister Laura's.

It's great to know that everyone is doing fine.

December 1st is a big day for us. Three birthdays plus Dale and Johnet's wedding anniversary.

We will see our new granddaughter soon. Mother and I have reservations to fly to California on December 31st. We plan to stay a couple of months in the warm California sunshine away from the cold Iowa winter. This will be our longest stay away from our farm home. Craig has rented an apartment for us close to his home. We have quite a few friends there and perhaps Craig and his doctor friends can give us a medical check up.

Right now I think I'll head for the dairy barn

December 3, 1990

We have had our first real winter storm.
We were fortunate. Not a lot of snow, but quite windy.
Eastern Iowa and Des Moines got seven to twelve inches of snow.
So once again, we are very lucky.

Doug and Chris finished the corn picking yesterday afternoon (Sunday, December 2). It was snowing quite a bit when he brought the last loads in from the field. The 'Uni' once again did her job: only one broken chain all during the harvest.

The big job now will be to bring the cattle in from the west pasture and try to make them comfortable for the winter.

No school today due to the road conditions. Jennifer and Grandma are making cookies. One of the blessings of grandchildren is having them so close and living here on the Cumberland Stock Farm.

December 18, 1990

Morning, 7:20
Looks like winter has settled in here in western Iowa.
We have had rain, a bit of sleet and yesterday, wet snow.
No wind, thank God. Just a pretty straight-down snow.

The treachery of the weather and roads was brought close to home. Sometime Saturday, Mrs. Dan Miller (Velda Greer) was driving a pickup and went off the road a half-mile north and three-quarters mile west of our home. Not a lot of people travel these roads, even in good weather, so she wasn't found quickly. When she was found, she was in pretty bad shape with a broken pelvis and crushed chest. She was later flown by Lifeline helicopter to Omaha but we heard Monday, when Patty came home from her school lunch job, Velda Miller had passed away.

One never knows!

God is so good and offers so much, yet we still expect Him to do all the necessary work.

Sunday afternoon Trudy finally made up her mind to decorate a Christmas tree. It's just a small artificial one but with lots of lights and very pretty. Our youngest two grandsons, John and Matt, saw her working and came in to help. Then John and Mother sang Christmas songs and Matt and I played checkers. He is a sharp checker player for a second grader.

How wonderful for Trudy and me to be able to enjoy our home and family. It is all the more enjoyable to do it on the same spot where we had our first Christmas in the winter of 1934.

Things here on the farm are busy as usual. On the last nice day, Doug managed to get his corn cobs ground, loaded on wagons and backed into the machine shed to keep them sheltered from the winter storms. They will be used to make nice dry bedding for the livestock this winter. The next day, Friday, he and veterinary David Slavic, took horns off the larger calves and vaccinated the larger heifers. In the meantime, he has loaded the big manure spreader.

What a difference!

It used to be that when the snow got so deep we couldn't use the spreader my Father and I would use a team of horses and a bob-sled. We loaded and unloaded it by hand with a pitch fork. Now, we use a two ton New Idea tandem wheeled spreader, an Allis 7000- tractor with the power of 100 horses and a heated cab. What would Grandfather and Father say and think? Even a hydraulic skid loader and a special tractor with a big front mounted scoop to load the spreader.

What a change here on the farm during my lifetime. From walking a plow behind a team of horses, a one-row cultivator and husking corn by hand to a farm with four automobiles, a pickup truck, five tractors, a Uni Harvester for harvesting hay to be put in three 360 foot tall silos and a four-row corn picker. To top it all off, a thirteen year old grandson, Chris, who can handle most all of the equipment.

What a change, and what an opportunity for the future. I almost wish I could see twenty-to-thirty years into the future from this 1990 Christmas season.

Mother and I have just finished our breakfast.

Four grandchildren off on the school bus at 7:40 am. They will be back on the bus at 3:45 this afternoon. Seventy years ago those children would walk and carry lunch pails to a country school.

The sun is beginning to break through the winter haze and it is a beautiful winter sight.

December 25, 1990.

Christmas Morning.
Just finished breakfast,
It's been very cold the past week. Yesterday, the temperature did get up to eighteen degrees above zero. Looks like a fairly nice day for Iowa in December
Finally got the 7000 AC tractor started. The diesel tractors don't start very well even when using electric heaters.

Another Christmas for Mother and me here on the Cumberland Stock Farm No. 2, Shelby County, Iowa. I know I keep repeating it but we are on the exact same spot, Section Two, Greeley Township, of the farm where we observed our first Christmas as a married couple. We were in our little house constructed of used lumber in 1934. The next year we had a little boy to share Christmas. Dean Arnold Saunders, born June 13, 1935.

I got to thinking of the accident here on the farm the year Dean was a senior in high school. We talked about it before but these things, as we grow older, bring home to a person how God works and how he looks after us.

Today, Dean, his wife Rosemary and his two sons, Kevin and Keith, will be sharing Christmas dinner with us. Their daughter Karen and her husband Dan Hanson will join us later.

Our youngest son Doug, his wife Patty Fisher Saunders and their four young children will join us in the mid-afternoon – Chris, thirteen , their beautiful blonde daughter Jennifer Ann, twelve , and the two younger boys, John, nine, and Matt who is eight-years-old. This family lives in the home my Father and Mother built on Section Three of the farm, directly across the road from our new home built in early 1980.

Doug and his family operate the whole Saunders farm, four-hundred forty acres and a large herd of Holstein dairy cattle.

Son Dale and wife Johnet have been asked to join us for dinner, but due to prior obligations, they may opt to come later in the day.

I phoned my sister Wilma and had a nice Christmas morning visit. She lives in Archer, Iowa, near Sanborn, in northwest Iowa.

She is in fairly good health and is planning on joining some of her family in Sioux City.

We are all getting older but we enjoy the youngsters so much.

Trudy is busy getting things around for dinner and she has just called her brother Bob and asked them if they care to eat dinner with us. In my opinion, she has always been the one in her family who is the most concerned for the family. She seems to harvest more than her share of heartaches, and now the rest of the family depends on her when problems arise.

I guess its good to be able to help.

March 26, 1991

Early morning, 2:35. Sometimes we awaken and can't possibly find the key to sleep. This is one of those mornings.
I can't believe it has been six months since I last wrote to my family.

Yesterday was a trying day for both of us, especially my life mate. Trudy is scheduled for knee replacement surgery on Thursday of this week. Yesterday was her day to see the doctor for a physical exam. Even though we have a son, Craig, who is a heart surgeon, Trudy seems to have a horror about visiting and consulting doctors of any kind. I really feel sorry for her and continue to be concerned about her well-being. It's hard for me to communicate with her. Even though many people tell her how successful their replacements have been, she is still nervous.

We pray to God for His divine guidance. We have a wonderful family, but we realize we are nearing the end of our lives and know they will miss us for a while. We all hate to see the time come when we must pass the torch to others.

Trudy and I have had more years together than many others, and kids, grandchildren and now a great-granddaughter. Please realize our family wouldn't have been possible without God and Trudy Arnold Saunders.

May God and all of you be in her corner when she needs you and I'm sure that God will bless you all for your help.

March 27, 1991

What a wonderful year we have had.

A year ago, at this time, we were visiting son Craig and wife JoDee in California. Then in June we flew out again and after three days rode to St. Helens, Oregon with Clarence and Verona (Niewoehner) Nickles, Trudy's cousin. From there we attended granddaughter Laura's high school graduation then flew from Portland to Omaha where Patty and family met us at the airport and brought us back to the farm.

In late June, Doug and family made a trip to Jackson, Michigan to the Penske Auto Races. The kids will never forget the time together. A busy, busy summer and rain enough for a real good crop.

In the meantime, we found out we had a grandchild and a great-grandchild on the way from God's heaven.

A busy summer!

On December 1, 1990 little Hilary RaeAnne Saunders came to live with Craig and JoDee. On the last day of December, Mother and I flew to California to see her and her parents.

Patty took us to the airport in Omaha in a four-wheel drive pickup through ice and snow in five-to-ten degree weather. A few hours later, dry sunshine and forty or fifty more degrees added to the thermometer and what a thrill to walk into the airport and be met by a four-week-old beautiful granddaughter and her parents.

Craig had rented us an apartment at Columbus Estates, a sort of a retirement home, a wonderful and nice place. We stayed and watched Hilary grow until March 2nd, and how she grew. Such a blessing to share the first few months of her life. We had a great two months.

How can we ever repay our family?

We were back in Iowa to enjoy March's spring snow and rain. On March 10, 1991, a few minutes after we got home from church, the phone rang and another milestone in our long lives on the Cumberland Stock Farm occurred.

Granddaughter Karen, who lives in Des Moines, called and informed us that we were now officially Great-Grandparents. Emily Rae Hanson had arrived while we were in church. Karen called her grandmother right after telling her Mother and Dad.

The next Saturday, Mother and I took granddaughter Jennifer and drove to Des Moines to see Emily Rae, our first great grandchild. The new parents, Karen and Dan, were celebrating. Dean and Rosemary were there and were, of course, proud and happy new grandparents.

Isn't it something!

My thoughts wandered back to the elevator ride with Grandma Arnold on that hot June day over half a century ago when we brought Dean into this world. I vividly recall the needle slipping into my vein as I gave blood for my new son and again eighteen years later when a tractor accident brought him so close to heaven's gate.

Isn't it something to live long enough to see your first-born, the one that taught you to be a parent, the one you shepherded through the early years, now a grandparent himself.

What greater cause for celebration?

We also celebrated Trudy's birthday, which was the next day, March 17th.

That Sunday Dorothy Theobald joined us at Cronk's Cafe for dinner.

> ## *"Isn't it something*
> *to live long enough . . . to see your first born . . .*
> ## *now a grandparent himself."*

March 30, 1991

Four o'clock in the morning

Dear kids,

Sons, wives, grandchildren, all of you, great granddaughter included.
We love you all. I'm sure this Easter, tomorrow, will be one of the happiest days for our family.
God has been so good to our family. We must continually thank Him.

As Ever.

Your Dad

Yesterday, March 29, 1991, Good Friday, Grandma Trudy had her right knee joint replaced by Dr. Ron Miller at Jenny Edmondson Hospital in Council Bluffs, Iowa. She was so scared; I'm sure she thought she had a look through the "gates of hell." She had so much pain when son Dean and I left her yesterday afternoon. I called the nurse about nine o'clock when I went to bed. She seemed to be resting better, but still had to have the therapy appliance on which keeps the knee from getting so stiff.

I'll call again around eight o'clock this morning.

Our family has been so good to us. Patty took us to the hospital on Thursday then Dean came from Spencer and spent the night here at our home on the farm. We left early and were able to spend some time with her before her eight o'clock date with Dr. Miller.

Like life, God didn't say it would be easy. I felt so helpless. It was so great to have part of our family present and to know they were all there with their prayers.

Dean and I arrived back home at the farm about six o'clock and Patty and her family had a nice chili supper for us. After supper, granddaughter Jennifer walked across the road with me to our little home.

After living together for nearly sixty years, regardless of the difficulties, the arguments, regardless of the good times or the bad, when your mate is not there, there is a great void. To help fill it, I phoned California and got to talk to granddaughter Laura. She can always cheer one up.

What more could a person ask?

If anyone should drive down to the hospital today, we have some cards and a gift from JoDee and Hilary for Mother. Doug's family is planning on visiting her on Easter Sunday. I'm sure it will be a day we will all remember.

Weather is nice, but quite cold.
More later.

April 1, 1991

April Fool's day.
A beautiful morning. I have been out raking leaves in our front lawn.
It's now 8:30

I wonder if all my grandchildren and great-grandchildren know why we call today April Fool's Day?

Well, I'll tell you.

It may come as a surprise to you that January 1st was not always New Year's Day. In fact, up until the middle of the 16th century New Year's Day was celebrated on the first of April. This probably made some sense, especially to us farmers, because it was the beginning of Spring, the reawakening of the earth and the beginning of the new crop season. The long cold dark winter was over and the earth was ready to start anew again for another year. However, for lots of other reasons, the old calendar was inaccurate and in the middle of the 16th century more than 100 years after Columbus discovered America, the Pope and his advisors saw fit to introduce a new calendar called the Gregorian calendar.

This new calendar placed New Years day on January 1st. However, in those days there were no newspapers and, God forbid, no TV. Add to this the fact that few of the people could even read or write. So, when the calendar was changed, not everyone heard about it and even some of those who did, didn't believe or maybe didn't want to change. These are the people who continued to celebrate New Year's Day on April first. The people in the know laughed at those who didn't and they became the world's first April Fools.

Yesterday, Doug, Pat and family took me to visit Mother in Council Bluffs. One of those pleasant Easter Sundays.

Mother is recovering from her total knee replacement. She is sort of a sick girl. Seems to be carrying a temperature and is sick to her stomach. Surgery was done Friday morning, so hopefully yesterday was her worst day. I plan on visiting her tomorrow, Tuesday, with her Cousin Mervin Arnold.

Not a whole lot more to talk about. A new heifer calf yesterday before we left for the hospital. There is always so much for Doug to do.
I will finish the front lawn today.
The family is great.

> # "The first of April is the day we remember what we are the other 364 days of the year"
>
> *- Mark Twain*

April 12, 1991

4:00 am
Having an early morning and a strong thunderstorm.

Another mile marker passed in our journey through life.

Mother came home from Jenny Edmondson Hospital yesterday. One of the windiest April days we have had for many years. Dale consented to drive the Chrysler to the hospital to pick up Mother. It was very, very windy on the highways with several large trucks off the road due to the strong winds.

Good to have Mother home. All the kids were happy to see Grandma home again as well. This little note was found stuck on our front door the day Mother returned home from the hospital.

Jennifer's little note says it all. We all were happy to have her home and beginning to enjoy the grandkids again. I've heard her say many times that the severe pain in her knee is gone. She uses a walker but gets around amazingly well.

Everyone has been good to us. Pat and Doug brought us a big bowl of chili for supper. Dean called. It was Rosemary's birthday yesterday the 11th. We had forgotten it in all the rush and confusion.

I hope after a couple weeks of therapy in Denison, Mother will be much better. She was a very, very sick person immediately after surgery. Whether it was the flu, worry or the effects of the surgery, she was very ill the first week.

We are all happy and thankful to God to have her home. One highlight – Frank and Helen Christ, former ministers at the Manilla Presbyterian Church and now in Sydney, Iowa, stopped in to see mother.

Always great to see and hear from old family friends.

April 14, 1991

Another early morning.
Seems Mother had a fairly comfortable night. At least I didn't hear her and she seems to be sleeping well now.
We have had a week of stormy weather. Thursday, the day we brought mother home from the hospital, we had very strong southeast winds. Some damage to fences and feed bunks.

Today our great-granddaughter, Karen and Dan's little Emily Rae Hanson, will be baptized. Dean and Rosemary were planning to take us with them to Des Moines for the great event, but Mother's leg has developed a slight fever spot. Dr. Hennessey came out yesterday at noon for a house call and examined her. He called Dr. Miller and we decided she had better stay off it for a day or so. He will have to check her again on Monday.

Meanwhile, sort of quiet and disappointing. Mother and I so wanted to be there. Emily represents the first of the fourth generation of Trudy's and my family, the sixth generation with which I have lived and the seventh generation of this Saunders family in America.

Our "preacher lady" finally visited us yesterday afternoon and Zona Saunders stopped by with one of her angel food cakes.

We received a photo of little Hilary this week. JoDee and Craig have one of God's blessings, too.

April 16, 1991

4:30 am
We have had four-and-a-quarter inches of rain this past week of stormy weather.

Yesterday was a great day for Doug and Patty. Chris had his first track meet, a meet between Manning, Charter Oak and Manilla. He placed third in the mile- and-one-half run. He was so happy when he came home, he came over to tell Grandpa and Grandma as soon as he got home. We were so happy for him.

Doug sold fifteen or sixteen steers for good money, $.71 per pound, right here on the farm. No hassling, no commission and no fuss, to the same man who bought our steers a year ago.

Mother went to Denison for therapy. Dale took her. Her knee is doing well. Hopefully she will be able to go full-steam-ahead before too long.

It's been a great day for us all.

We are so thankful to God for all of His blessings.

Emily Rae Hanson. . .
Our great-granddaughter. . .

represents the *first* of the

fourth generation of Trudy's and my family, the

sixth generation with which I have lived and the

seventh generation of this

Saunders family in America.

April 19, 1991

3:45 am. It rained a good share of the day yesterday. Real Iowa April showers.

I know I have said this a lot but yesterday, April 18, 1991 was truly one of the great days here on Cumberland Stock Farm No. 2. It was granddaughter Jennifer Ann's twelfth birthday. Grandma Trudy gave her a beautiful long-stemmed artificial rose she had brought back from California.

Well, I guess we are not the sophisticated travelers we thought we had become. The long-stem red rose we bought in the LA airport turned out to be a beautifully packaged pair of red lace panties, just about the color of Grandma's face. Poor Jenny was so embarrassed but everyone had a good laugh. She will long remember her twelfth birthday at Grandma's house.

Doug has sold his Holstein steers to a man near Earling, Iowa. Yesterday he came to get them but couldn't get them all in his truck. Doug helped him out by taking four head in his own trailer behind his pickup. Another example of the Saunders being helpful to his neighbors.

Before he left, Alice and Tom DeJong Jr., dairy farmer friends of ours from Porterville, California, stopped in for dinner with us. They were driving through in their motor home on their way to Michigan to visit their daughter. Tom had bought some of Doug's heifers during the dry summer of 1989.

Tom and I joined Doug on the 25 mile trip through western Iowa to deliver the steers. Then, upon arriving back home, Mother and Patty had a great ham dinner, corn, potato salad, angel food cake (baked by Zona Saunders) and ice cream.

The visit was really good for Mother. Her knee is doing much better and she is gaining strength. She got tired, but really enjoyed the visit.

To top off the day, the steers outweighed everyone's guesses by one-hundred pounds and brought about $2,000 more than Doug had estimated.

April 22, 1991

Our 1991 spring is beginning to calm down. We have had lots of April showers and the pastures are coming along. We will see what Tuesday is like.

Today was another of those great days of our lives. Mother drove her car to Denison for therapy on her new knee. She didn't want to admit how great it was, but to me it was one of our great days together, one I have lived for. She gets tired but she has been a pretty sick lady. Also, she worries so much. I wish she would begin to look more at the great blessings God has given us and not so much at what might never be.

Doug finished putting nitrogen fertilizer on the pastures today. Now he will finish the four or five acres of alfalfa and get on with his work on corn and beans. His steers brought more than he figured and the young cattle look good.

We enjoyed the short visit with Tom and Alice DeJong of California. Doug's comment was, "Why don't we have neighbors like them here?" My answer, "They are very special Dutch. They came to this country with their parents at the onset of World War II with only a few dollars in their pockets and the clothes on their backs but those backs were strong and not afraid to work. They are wonderful people who care about their families and farm and homes."

Chris has a junior high track meet in Manning this afternoon. We may get a chance to see him try out his new track shoes.

It's wonderful to be a Grandpa.

> *"... look more at the*
> *great blessings God has given us*
> *and not so much at what might never be."*

April 23, 1991

We still have quite cold weather.
Doug has a couple of hours and he will have his alfalfa seeded.

Today Grandpa Saunders had one of his enjoyable days. Doug and Patty took me along to Manning, Iowa to a junior high track meet.

Grandson Chris, only a seventh grader, was running in only his second track meet of his life. He ran 1,600 meters (metric mile). He placed second to a big eighth grader from Manning with just a short distance between them.

He also ran the 800 meters and came within a few inches of winning that one, also against eighth graders who were much more mature. I hope I'm around to see him run when he is a junior and senior in high school. His two younger brothers will be in junior high at that time.

Trudy's knee is improving. It seems to be coming along nicely. She and I went to Denison Wednesday afternoon where she had a couple hours of physical therapy. She walks real straight and without that nagging pain. She is able to drive her car and that means so much to her.

We are looking forward to a visit from Craig, JoDee, Emily and baby Hilary, during the first week of July. JoDee called yesterday morning with the news.

I believe little Hilary will be baptized July 7th in the same church where her dad was baptized over forty years ago.

We hope to have another great family gathering.

Much to be thankful for!

Life goes on and how great to be able to enjoy it with one's family.

May 14, 1991

It was Mother's Day last Sunday. We enjoyed dinner with Pat and Doug's family. Later, Dean, Rosemary, Dale and Johnet, Karen and Dan and new great-granddaughter Emily Rae Hanson all enjoyed a nice day together.

Chris and Grandma Trudy attended church together, Chris will be confirmed next Sunday.

After church, Doug let Chris drive the big tractor, a 165 horsepower Allis Chalmers 7060 and a five-bottom plow, cutting seven-and-a-half feet of soil. Chris's Great-Grandfather had plowed that same field years ago with a one-bottom walking plow and two horses. I had used six horses on a twenty-eight inch gang plow and both his Grandmother and I have driven a 1937 WC Allis with a two-bottom plow on the same field. I know that I sometimes repeat myself, but this is what I think about and continuously marvel on how much change I have seen in one lifetime.

Doug finished up the field before starting his milking chores. Had Chris not done his bit, the field wouldn't have been finished.

Son Dean behind the plow share of my double bottom plow pulled by my 1937 model WC Allis Chalmers.

It gives his eighty-year-old Grandpa a great feeling of pride to see young people following the old generations' footsteps. I sincerely hope God continues to point the way for them, as he did for Mother and me.

We had a great weekend. Mother is feeling so much better. She walks straight and her knee seems to be so much better. She says she has no pain, but boy oh boy, that first week after the joint replacement she was sicker than she's ever been. We see both of her doctors a week from today on May 22. It's great to see her able to walk and begin to enjoy being with the rest of the family.

Yesterday we drove to Audubon, picked up a repaired silo unloader blower for Doug. Southside Welding does a great job, expensive, but good.

We then drove to Elk Horn, Iowa to watch a junior high track meet. Chris again ran the 1,600 meters and brought home a fifth-place ribbon. He is such a slender little thirteen-year-old. There were six schools competing, boys and girls in seventh and eighth grade. Chris's school brought home the 2nd place boy's trophy and the 1st place girl's trophy.

Today I hope to be able to help Doug with his field work. He finished spraying pasture thistles yesterday, a job lots of people let go when the field work schedule gets crowded.

It's great to have a family and Mother feeling better!

So long for now.

May 18,1991

Saturday morning.
It has been a frustrating Spring. Lots of wind and flooding, but here, just rain. No bad storms.
I thank God for moisture. Dry weather in Iowa can be devastating to our livelihood.

There has been so much to do. We haven't planted corn yet but we will as soon as there is a break in the weather.

We need to move cattle to the pasture. Doug got it all sprayed for thistles and I guess the good thing is that with all the rain the grass is growing and there will be plenty of water in the well.

Today Mother and I plan to make a trip to Harlan to get a couple of tires repaired for Doug and the muffler repaired on his pickup.

It's great to have Mother feeling well enough to drive a bit. She drove to Breda, Iowa Thursday for her Club Ladies Luncheon. Then in the late afternoon she joined us at Dunlap where Chris ran the mile and the half-mile race in another junior high track meet. He came home with two ribbons. He has placed in every race he has run. He's in seventh grade and only thirteen-years-old. He has one more track meet at Exira the following week and then that will be all for this year.

They are growing so fast!

June 17, 1991

Spring in Iowa 1991 has been wet.
Doug just started planting beans yesterday. He has a full-time job with his dairy herd.

We had quite a day on June 16, 1991. Mildred, Don, Chuck (Buzz) and his new wife Lynn spent the afternoon with us. They are my cousins, Uncle Chuck's (dad's brother) children. They grew up right here on grandfather C. A's Cumberland Stock Farm, going to school at Greeley No. 2, a one-room school house on the southwest corner of the old Saunders farm. We kids used to walk to school together, seven Saunders cousins in a one-room schoolhouse.[66]

Buzz, Mildred, Ray and Don Saunders.

Mildred is about eight months older than I, born on July 10, 1910. We were in the same class through Manilla High School, Class of 1928. Buzz was about three years younger and Don was born between 1921 and 1923. Merle was their other brother born between 1917 and 1918. After a full farming career, Merle and his wife Jean lived in Manning and ran the Saunders Steak House.

[66] Uncle Chucks Mildred, Don, Buzz and Merle plus my two sisters Margaret and Wilma and me.

Merle has passed on and Jean is now living in Fort Madison, Iowa, close to their son Carl, an attorney there.

Don is a family physician in Lodi, California. He has lost two wives, the first soon after their marriage, due to Leukemia and Gwen, about two or three years ago. Mildred's first husband Causby Blount (C.B.) died of a heart attack in 1969 and her second husband Elmer Lang, three years ago. Buzz and Phyllis built a world famous archery company and raised three boys. Phyllis died quite suddenly five years ago. Buzz and Lynn were married Saturday, June 15, 1991 in Omaha.

Of Dad's and Uncle Chuck's family, Trudy and I are the only couple still together.

God has been so very good to us. I hope we will be able to bring a good part of our life to a happy finish.

There is so much we need to do yet so that young people can carry on without too many conflicts or trouble.

Mother and I spent the day in Harlan. We consulted with Dr. Shafer who helped me with a tough bleeding ulcer last fall. He is going to examine my colon on July 1st. I sure hope he finds no major problems.

Mother and I are both in good health for eighty-year-olds. She has had eye surgery for a cataract about a year ago and a knee joint replacement this last spring. She walks without pain, doesn't use a cane and is still able to walk straight.

While we were in Harlan we also spent some time at the courthouse looking through some family and farm records. We found Grandpa and Grandmother's record of marriage and records from when he bought the first part of the farm from the railroad. We also found the records when they acquired the second part of the farm from Charles Cornelius and his wife Alma. They worked for the Milwaukee and Saint Paul railroad, he as a conductor on a passenger train. I am not sure what she did. These 160 acres were bought in 1917, just before my Mother and Father built their home (where Doug lives now). Mr. Cornelius held the mortgage for $16,000. The farm was owned by C. A. Saunders and Sons until 1925 when the bank in Denison and the one in Manilla closed.

At that time my Mother and Dad took possession and the home and farm were refinanced with Bankers Life of Des Moines, Iowa. Then the farm my Father rented from the Goddard Estate was bought in about 1926, and added to Dad and Mother's farm, giving them one-hundred twenty acres in Section Three and one-hundred and ninety-five acres is Section Two of Greeley Township.

Equitable Life of Des Moines held the Mortgage of about $10,000 to $12,000 on this land.

In 1928 Herbert Hoover was elected President and the Great Depression set in. Corn sold for 10 cents a bushel and hogs, what we thought would be the 'mortgage lifters', went to 2 1/2 cents a pound. Hay, straw and oats were worth nothing. Farms and businesses folded.

The Federal Land Bank was set up and my Father, Mother and I managed to pull the farm together and secure a Federal Land Bank Loan for $20,500 and as a result were able to hang onto our home.

Grandfather and Uncle Chuck secured financing through Production Credit and Wilmer Peterson ended up with the original C. A. Saunders' Cumberland Stock Farm. The farm is now in the Federal Farm Program and is in conservation reserve acreage, which means that Wilmer is getting paid not to farm it. I understand that when Wilmer Peterson dies, it will go to the State Wildlife Commission.

What a shame. All the buildings will be torn down when it should be made into an historical site. It was once recognized as the nation's top breeding farm for Shorthorn Cattle.

Mildred, Buzz, Don, Trudy and I spent some time looking through the big old house. It has been empty for some years now but Cumberland Stock Farm was once the scene of all our Thanksgiving and Christmas parties for the Saunders' families.

My hope, my dream is that Doug, Pat and their family can continue to have hope on this land, Cumberland Stock Farm No. 2. C. A. and Bertha, John and Marie, and my wife Trudy and I have spent our lives trying to hold this farm together. Now we will pass the legacy to Doug and Patty.

Just remember, son, it's okay to make a mistake but there isn't time in life for too many, especially if you don't learn from them. Hopefully, the year will be more profitable than it appears at the present time. Your Mother and I hope and pray your family can learn to enjoy the Saunders farm tradition as we have, even through all the frustrations and hard work it promises.

Cumberland Stock Farm, Manilla Once Internationally Known

Manilla, Ia. Times Thursday, April 10, 1986 Page

By Carole Chapman

Cumberland Farms was located in Section 3 of Greeley Township, Shelby County, about two miles south of Manilla. Charles A. Saunders was the grandfather of Ray Saunders. Ray now lives on Cumberland Stock Farm No. 2, although only the buildings of Ray's farm are on 12 acres of the original farm. Mr. C.A. Saunders was the son of Mr. and Mrs. Charles A. Saunders, who were married in 1863 in Brighton, England. The senior Mr. Saunders served in the Wisconsin Infantry in the Civil War. Both parents died in Wisconsin leaving their children orphaned. Young C.A. Saunders, at the age of 11, came to live and work for the Will Theobald family. He also had brothers, Will; Fred, father of Austin; and Ed, father of Harry; and sister ...

The Cumberland Stock Farm is no more. It exists only in the hearts and minds of a very select few people still alive today. Once the scene of international commerce and family celebrations, all the buildings have been torn down and turned into a wildlife preserve. The land is slowly turning back into the condition my grandfather found it nearly 125 years ago.

466

August 25, 1991

Late August on an early Sunday morning, 4:45 am. A car just went by. Someone getting home late or starting early?

Last evening Mother and I enjoyed a dinner out with Doug and Pat's family. We all had a fine meal in Manning. Steak, red snapper, shrimp and fried oysters plus the salad bar. This was an end of bean walking and back to school celebration. Tomorrow they all start school. Even Patty will be filling in at the school lunchroom as a cook.

Where has the summer of 1991 gone?

Seems like only a few days ago when Doug and Patty were planning their wedding.

Mother and I are fortunate to have this young family so close. We could never ask for a better gift from God.

Friday, Mother and I drove the pickup and stock trailer to Des Moines and met Tom and Mary Sullivan of Jessup, Iowa. They brought us a young Holstein bull to take over the "bull duties" here at the Saunders Dairy. Doug breeds most of the older cows artificially but uses a good bull on the heifers.

We seem to have been busy this past summer and looking forward to another California winter. It's expensive but nice.

Speaking of California, Craig, JoDee and his family were here as planned this summer. On July 7, 1991 at the First Presbyterian Church in Manilla, Hilary RaeAnne was baptized at the same altar where her Dad was baptized so many years ago. Little Hilary was and is a little lady, so pleasant a disposition. Grandma played the organ, Chris and Jennifer were ushers and "old grandpa" stood proudly beside them as the Elder representing the church in the ceremonies.

It was quite an honor, and a very emotional time for me. I don't know that I could do it again.[67]

I love my family and home!

Thank God for perfect gifts.

---

[67] He did it twice more, for Stevie Marie Reece Saunders in 1992 and for 'Boomer' Ryan Douglas Saunders in 1994 - CRS

On August 8, Mother and I drove to Des Moines and stayed overnight with granddaughter Karen and her husband Dan. Early Friday morning, Dean, Rosemary, Karen, Dan, great granddaughter Emily and Dan's nephew and our grandson Chris all drove to Chicago to see the Cubs play the NY Mets at Wrigley Field. We stayed overnight, had breakfast in Chicago and drove back home. We arrived in Des Moines at about four o'clock Saturday evening.

It is so great to be with family but, oh, so much greater just to know that these young people want to include Grandma and Grandpa in their lives.

November 10, 1991

Early morning and cold this early November.

Our '91 Halloween will long be remembered for the severe ice and snow storm in western Iowa.

We have approximately six inches of snow along with a thick coating of ice. Many power lines are still out and many others in temporary repair.

Our farm was without lights and power from Friday morning about 7:30 until Monday evening at 8:30. Thank God we owned a tractor-powered generator. Doug was able to operate the barn so that we could get the cows milked and then with what was left over, give the houses a bit of power.

No school, of course, so the grandchildren came over to enjoy our fireplace. Because the generator could only supply the barn Patty filled her electric crockpot and took it to the barn when she helped Doug with the morning chores, later we all shared a hot meal at noon.

Two heifer calves were born during that time. The kids named them "Stormy" and "Zero Degrees."

Certainly a lot of extra work on the farm when we have weather like this. The roads are snow-packed and icy. Dale used Doug's stock trailer to move some cattle and tried to bring it home Friday about noon. Doug ended up taking the Allis 7000 tractor with a chain and pulling them up the last hill one mile west of the farm.

Saturday, Doug came in and said. "I have the cattle shed finally cleaned out. Now I have to go up on the east hill and grind some calf feed and tomorrow I have to grind cattle feed." On top of all that, we still have eighty acres of corn to harvest.

God has ways of teaching us, but sometimes we are pretty slow learners.

Mother spent a part of yesterday in Denison shopping for groceries and doing some other business, plus a craft show at one of the churches. She gets lonesome here on the farm. Today, she has church services at nine o'clock and still heads the Presbyterian Women's Association so will have to take care of the potluck harvest dinner at noon. It all keeps her busy and challenged but it seems she is about the only one who will take the responsibility. That strikes me as a bit strange. We are both close to eighty-years-old but we are still enjoying good health for our age.

Craig and JoDee and Hilary are making plans for us to spend a part of the winter in California. We enjoyed two months there last year and have an apartment available December 1 this year. It will be our first-ever Christmas away from our home here on the old Saunders farm.

My heart is deeply embedded here.

I love our home!

God has been good to us. He somehow brought Trudy and me together and gave us our four fine sons. We were able to work with Mother and Dad and we all gained in life.

It's a very, very good feeling to be needed and wanted.

It's my hope that Doug and his family can enjoy the Saunders farm home as I have.

It is 5:15.
I'll sign off for now and hope to write more later.

> *"Thank God for my wife, my family, and my home in America."*

December 14-15, 1991

We have had a wonderful early Iowa Christmas here on the Saunders' Cumberland Stock Farm No. 2. I say early because today we, Mother and I are leaving to spend a couple of months in California with Craig, JoDee and granddaughter Hilary

Patty and her family drove us to the airport in Omaha. We had planned on eating a nice Christmas dinner at the Bishop Cafeteria. For as many years as I can remember, dinner at Bishop's was as close to a tradition as anything this family had. Every trip to Omaha included dinner at Bishop's. It was an inexpensive way of feeding our young boys. They loved pushing their silver metal trays along, having the luxury of selecting their own special favorites from the long row of cafeteria food, always ending with a big bowl of chocolate pudding from the dessert section.

Before dinner was over, they would all be given a Bishop's balloon of the color of their choice, blown up and fastened to a cardboard cut-out of a pair of clown shoes. The clown shoes made the balloon stand upright beside their plates. The balloons rarely survived long enough to make the trip home, but no trip to Omaha was complete without them.

What a disappointment to find Bishop's closed and the place vacated. It marked the end of an era. We ended up at Hardee's fast food – it's not the same.

Life continues to change, not always necessarily for the better.

It's always hard to leave our Iowa home, and hard to leave Doug with all the work. I feel like the rest of us seem to be running out on him. No one ever had a better son and daughter-in-law. The family is super and God knows it.

We arrived in California at eight o'clock, JoDee and Hilary met us. Craig was on call at the hospital in Ventura. Hilary is a happy one-year-old and JoDee her old self, always worrying about all of us. Craig is a lucky man to have found her; they are so full of life.

We found Columbus Estates much the same as when we left last March. Craig and JoDee have the rented furniture in place and food in the refrigerator.

Our family is so good to us.

We attended church at 8:30 today. It's always nice to go to the big Presbyterian Church here. They have a big choir and the music is so nice, and there are lots of kids around. Even at 8:30 in the morning, it is nice to have the young ones around.

December 29, 1991

On December 22, we attended the eleven o'clock pre-Christmas service at church and then on Christmas Eve we attended the 7:30 pm service. Twelve Elders served communion. Very impressive, I thought. There were lots and lots of young people present. Santa Claus even took time to talk to the youngsters and explain the real meaning of Christmas. When I called home and talked to Doug and Pat's family, I was told by grandson Matt that Santa had already been to his house.

We ate Christmas dinner at Columbus Estates. The management asked Trudy if she would play the big grand piano in the dinner hall so we had beautiful live Christmas music with our meal.

Craig was doing surgery, always busy and was called to Ventura for more on Christmas Day.

We are looking forward to seeing Emily. She will fly in from Oregon about midnight on the 26th and then we are all planning on flying to Ventura and having Christmas there. I believe this is the first Christmas with Craig since he joined the heart team here ten or twelve years ago. Laura was here a few days before she left the University of Southern California for her Christmas vacation in Oregon. She is a very outgoing young lady.

Christmas at "Windy Gables," Craig's home on Hollywood Beach just south of Ventura, was wonderful. Legend has it, the house, which is actually just a small cottage, once belonged to Clark Gable who used it when he came up from LA to go duck hunting. A few blocks down the street is a cottage once owned by Rudolph Valentino.

We sat and watched the sun sparkle on the waves. As they crashed on the beach, our eyes followed joggers and lovers as they made their way up and down the sand outside our dining room window while we ate our Christmas turkey roasted with all the trimmings. Later we opened the traditional gifts, but oh, we couldn't compare our meager gifts with what Craig and JoDee have shown us. They do so much for us.

The house was so small that we stayed two nights at the resort hotel just down the beach from their house. What a strange sensation to awaken in the middle of the night and hear the cold winter wind of a genuine Midwestern blizzard howling through the trees, only to go to the window and see the moonlight reflecting off the pounding California surf. The two sounds are eerily similar.

Craig was on call and did surgery on Sunday. Mother, JoDee, the baby and I flew back to Bakersfield at six o'clock. Sunday evening was rainy and cloudy but after we were above the storm clouds we were treated to one of the reddest sunsets I have ever seen, really very red.

Blessed

January 6, 1992

What a weekend.
What a Christmas 1991.
We have been here in California since December 14th.

There is so much going on for a pair of grandparents. We have enjoyed Craig and JoDee and our granddaughters Laura, Emily and Hilary so much. Emily wanted so much to leave on an early flight for home in Oregon, but due to that heavy winter fog they get here in the central California valley, her flight was delayed until 11:00 am. That gave Grandma and Grandpa a chance to take her out for breakfast. It's been a while since we had been alone with her. We enjoyed it very much.

We bid her goodbye after breakfast and her Dad was there at 11:00 to see her off. Because of the delays, the plane was overcrowded and she was given a later flight plus a coupon good for $250 to use on another flight. What an experience for a young girl, just a junior in high school. When my sisters and I were juniors in high school, our only transportation problem was where to board our horses while we were in school.

Seems to me that God looks after us in odd ways. For some reason, God did not care to have her home in time to meet her friends who were driving one-and-a-half hours to a rock concert.

On Sunday, January 5th we attended the First Presbyterian Church, another nice service and communion. Afterwards, we picked up JoDee and baby Hilary for dinner at Marie Calendar's. Craig was at the hospital again.

How nice to be with this young family.

While waiting for our table at the restaurant, we visited with a man and his family who were also waiting for a table. You learn so much and meet so many nice people if you are only willing to visit and listen. Turns out the man had open-heart surgery and my son, Dr. Craig R. Saunders, was his surgeon. They were so happy to meet his wife JoDee and little daughter Hilary.

During the conversation I found out he was originally from North Dakota, not far from where my Mother homesteaded and his wife was from the same area in Montana where Trudy's uncle and cousins lived. She was acquainted with them.

This would be Trudy's Uncle Roland Niewoehner. His son George had visited us in Iowa years ago. George's son Dirk Niewoehner is better known as Dirk Benedict of TV's "The A Team" and "Battle Star Galactica."

Through further conversations, we found out that he and his wife are going on the bus to Universal Studios for a taping of Johnny Carson's TV show. JoDee's Gone with the Wind Travel Agency is putting this trip together. We are looking forward to a good time, this is something Mother has always wanted to do.

Craig and JoDee do so much for us.

> *"Seems to me*
>
> # *God looks after us*
> *in odd ways. . .* "

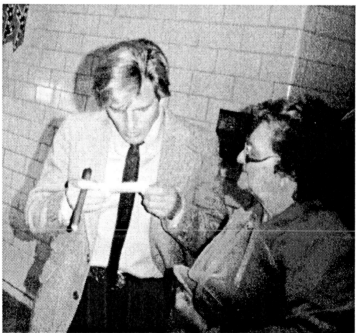

Trudy with her cousin's boy Dirk Benedict (Niewoehner), our only movie star relative, looking at family photos.

January 8, 1992

What a day!

About 4:30 in the afternoon we left our Columbus Estates apartment and enjoyed dinner with Craig and family. When we came back to the apartment at about 8:30, our apartment had been broken into. The thief had kicked in the patio door and went through our drawers. Several things were taken including my Seiko wristwatch, a present Craig brought back from Japan about twenty years ago when he was in the Air Force. We had quite an evening with the Estates manager, Mel Young. He called a police officer and we had to file a report and all those good things.

The next day, the caretaker repaired the door jam and casing and planned a more secure lock but he did not have the time to completely finish. The door could be locked, but the weather stripping and the inside chain were not yet in place.

We found we were covered by insurance up to $3,000 by our policy on our home in Iowa with Shelby County Farm Mutual. So, we proceeded with the reports.

January 11, 1992

Saturday evening we left our apartment to go to the main building to play Bingo. We were gone from 6:30 to approximately 9:00 pm. Again we were broken into. This time it looked like the lock had been picked. Our TV was taken and drawers ransacked again. So, back to the same routine, police report and conference with the manager and all that good stuff.

What an experience – two break-ins in one week, Trudy was about ready to go home.

Isn't this something?

We have spent eighty years in our Iowa farm home and never once felt the need to lock a door. In California after less than a month, we have had two break-ins.

Oh, did I tell you about our Christmas present? We will be joining Craig and family for a three-day cruise to Puerto Vallarta, Mexico with a stop at Santa Catalina Island, we are leaving on January 17th. It will be another first for Grandma and Grandpa.

January 25, 1992

We enjoyed the weekend with Craig and his little family so much. So very different from our way of life in the Midwest.

Craig and JoDee are so gracious. They take so much time and patience to see that old Dad and Mother are not wanting or needing a thing. They have given us so much since our arrival. Christmas was so much and so nice to see and be with Laura, Emily and the new family.

Hilary is such an active one-year-old and a great little traveler, too. We have spent quite a bit of time baby-sitting her this past week. Craig is always too busy and JoDee has been working on arrangements for her tour of the Johnny Carson Show. She works out of her home. When the new baby arrives in April, it will be a pretty busy home.[68] I almost wish they lived in the Midwest where things move at a slower pace.

But, looking back, Doug handled two babies eighteen months apart. Not once, but twice. Once in their small Midwestern trailer home and then again after moving into the big Saunders house. And oh, what a joy they are now. Chris, 14; Jennifer, 13; and John and Matt almost fourteen months apart.

God loves them all.

---

[68] Stevie Marie Reese Saunders was born April 7, 1992. There would be one last grandchild, a boy, Boomer (Ryan Douglas) born October 1, 1993.

January 27, 1992

Early Monday morning. It's not quite yet 3:30 am. As usual I wake up real early.
It's cold and foggy here in California, 30 degrees cold.

Craig and family were in Ventura this weekend. He was on call at the hospital there. Yesterday, Mother and I went to church at 8:30. Afterwards we drove up near McFarland for an afternoon with Grandma DeJong. On the way we stopped in Shafter, a small California farming community for lunch about 10:30 or 11:00. We spent the afternoon on the DeJong's dairy farm with 'Grandma', her daughter Nellie and her family of five; a pair of sixteen year old twins, a boy and a girl, and three other boys. Makes us think of the family at home.

They are all enjoying good health. Grandma DeJong makes her home with them. Chris, Tom's boy, was there and remarked that they wanted us to go to the big machinery and dairy show in Tulare, California on February 11th through the 14th.

Afterward, Mother remarked how much she wished we had waited to eat dinner with the DeJong family. I sure wish she would say what she really wants to do and not be so critical of me on so many things when I finally do voice my decisions.

Seems to me that once it is all over and done, and you know how things have turned out, it is pretty easy to wish for something different. The difficult thing is to live with the decisions that you have made and to be satisfied with them. It is such a waste of time to worry about or be unhappy with the past. The past is either something that was completely out of your control or something that you chose; either way there is nothing you can do about it and your time is better spent planning for the future.

I haven't been very efficient this morning. It's almost five o'clock already.
I'm going to try to go back to sleep.

February 23, 1992

We went this weekend to Ventura and the wonderful beach house, "Windy Gables." JoDee, baby, Mother and I drove over Friday morning. JoDee and baby had a party to go to Friday afternoon. Craig was busy at Memorial Hospital in Bakersfield and flew over in the early evening to take call over the weekend at the Ventura hospital. He is a busy surgeon and a very understanding dad to his older girls and one-year-old Hilary. They all worship the time they have with him.

Saturday morning Mother, Craig and I took time to walk on the beach and gaze out across the Pacific Ocean at the Channel Islands in the distance. I had waited eighty years for this. Mother had been there a year ago but it was another first for me. The waves were coming in as we strolled at water's edge looking for sea shells. I had a hold of Craig's hand and before we realized it, a big roller came in and soaked me half-way to my knees. Not many Iowa farmers have had that kind of experience at eighty-one-years-old. Quite an experience; it took quite a while for us to get the sand out of our shoes. Meanwhile, JoDee threw our trousers and socks in the washer.

Soon after getting dried out and making plans for breakfast, Patty called from Iowa. She gave us the news of the death of our closest and dearest friend, Jim Theobald. He had been in the Manilla nursing home for years, suffering from Parkinson's Disease.

Dorothy, his wife of sixty years, told us he had been real good the past couple of weeks and enjoyed several rides through the countryside, and then he just slipped away in his sleep between 4:00 and 5:00 in the morning.

Another of God's many blessings.

Immediately, Craig began to make arrangements for us to fly back home. We made reservations to fly to Omaha Sunday morning and for Patty to meet us and bring us back to Manilla so that we could be with Dorothy and family on Monday morning.

After an outdoor breakfast at the Harbor Inn and a bit of discussion, we cancelled our plans. We decided it was just too much unnecessary stress on a pair of eighty-year-olds, and much easier on all our families.

We made long-distance phone calls again and settled down and drove home with Craig and JoDee on Sunday afternoon. This was much easier on Craig and JoDee and also much better for Mom and Dad, not to mention the families back in Iowa.

We made plans to head back to Iowa about March 7th or 8th. We'll be with Dorothy then, when I am sure she will need someone as much as we will.

We will miss visiting with Jim, but he is at rest now and I thank God for taking him so carefully.

The Theobald family were the people who gave my grandfather, Charles A. Saunders, a home the year after he was orphaned in Wisconsin. He was fifteen years old when he came to Astor; his brothers and sisters came later. Grandfather and his brother Fred later married Theobald sisters, Bertha and Ruth.

The Theobalds have been more than friends of the Saunders' family for as many years as our family has been in this country.

> *"It's great to have family, without them, life would be worthless."*

February 29, 1992

Today we had a wonderful day with Craig and family.

One of the greatest.

We drove to a small ranch in Shafter, California, a sort of half-way home for troubled young men, 18-24 year olds, mostly from the inner city. The ranch was started on a shoe-string budget by a retired judge named Earl Gibbons as a home for three boys a few years ago. Now there are many buildings and as many as 78 boys participating in a one-year program which includes one half-day of work with the other half-day for study and worship.

The ranch is totally self-supporting, relying on donated labor and funds. Today's event was a Walk-a-thon fund raiser on a one-fourth mile track roped off in their pasture. It attracted a large crowd and lots of sponsored walkers and runners with pledges of money for each lap completed. For those who couldn't manage the track, there was also a rock-a-thon with participants in rocking chairs.

Dr. Saunders sponsored an eighty-seven-year-old lady, Mrs. Gibbons. She was Earl Gibbons' mother and about a year previously Craig had done open-heart surgery on her, replacing or repairing three heart valves and doing two or three bypasses. When she called Craig asking him to be a sponsor for her son's charity, Craig thought that someone else was going to do the walking but when he finally understood that she was to be the walker he pledged $100 per lap.

I don't know if he underestimated Mrs. Gibbons, his surgical skills or both but at the end of the day she had walked fourteen laps or three-and-a-half miles and it cost the doctor $1400. Both she and her doctor were interviewed and were on the Six and Eleven o'clock Channel 23 News.

Mrs. Gibbons received the prize for the oldest walker. Little Hilary, who has just learned to walk, walked one lap with her Dad and received a prize of five passes to a local roller-skating rink for being the youngest walker. It will be some time before she uses those passes.

Incidentally, it cost her Grandpa $25 for that lap but it was priceless. We had a great day and a great barbecue beef dinner.

I hope we can attend next year.

It's great to have family. Without them, life would be worthless.

God bless them, please!

March 3, 1992

A year of changes.

Today we had planned to fly to Eugene, Oregon with Craig to be with Emily for her Spring Musical Concert. We received word that it has been postponed until March 10, so we will be staying in California for one more week. Our plans are now to fly home to Iowa on March 15. Thank God we did not go home for Jim's funeral. We will enjoy a grand day with Craig and his daughter, Emily.

Last evening we had dinner with Craig and JoDee, she did a fine job on good old Iowa-style pork chops and all the fixin's. I think her Midwestern background shone through with that meal and I have no doubt that she could have been a good farmer's wife.

Craig and family also gave Mother her birthday present a little early,[69] a beautiful matched set of dark gray tweed luggage. This is something she would never consent to look at herself, let alone buy. We will use it on our upcoming trip to Oregon and I sincerely hope we live a few more years and can manage to use it often.

Little Hilary modeled her first Easter dress for us. She is having her picture taken in it today and as I understand it, with real live Easter bunnies. As I sit here in the darkness of this early March morning in the year 1992, I wonder if in 2092 some as yet unconceived descendent will be sitting at their breakfast table in the wee hours of the morning writing a new history of their family and including this antique photo of their great grandmother.

Oh, Hilary, you have such a future ahead of you and you are so fortunate to have such devoted and loving parents to get you off on the right foot. And, although you don't understand it now, you are also in line for another of God's blessings in the form of a baby sister next month.

God will be good to you as he is to all those who try to obey him and help others.

This has been a wonderful three months with our family in California.

Thank God, He has been willing for us to enjoy it together.

---

[69] Trudy's was born on Saint Patrick's Day (March 17th) in the year 1914.

Good night again. It's 4:15 in the morning and I am going to try to get some more sleep.

We have had some badly needed rain and I hear that there is more in the forecast.

Hilary RaeAnne Saunders, Easter 1992.

March 10, 1992

A wonderful winter in California in 1992

We arrived at Columbus Estates, our home away from home, on December 14th. We met friends we had made a year ago and renewed acquaintances with our lively granddaughter Hilary who was one-year-old on December 1st.

We were joined by granddaughter Laura and then Emily on December 26 and spent the weekend at Windy Gables where we had our Christmas with Craig's family.

We embarked on a cruise ship to Catalina Island and Mexico.

Our apartment was broken into two times in January.

On February 15th we had a great surprise when we were joined by Dean and Rosemary. He was in California to attend a school board educational meeting in San Diego but he came a bit early and spent my birthday with us. How wonderful!

We visited JoDee's stepfather, Stan Coleman, who spent several days in the hospital due to a real bad case of pneumonia.

We joined a busload of people on a trip to Universal Studios to watch the taping of Johnny Carson's Tonight Show.

A year ago on March 10, 1991 we received a phone call that our first great- grandchild, Emily Rae Hanson had just arrived. This year on February 12th, Dale's boy Jay and wife Laura Saunders of Pella, Iowa called to let us know of the arrival of Matthew Saunders, our first great-grandson.

Last evening we had a wonderful dinner with Craig and family. JoDee has quite a cold and their second baby is due April 6-7-8th, so she was uncomfortable. Hopefully she is much better today.

Craig took the dressing off my arm last evening. Guess I forgot to tell you that I tripped and fell through a plate glass door at his house and had to have twenty stitches in my arm. It's coming along well but I wish my eyes were as good as Mother's. I am thankful though for the health I have.

Today was one of the most memorable days of our winter in California, 1991-1992. We left Bakersfield about noon for Eugene, Oregon in son Craig's business plane. The flight was simply wonderful, so smooth and pretty. We saw Yosemite National park, Lake Tahoe and Mt. Shasta, all covered with snow. Very, very beautiful. Again, I wish my eyesight was better, but I am thankful for what I have.

After about a three-hour flight, Emily was waiting for us at the airport parking lot, all smiles, but no more happy than her grandparents. We had dinner with Emily and then attended her spring music concert. Emily performed with three or four other students in a string group. This was a special time for both granddaughter and grandparents. How great it is to be able to share these few moments in life with a son and his daughter. Not every young person has this kind of opportunity. I am sure Emily is beginning to realize the things her Dad has and what he is doing for her.

What a great day, March 10, 1992. A great-granddaughter turning one-year- old and a granddaughter who had her junior high school music concert and Grandma and Grandpa could be there with her, however short the time.

What's more, little did Mother and I ever think this kind of thing would ever be available for a pair of eighty-year-old farm kids from Iowa who decided to put their lives together back in the days of the "Great Depression."

We will be flying home on Sunday morning and using our new travel luggage. What a wonderful winter! We are sort of anxious to get back home and visit folks there.

We have to spend some time with Dorothy Theobald and come to closure with Jim's passing.

We have to remember we are eighty, I guess.

God has opened a lot of doors for us. We just have to have the faith to walk through them.

We have to assure that the entire Saunders family will always have Cumberland Stock Farm to come home to.

March 15, 1992

Weather is real nice for mid-March.

Today was another great day in our lives. At six o'clock am son Craig, JoDee and little Hilary took Trudy and me to Meadows Field in Bakersfield, California to board an American Airlines jet. We were heading back to our Iowa farm, my home since February 15, 1911, where I was born less than a half-mile from our present home.

Little sixteen month old Hilary was so wide awake, "Bye, bye, Papa" were her parting words. How wonderful life is to be 81-years-old and have family, as Trudy and I have, who cares for us.

We were met in Omaha at Epply Air Terminal by Doug's family. How pleasant again after three months in California to see their happy smiles. We all enjoyed ice cream at Mickel's Restaurant in Harlan and were back in our home on the farm before dark.

Monday we visited Gene Saunders at the Manilla Manor and Fred Rabe at the Denison Hospital. We picked up some Kentucky Fried Chicken and ate an early supper with Dale and Johnet. She is doing fairly well recovering from a broken ankle.

It is so great to have such a nice house to come home to and grandchildren.

> *"We have to assure that the entire Saunders family will always have Cumberland Stock Farm to come home to."*

April 7 1992

Today our 13th grandchild came to make her home with Craig and JoDee. Her Dad called us here in Iowa around 10:30 am telling us Stevie Marie Reese Saunders had arrived weighing 7lbs. 9 oz. and 21 inches long.

Baby Stevie came by cesarean section in Ventura, California. She brings our Saunders grandchildren to seven boys and half a dozen girls. We are very fortunate all our family is living and well, including 2 great-grandchildren.

Another one of God's blessings!

> *"...our 13th grandchild...*
>
> ## *Stevie Marie Reese Saunders*
>
> *... brings our Saunders grandchildren to*
>
> *7 boys and half a dozen girls."*

April 10, 1992

Mother and I joined John and Matt (Doug's boys in the 3rd and 4th grades) at the Manilla School for Grandparent's Day. We had a Spring Musical Program with cookies and juice.

Then we drove to Des Moines to visit Karen and Dan Hanson and great- granddaughter Emily, a year old March 10th. She and her parents were so kind and gracious to two old grandparents. The baby is growing so fast and both parents so busy.

After breakfast we drove to Pella, Iowa and visited Dale's boy Jay, his wife Laura and their new son Mathew David Saunders born February 13th. Mathew David is our first great grandson and will be the first to carry the Saunders name into the next generation. He is a happy, bright-eyed little fellow and growing. He weighs almost twelve pounds. He also has a proud pair of young parents.

Mother and I had supper in Des Moines and were home before it was very dark.

It was a wonderful and enjoyable Grandpa and Grandma's weekend.

" Mathew David Saunders. . .

our first great grandson. . .

will be the first

to carry the Saunders name

into the next generation."

April 21, 1992

We had a wonderful 1992 Easter with our family. Saturday was a birthday dinner with Doug's family. Their daughter Jennifer is thirteen years old.

Sunday we attended sunrise services with the young people at church and then drove to Spencer and had dinner with Dean's family including one-year-old great-granddaughter Emily Hanson.

We came home for Trudy's Monday Night Ladies Club bridge game and awoke this morning to "The Great 1992 Iowa Easter Snow", about 4-5 inches. Easter was white, not green.

On April 9th I had a wonderful experience. Doug and Patty took me to Audubon to attend Chris' first 1992 track and field meet. Chris is in 8th grade and this year is running the 800 meters, it's his first try after having run the mile last year. His first race was anchoring the Medley Relay and he ran a very close second.

In the open race he took command from the start and won his first 800 meter race. His time was 2:31, a respectable time for junior hi and it will build his confidence. There were five schools competing in the meet and Chris' team (IKM –Irwin, Kirkman and Manilla) brought home the 1st place trophy.

His sister Jennifer, now a 7th grader, came home from practice Monday night overjoyed. It was her first try with her new track shoes and she cut about one minute off her best previous time. We are looking forward to a lot more enjoyable track meets.

We learned today that Fred Rabe has been transferred from the Manilla Nursing Home to a Des Moines hospital. Guess he has heart failure and perhaps more of his old stomach problems.

Garnet Arnold (Bob's wife) hasn't been real well all winter either. She has had some x-rays of her stomach in the past week. Bob called Trudy Monday afternoon. Trudy drove over immediately and stopped in again Tuesday afternoon.

They all seem to be so resistant to really try to get to the real root of their problems. Seems to me early attention and care is not to be overlooked.

But we must remember we are all getting old.

May 6, 1992

3:58 am. Another early morning.
A much different spring. We like to say typical Iowa weather. It has been foggy and wet a few days and HOT but now, on the night of May 5th, we covered our young flowers to protect from the frost. It's cold and dry.

Doug finished applying his anhydrous ammonia to his corn ground yesterday and now will disk his corn stalks in preparation for herbicides and corn planting. Doug Backhaus started planting corn on the rented ground. The calves seem to be doing well; the new hutches are great. We still haven't taken the old silo down but will soon, then the men can get started on the new milking parlor.

We have had some young men taking out wild trees from the fencerows. This was one of the things I so wanted to get done. It will improve the appearance of the farm so much. The fencerows may look sort of naked for a while but it will be better in the future. I hope I can get some pine and fir trees established before I have to leave. It could be something to help the grandchildren remember Grandpa.

Trudy and I have spent many happy hours here with our family; many frustrating and trying times, too. It's hard to justify the cost and time involved in some of these projects. A person has to have an undying faith in home, family and the future. I sincerely hope I can see the new milk parlor completed, the fence repaired, feed stations installed and some evergreens started along the north road. Big order?

On May 2nd we drove to Norwalk, Iowa to attend Robb Theobald's wedding. He is Jim and Dorothy's grandson. We have known the family forever; they are like our own. We then spent Saturday night with Karen and her family. Dan is also like one of our own and baby Emily, what a joy. We enjoyed church Sunday morning with them and then drove home. On the way we stopped to visit Ingrid Bro in Exira. Their son Doug worked with us the first summer son Doug was in the Navy.

May 19, 1992

Beautiful sunrise just lighting up the silos and calf pasture. Cool 55 degrees.

Had another of "God's Blessings." Over one inch of rain over the weekend.

Doug sprayed thistles in the pasture yesterday then took time out to attend Chris' last junior high track meet in Manning. Another beautiful sunny warm day. The boys won their meet and were a happy, whooping, yelling crowd of boys as they all took off on their victory lap.

It was a team effort. Even one of the smallest boys, the son of an Irwin preacher who also drives their bus, was so happy he shouted, "I can't believe it. I placed in both my races!" Happy boys – they gave their coach a bath with a big water balloon.

Chris filled in for an injured boy who pulled a muscle in the Carroll meet a week ago. Chris placed 3rd or 4th. Their Medley Relay placed first with Chris running the anchor half-mile. He also placed 2nd in the open 880. He had a good fast time for an 8th grader, 2:22.

The IKM Jr. High track team had a good 1992 season. The IKM girls took 2nd place again with several point winners out because of pulled muscles and the flu bug. Granddaughter Jennifer was one of them. She ran the 440 in Carroll, placing 3rd with a hurt foot. She is back walking normal after being on crutches for a week. The whole team has learned life is not always easy but it still has its rewards. I hope I am able to see the kids run again next year.

We stopped in to visit Fred Rabe Sunday. Bob and Garnet went along. Fred is in the Manning Hospital. He is very weak. I hope Mother and I don't have to face too much of that kind of life. I think back over the years how wonderful my wife was in helping care for Mother and Dad Saunders. She was with both parents when they departed this life.

There are few people like your Mother, boys.

Always remember whose son you are.

May 24-25, 1992

Memorial Day weekend.
Cold. Very cold and rainy.

Mother and I visited the Denison Cemeteries Sunday afternoon. Driving out of the Denison Cemetery we met Trudy's cousin, Wilbert Bergstead of Omaha. Trudy had not seen him for ten years or more. We all went for lunch at Cronk's Café. We had quite a nice, but short visit with Wilbert.

The big surprise is that Fred Rabe is back in Manilla Manor from the Manning Hospital. Fred surprised us all. He is a long way from 100% but such a change. One wonders how long he can keep coming back. God knows and must have more work for him.

His daughter Joan and family were here from Sioux City. They came out to our home, it was a big treat for Joan's three Sioux City kids. Doug's children really enjoyed hot dogs with their city cousins. Little four-year-old Joey couldn't get enough 'real cow milk.'

Monday the 20th Trudy and I took flowers to Mom and Dad's graves in the Astor Cemetery. It was cold, rainy and forlorn. Such is life here on Earth.

It was good to see Fred as good as he is. We heard nothing from Bob and Garnet. I talked to my sister Margaret; her diabetes is really bothering her. I wish I could visit her for a few hours. She is so alone.

Mother and I are so fortunate to have family close by and able to get about as we can.

June 4, 1992

Today marks the first real start of remodeling and rebuilding the dairy equipment here on the Cumberland Farm No. 2. Carroll Kalvig and son-in-law Al Peterson began the process of laying a new water line. We are using a two-inch PVC plastic line that will replace the one-inch galvanized water line put in by my father, John Saunders, when he started the home place on a bare alfalfa field in the spring of 1917.

A lot of hard work and many tears went into the farm by my Mother and Dad. They started with a dream and thank God they were able to live out their lives in the home they built for us. I'm glad my wife and I were able to stick with them. We have had our problems but have a nice home on the spot where we built our first little home in 1934 using the same two rooms Dad and Mother used in 1903. I have told you before of adding on using part of the old Milwaukee Depot in Manilla. We bought that 40 X 22 foot building for $40 and tore it down to use the lumber.

We raised four sons in that house, all good honest men. No big problems and all with wonderful families. Mother and Dad would be proud of them all and very happy to see Doug, Patty and their four children in the house they built, lived and died in.

Hopefully the new water line will relieve most of the problems of enough water to the house. Patty has been short on days when the cattle demanded so much water.

I have spent most of my spare time the past week cleaning up the used stainless steel dairy equipment Doug bought for his milk parlor. It is cleaning up nicely but it is slow and takes lots of elbow grease. There is no way he could have had new equipment. The cost is just too prohibitive.

More later, I hope.
Good night.
12:45 am

June 28, 1992

Early Sunday morning. It looks like another beautiful June day. Cool.
The night security light on the silo just turned off so sunrise is just a few minutes away.

We have had a busy couple of weeks. Sunday, June 14th, Mother managed a musical concert and lunch at our church. Christy Humphries of near Iowa City and two accomplished violinists, Bryce Christensen and Michael (?), came on Saturday evening and had a wonderful dinner with us here on the farm. Granddaughter Jennifer helped and her Grandmother Fisher also ate with us.

Christy had been a concert pianist and a bride of three months when she was badly burned in an apartment fire in Florida when she was only nineteen-years-old. Her husband at that time was charged with arson and attempted murder but was later acquitted because there was only circumstantial evidence.

After 74 skin grafts and operations, Christy, badly scarred and hands deformed, has resumed playing the piano and organ and has given her life to her God and the people. This concert at our church brought a standing ovation for both Christy and Trudy who had worked so hard to bring the musical to our church.

The next weekend started off with Ken and Mary Keats' 50th Wedding Anniversary held at Pastimes Banquet Room in Denison. It was great to see the family who grew up just about two miles from our home and who went to school with our boys. Ken Jr., who ran on Craig's high school relay team, is a Lutheran minister and Chaplin at the Arizona State Prison. Dan is a chiropractor in Des Moines. Jim is also a minister in a church in eastern Iowa and Deb lives in Denison with her family.

A great afternoon.

Then on Sunday another Golden Wedding Anniversary, this time Dale and Phyllis McCone's at the Presbyterian Church in Manilla. We have known Phil and Dale forever. Their son Stan was born the same day as our son Craig. Pam and Gary Hall, Patty and Dan Muhlbauer and families are all a part of our great family of friends.

On Father's Day Dean and Rosemary, Keith and Doug and his family all had Sunday dinner with us before we all attended the McCone's 50th.

Wednesday, June 24th, Phyllis and Trudy got their heads together and we celebrated our 58th wedding anniversary with dinner at Pastimes. We were joined by a young couple from Minnesota who were visiting the McCones. Very enjoyable.

To top off a busy time, on Saturday Trudy and I drove to Council Bluffs. Trudy had an appointment with Dr. Miller who a year ago rebuilt her right knee. She has been having a lot of pain in her hips.

I think we got good news. Something connected to 78 years of age and 58 years of marriage. X rays only showed some build-up of arthritis in the hips and back. Dr. Miller ordered therapy three times a week for a month. We are so happy that it is nothing more serious and that we are as well as we are.

June 30th will be Craig's birthday and this weekend Patty and her family are going to Davenport for her mother's family reunion.

I sincerely hope for God's guidance and a safe trip home for all.

July 9, 1992

Today will be a day remembered. Uncle Fred Rabe, Trudy's sister's husband, passed away at Manilla Manor. Fred had been in poor health since before Anna Marie passed two years ago. His passing leaves quite a burden on his family in the sense of dealing with his property in Denison.

Here on the Saunders' farm the old silo built for my father in 1917 by Add Morgan was hauled to a landfill west of the house. This silo had been taken down earlier to make room for the new milking parlor being built by Doug, grandson of John and Marie Saunders who built the original farm buildings in 1917 then moved into their new home complete with running water, a furnace and indoor toilets on that cold winter day, February 2, 1918.

There are three generations of the Saunders family still on the farm – Trudy and myself, Doug and Patty and four of their children. Chris, fourteen, Jennifer, twelve, John, eleven and Matt, nine.

July 10, 1992

Ten years ago I was in 7th heaven. My four-year-old grandson rode in the cab of the big 704 New Idea Uni Harvester. We cut many loads of haylage and corn silage together and Grandpa enjoyed every precious minute.

Now, using the immortal words of John F. Kennedy in his inaugural speech as President of the great United States of America, "The torch has passed."

Today that four year old is fourteen and he is handling the 709 Diesel wonderfully by himself.

I would like to take credit for teaching him but his father has done far better than I ever could. Chris Douglas seems to be a capable young boy. I am glad to have him seemingly taking my place.

July 12, 1992

What a wonderful Early Sunday morning. Just beginning to get light and a steady rain. No storm, just that wonderful sound of raindrops. Very, very welcome.

We had a mid-morning shower yesterday, approximately half an inch.

Carroll Kalvig and son-in-law Al Peterson were here last week working on the new water line. It is a big job but when the new milk parlor is finished and in use, I'm sure all will enjoy and profit by the undertaking.

Friday was a good day of hay harvest for Doug and Chris.

Today Mother has to substitute as organist at the Methodist Church so we will leave early.

Next Sunday, granddaughter Stevie Marie Reece Saunders, Craig's baby, will be baptized as was her sister Hilary RaeAnne a year ago. Baptized into the Christian faith in the Manilla Presbyterian Church in which her dad grew up, with her Grandfather as the presiding Elder and Grandma playing the organ. To me this is quite an honor, Chris, Jennifer and now Craig's daughters. Not many grandpas have that honor.

Craig and family will be here at the farm on Thursday afternoon and will leave for home Sunday afternoon. As we plan, Saturday will be our family get together.

More later.

July 21,1992

Monday, 6:30 am

What a great family weekend.

We saw granddaughter Stevie Marie for the first time on Thursday afternoon. Curly blonde hair, and huge, no giant blue eyes only slightly smaller than the beautiful big smile that is always on her face, always, that is, when there isn't a thumb stuck in her mouth. Her 'big' sister Hilary enjoyed showing her off and is so proud of her, as is her Mom and Dad.

Saturday Karen and great-granddaughter Emily joined us along with grandpa Dean, wife Rosemary and their sons Keith and Kevin. Then after dinner Dale spent some time at our home. All four boys were home plus Doug and Patty's four children.

It was all over too soon.

Sunday morning Grandpa again had the privilege and honor of taking part in the baptism of a grandchild. Stevie was a "little angel."

Doug, Patty, their children, Craig, JoDee and girls all had dinner at Cronk's smorgasbord in Denison. Craig and family then left for Omaha and their flight back to California.

Again it was all over too soon but all is well and we are happy to be God's children.

I will be 82-years-old in February 1993. I don't have very good eyesight and my legs bother me a lot. This summer my main concern is to help clean up the used milk equipment and see it installed and working. Then, I will almost be satisfied with my life her on Cumberland Farm II.

I trust God will see to it that I'll have a few more years with Trudy and the family.

Chris – take a few years at Iowa State and find a girl who comes as close to your mother as possible. One like Grandma would not be bad.

Best of everything to all!

July 27,1992

Monday.
Looks like a clear day.

A great July week in Iowa. It all started Monday morning. It was lonesome; our company and family had all gone home and once again we were left with an empty house. Craig, JoDee and the girls had a rough flight from Omaha to Dallas and were about an hour late. The plane from Dallas to California was about an hour-and-a-half late so they arrived home with two very tired little girls.

Thank God all are safe and home. It was too much to crowd into such a short time.

Doug decided Monday an older cull cow should go to market. She had been kept because she had been carrying an A. I. (artificially inseminated) calf. So Tuesday morning Doug and Chris loaded her into the trailer and left for Dunlap but not before they got a big wagon ready in the field for Doug Backhaus who was ready to start combining the oats.

On the way home from the Dunlap sale barn, Doug's pickup developed a leak in the radiator. They were only about half a mile from Pete's Repair Shop but Pete was on vacation so Doug started the walk home, almost five miles and not one car met or passed them. Quite unusual even for Iowa.

After arriving home the wagon in the field was full of oats so another one had to be gotten ready. By late Tuesday evening three wagons were full of grain. This was perhaps the best oat crop Doug has ever had, eighty plus bushels per acre by measure and very heavy. It was late by the time the wagons were under cover and the milking chores done. By morning we had three-fourths inch of rain.

On Monday afternoon Chris had been invited to go with the F.F.A. class to attend the F.F.A. judging at the Shelby County Fair. Four kids showed up. Chris was the only freshman and they came home with the 2nd place trophy. It was a great learning experience for a boy who I hope will take my place here on Cumberland Stock Farm No. 2.

The milk parlor progress is slow. I have about 7/8ths of the used equipment cleaned and painted with primer.

By Saturday evening we had a total of four and three quarter's inches and very little if any had run out of the fields. During this time Doug had three artificially inseminated heifer calves born, so all in all, quite a week.

August 14, 1992

Another cool day ahead. Sun is beginning to show on the silos across the road.

Record low temperatures across the Midwest; 46 degrees reported at Spencer.

Very unusual.

Showers almost every night.

The boys are progressing with the milk parlor. Yesterday the big bulk tank was moved to the new location in the north end of the barn. A big day's work but a good one and things are progressing with the building, too.

Dean stopped in Wednesday afternoon and Mother and I ate dinner with him in Denison. Afterwards we went to the auto dealers and saw a nice 1989 Chrysler New Yorker with only 48,000 miles. The asking price was $10,500. They were willing to take $7,750 and our 1985 in trade in. Mother and I took it for a test drive last evening. It is a nice auto but we are still undecided.

Doug and the boys got the straw baled and undercover but still have one load to unload. The New Holland Bale Wagon saves a lot of heavy work but for it to work right it must be tuned like a violin.

Mother has quite a cold so I'll eat breakfast alone this morning. Will write more later.

August 22,1992

It is with a heavy heart that I write tonight. Today Mother and I took an old iron bed that used to belong to my Mother, a buffet Trudy bought when we were first married and a few other items to put in Fred Rabe's Estate Sale.

This evening Fred's children, Arnold and his wife Shirley, Joan and her husband John with their three children Jill, Jim and Joey ate supper with us here at the farm. We don't realize it now but the real family ties are getting stretched thin.

Fred and Anna Marie are gone. Bob and Garnet are very much alone. Trudy and I are now in our 80's. Thank God for our family and the fact that Doug and Pat and kids are so close and good to us.

We have so much yet always want so much more.

We need to stop and count our blessings.

August 23, 1992

The Rabe sale is now history. Son Dale was one of the auctioneers.

Arnold, Joan and families did a great job over the past few weeks gathering all the old items to be sold. Many boxes of small items at $1, $2 or $3 but things had to be cleaned out.

One bit of irony – Dean bought the old buffet of his Mother's for his daughter Karen. Had we known, we would gladly have given it to her. It had been in Doug and Pat's storeroom for years.

The sale is over.

The house up for sale.

The kids have gone back to their homes.

Only memories left.

August 24, 1992

My Father's birthday.

Dad was born here on the home farm in 1880 and spent his life on sections Two & Three of Greeley Township, Shelby County, Iowa. He would have been 112- years-old today.

I wish my grandchildren could have known Mother and Dad. They have great opportunities ahead and seem to be willing to work at life.

So far, no drugs, no alcohol, no tobacco.

I'm sure Trudy and I thank God every day for our life even though there are numerous problems and disagreements.

My father, John Raymond Saunders. The lapel pin is a picture of my mother.

August 27, 1992

The sun is beginning to show across the road.
In the silo pasture a young Holstein calf and its mother enjoying the green grass.
We have had so much cool weather and rain that the crops are slow.

The new milk parlor is progressing but there is still so much to be done. Carroll Kalvig and son-in-law Al Peterson are busy with drains and water, etc. Mother and I brought the rest of the repaired equipment from the welding shop in Audubon yesterday. It was so cool we needed a jacket.

Mother is up.
Will write more later.
Breakfast now.

> *"Life is wonderful*
>
> *for those who work at it."*

Blessed

September 5, 1992

Saturday morning.
No rain yet but showers in the forecast. We here in Iowa could use four-to-six weeks of warm sunny weather.

Four years ago Craig and JoDee were married in San Francisco. Last evening we talked to them and their two daughters. Hilary is almost two years old and little Stevie Marie was born last April 7th.

Time flies and even though we complain, God is good.

Much has been accomplished here on the farm. The milk parlor is progressing. The return alley cement has been poured. Carroll and Al set the drains in the pit floor and Robert's Construction got the pit walls formed and poured the concrete then striped the forms and hauled fill sand.

Thursday Carroll and Al put in the side drains. Friday was a big day. John Herbst of Rock Valley, Iowa, a milk equipment dealer and helper, came and set the stalls. Jim of Robert's Construction finished the forming of the cow platform. About 4:30 Carroll and Al came with a back hoe and tied the drain lines together.

Everyone worked late.

The boys hope to pour cement for the cow platform Tuesday. There is a lot to do but all the pieces are coming together and things are taking shape. Patty and Chris have most of the parts painted and they look good.

Last evening was Chris' first football game as a member of the IKM Marching Band. It was his first time wearing his new band uniform. He was a proud fourteen-year-old freshman.

Life is wonderful for those who work at it.

It is beginning to get light. The silos are showing up across the road. Looks like we have escaped the rain so far today.
The summer of 1992 has been Iowa's 2nd coolest in this 20th century. So long for now.

September 15,1992

Still a wet September.
Several early morning rains of one inch or more.

We are fortunate where we live. There has been no flooding. Several southern Iowa counties have suffered severe flooding. Many highways have been closed and bridges washed out. Interstate 35 is closed south of Des Moines. The Burlington Railroad, on which Amtrak passenger trains run, washed out in several places also.

Those poor farmers in that seven county area sustained severe crop damage. It was a total loss in some parts. We are fortunate even though work has been delayed on the new milk parlor.

In the spring we wanted to get the corn planted before work started on the parlor. Now we wonder if we will be ready to go by the time the snow flies. Hopefully things will progress much faster once all the concrete work is finished.

The new water line to Pat's house is one of God's blessings and Carroll and Al have the new furnace about half completed. We will move the old furnace to the barn.

Will write more as work progresses.

September 17, 1992

These past few days have had their bright moments.

We received one of the nicest letters ever received from anyone. Granddaughter Laura, Craig's first daughter, wrote us from college at the University of Southern California. A wonderful, wonderful letter.

About the same time a letter from her Aunt Janet Clevenger who lives in or near Des Moines. She and Murray are the parents of five year old twin girls, Kim and Katy. Two beautiful little girls. Their mother Janet teaches in Carlisle, Iowa and is taking a year's leave to be with the girls full-time before they start school. How wonderful to know these kind of people and to be able to include them in our family.

Yesterday, Thursday the 16th, Dale and Phyllis McCone, Trudy and I drove to Spencer for a day at the Clay County Fair. Our son Dean is following in his great-grandfather's footsteps and is on the fair board. We had a nice visit with Dean and his wife Rosemary. This is not the first time for the McCones and us to share a fair, we both used to raise shorthorns and we always enjoy being with them.

On the way home we stopped in Storm Lake, Iowa and had dinner. We were joined by Floyd and Phyllis Fanning of Nemaha. It is always nice to visit with old Shorthorn cattle friends.

> *"How wonderful to know these kind of people and. . . include them in our family."*

September 22, 1992

*Summer of '92 is over. Fall started at 2:40 this afternoon.
It is a beautiful day.
The forecast is for a few sunshiny days.*

Hope they really get started again on the building. We poured some more cement Monday and Carroll and Al set the drains and heat pipes so the floor of the pit can be poured.

Tuesday was another no-show day.

Today, Wednesday, is so bright and pretty at 7:30 am. Sure hope the builders get on the ball.

How time slips by and how we would like it to be only the end of August. Three more days should about finish the carpenters work, then installation of the electricity and some more of the cement work, this time the pit floor.

It will be very nice. I know Doug and Patty will breathe a deep sigh of relief when they have used the parlor a week and know things are working. It has been an enormous undertaking with used equipment.

Last Sunday of September 1992

This has been one of the great days of being a grandpa. John and Matt helped me clean up a bit at the new parlor this afternoon. Jennifer painted the two used cow entry doors and Patty painted the gates inside the parlor. Doug, who is nursing a badly sprained knee, chopped more hay and tended chores. A good hired man would be a great asset for the farm for the next three months but it is almost impossible to find someone who wants to work.

Chris and his classmate Aaron Nelson have been working on their freshman science project. They are to devise a way to strike a match using a combination of wheels, axels, levers and inclined planes, etc. They accomplished this today and it will be demonstrated in class Monday or Tuesday. Mother went over to see it late last evening, her comment "A lot of work to light a match."

About four o'clock Mother and I took Jennifer, Matt and John over to Manteno County Park as a reward for their help in the milk parlor. They really enjoyed the time. We walked across a floating bridge and tried all the various rides and slides. They brought home frogs, snails, clam shells and various other things. After arriving home they went right to work feeding the young calves.

We made a few plans to try to organize a wiener roast at the park next weekend.

On September 25th, Brian Nicolas, Robin and Sue Saunders' baby boy arrived at their home in Oskaloosa, Iowa. This makes three great grandbabies joining our Saunders family.

They are all a joy and thank God for our whole family.

Bye for now.

October 4, 1992

Sunday Morning.

Yesterday afternoon I thoroughly enjoyed a few hours with my grandson Chris. He used the big Allis Chalmers 7060 tractor, the big New Idea manure spreader, the Hew Holland skid loader and hauled fertilizer (cow manure).

The afternoon was one of those October days poets write about, clear, warm and with very little breeze. Chris did all the work. He handles the machinery so carefully, it is a joy. I used a long-handled shovel and cleaned around the fence and water tank. What a way for an 82-year-old grandpa to enjoy a few hours of his last days!

Another day, long ago. My dad hauling manure with Fox and, I believe, Margaret along for the ride.

My Dad and Mother, Trudy and I have spent long hours of work here on the Cumberland Farm No. 2 and made nice homes for ourselves. I just hope and pray the grandchildren can build on the foundation of life laid out years ago and that they can enjoy these same pleasures with their families.

These are God's blessings.

Kids, learn to enjoy them.

This past week has been beautiful October weather. The milk parlor is progressing. The pit floor has been poured and about half the cement for the holding pen and wall. Friday we laid the cement for an extension of the feed yards and the pads for the feed bins.

We are almost ready to set the new computerized feeders. The cows will wear an ID around their neck and each time they are milked it will record how much milk they give and it will give them their individual feed ration. We need the doors on the milk room, etc. I hope I am here next summer to see the whole system working.

Today Doug plans to have his family help him bring the cattle from the west pasture, sort out some, add a few heifers and then take them back. It is a lot of work. Afterwards hopefully we all can go to the picnic area for a wiener roast.

How I wish I could really be of good help to them!

Hopefully, we have a month or six weeks of nice weather for the final hay and silage harvest.

Thank God for all my family.

October 16, 1992

Today is my sister Margaret's birthday. We are all getting older, thank God. I had hoped Wilma and I could have got together and spent a weekend with her this summer.

It's been a rewarding but frustrating summer. It started in early April and May, which were dry, June had little rain and was very cool. Then came July. It was the wettest and coolest July in 100 years. August was about the same and September, more of the same. We are now in mid-October and we have hardly had a frost.

The corn and beans are bumper crops.

Doug has cut very little corn silage to date but what he has cut is good. Hopefully this coming two weeks he will find the time to really harvest.

Work on the new milk parlor is like the crops – late, late, late. We are about six weeks behind on construction. Yesterday, though, a lot was accomplished. Carpenters, electricians and John Herbst with his helper were all here. John is installing the milking and feeding equipment. The machinist from South Side Welding in Audubon was on the job, too.

Doug didn't get much more than his cattle looked after while supervising the work and plans but at last a new permanent steel roof is on the silo shed and the feed bins.

The automatic feeding system is beginning to shape up. Herbst has set a goal of milking in the new parlor two weeks from last night. That will still be two months late but it will be great. It is as big a change as when we went from buckets to the old parlor in 1967, just before Doug left for the Navy.

A lot has happened since that dark and rainy September night!

November 6, 1992

Last evening son Dale and grandson Chris, who both have birthdays on November 5th, joined us at the new Country Café in Manilla for birthday dinner. We enjoyed a nice dinner; it is wonderful to have the new generation active.

The new milking parlor is now in use. We still need some more electrical and plumbing work done but it is going to live up to its expectations.

The great presidential campaign of 1992 is over. We have a new young President and Vice-President. I'm hopeful the U.S.A. under new young leaders, President-elect Bill and Hilary Clinton and Vice-President Al and Tipper Gore, will bring a new young out look for America. They defeated a good man in George Bush; I hope America's trust has not been misplaced; even so there will be more good young men to follow.

Thank God for all the young people with mission and willingness to plan and work for the future.

Breakfast time on Cumberland Stock Farm No. 2

> *"God's great gifts –*
> *family,*
> *friends and*
> *good health."*

November 27, 1992

5 am. Thanksgiving Day 1992 is history.

Dean and Doug's families joined us again for a great day. I am 81 and Mother is 79. Just a pair of kids married in the great depression years, June 24, 1934, just a few short years ago.

It has been sort of a tradition for Thanksgiving Dinner at Grandma's house. We are thankful that our family is all living. Our great-granddaughter, Emily Hanson, Dan and Karen's little eighteen-month-old baby was the center of attention – such a darling and so good. She and her dad are the only ones who do not answer to the name Saunders!

We were joined mid-afternoon by Trudy's brother Bob and wife Garnet Arnold. Garnet has just had abdominal surgery and looks great and feels very good. We had phone calls from Craig and JoDee, Ginny and her two daughters Laura and Emily of Eugene Oregon and Russell Halliday of Reno, Nevada, my sister Margaret's son. It was quite a full day and as usual Mother put together one of her better dinners.

To finish off a perfect day, the sun came out. We have had very little sun this fall. It's been wet and rainy. This has made our harvest late and, of course, the corn is wet. The forecast is for three or four sunny days, they will be very welcome.

One final important part of the day – about 7:30 pm, Dale came and spent some time with his Dad and Mother. We both enjoyed his brief visit.

Dale's two boys, Rob and Jay, live southeast of Des Moines in Osceola and Pella, Iowa. They each have young sons born in 1992 so they were unable to be with their Dad and Mom due to the distance of travel and road conditions. Southwest and central Iowa 'enjoyed' a great six-to-ten inch snow storm, making roads treacherous and causing many accidents. It's good they stayed home; we don't need more problems.

So this is our 1992 Thanksgiving. God's great gifts – family, friends and good health. God Bless us all.

December 10, 1992

Early Thursday morning.
Granddaughter Emily's birthday.

This has been a long, wet fall. Rain and some snow but not real cold. However, it's nothing like last year's Halloween ice storm when we were without electricity from Friday to Monday evening. The portable generator and our wood burning fireplace were well used then with Doug's family sharing our fireplace and us sharing their soup. It was a trying but lively weekend.

This year has seen little sunshine, from the day the rain started on July 2nd it has been a cool wet summer. The corn and bean crops have been late maturing. There are lots of crops still in the fields and the grass is still green even though we now have some snow on the ground.

All in all, a trying fall for both grain and livestock farmers. Corn is coming out of the fields well above 20% moisture, making drying and storage very expensive. The current price for 15% corn is now $1.78 to $1.85. When drying and shrinkage is considered, corn brings from $1.30 to $1.50 per bushel. This won't pay farmers much for their work and worry even though yields are exceptional with lots of yields over 150 bushels per acre.

It's been a trying year here on Cumberland Farm No. 2. The builders were so slow getting started on Doug's milk parlor. Originally we wanted to be started in April or early May but it was almost August before the crew showed up and then they were delayed by rain and other commitments. We spent the rest of the summer in a mess trying to make hay, cut silage and keep an eagle eye on the builders, plumbers, electricians and equipment men. Hopefully by next May or June all the loose ends will be tied together.

One thing we have is an A1 water system with a new two-inch line to the barn and a one-and-a-half inch line from the barn to Doug's house and lots of good water. This is one of God's blessings for a livestock farmer.

Mother and I will be leaving by plane December 19 to spend another Christmas with Craig, JoDee and family. We have spent only one Christmas with Craig (1991) since he went to work in Bakersfield, California although we visited him often.

Our family is wonderful but they all seem to work too hard; however, grandkids and all, they have managed to stay out of trouble. We thank God many times every day for this. The fact that they had good grandmothers and mothers for several generations has been a contributing factor. A man can accomplish nothing without God and His greatest gift to man – the right woman.

December 13, 1992

Yesterday was one of the nicest days of my life. Two grandchildren, Chris and his sister Jennifer, ate dinner with Grandma and Grandpa.

Doug, Pat and the two younger boys, Matt and John, took the pickup and livestock trailer to Ames, Iowa to pick up the new Halst bull. Chris stayed home and hauled in big bales of hay and Jennifer cleaned house.

We had a wonderful time eating spaghetti and home-made ice cream.

Grandchildren are God's gifts to Grandpas.

"Grandchildren are

God's gifts to Grandpas."

December 26, 1992

On Saturday, December 19, Doug, Pat and family took us to the airport in Omaha to meet the American Airline plane that took us out of the Iowa winter. We all had dinner together at Shoney's Restaurant in Council Bluffs. They are noted for quality and quantity; it was a dinner I will long remember. The young family really enjoyed the salad and dessert bar and the weather was nice for mid- December in Iowa.

We had our reservations and tickets bought and were to leave Omaha at 3:50 in the afternoon only to find out there was a one hour delay in and out of Dallas/Ft. Worth due to fog. After what seemed like a long, long flight we were met in Bakersfield by Craig and JoDee and his two older girls, Laura and Emily. They are two beautiful girls. Laura is a junior at USC and Emily a high school senior in Eugene, Oregon.

Christmas was planned with them for Sunday the 20th. We had a wonderful turkey dinner. Just as we were about finished, Craig got a call from Memorial Hospital. An emergency patient was being helicoptered in so he immediately left to make his preliminary assessment. He came home soon and we all opened our gifts and then Dr. Craig was off to the operating room.

JoDee told us the surgery went well. Craig slept two hours at the hospital and arrived home about 5:30 am, got cleaned up and went back to start a normal Monday morning.

What a full life and how wonderful to be able to share time with others. First Iowa then California, then sharing a father, husband and son with someone I will never meet or know.

After Sunday, another Christmas with JoDee's Mother and stepfather Stan, her sister and niece. More Christmas.

Christmas Day we shared another Christmas dinner with a young German family who works with Craig. He is a physician's assistant and they have two youngsters, a boy Hilary's age and a girl about the same age as Stevie. It was a wonderful afternoon and also the end of our longest Christmas ever.

God bless you all for sharing your time with us.

January 31, 1993

Yesterday, January 10th, Craig and JoDee took Mother and me to Los Angles for something completely out of our world.

We picked up granddaughter Laura at USC and all went to the theater to see "The Phantom of the Opera." Never in our life had we ever expected to see such a production. It was wonderful to be able to enjoy something such as this. It was so far, far removed from our wonderful Iowa home and the people we have grown to love so much.

This enjoyable afternoon could never have happened had it not been for that little fellow who came into our life back in Iowa on June 30, 1944. Craig and his family have done so much and opened so many doors for us.

Our day ended on one sad note. Little Stevie Marie had contracted a slight ear infection and was pretty uncomfortable when we arrived home. She and her sister Hilary (two) had been left in the care of a nurse friend, Misty Pfannmueller, so they were in the best of care.

The last weekend of January '93 we joined Craig and JoDee at the beach house, Windy Gables, in Ventura. Craig was on call at the Ventura hospital. Saturday, after hospital rounds, Craig and Hilary took us to Semi Valley where we visited President Ronald Reagan's Presidential Library. Again, it was a great opportunity for Grandpa and Grandma. Among the many things there was an eight-foot piece of the Berlin Wall, originally built by the communists to keep people from East Berlin from fleeing to the free world.

What fools the people here on God's earth have been.

Again, thank God for family and thank God for America.

Spring of 1993

A frustrating spring, cool and wet. So far no bad storms but fog, mist, rain, snow, then more rain and fog.

Seldom have we had more than two days when a clear sunrise greeted us since we came home from California. All of March continues wet, foggy and with more rain.

Doug managed to get his big steers over to the Dunlap sale barn the first part of April. The weights were good considering the kind of winter we had. The prices were in the high 70s cents per pound. For Holstein cattle who came through a tough winter and the kind of cattle (Holstein) which thirty-to-fifty years ago people thought were almost worthless, $13,000 looked great to an old grandpa who had sold good cattle at six-to-eight cents per pound and hogs at $2.65 per cwt in Omaha.

One of the early April days when it looked like it might not rain all day, Mother and I took the steer money to the Lytton Bank for Doug. He paid for his 'new' used John Deere grain drill and made his 1994 farm note payment. If worse comes to worse, he is covered for almost two years, until 1995. I'm sure those Holsteins will be able to come up with the 1995 payments.

Things are so wet. Easter Sunday, Jennifer's birthday started out fairly nice but not much sunshine and more rain.

Doug still has 1992 corn standing in the field. He has been chopping a small load between rains and using it to feed the young cattle and the bred heifers, saving the haylage and corn silage for the milk cows.

He managed to get his '93 oat crop drilled about thirty days late, this went in on what I call the North Slope, the long hillside on the Wetzel farm below the long steep terrace. If it keeps raining they could surprise us all. No doubt they will need to be sprayed for button weed, sunflowers and broad leaf weeds. He also finally managed to get the new alfalfa seeded. Again, late but if it stays wet that, too, can surprise us.

Sometimes strange things happen here in Iowa.

May 20, 1993

Some way, by working nights and Sundays as well, Doug Backhaus, Doug Saunders and son Chris have managed to get a 100-plus acres of corn planted.

Then more rain.

Also by running the combine at night they managed to get the 1992 corn crop in the wagons but that, too, had to be held in the machine shed until a few hours of sunshine would allow unloading. The bright side is that the corn tested out at 14% moisture. Last fall it was 26% or more so leaving it in the field had some advantage even in a wet rainy season.

It is so hard to plan or get any work done but the continued rain ought to be God's Blessing to the late planted alfalfa.

> *"Sometimes strange things happen here in Iowa."*

June 1, 1993

Lots of light rain and a bit of sunshine.

It is still rainy and getting close to the time the two younger boys and Grandpa and Grandma are planning to see a major league baseball game, the Kansas City Royals vs. the Milwaukee Braves on Saturday night, June 5th. I will write about that later.

The past week has still been wet. Doug and Chris cleaned all the cement Sunday and Monday (Decoration Day) hoping the weather would break for a few dry days but more rain. Doug arranged for Southside Welding to take advantage of the weather so Wednesday and Thursday they put up the new crowd gate. This keeps the milk cows pushed up to the milk parlor door as we are doing the milking. They got it all done except for threading the cable.

Friday Doug took sixteen lighter weight steers to the Dunlap sale barn. Everyone went along. The boys, Doug and Dale, hauled these light cattle in their trailers. Sixteen head, all less than 600 pounds, sold for $83.50 per hundred weight.

It was one of the hottest, fastest moving sales I've seen Jim Schaben conduct. The sale ring was full. No one was able to be in the fields because of the rain and I guess they were all wondering what they would do to the grass.

Saturday we head for the ball game.

More rain?

> *"When God made our grandchildren*
> *He worked overtime."*

June 10, 1993

Our weekend in Kansas City was great.

Dean and Rosemary picked us up about eight o'clock Saturday morning. The two boys, John 12 and Matt 10 were more than ready.

We arrived at Mound City, Missouri about ten o'clock. Mother called Rev. Frank and Helen Christ, former pastors of our Presbyterian church, while in Manilla. We are told the little city of Mound City has nine churches so Frank's church is small. After a cool drink and a stretch of our legs we headed for Kevin's place in Kansas City, Kansas. We had a nice lunch with Kevin and his friend Jerry who works at Ford/New Holland with Keith. We were then driven to our hotel then back to Kevin's for grilled hamburgers and then on to the Arrowhead Stadium for the big game.

We had a nice 0–0 game going until K.C. fell apart in the 7th inning. It ended 7–1 Milwaukee. The boys really enjoyed it, though, and came away with a pair of souvenir K.C. Royals baseballs.

We didn't awaken too early Sunday morning but there was time for the boys to enjoy another swim in the hotel pool. Luckily it was indoors because we were having more rain.

Kevin arranged a brunch at a restaurant close to the hotel called Trotters. It was fine with lots of food, and then it was back in the car. We arrived home around seven pm, tired and wet in the never-ending rain. Dean and Rosemary still had two hours of driving left.

Monday, Doug had the carpenters here to enlarge three doors on the barn in order to get in with the skid loader for cleaning out the manure. It will take more finishing but with this many cattle things have to change.

The crowd gate is working well.

We do need dry weather so the corn and bean planting can be finished; then we can move on to making hay.

June 21, 1993

The summer of 1993 has just started. Its 4:15 in the early morning.

We have had a wet spring and it has been hard for the boys to get their crops planted. Some never will be planted. Thank God for the dairy cattle. The heifers in the west pasture are knee-deep in grass but, oh, the yards are knee-deep in mud. The pavement laid down years ago is paying dividends.

The past three weeks have been rewarding for Mother and me. First the Kansas City trip with Dean's family and the two young boys, John and Matt. They enjoyed it almost as much as Grandpa.

This was followed by a week in California with Dr. Craig, JoDee and family. We took Chris and Jennifer along to spend some time with their California cousins but the time was so short. They were so busy and such good understanding company. When God made our grandchildren He worked overtime. I thank him for our family.

Saturday the 20th we drove to Omaha to be a part of our cousin's family reunion, Uncle Chuck's family, Mildred, C.A. (Buzz), and Don. Merle has passed away. Mildred's son Wayne, now 62-years-old, was the ring bearer at our wedding June 24, 1934.[70] His son Bruce was our chauffer from the hotel to Buzz and Lynn's home there in Omaha, where we met the rest of the family. The 'kids' had all grown up here on the Saunders' Cumberland Farms and attended the Greeley No. 2 country school and all graduated from Manilla High School.

Next week we observe our 59th Wedding Anniversary.

---

[70] See wedding picture Chapter 8.

August 31, 1993

Not only wet – lots and lots of rain.

August 1993 will be remembered here on the Saunders farm for a long, long time. The first weekend we spent with Dean, Rosemary and Keith at their home in Spencer. We said goodbye as Keith left for school, his last year at the University of Northern Iowa. Then Sunday we drove to the Iowa Great Lakes and enjoyed a couple of hours at a concert given by "The Country Men," the group that sang June 27th at our 59th wedding anniversary. For a group of farmers they are super.

The next weekend we were getting ready to go to Des Moines to spend a day with Karen and her family. Dean and Rosemary were returning from a farm implement show in Nashville, Tennessee and we're going to be there, too. Early Sunday morning, Trudy in her rush to have everything perfect, fell and broke her right hip.

Thank God for the young family across the road. Excellent help was just a few minutes away. Doug called Lloyd Robinson and in a short time Mother was on her way to the Harlan Hospital, from there she was transferred to Jenny Edmondson Hospital in Council Bluffs under the care of Dr.s Miller and LaRose.

Patty and grandson Chris took care of me as we followed the ambulance to Council Bluffs. Jennifer took over for Patty looking after her Dad and two younger brothers. Patty, Jennifer and I returned Monday afternoon. Dr. LaRose had a heavy workload that day and pinned her hip late Monday afternoon.

Today, August 31, Dean, who is attending a meeting in Omaha, will be bringing her home.

It has been a long sixteen days but the whole family has been so kind and concerned. Again, I thank God we built our home here on the farm close to the young family. It is so great to have young kids who are concerned about us and so close and kind.

God is good to us if we are willing to listen and look.

October 2, 1993

I couldn't sleep.
Early morning and a beautiful new day awaits the sun to peek over the eastern horizon.

There will never be another October 1st like October 1, 1993. Our last grandchild was born on this day. We received a call from California about eleven o'clock Iowa time telling us that Craig and JoDee had a son. It was not unexpected that this new baby would be a boy. Early in the pregnancy JoDee had an ultrasound with what the doctors described as a 'turtle sign', which was a clear indication that the baby was a boy. For reasons not really remembered by anyone, that baby was soon known only as Boomer.

Friends and family seemed to know Boomer even before he was born and all were eagerly awaiting his arrival. At about 8:30 yesterday, Monday morning, Boomer weighed in at 7 lbs. 1 oz and 20 inches. The birth certificate will record Ryan Douglas Saunders but most people will only know Boomer. He has a big responsibility in life. Not only will he be our last grandchild, he will also be my last grandchild and Craig's only child to carry on the Saunders name.

This Saunders name is the only thing I can give him to pass on to his own children. I don't know if it will be a burden or a blessing for this young child. What I do know is that like his great-great-grandfather C. A., his great-grandfather John, his grandfather Ray and his father Craig, it will be what he, with God's help, makes of it.

"The birth certificate will record Ryan Douglas Saunders. . .

this **Saunders** *name is*
the only thing I can give him . . .

it will be what he,
with God's help,
makes of it."

November 2, 1993

What a fall 1993 has been.

Trudy is still having quite a bit of pain but when one realizes she broke the largest bone in her body and has a six inch stainless steel plate in her thigh it is quite understandable. However, she is improving each day. She is walking around the house without her cane and she is driving her car.

We have so much to be thankful for. We have a nice home right here on the spot we started in 1934 and a wonderful family.

God has given us a lot!

On November 21, we will baptize Craig and JoDee's baby boy Boomer (Ryan Douglas) Saunders. The event is planned in the same Presbyterian Church where I was baptized seventy years ago in 1923 and Craig 49 years ago in 1944. Boomer's two sisters, Hilary RaeAnne and Stevie Marie Reese, were also baptized in their Grandfather and Dad's church. All three had their Grandfather as the officiating church elder and their Grandmother playing the organ. Once again I am repeating myself but this will be the last time for all of us.

Craig's hard work in California has been recognized and rewarded. He and JoDee and kids are moving from California to Cleveland, Ohio where Craig will join the Cardiovascular Department at the Cleveland Clinic. The Clinic is recognized as the best heart hospital in the United States so this is a great honor and boost to his career to be invited to return to the institution that trained him.

We are looking forward to an early Thanksgiving as they stop on their way to their new home. What blessings and opportunities God has opened for our family.

The fall of '93 has been both trying and busy. Our crops are short but much better than some. I remember very well the short crop of '34 and the drought year of '36 when we had almost nothing for a crop, so 1993 is a year to learn from and thank Him for all His goodness.

We have had a few weeks of nice weather so Doug and Chris have been busy filling the silos and baling late cutting hay. They have twenty acres of corn yet to harvest. By cutting and chopping it, they can extend their feed supply. They plan to 'big bale' some corn stalks for winter cattle bedding, hopefully get some fall tillage done and then do what every farmer has done since man first learned to plant seeds – hope for a better year next year.

> *". . . (we) do what*
>
> *every farmer has done*
>
> *since man first learned*
>
> *to plant seeds –*
>
> *hope for a better year*
>
> *next year."*

Thanksgiving Day 1993

A season for the Saunders family to remember.

On November 17, 1993 Boomer, Craig and JoDee's little boy, arrived for his first visit to his grandparent's Iowa home. Craig and family stopped for a few days on their way to Cleveland where he will be joining the staff of the Cardiovascular Department of the Cleveland Clinic.

We baptized Ryan Douglas here at the same church his two sisters, Hilary RaeAnne and Stevie Marie, were baptized earlier. I know this is repeating myself but his Dad was baptized in the same church in 1944 and his Grandfather in 1923.

Grandpa Ray again had the honor of presiding Elder and Grandma Trudy played the church organ. It was a blessing for his 80-year-old grandparents and the last time we will ever have this great honor.

The weekend weather was letter-perfect for Iowa in November. Twenty eight Saunders were joined by JoDee's grandmother, mother, brother, sister, aunts, uncles, nieces and nephews from Nebraska. Twelve in all, joined us for an early Thanksgiving Dinner at Cronk's Buffet in Denison.

It made for a wonderful family gathering.

We may never again all be together.

Grandpa Ray with Grandson Boomer Ryan.

March 25, 1994

The long cold winter of '93-94 is history. It was a cold one but thank God only one real windy night and not much snow; only a few blocked roads.

Had the builders got their work done it would have been a fairly good winter here on the dairy farm. As it is, we have to work extra now to get last year's work finished.

Both Mom and I have had wonderful birthdays this year. For my 83rd, Karen and Dan brought our two great-granddaughters to the farm. Emily, who just turned three, and baby Sara who was born January 5th, 1994.

For Trudy's 80th on St. Patrick's Day, Jay and Laura brought their three-year-old Matthew, our first great grandson.

What a treat to have a lively, healthy family.

This week I go to Des Moines to see Dr. Johnson again about my eyes. I don't see very much. I don't expect Dr. Johnson will be able to do much but I have made up my mind if he can accomplish anything, it will be one of God's gifts to the both of us.

I pray God will guide his hands.

May 20, 1994

The month of May has been beautiful here in Iowa. The fieldwork here on the Saunders' farm is a bit behind the majority of the farmers in the area, but the dairy heard is doing nicely. A couple of new calves and yesterday Doug told me he had sixteen bred heifers to go to the pasture and twenty more to be mated in July.

So if we raise enough forage, the barn will be full a year from now.

It takes a lot of management. My hope is that Chris can attend college at Iowa State and take over the field crops. Doug seems to have a way with the dairy cattle. They would make a good combination, with plenty of room for the rest of the family in the future. They would always have a home and be their own boss.

I can sincerely thank my Mother for helping me establish my life. I also found a wife who, I know, has those same feelings. I don't blame her for being frustrated at times but we raised a great family of four boys.

The fifth of May Trudy flew to California and joined Craig and his family at the University of Southern California where Craig's daughter Laura was among 8,000 graduates receiving their diplomas. She is now a USC graduate.

The next weekend Trudy and I joined Dean's family at the University of Northern Iowa in Cedar Falls, Iowa where grandson Keith joined 4,000 graduates. He now has his degree in Political Science and will attend the University Of Iowa Law School this fall. We also met his girlfriend Greta who already has one year of law school behind her. I suppose Keith could spend the rest of his life trying to catch up?

The following week Mother and I spent at the University of Iowa Medical Center. We saw some doctors there in regard to my eyes. I have almost lost all my sight due to glaucoma. I saw doctors in Omaha for several years and when in California the past winter I checked with doctors there but somehow we have been unable to check the progress. I'll go back to the University soon and doctors there will do some surgery and try to save what vision I still have.

On the way home from the U of I we stayed overnight in Newton, Iowa. Dale's boys, Grandson Robin with wife Sue and son Brian and Grandson Jay with wife Laura and son Matt, joined us for supper. What a great pair of little boys.

In the meantime JoDee, Craig's wife, and their three babies, Hilary three, Stevie Marie two, and Boomer Ryan eight months, spent three days here on the farm with us. They are on their way from Cleveland to Ainsworth and Grand Island, Nebraska to visit her family.

Now for the month of June, Doug and Pat's boys John and Matthew along with Grandma and Grandpa are flying to Cleveland to spend a week with Dr. Craig and family.

So, during the months of May and June we will have had the privilege of visiting all our family.

Surely this is one of God's gifts to any couple that have spent sixty years together.

I may be losing my sight but these are visions I will see forever.

I am so blessed!

March 1, 2003

One last word.

Many times we have gathered together and I have said it may be our last. So far, by the grace of God, I have been 100% wrong. With His blessing we are gathered again today.

Since these are relatively rare occasions, on this one day we are commemorating our 69th wedding anniversary (June 24, 1934), my birthday of 92 years (Feb. 11, 1911), Mother's birthday (March 17, 1914), four sons, Dean Arnold, Dale Allen, Craig Raymond and Douglas Lee, wonderful daughters-in-law, grandchildren and great-grandchildren, so many that it is hard to remember. We are so thankful all are alive and healthy and solid citizens.

The importance of family cannot be overestimated. I have recently survived a near brush with death. It seems old Grandpa's legs don't work very well and his eyes don't work at all. These two minor annoyances teamed up to put me back in the hospital with a broken hip. The surgery went fine, the surgeon's only real comments were those of amazement of how big my bones were, but the recovery was less than routine. It seems I had a young internist (there're all young at my age) who just couldn't listen and a set of Medicare regulations that just couldn't grasp the nuances of a 90 year-old blind man with two legs that over the years had been attacked by bulls, tractors and father time.

Finally, after all the overmedication was out of my system I was able to take the few short steps necessary to keep me from being forever relegated to a nursing home bed. With the aid of an attentive family and a caseworker by the name of Deb Van Gundy Lowndes, I was able to be transferred to Harlan's Myrtue Memorial Hospital under the common sense care of Dr. Tim Brelje and a wonderfully helpful physical therapy department. Thanks to my devoted family and these few professionals who were able to see beyond "cookie cutter" medicine to provide the much-needed personalized attention I required, I have returned to the only home I have ever known – Cumberland Stock Farm II.

I am so thankful to God for such a wonderful long life. You have heard me refer to God many times and from that you may think I know Him well.

I don't.

I do, however, have faith that He exists.

We humans are set apart from the rest of the animal kingdom. It is not the ability to think and reason that sets us apart, my lifetime of working with animals leaves no doubt in my mind they possess these capacities. However, the simple fact that we, as human beings have the additional ability to distinguish between good and evil tells me these forces exist.

The Bible tells us that man was created in His image. Not Him in man's image.

I believe we too often error and it is far too short sighted to limit God to those images our mind conceives. As comforting as it may be to think of God as a kindly white bearded old man, I believe and trust He is so much more.

Though less comforting and more difficult to explain, I have faith that God is so much more. Since man first walked upright he has had an innate need to acknowledge this supreme force. I have faith this force exists. I am a man of faith though I would not consider myself an overly religious man.

Religion is faith plus man. To me, religion is faith with a human stamp on it and this is where my concerns begin. When men become insistent their stamp is the only true path to God, well, that's when all hell can break loose.

Religion; the church, the synagogue, the mosque is there to help us all know Him better, not to divide us. I believe it is important to be part of a faithful community; to participate, to commit and to profess however, my faith is more with that universal force we call God than with a church of human origin. A God with whom I live and work everyday, not just visit on Sunday.

Perhaps the little Sunday School boy said it best. When asked to explain God he put it this way:

Blessed

I have two Four O'clock seeds,[71]
both are black, they are identical.
I put them in the same dirt,
the same water and the same air.
Both grew green stalks then bloomed,
one red, one yellow.
That's God.

I can't explain it any better. If my 92 years on Earth has taught me anything it is the realization that I have reached the point where I know less, but understand more.

In reading these pages and viewing these images you have been witness to generations passing from youth to old age and beyond. In doing so you have realized each generation's prime is fleeting and their possessions but temporary holdings.

However, the wise amongst you will realize it is family and most importantly the power of the thoughts and dreams you instill within them that are your most prized possessions.

He has given us all the same things to work with. I know some men have accomplished more in life but for me this has been a good life's work. The life of a farmer is hard, but it is good and honest work.

The life I chose is close to Mother Nature. It is filled with cycles of birth and rebirth. Each cycle brings with it the optimism of new life. Year after year after year I have been blessed to watch as newly planted seeds emerge from the spring soil warmed by a sun growing stronger each day as it lights the way for the newborn animals taking their first wobbly steps.

As each cycle completes itself I have participated in bountiful harvests but have also experienced great personal losses; losses that are necessary to complete the rich fabric of our human experience; losses that give value to the days with which we have been entrusted.

---

[71] Four O'clock flowers were popular in my grandfather's time. The multicolored flowers open in mid summer afternoon (Four O'clock), stay open all night and close in the morning.

I have been blessed to live long enough to witness the future become history. Through it all, I have been blessed to watch my family grow. I have been blessed to keep alive the dreams of my parents and grandparents and I have been blessed to pass them on.

May He be with my family in the future as He has been with us in the past.

I am so damn grateful . . .

> " *Be joyful and always*
>
> *pray continually,*
>
> *give thanks*
>
> *in all circumstances*
>
> *for this is God's will for you."*
>
> **First Thessalonians 5 16-18**

Printed in the United States
23731LVS00002B/46